Religion and Reality

Religion and Reality

An Exploration of Contemporary Metaphysical Systems, Theologies, and Religious Pluralism

Darren Iammarino

◥PICKWICK *Publications* · Eugene, Oregon

RELIGION AND REALITY
An Exploration of Contemporary Metaphysical Systems, Theologies, and Religious Pluralism

Copyright © 2013 Darren Iammarino. All rights reserved. Except for brief quotations in critical publications or reviews, no part of this book may be reproduced in any manner without prior written permission from the publisher. Write: Permissions, Wipf and Stock Publishers, 199 W. 8th Ave., Suite 3, Eugene, OR 97401.

Pickwick Publications
An Imprint of Wipf and Stock Publishers
199 W. 8th Ave., Suite 3
Eugene, OR 97401

www.wipfandstock.com

ISBN 13: 978-1-62032-244-4

Cataloguing-in-Publication data:

Iammarino, Darren.

    Religion and reality : an exploration of contemporary metaphysical systems, theologies, and religious pluralism / Darren Iammarino.

    xx + 268 pp. ; 23 cm. Includes bibliographical references.

    ISBN 13: 978-1-62032-244-4

    1. Religious pluralism. 2. Religion—Philosophy. 3. Religions. 4. Globalization—Religious aspects. 5. Metaphysics. 6. Whitehead, Alfred North, 1861–1947. 7. Cobb, John B. 8. Griffin, David Ray, 1939–. I. Title.

BL65 G55 I26 2013

Manufactured in the U.S.A.

To all who are seeking truth . . .
in need of hope . . .
striving to flourish . . .
longing for love . . .
and pursuing creativity and novelty

Contents

List of Illustrations | x
Acknowledgments | xi
Introduction | xiii

Part I **Five Possible Global Metaphysical Systems for the Twenty-First Century**

  1 Cobb and Griffin's Conception of Three Religious Ultimates | 3
      Whitehead and Multiple Ultimates
      The Three Complementary Religious Ultimates
      Enriching and Purifying the Depths
      Summary

  2 Four Additional Contenders for a Twenty-First-Century Global Metaphysical System | 13
      The Perennial Philosophy or the Traditionalist School
      Emanationism
      Classical Theism
      Emergent Theism
      Summary

Part II **Cosmosyntheism: A New Option**

  3 The Five Mutually Grounding Ultimates and Cosmosyntheism's Nine Key Advancements | 59
      The Nine Advancements
      The Five Mutually Grounding or Presupposing Ultimates
      Definitions of the Five Ultimates
      How They Ground One Another
      Reality: A Complex Adaptive System?
      Cosmosyntheism and Creation
      Summary

  4 The Forms | 71
      Why the Forms?
      Plato and the Theory of the Forms
      Whitehead's Eternal Objects
      Cosmosyntheism's Expanding Set of Forms
      Why Not Just the Forms?
      Summary

5 The Dipolar Deity | 82
   Why a God?
   Whitehead's Dipolar Process Theism
   Hartshorne and Griffin's Dipolar God as a Serially Ordered Society of Actual Occasions
   The God of Cosmosyntheism
   Summary

6 A World/Cosmos | 92
   Creation out of Chaos
   Aristotle and Prime Matter
   A World of Strings
   Cosmosyntheism's Primordial World
   Why Not Just a World/Cosmos?
   Summary

7 Creativity/Eros | 102
   Why Creativity?
   Creativity, What It Is and What It Isn't
   Creativity/Eros in Cosmosyntheism
   Why Not Just Creativity?
   Summary

8 The Plane of Mutual Immanence | 107
   Why a Receptacle or Plane of Mutual Immanence?
   Plato's Timaeus
   The Receptacle in Whitehead's Adventures of Ideas
   The Plane of Mutual Immanence in Cosmosyntheism
   Why Not Just the Receptacle?
   Summary

9 The Logical Inconsistencies of All Other Possible Combinations | 117
   The Problems
   The Possible Combinations
   Summary

Part III Cosmosyntheism vs. the Five Rival Contenders: Assessing the Strengths and Weaknesses of each System

10 Free Will | 133
    The Free Will Problem
    Free Will and the Perennial Philosophy
    Free Will and Emanation Theories
    Free Will and Classical Theism
    Free Will and Emergent Theism
    Cobb and Griffin on Free Will
    Cosmosyntheism and Free Will
    Summary

11 Conflicting Religious Truth Claims Part 1 | 157
The Problem of Conflicting Religious Truth Claims
The Perennial Philosophy and Conflicting Religious Truth Claims
Emanation and the Problem of Conflicting Religious Truth Claims
Classical Theism and the Problem of Conflicting Religious Truth Claims
Emergent Theism and the Problem of Conflicting Religious Truth Claims
Cobb/Griffin and the Problem of Conflicting Religious Truth Claims
Summary

12 Conflicting Religious Truth Claims Part 2 | 175
The Forms
Cosmosyntheism and the Forms in Other Religions
God
Cosmosyntheism and Other Theisms
A Cosmos
Cosmosyntheism and the Traditions that Focus on a Cosmos
Creativity
Cosmosyntheism and the Religions that Focus on Creativity
Receptacle
Sikhism and the Akashic Records
Cosmosyntheism and the Religions that Focus on the Receptacle
Summary

13 The Problem of Evil | 202
The Problem
The Perennial Philosophy and the Problem of Evil
Emanation and the Problem of Evil
Classical Theism and the Problem of Evil
Emergent Theism and the Problem of Evil
Griffin on the Problem of Evil
Cosmosyntheism and the Problem of Evil
Summary

Part IV **Implications and Applications of Cosmosyntheism**

14 Ethics | 223
The Cosmic Aim of Life
The Social Aim of Life
The Individual Aim of Life
Summary

Appendix: Cosmosyntheism and Applied or Practical Religion | 237
Final Meditations | 263
Bibliography | 265
Subject Index | 269

Illustrations

Figure 01 Different Paths, One Summit | 15
Figure 02 Different Ultimates, One Global Ethic | 16
Figure 03 The Chain of Being | 19
Figure 04 Daoist Emanation | 25
Figure 05 Hermetic Cosmology | 28
Figure 06 Sethian Myth | 32
Figure 07 Plotinus' Emanation/Ontological Dependence | 36
Figure 08 3 Story Universe vs. Emanation | 39
Figure 09 Key Emergent Levels | 52
Figure 10 Cosmosyntheism's 5 Mutually Grounding Ultimates | 67
Figure 11 Plato's Divided Line | 73
Figure 12 Cosmosyntheism's 5 Mutually Grounding Ultimates and the Religions | 177

Acknowledgments

THERE HAVE BEEN TWO formative periods in my academic life, which can be defined as initiation and cultivation. In each of these two stages, three figures stand out for the impact they have had over my interests and creative expression. I will however, acknowledge them in a reverse order, beginning with the three most recent individuals and concluding with those whom I have had the great fortune of knowing even longer.

This current work would truly not have come to fruition without the expert guidance of my mentor and friend Dr. Philip Clayton. I am indebted to Dr. Clayton not only for his principal role in steering this project, but even more so for introducing me to emergent theism in its various forms. I find myself inclined towards this novel philosophy and I view it as one of the primary contenders for a new paradigm going into the twenty-first century. Dr. Clayton has functioned as a paradigmatic figure for what the ideal scholar should look like for this new millennium, mainly: interdisciplinary. Not only do I wish to acknowledge his assistance and leadership within my life and career thus far, but I also look forward to a lengthy future relationship in the hope that he will continue to expand my horizons and inspire me to always remain creative yet respectful.

Dr. Anselm Min has opened my eyes to hidden levels of depth and philosophical insight that lie within the realm of classical theism. I now realize that earlier in my life, I was too quick and eager to discount or write-off many of the beliefs expressed in the Catholic faith. Dr. Min has helped to illuminate the true meaning of some of the central dogma and principles within Catholicism. Now that I have looked again with a fresh pair of eyes on this traditional material and grappled with it on a deeper level, I have gained a growing respect for the men of genius that articulated this extremely well thought out system.

I have only had the pleasure of knowing Dr. Monica Coleman for one year; however, in this brief time she has highlighted the importance of the practical domain for any successful constructive theology. Far too often philosophers set up a complex and abstract system that ends up having little or no bearing on the everyday lives of most people.

Concerning the current book, I must also recognize the key intellectual influences that have served as dialogue partners. John Cobb Jr., whose work on Alfred Whitehead and interreligious dialogue played a major formative role in this work, was gracious enough to look over my original outline and to offer his help with further consultation.

Acknowledgments

David Ray Griffin, another Whiteheadian and process theology scholar, posits a process-relational framework that is the most similar to my own. Due to the similarities between Griffin and myself, his work has served to help me frame my own thoughts and to lend clarification on certain highly complex points of Whiteheadian philosophy.

In regards to my earlier initiation into the fields of religion and philosophy, three names rise far above the rest. The first name is Dr. Mark Wheeler with whom I have maintained a very close friendship. Dr. Wheeler was the first major influence I had within the field of philosophy and he taught me how to think and write in a succinct, clear and logical way. Over the years and after many discussions, we both came to the conclusion that it was time to start a collaborative project on religion within the limits of hope alone. Working on religion and hope has not only been academically rewarding, but spiritually in a way that I imagine neither one of us would have anticipated when the project began.

When it comes to overall guidance and tireless assistance, no one stands out like Dr. Rebecca Moore. Dr. Moore has been the quintessential mentor and has guided me through more tough and uncertain situations than I care to even try and remember. On a professional level, she has always pointed me in the right direction and always at the perfect time; she has an uncanny ability to intuitively grasp when and how to divulge information.

Last, but certainly not least among academic influences is my good friend Dr. Howard Mueller. Way back as a sophomore in college, Dr. Mueller introduced me to what would over time become my profession and obsession: religious studies. It was because of his moving lectures that I first decided to pursue religious studies full-time. For twelve years he has been there for me and I can always count on the fact that whatever problem I am having he will not only have the best solution, but he will be able to articulate it in his typically poetic yet clear fashion.

In addition to the above-mentioned academic influences, I would be remiss to leave out the many family members and friends without whom I could not have completed this present work. Therefore, I wish to thank my family for the continued support both financial and motivational. I also must mention the key role that my fiancé Erica Stark has had on this project. Erica has been forced to endure hearing all of the miniscule details of this project a thousand times and thus, she probably knows it almost as well as I do. Finally, I thank, as always, my inner circle of friends whom I have known for almost thirty years now; their loyalty and friendship is one of the greatest gifts I have ever and will ever know.

Introduction

No peace among the nations
without peace among the religions.

No peace among the religions
without dialogue between the religions

No dialogue between the religions
without investigation of the foundation of the religions.

—HANS KÜNG, *CHRISTIANITY: ESSENCE, HISTORY, AND FUTURE*

OUR WORLD IS CHANGING . . . shrinking, expanding, pulsating. A global age has already dawned. Yet the world holds its breath, waiting to see if the faint and delicate rays of this new light will attain to the full clarity and radiance that will only arrive at the zenith of midday. With each passing year, the earth's pulse seems to beat more rapidly. Will this pivotal age make it past the crowning of the dawn or will it quickly become eclipsed, only to fade back below the horizon? One thing is for certain: if we can achieve peace between the religions, we can at least give this new day a fighting chance to break through the uncertainty and obscurity of the early morning fog. However, peace between the religions is no small task. This is a work that is nonetheless, grounded in that hope. There will be an investigation of the foundation of the religions. The religions will be placed into a dialogue. There *can* be peace . . . let us hope that there *will* be peace.

Hans Küng has defined the problem of conflicting religious truth claims as plainly as it can be presented.[1] It is not merely my problem. It is not simply your problem. It is *our* problem. The haunting issue of religious conflict continually creeps up into the forefront of our everyday lives. It seems the more one tries to repress, evade, or avoid dealing with the problem, the more *violently* it rears its head again. In short, it will not be ignored and it will not just go away. It bears down upon the atheist just as much as it does on the religious believer.

The reason for its persistence should be obvious—the problem is as ubiquitous as it is *multifarious*. Religion is so finely interwoven into the fabric of human life and society

---

1. For an interesting treatment of conflicting religious truth claims, see Küng, *Christianity: Essence, History and Future*.

Introduction

to the degree that if you try to pull on any other "string" that constitutes human culture, the thread of religion will tighten up and provide resistance. Given this apparent fact, the solution to the problem is never going to be solely theoretical, to be provided by philosophers or theologians. The sociologist, anthropologist, biologist, and political scientist all have their respective roles to play in approaching a solution. Nevertheless, the task should fall to the philosophers of religion and theologians to suggest frameworks that can facilitate a peaceful exchange of religious ideas. *This book provides one such theoretical approach to dealing with religious pluralism that simultaneously results in a broad range of philosophical and practical advantages over prior solutions.*

One major goal of this work is to unravel the modern day Gordian knot that is religious pluralism. This knot was initially created by *exclusivist* approaches to dealing with pluralism. Exclusivists have little interest in interreligious dialogue or acknowledging religious pluralism, because they believe that their view contains the ultimate truth and this "excludes" other ways. Exclusivism has led to wars between the faiths and so it happened that the knot began to take shape. In our current age, *inclusivist* approaches have attempted to incorporate other religious views into their paradigm and in so doing, to untangle the knot. Unfortunately, inclusivist attempts have frequently *integrated other faiths by ranking the religions* as Hegel did, or by *unintentionally subjugating one religion to another religion or to a philosophical abstraction* as John Hick's conception of the "Real" did. Inclusivism sometimes bordered on "convolutionism" and so the knot only grew larger.

Finally, some new-agers and perennialists like Fritjhof Schuon and Huston Smith have taken this large loose knot and attempted to show that all the religions are the same at the esoteric level and so *in reality, there is no knot*. By assuming that all the religions lead to the same summit (religious object), the perennialists actually just took the knot and attempted to tighten it so taut that it would just flatten away at the infinite point of the summit of the mountain. Sadly, this seems to have only put the proverbial nail in the coffin for dealing with religious pluralism, making it an unimaginable mess.

With so many seemingly conflicting religious truth claims out there, it is not shocking that some scientists and secularists would just have us cut the knot entirely with the sword of science and technology. However, as was mentioned above, religion is a crucial part of the fabric of society and even if one could completely eradicate religion, it is unlikely that this would represent an improvement for humanity. *The over zealous application of Occam's razor is not without its dangers.* As with any blade, literal or metaphorical, the risk of causing scarring or disfigurement is always present.

Cutting through the Gordian knot may have been an ideal solution for Alexander the Great, but it is not a viable option for us now given the deep embeddedness of religion within culture. Religion often deals with the future, hope, and salvation. Science is frequently concerned with truth and the present or past. Hope—being one of the quintessential human virtues—is imperative for the continued well-being of humanity. Due to the fact that religions are sciences of hope, it only makes sense to address and incorporate these systems of hope and salvation, as they provide us with purpose, values, and meaning. Therefore, religion, in its own way, is equally as valuable as science.

Dissolving the Knot

What is intriguing is that all the former attempts to solve the problems posed by religious pluralism have had the same built in assumption: *there is only one ultimate, whether religious or secular*. Therefore, the debate has been over *which* ultimate is truly ultimate. Is the ultimate a personal God; an impersonal force, such as the Dao, Nirguna Brahman, Sunyata, or the Real; or is the ultimate simply the world or nature? With all these contenders for religious ultimacy having solid arguments on their side, perhaps a deeper truth is beginning to unveil itself; what if they all had an equally valid claim to ultimacy? This book pursues an alternative and novel possibility: *there might be multiple religious ultimates*.

Before taking even one more step forward, the word ultimate must be defined. I will be using this term to mean: that which is constitutive of all there is; the terminal point(s) of a chain of regression, the necessary elements that allow for there to be a universe the likes of which we find ourselves presently in, the primordial ingredients. Given this somewhat prolix definition of the term ultimate, any reality constituted by multiple religious ultimates would necessitate an intricate balance of *mutually grounding, co-necessary and co-equal basic elements or components*. If this claim can at least be accepted as possible, then a new approach to dissolving or untying the Gordian Knot can be pursued. Upon closer examination, it may be discovered that the hypothesis of multiple religious ultimates is not the most probable solution, but it certainly appears possible to me and this possibility opens up entirely new vistas for religious studies.

One thing I am convinced of is that the idea of multiple religious ultimates can yield systems of tremendous explanatory and pragmatic power. For example, the concept of multiple religious ultimates may be able to shake loose this seemingly intractable knot once-and-for-all. What if that knot that for so long appeared to be unbreakable is not really a knot at all? What if the appearance of knotting and incompatibility was simply due to the fact that all these different religions or "threads" were going off in various directions and it merely seemed to be a knot because from our single vantage point in space and time all the "threads" appeared to cross paths at one precise location? In other words, if one could take a 360-degree virtual tour around the threads, one would see there is no knot; instead, there are just strings crisscrossing each other's paths.

If this is at least feasible and all the "threads" lead to different "ultimate" destinations and have unique valuable insights, then the next question becomes, what if one were to twist some of the end points of the threads in a clockwise motion and the other end points in a counter-clockwise motion so that rather than a knot, a cable of increasing strength began to emerge? In this analogy, the end-points do not vanish

Introduction

into a singularity, as in the perennial philosophy, but they do become much closer together and they serve *to strengthen one another into a greater whole*. The concept of multiple religious ends and ultimates may be a difficult pill to swallow for many philosophers of religion and theologians, but the implication that these multiple religious ultimates *may be mutually grounding* could border on unpalatable. I understand; it is challenging to envision—let alone accept—but the demands of the twenty-first century and the reality of increasing globalization should at a minimum warrant us in examining this new approach to handling the issue of religious pluralism.

I call the paradigm that emerges from spinning the multiple ultimates into a unified cable: *Cosmosyntheism*. The word "Cosmosyntheism" literally means a world or (*cosmos*) with (*syn*) God (*theos*). I will argue throughout this work that Cosmosyntheism has numerous theoretical and practical advantages over prior systems, not only in its solution to the problem posed by religious pluralism, but also in the areas of metaphysics, epistemology, ethics, salvation and theodicy.

Three Objectives, Four Assumptions, and Four Arguments

There are three main objectives for this book. (1) *To completely elucidate the importance of the idea of multiple religious ultimates, specifically as laid out in the system of Cosmosyntheism;* (2) *to prove that Cosmosyntheism has numerous advantages over prior models, even previous systems that posit multiple, complementary religious ultimates;* and (3) *to demonstrate how Cosmosyntheism can incorporate key insights from all the religions without denigrating or subjugating any one of them to any other*.

In order to further justify the importance of this work, I propose four assumptions and four arguments that the remainder of my work is based upon. I imagine that the four subsequent assumptions would hold true for peoples of most—if not all cultures—at least among those who have a *progressive* and *realistic* mindset about the current status of world affairs and the anticipated trends for human advancement. *It must be stated explicitly here that the audience for this book are individuals with a forward-thinking outlook, as none of the novel concepts introduced here will likely persuade a staunch fundamentalist from any of the religious traditions.*

Although I seek a global audience, I realize that some of the assumptions betray a Western emphasis or bias. For example, assumption two below proposes that modern science should be taken into account and many would disagree with this point. Again, in assumption three, I suggest that ideally we should seek to overcome prior paradoxes; however, many forms of Western mysticism and Eastern religions, such as Zen, thrive on paradoxes. Nevertheless, when dialogue and mutual transformation are required, there must be give and take, so I still feel these assumptions to be both fair and useful for constructing contemporary theologies. *Therefore, the following four assumptions act as the minimal criteria for any successful constructive theology of the twenty-first century.*

Introduction

The Four Assumptions

1. *Assumption*: As we enter an era of complete globalization, we must seek peaceful resolutions to the reality of religious pluralism if we are to continue moving upward and forward as a civilization. (*Criterion*: Deal with Religious Pluralism)

2. *Assumption*: Any new theologies, metaphysical systems or religions proposed, should try their best to present the most complete version of the truth about Ultimate Reality. This should entail taking into account the achievements of modern science, contemporary work within the humanities, and especially the advancements made in current religious studies and philosophy. (*Criterion*: Interdisciplinary Approach)

3. *Assumption*: In its attempt to elucidate truth, any new system should seek to overcome as many paradoxes and problems that have been pointed out in prior religions, philosophies, or paradigms. (*Criterion*: Logical Consistency)

4. *Assumption*: Only by incorporating the wisdom and traditions of the past with the insights of the present along with forecasts of the future can one present a novel system with a holistic appeal: emotional, intellectual and spiritual. (*Criterion*: Multidimensional)

Before proceeding, it seems prudent to provide a brief argument for these four assumptions to bolster the claim that they are the minimal criteria for a successful constructive, global theology. The first criterion of dealing with religious pluralism is an unavoidable issue for all peoples of faith in a globalized society. One can deal with pluralism in a variety of ways ranging from war, to exclusivism, to a denial of essential differences, to dialogue and tolerance, to dialogue that seeks mutual transformation. However, my assumption is that we cannot move forward and upward as a society unless we adopt one of the peaceful routes. At a minimum, a sort of neutral cease-fire and uneasy tolerance is required. *Ideally, I feel that the best route is dialogue seeking mutual transformation.* I do not believe that a person of any religious persuasion would be troubled by my first assumption, as it seems self-evident that seeking peaceful solutions to the problem is a more civilized approach.

The second criterion of employing an interdisciplinary approach is likely to be far more contentious. Regardless, the fact remains that if one is seeking a broad acceptance of a new system or solution to religious pluralism and interreligious strife, then it must reach beyond the field of religion. If it does not, then it can never go further than the sphere of religion. *Since most humans' lives, personalities and decisions are interrelated with other fields of interest and commitments, it is necessary to be interdisciplinary.* Any new constructive theology must be capable of articulating why religion is still relevant and necessary in a globalized society. This second assumption is especially important for reaching an audience that is progressive, because they are

Introduction

often positively inclined towards the insights and the benefits science and technology have bestowed upon us.[2]

The third criterion of logical consistency may be even more controversial than the second criterion of the necessity for an interdisciplinary approach. It is not that paradox should be avoided or eliminated. My point is that any system, as it is elucidated for the general audience, must have straightforward assertions and ideas that can be articulated through everyday language. I am personally a huge proponent of symbolism and paradox and their power to convey large amounts of data instantly, to awaken creativity and to breakthrough the, at times constricting, concrete wall or box of reason and logical thinking.

Perhaps it is more productive to relegate ambiguity, paradox, and symbolism to the realm of techniques, methods and exercises and to abstain from employing them in the domain of discourse. Dialogue is already difficult enough without the added obscurity that paradoxical statements and equivocal claims bring to the table. Two problems can result from using paradox in either dialogue or a written system: (1) decrease in the probability of accurate information transfer and (2) disinterest and a reduction of credibility beyond the field of religion. So it appears that criterion three is interrelated with the second criterion as well. Any new system should represent a real improvement that can be disseminated to a large group of individuals. Successful dissemination and acceptance appear to require at least the attempt to overcome prior philosophical and religious problems and the minimizing of the use of riddles, encryptions, and intentional paradox. *If no one can understand how or why this is an improvement, then they will stop listening to you and will not accept any of your claims.*

The fourth and final criterion of multidimensionality is essential for a successful global theology because humans are themselves emotional, intellectual and spiritual beings by nature. The three previous criteria are primarily concerned with satisfying the intellect, but this last criterion is crucial because it is the only way to truly reach a global audience. Any global theology or philosophical system must be logical, but it must also incorporate tradition, which appeals to our emotional and sentimental side, as well as provide a comprehensive or perhaps syncretistic form of worship to appease our spiritual side. *If the system only satisfies the intellect, it will fail.* I will be arguing that Cosmosyntheism represents one such global theology that incorporates all of the above four criteria.

Cosmosyntheism meets all Four Criteria:
Four Arguments Sustained throughout the Book

1. *Argument*: The novel paradigm that I call Cosmosyntheism can integrate the main concepts of all the world's religions due to its pluralistic metaphysics, combined

[2]. Some religions, like the Baha'i faith, advocate dialogue between science and religion as a central tenet.

Introduction

with its unique epistemology and corresponding ethics and soteriologies. I argue that Cosmosyntheism follows *a metaphysical primary objective: Constructive or Balanced Creativity*. However, I show that Ultimate Reality is actually composed of *five mutually grounding Ultimates*, of which, Creativity is only one aspect of this overall Ultimate Reality. This framework of five mutually grounding Ultimates helps to eliminate the apparent conflicting truth claims among the pre-existing religions. *If different religions are focusing on diverse elements of Ultimate Reality, which presumably lead to varying ethical systems and soteriologies, then the door is opened for true dialogue and enrichment between the many faiths.* I call this type of dialogue both multi-perspectival rationalism and differential non-hierarchical pluralism.

2. *Argument*: Cosmosyntheism is compatible with many cutting-edge scientific theories in cosmology and physics, such as, string theories, the inflationary big bang scenario and the multiverse or many worlds hypotheses. In addition, Cosmosyntheism is not only in agreement with biological theories like evolution and emergent complexity, it can go further by refining and elucidating some current problems with the various forms of evolutionary theory.

3. *Argument*: The third argument I will uphold and defend is that the major atheistic arguments brought to bear against classical theism (problems of evil, freedom and conflicting religious truth claims), do not apply to Cosmosyntheism. Also, Cosmosyntheism avoids the critiques of many philosophers and ethicists, that all process-based ethics are incomplete, overly aesthetic and elitist.

4. *Argument*: The final argument is that Cosmosyntheism has a stronger explanatory power of Ultimate Reality and the aim of life than other contemporary theologies, because it is multidimensional. It is grounded in multiple religious traditions, pluralism and interdisciplinary studies. Due to this fact, Cosmosyntheism is capable of appealing to a global audience that values harmony and progress. As one example, prior attempts at positing a World Ethos have been deemed problematic because they have glossed over real differences in ethical views. It is true that there are many similarities between ethical systems within the world religions: don't kill, don't steal, the golden rule. However, there are still disagreements and previous systems have failed to provide a way of arbitration between these differences since all the religions are viewed as equally valid. Cosmosyntheism manages to go beyond former attempts at providing a World Ethos—like that of Hans Küng—by advocating that a balanced Creativity and forward progress provide a way of resolving any lingering ethical disputes between the religions. If a proposed law or axiom goes against the metaphysical or cosmic objective/aim, then it is misguided and should be eliminated. Furthermore, Cosmosyntheism suggests a complete bottom-up system for self-cultivation and extension that could appeal to an individual's emotional, intuitive, rational, and spiritual nature.

Introduction

A Brief Outline

I argue in this book that there are solutions to the problems posed to religion and religious pluralism by globalization, science, and secularism. However, in my pursuit for the best answer, the book will first cover in part I, chapter 1, two current answers that are based on the work of the philosopher Alfred Whitehead. *These contemporary solutions both employ the idea of multiple, complementary religious ultimates.* These first two positions are those of John Cobb Jr. and David Ray Griffin, both of whom seek a new paradigm for understanding reality; for ameliorating the problems posed by religious pluralism in a globalized age; and a system that can overcome some long-standing philosophical problems, such as, the problem of evil. Concerning the practical implications and applications of Whitehead's theories, I have chosen Cobb and Griffin as models and allies because I am highly indebted to their prior work and Cosmosyntheism most closely resembles their positions. Put briefly, I align myself with Cobb and Griffin's advances, *which can be identified as a distinct school of thought* because the three of us all share the belief in the importance for multiple *religious* ultimates.

The central concepts of four other rival contenders for a global metaphysical system will be outlined and explained in chapter 2: the perennial philosophy, emanationism, classical theism, and emergent theism. The reason for including four rival options is for the sake of fairness and consistency. *Too often one position is argued for and is contrasted with only one other system, which likely lies on the far opposite extreme of a continuum of possibilities.* However, I must state explicitly here that my goal is not to falsify these other schools of thought, but rather to use them as examples, which help highlight and orient the differences between Cosmosyntheism and the other preexisting systems. Chapters 1 and 2 comprise Part I.

The main goal of part II is to present my new solution, which I call Cosmosyntheism. As I will show, one reason why this paradigm is valuable is because it is sufficiently interdisciplinary: religiously, scientifically, and philosophically. Due to limitations of space, the science content will be kept to a minimum, whereas religion and philosophy will act as the primary focus. *Throughout the second part, I will address some of the technical ways in which my system differs from those of Whitehead, Cobb and Griffin. However, the full import of these key advances to the work of Whitehead, Cobb and Griffin will be delineated thematically throughout Part III.*

The third part brings the philosophical systems outlined in the preceding two parts together in order to assess their strengths and weaknesses when confronted with three major problems within the field of philosophy of religion: the problem of free will; the problem of conflicting religious truth claims and the problem of evil. Part III contains four chapters, one for each of the above problems, but two full chapters are needed to cover the problem of conflicting religious truth claims.

PART I

Five Possible Global Metaphysical Systems for the Twenty-First Century

CHAPTER 1

Cobb and Griffin's Conception of Three Religious Ultimates

Reflection on these matters has led me to speak of three ultimates. Perhaps there are others, although at present I have no idea what they might be. Thinking of these three has helped me to understand the diversity of religious traditions more deeply.

—JOHN B. COBB JR., *TRANSFORMING CHRISTIANITY AND THE WORLD*

THE IDEA OF MULTIPLE religious ultimates is not entirely without precedent in both the West and the East.[1] This initial chapter provides an overview of the pioneering work done by John B. Cobb Jr. and David Ray Griffin in the field of religious pluralism. The chapter is divided into three parts. The first part highlights how John Cobb and David Griffin's insights on multiple religious ultimates are indebted to Alfred Whitehead's pluralistic metaphysics. My discussion of Whitehead's philosophy *in this chapter* will be limited to how his ideas can support a system of multiple religious ultimates and pave the way for a novel solution to dealing with the problems posed by religious pluralism. The second part addresses how John Cobb's position has incorporated and elaborated upon Whitehead's philosophy. The final part examines Griffin's philosophy on pluralism known as deep religious pluralism. Throughout the second and third parts, I will cover the ideas of complementarity, mutual transformation, deep religious pluralism, enrichment and purification, which taken together constitute the core message of the Cobbian/Griffian school of thought on the issue of dealing with religious pluralism.

---

1. I will be examining the approach taken by two Westerners, John B. Cobb Jr. and David Ray Griffin; however, there are major Chinese scholars like Fung Yu-Lan who have proposed something similar to multiple religious ultimates. See Fung Yu-Lan's *Hsin li-hsüeh* for an example of four religious ultimates. In addition to the Chinese, Indian philosophers like Sri Aurobindo have suggested the plausibility of multiple religious ultimates.

Part I: Five Possible Global Metaphysical Systems for the Twenty-First Century

Whitehead and Multiple Ultimates

The philosopher Alfred North Whitehead is perhaps the most underappreciated thinker of the twentieth century. Whitehead, originally a prominent mathematician, made the shift to systematic metaphysician late in life while he was teaching at Harvard. His philosophical goal is clearly enunciated at the outset of his magnum opus, *Process and Reality*: "Speculative philosophy is the endeavor to frame a coherent, logical, necessary system of general ideas in terms of which every element of our experience can be interpreted."[2] Whitehead's desire to include every element of our experience within his system led him to argue for a pluralistic metaphysics. This pluralistic metaphysics includes three elements, which are interrelated and when combined, constitute what could be called Ultimate Reality. The three ultimates are: Creativity, God, and a World. It should be mentioned that his metaphysical scheme can be interpreted in various ways, but no matter which route one pursues, the idea of multiple ultimates is unavoidable in the interpretation. The question becomes how many "ultimates?"

As far as *Process and Reality* is concerned, a picture of three ultimates appears to be the dominant interpretation. The key passages to bolster this view are as follows, "Creativity, many, one are the ultimate notions involved in the meaning of the synonymous terms, thing, being and entity. These three notions complete the Category of the Ultimate and are presupposed in all the more special categories."[3] Towards the end of *Process and Reality*, one encounters what is known as the six antitheses, which clearly show the interrelated nature of the ultimates, God and the World.

> It is as true to say that God is permanent and the World fluent, as that the World is permanent and God is fluent. It is as true to say that God is one and the World many, as that the World is one and God many. It is as true to say that, in comparison with the World, God is actual eminently, as that, in comparison with God, the World is actual eminently. It is as true to say that the World is immanent in God, as that God is immanent in the World. It is as true to say that God transcends the World as that the World transcends God. It is as true to say that God creates the World, as that the World creates God.[4]

One final example follows shortly after the above quote: "Neither God, nor the World reaches static completion. Both are in the grip of the ultimate metaphysical ground, the creative advance into novelty. Either of them, God and the World, is the instrument of novelty for the other."[5]

I must briefly explain the main functions of these three ultimates as Whitehead conceives them because John Cobb and David Griffin *find strong parallels between these three ultimates and the insights of the religious faiths of the world*. God is understood

2. Whitehead, *Process and Reality*, 3.
3. Ibid., 21.
4. Ibid., 348.
5. Ibid., 349.

as "dipolar" meaning that God's nature consists of both a mental pole and a physical pole. The mental pole envisages all the "eternal objects," Whitehead's term for the Platonic Forms, and provides relevant possibilities to the "multiplicity" of other entities that comprise the World. God's physical pole is known as his "consequent nature." This aspect of God is the receptive side that takes in the physical enjoyment of each moment of every creature and stores it everlastingly in God's overall nature.

The World is a multiplicity of what Whitehead calls "actual occasions of experience." The function of the World is *to actualize the novel possibilities* that are provided by God in each moment. This actualization brings *experiential knowledge* and physical enjoyment or "satisfaction" to the creatures and back into God where it is forever retained, "objectively immortalized." The final piece of the puzzle is Creativity, or the creative advance into novelty. Creativity is akin to the power of Being; it is an ultimate principle that brings God and the World together again-and-again for the sake of issuing in novel forms of value from a state of potentiality into full-blown actuality. In his later work, *Adventures of Ideas*, Whitehead adds another element to his system: the *Khora* or place. This concept is nearly identical to Plato's Receptacle as expounded in the *Timaeus*. However, I will address that later when I reach my own system, as both John Cobb and David Griffin focus their attention on the parallels between sacred Scriptures and the accounts of religious experiences, and the three ultimates delineated by Whitehead in *Process and Reality*. It is to John Cobb and his portrayal of three ultimates that I now turn.

The Three Complementary Religious Ultimates

John Cobb follows Jack Hutchison in identifying three religious ultimates: theistic, cosmic and acosmic. Cobb's definition of an ultimate is, "that at which a line of questioning ends."[6] He demonstrates that religious history cross-culturally has identified at least three terminal points. "Religious interest in the West centered overwhelmingly on the ultimate in the line of efficient, formal, and final causation."[7] In other words, the West was concerned with the theistic dimension of reality. Indian philosophy and religion however, dwelled on the acosmic element. "Brahman/Atman seems to be the ultimate in this line of reflection. The goal in some forms of Vedantic practice is to realize that at the deepest level I am what all things are, Atman is Brahman . . . Questions of efficient cause, formal cause, and final cause, belong to a subordinate sphere."[8] Cobb says of the cosmic ultimate, "It has deep roots in many cultures. Much of primal religion has this form. It expresses itself in some forms of Taoism. Western pantheism

---

6. Cobb, *Transforming Christianity*, 184.
7. Ibid.
8. Ibid., 185.

Part I: Five Possible Global Metaphysical Systems for the Twenty-First Century

has sometimes had this character. Surely we cannot deny that in some sense the totality of the things that are is ultimate as well"![9]

What distinguishes Cobb from nearly all of his colleagues is that he believes that these three religious insights into the nature of reality can be and are complementary and interrelated. "I would propose that without a cosmic reality there can be no acosmic one, and that without God there can be neither. Similarly, without both the cosmic and acosmic features of reality there can be no God."[10] However, for practical purposes they can be examined and experienced as distinct. "It need not be nonsensical to suppose that one immeasurably complex reality contains theistic, cosmic, and acosmic features that can be related to in some separation one from the other."[11] One may be tempted to ask why various religions have stressed one or more of the three. Cobb's answer is that "cultural differences deeply influence which features are attended to, but the resultant relativism does not invalidate the diverse experiences. Each of the great types of experience can be seen to be veridical."[12]

What does this radical new paradigm for understanding religious pluralism offer us? What are the advances and advantages over prior interpretive frameworks? Cobb tells us that, "When we understand global religious experience and thought in this way, it is easier to view the contributions of diverse traditions as complementary, this approach reduces the tendency to reinterpret what others say to make it fit into what one already believes. It avoids the need to assert that behind the realities to which the traditions attest there is another that unifies them."[13] This last sentence is in reference to what Cobb views as the most distressing situation, *a deeply rooted tendency that one ultimate is somehow more perfect and necessary than two or three ultimates.*

All prior solutions to dealing with religious pluralism have not been content to rest with multiple religious ultimates that are equally valid. Instead, the dominant view in the field of religious pluralism has been to assume that all the religions are actually aiming at and attempting to describe the same religious object and end. This way of pursuing pluralism is known as identist pluralism. "According to identist pluralism, all religions are oriented toward the same religious object and promote essentially the same end (the same type of salvation)."[14] Approaching interreligious dialogue from an identist paradigm frequently results in an inclusivism that is automatically hierarchical or subjugating because the starting point is normally one's own tradition, which is assumed to be the best at articulating what all religions are ultimately about: describing the one ultimate object and goal. One can find this hierarchy and rating system beginning with

9. Ibid.
10. Ibid., 121.
11. Ibid.
12. Ibid., 123.
13. Ibid., 186.
14. Griffin, "Religious Pluralism," 24.

Hegel and running all the way up to the present day with far more subtle and nuanced proposals from people, such as, John Hick, S. Mark Heim, and Paul Knitter.[15]

Pursuing an interpretive framework that operates from multiple religious ultimates has at least the two advantages Cobb has outlined. First, it allows the variety of religious experiences to be equally valid insights as opposed to one being truer than another form. Second, it allows us to broaden our individual, culturally conditioned paradigm to include these other equally plausible windows onto the depth of reality. Finally, this system claims that if one does exert the effort to broaden their view and include these other avenues for experiencing the holy, then an enriched and purified image of reality begins to unfold. Slowly, as if constructing the supreme jigsaw puzzle, a picture of reality presents itself that is more than we could have imagined when the pieces lay before us jumbled and disjointed. The beauty of this puzzle is that, unlike the one in your closet, this puzzle can be fit together in more than one way. The process of experimenting with the different combinations is defined by David Griffin as deep religious pluralism.

Enriching and Purifying the Depths

I have shown above how some process thinkers have interpreted Whitehead's philosophy as advocating or at least suggestive of three religious ultimates. This line of reasoning is also taken up by David Ray Griffin, a former student of John Cobb, and a like-minded process thinker. However, Griffin's earlier interpretation is that there are two ultimates: God and Creativity. This position is explicated in chapter 7 of his book, *Reenchantment without Supernaturalism*. What is important for my purposes is that he undertakes a prolonged and thorough critical analysis of these two ultimates, identifying God as the personal ultimate experienced within the Western monotheistic faiths and Creativity as the impersonal ultimate realized primarily within the Eastern religions. For Griffin, there are two fundamental types of religious experience: personal and impersonal. He explains that,

> In religious experience of the one kind, the experience is said to be of a personal, perfectly good, loving, Holy Being distinct from the experiencer. In the other kind, the experience is said to be of an ultimate reality, finally identical with one's own deepest reality, that is impersonal, indifferent (beyond good and evil), and in some Buddhist accounts, wholly empty.[16]

---

15. Hick's implicit hierarchy runs from the pre-axial at the nadir, to the monotheistic faiths, to non-theistic religions, to the Real *an sich* at the apex. To be fair, Heim is not an identist soteriologically, in that he recognizes different religious ends, but his system is subjugating and hierarchical because he claims that only Christianity, and Catholicism in particular, understand the mystery of the Trinity; all other religions are focused on only one or two of the three personas of the Trinity. Knitter is also a Christian and approaches pluralism from within typical Western categories and terminology, such as God being love and justice as an impartial and supposedly ubiquitous norm for evaluating religions.

16. Griffin, *Reenchantment without Supernaturalism*, 273.

Part I: Five Possible Global Metaphysical Systems for the Twenty-First Century

By-and-large, the personal accounts come from monotheistic religious experiences and the impersonal come from Advaita Vedantic Hindu accounts and many Mahayana Buddhist practitioners. However, this sharp delineation is blurred by the fact that many Hindu's follow the path of Bhakti or devotional Yoga as found in the Epics and some Upanishads and some Western mystics provide accounts that sound impersonal, like Meister Eckhart's "Godhead" or the *Ain* of Kabbalists. Nevertheless, the point is that worldwide, two momentous forms of experience are occurring that can clearly be called religious. This apparent fact of two distinct types of experience provides ammunition for neo-atheists and secularists who point to the fact that the various religions say conflicting things, whereas it would seem that if religion and religious experience were true, then there would be a consistent form of insight.

Griffin provides poignant examples from earlier authors who have made the problem of conflicting religious truth claims glaringly apparent. "How can ultimate reality be both a personal being and an impersonal principle, identical to our inmost self and forever other, loving and utterly indifferent, good and amoral, knowable and unknowable, a plenitude and an emptiness?"[17] And again, "There is no intelligible way that anyone can legitimately argue that a "no-self" experience of empty calm is the same experience as the experience of intense loving intimate relationship between two substantial selves."[18] Griffin explains that this paradox within the philosophy of religion simply dissolves away when one realizes that reality consists of multiple elements or principles, one of which happens to be experienced as personal, and the other as impersonal. In other words, the Buddhist experience of emptiness is equally as valid as the Christian, Jewish or Islamic experience of a loving God who is wholly other.

I agree with the majority of Griffin's Whiteheadian solution based on two ultimates, but one is still left wondering, what of the religions that appear to dwell on the element of "the Many" rather than "the One" or God and "Creativity?" Before I answer this question, I feel a brief digression and foreshadowing is in order. Simply identifying Buddhism and Advaita Vedantic experience with Creativity is an inadequate solution. I will show later on that Whitehead's system and my own, posit another element: the Receptacle, Storehouse, or the Place. This principle, one of the five ultimates of Cosmosyntheism, along with Creativity, provides a more adequate account of the impersonal religious experience.

Returning to the above question of what to do about additional forms of religious experience, Griffin's answer is to be found, like most intriguing answers, in a lengthy footnote. The aside is a response to a challenge put forth by Gene Reeves, a Lotus Sutra Buddhist and a Unitarian Universalist who, like Cobb, thinks that Whitehead's philosophy consists of three ultimates, with finite actual occasions constituting the third ultimate. Reeves's fear is that, "a religion oriented around God and/or Creativity

---

17. Davis, *The Evidential Force*, 167.
18. Katz, "Language, Epistemology and Mysticism," 39–40.

as such might encourage a religiosity in which this world is trivialized."[19] This is a valid concern, which Griffin recognizes, but in 2001 is still inclined to dismiss.

David Griffin lists four reasons why he has not spoken of three ultimates.

> First, simply getting a hearing for the idea that there may be two ultimates is difficult enough. Second, the chapter was already sufficiently long and complex. Third, even though "the world" is ultimate in the sense that some world or other exists necessarily, our particular world, our cosmic epoch, does not exist necessarily and will not endure forever. Fourth, many of process philosophy's doctrines, such as the doctrines that all actual entities have intrinsic value, that the divine purpose is to maximize important experience in the world, and that all experiences are preserved everlastingly in the divine experience, make clear that it does not support a world negating spirituality.[20]

The first two reasons are merely pragmatic, but the third and fourth bring out a key issue that I must discuss somewhat in depth here. Process thinkers frequently point out that Whitehead believes *a* World must exist co-eternally with God, not *this particular world* or as Whitehead says, cosmic epoch. What this means is that our universe and our Earth are not metaphysically ultimate. What is ultimate is that there must be *a World of finite actualities*, a Many, a multiplicity, co-eternal with God.

It is at this point that I must briefly digress once again in order to clear this critical ambiguity up. *The earth, even our particular universe is not ultimate.* For this reason, I struggled with applying the term Cosmosyntheism to my philosophy, as it could become misleading. I do not mean to say that *this* universe or cosmos was ultimately with God at the beginning; rather, I follow Whitehead, the Bible and most ancient myths in saying *a* World, primeval waters or foam, meaning some type of chaotic and inchoate primordial multiplicity. It is because of this point that at times I may employ the alternative neologism, Chaosyntheism, to avoid the above confusion.

Now to tie all this back to the above block quote, Gene Reeves brings up an important point: we must view the cosmos optimistically and have a world-affirming theology. Griffin just does not want to fall into the trap of saying that the earth is somehow ultimate. What is interesting is that some religious experience, like that of contemporary pagans, Native American religions, and other indigenous religions claim to have religious experiences of the earth as sacred. We must not lose sight of this critical insight especially in an era of increasing ecological crisis; it can save us. Whitehead believed the point of life is to issue into the world novel forms of value and experience. The earth is the only stage we currently have to bring these forms into the world and seeing as how the cosmic aim of life is to do just that, a revitalized reverence for the earth must come about. However, the earth is not ultimate and it is not one of

---

19. Gene Reeves, personal communication with David Griffin quoted in Griffin's *Reenchantment without Supernaturalism,* 281.

20. Ibid., fn. 16.

Part I: Five Possible Global Metaphysical Systems for the Twenty-First Century

the five elements making up Ultimate Reality. *It is imperative that this point has been clarified, Reeves is right that a multiplicity of finite actualities is one of the ultimates, but Griffin was right in making sure to clarify what is meant by a world-affirming religion.* I now turn to Griffin's next major shift in thought, which can be found in *Deep Religious Pluralism* of which he was the general editor.

The first major advance to be found in *Deep Religious Pluralism* follows closely on the heels of the solution provided by Cobb and Griffin regarding the problem of conflicting religious truth claims. Griffin explains how the recognition of two genuine forms of religious experience necessarily leads to two forms of interreligious dialogue: *purification and enrichment*. "Dialogue with those from other traditions that are attending to the same ultimate, as when Christians talk with Jews, Muslims, and theistic Hindus, can be a dialogue of *purification*. Dialogue with those who focus on the other ultimate can be a dialogue of *enrichment* in which one's comprehensive vision is enlarged."[21] For example, Christians can discuss with Jews about exactly what they mean by the messiah and Christ, or God as law-giver and covenant maker and God as love and come to a *clearer* understanding. Christians can dialogue with Muslims about a Triune God and a God that is strictly One and merciful. In a dialogue of enrichment, the idea is that another religion's insights can *complement* your own and as a result, both you and the dialogue partner can be mutually transformed and therefore, be enriched.

Enrichment and purification goes beyond discussing personal and impersonal accounts of religious experience. In *Deep Religious Pluralism*, Griffin admits that he was wrong to deny the suggestion of three ultimates by Whitehead, Cobb, Reeves, and religious experiences. "Reeves favors a religion in which all three ultimates are emphasized. Although for various reasons I there [*Reenchantment without Supernaturalism*] resisted Reeves's suggestion, I now wish that I had incorporated it."[22] Griffin explains further that, "what exists necessarily is not simply God, as in traditional Christian theism, and not simply the world understood as the totality of finite things, as in atheistic naturalism, but God-and-a-world, with both God and worldly actualities being embodiments of creativity."[23] He follows by agreeing with Cobb that although these three ultimates are distinct, they are not in fact separable from one another.

The final advances that Griffin makes come in his most recent book on process thought, *Whitehead's Radically Different Postmodern Philosophy*. Griffin's position changes once again to now include *four ultimates*. "I hold with Whitehead that eternal objects, creativity, God, and some finite actual entities all presuppose each other, that they obtain eternally and therefore necessarily. What exists necessarily is God-and-a-world, along with the embodied creativity and the objective and subjective species of

---

21. Griffin, *Deep Religious Pluralism*, 47.
22. Ibid., 51, fn. 44.
23. Ibid., 49.

eternal forms."[24] In addition to accumulating another ultimate on his list, Griffin argues that there is a way to avoid any potential debilitating relativism of religious beliefs.

In chapter 5 of *Whitehead's Radically Different Postmodern Philosophy*, Griffin provides two formal criteria for avoiding a simple relativism of beliefs. "I have already suggested that there are at least two formal notions of this type: the idea of truth as correspondence and the law of non-contradiction."[25] However, Griffin admits this is a rather limited basis for judging the adequacy of different systems of thought. Therefore, he adds four substantive hard-core common sense notions,

> the existence of an external world, of the past, of causation as real influence, and of human freedom. And elsewhere I have suggested that there are several more universally presupposed substantive notions, including the distinction between better and worse possibilities, the idea that some things are important, and the reality of something sacred or holy.[26]

Griffin explains that if at least some of these notions are universal then we cannot verbally deny them without violating the law of non-contradiction.[27]

What does all of the above mean? How is it valuable for this study? The value lies in the fact that *it can help to set unbiased parameters for interreligious dialogue*. Certain religious claims that go against the above criteria should be either outright dismissed or viewed with a high amount of skepticism. Griffin states that, "Insofar as my list is accepted, we could rule out, for example, any systems espousing acausalism, determinism, solipsism, nihilism, or the unreality of time."[28] However, Griffin goes further to suggest that the different religions of the world may each have lifted to consciousness another set of hard-core common sense notions. "It is very difficult to become aware of the notions that we presuppose in every moment, in every act, in every thought. However, if each tradition has become consciously aware of a different set of these notions then we can learn from each other."[29] In other words, interreligious dialogue is imperative because it helps us to enrich our understanding of the common ground of human experience and we do at least have some formal criteria for judging the adequacy of the various insights, which allows us to avoid a debilitating relativism throughout the course of dialogue.

The position that there are multiple religious ultimates is rather new and obviously there are contending metaphysical systems, some of which have a very long intellectual

---

24. Griffin, *Whitehead's Radically Different Postmodern Philosophy*, 195.

25. Ibid., 101.

26. Ibid.

27. By the law of non-contradiction, Griffin has in mind the idea of performative self-contradictions where one cannot simultaneously state for example, that they are alive and dead because the very act of speaking the words "I am alive and dead" would prove that you are not dead. He is obviously aware that one can verbally say they are both p and -p, but they cannot prove both claims because the very act of living, existing and acting in general prove otherwise.

28. Griffin, *Whitehead's Radically Different Postmodern Philosophy*, 101.

29. Ibid., 102.

Part I: Five Possible Global Metaphysical Systems for the Twenty-First Century

history. Perhaps there is only one ultimate, one truly Real element at the base or ground of all things. Maybe some religious insights are derivative or even completely false and illusory. In the following chapter, I will be covering four of these alternative and rival positions, each of which is still a live option and strong contender for a global theology or metaphysics. However, before proceeding to that task, it is worth summarizing the main points of the current chapter so that the differences between a system based on multiple ultimates and a system based on one ultimate can be more clearly visualized.

Summary

John Cobb:

- There are three religious ultimates that roughly correspond to Whitehead's God, Creativity, and a World.
- There are three main forms of religion: theistic, cosmic, and acosmic.
- Each of the three main forms of religion primarily focus on one of the religious ultimates, either on God or on Creativity or on a World of finite actualities.
- The reality of multiple ultimates would allow for a new form of interreligious dialogue where each religion can mutually transform one another and thereby grow in depth.

David Griffin:

- There are two forms of pluralists: identist and deep or differential. Identist pluralists believe all religions are oriented towards the same religious object and the same salvation. Differential pluralists suggest that religions promote different ends and are perhaps oriented towards different religious objects.
- There are actually two forms of interreligious dialogue: purification and enrichment. Purification is dialogue with other faiths that focus on the same ultimate as you do, whereas, enrichment is dialogue with religions that dwell on a different ultimate than your own tradition.
- There are some universally valid criteria for judging the adequacy of various systems of thought. Two formal criteria are: the idea of truth as correspondence and the law of non-contradiction. Four substantive criteria are: the existence of an external world, of the past, of causation as real influence, and of human freedom.
- Truth is correspondence with reality, but knowledge is necessarily limited by human constraints and therefore, dialogue is an imperative in order to achieve a fuller picture of the whole of reality.

CHAPTER 2

Four Additional Contenders for a Twenty-First-Century Global Metaphysical System

In this age of flourishing futurists when almost the only way to get attention is to claim to be privy to some new discovery, it gives us the most exceptional pleasure, the most piquant delight, to announce what in today's climate of opinion may be the most novel, original, and unexpected prediction imaginable. The wave of the future will be a return to the past.

—HUSTON SMITH, *FORGOTTEN TRUTH*

There is a nisus in Space-Time which, as it has borne its creatures forward through matter and life to mind, will bear them forward to some higher level of existence.

—SAMUEL ALEXANDER, *SPACE, TIME AND DEITY*

IN CHAPTER 1, I outlined two views of Ultimate Reality that argued for the existence of multiple religious ultimates. The purpose of this chapter is to examine four alternative models for comprehending Ultimate Reality that all share one thing in common—*there is only one true ultimate*. The four metaphysical systems are: the perennial philosophy, emanationism, classical theism, and emergent theism. For each of these systems, I will provide a few of what are frequently accepted as paradigmatic examples, but this chapter is not meant to be an exhaustive account of all versions of the perennial philosophy, emanationism, classical theism or emergent theism, since that would result in an encyclopedic-length work. The goal of this chapter is instead, to layout the central tenets of each of these systems in as unbiased a fashion as possible. I have a great deal of respect for all of these options, as I strongly feel they are or will become on the short list for viable and live options for understanding both reality and religion in the twenty-first century. It is not until part III that I will argue for what I believe to be the superiority of positions that assert multiple religious ultimates.

Part I: Five Possible Global Metaphysical Systems for the Twenty-First Century

The Perennial Philosophy or the Traditionalist School

I will begin by discussing what is variously known as the perennial philosophy or traditionalist school of thought. There have been a number of famous individuals that claim allegiance to this viewpoint, such as René Guénon and Aldous Huxley; however, I will focus my attention on the two figures that have most recently and exhaustively articulated the central tenets of this position: Frithjof Schuon and Huston Smith. The latter author is perhaps most well-known for his bestselling introduction to religious studies, *The World Religions*. The fact that Huston Smith has had such a vast influence on the field of religious studies makes it all the more important that one comes to understand his personal beliefs about religious pluralism.

The bulk of Huston Smith's writings on the subject of the perennial philosophy are to be found in a single book: *Forgotten Truth: the Common Vision of the World's Religions*. As for Frithjof Schuon his most acclaimed work is the *Transcendent Unity of Religions*. The titles of these books are revealing in that they point to the first and main tenet of the perennial philosophy.

Point 1: *All of the religions at the esoteric level are describing the same "Reality."*

"There is a unity at the heart of religions. More than moral it is theological, but more than theological it is metaphysical in the precise sense of the word earlier noted: that which transcends the manifest world."[1] This one quotation contains so much of the essence of the perennial philosophy that it must be unpacked point-by-point. First of all, it explicitly states that there is a unity to the religions, but more importantly, it suggests that the unity *is not to be found on the moral level*. This is a major claim because there are many out there including Hans Küng and Paul Knitter that would like to argue that this is where the most plausible unity between religions is to be found. Next, one learns that it is a theological unity, but even that is not correct; it is a metaphysical unity in the literal sense of the word. This strong claim implies that the unity is to be found on the esoteric or metaphysical level of all the religions and it is a concord of insight *into the nature of Ultimate Reality, not merely ethics.*

---

1. Frithjof Schuon, *The Transcendent Unity of Religions*, xxiii.

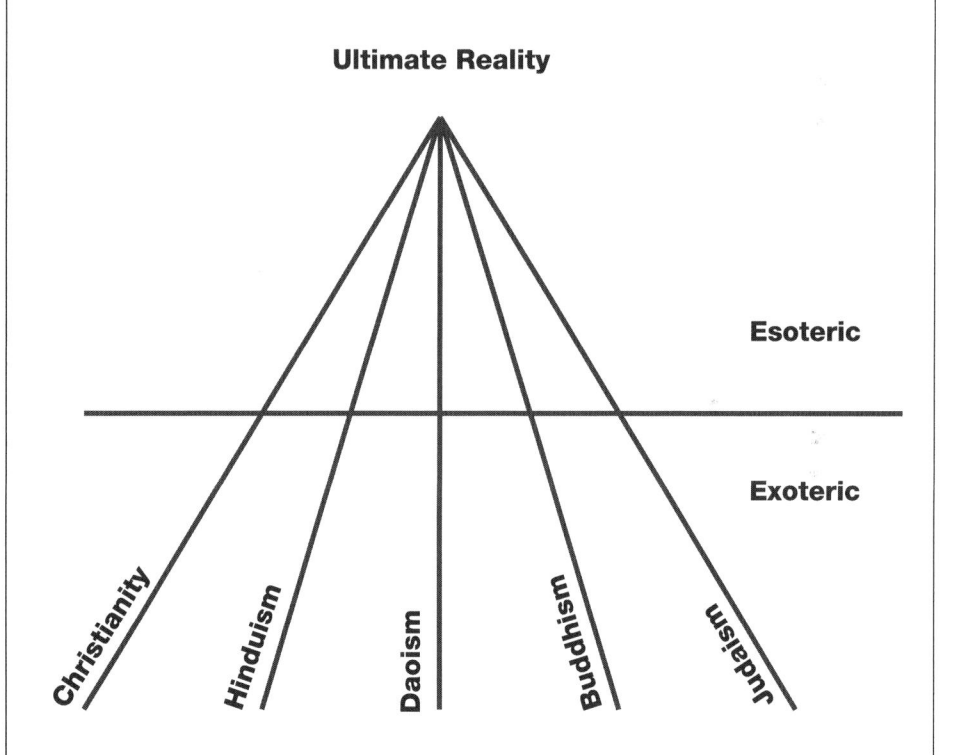

Different Paths, One Summit

Ultimate Reality

Esoteric

Exoteric

Christianity

Hinduism

Daoism

Buddhism

Judaism

Different Ultimates, One Global Ethic

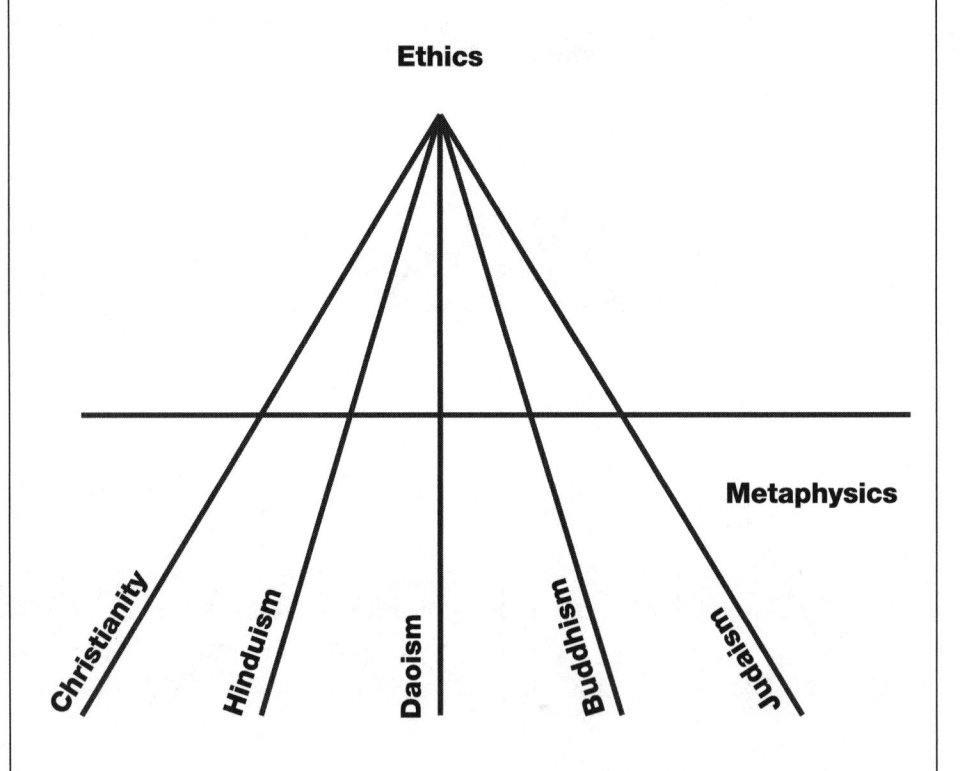

Ethics

Metaphysics

Christianity Hinduism Daoism Buddhism Judaism

Four Additional Contenders for a Twenty-First-Century Global Metaphysical System

Point 2: *"Forms for exoterics are relatively non-negotiable. Esoterics ride them more loosely."*[2]

For Schuon and Smith, the distinction between theological and metaphysical parallels the dichotomy between exoteric religion, with its outward forms, dogmatism and large following, and the esoteric or metaphysical level, with its more profound insight into the direct knowledge of the Infinite, its symbolic use of the religious imagery, forms and dogmas and its elite group of adepts.

> If an example may be drawn from the sensory sphere to illustrate the difference between metaphysical and theological knowledge, it may be said that the former, which can be called esoteric when it is manifested through a religious symbolism, is conscious of the colorless essence of light and of its character of pure luminosity; a given religious belief, on the other hand, will assert that light is red and not green, whereas another belief will assert the opposite; both will be right insofar as they distinguish light from darkness but not insofar as they identify it with a particular color.[3]

What this amounts to saying is that an individual grounded in the esoteric or metaphysical point of view is capable of shifting more loosely between various religious forms. He or she can comprehend the hidden meaning behind the rites and forms of the outward exoteric level. For this reason, they can jump between the varied outward forms that appear different between the numerous religions without falling into a feeling of contradiction and inner turmoil; they recognize the "transcendent unity" behind all the forms or expressions of the one truth. In contrast, theological knowledge is purely exclusivist knowledge and "will of necessity confuse the symbol or form with the naked and supraformal Truth."[4] In short, the exoteric must absolutize what is actually only one relative revelation of truth.

Schoun provides us with some additional definitions to distinguish the exoteric from the esoteric. "This brings us to what is really the definition of the exoteric perspective, namely, an irreducible dualism and the exclusive pursuit of individual salvation."[5] It is this dualism of feeling distinct and separate from the Infinite that really demarcates the average religious believer from the esoteric. This dualism is reflected in the common belief among many religious people that Ultimate Reality is the personal God, which is distinct from us in some radical and fundamental way. Schoun concisely makes this point by quoting a Sufi maxim: "The exoteric way: I and Thou. The esoteric way: I am Thou and Thou art I. Esoteric Knowledge: neither I nor Thou,

---

2. Ibid., xxvi.
3. Ibid., xxx.
4. Ibid., xxxi.
5. Ibid., 47.

Him."[6] This discussion of various degrees of religious insight between the exoteric believer and the esoteric adept leads us to our next key point.

So far, one has learned that for adherents of the perennial philosophy, all of the religions are the same *only in their essence*, which refers to their metaphysics or their esoteric interpretation of Ultimate Reality. It has also been shown that all religions have an exoteric side, which the majority of members cling to as their vehicle for personal satisfaction and individual salvation. The big question still looms: what is the actual *content*, the secret message that all religions unveil at their deepest core?

Point 3: *Reality is hierarchical, admitting of higher and lower degrees.*

Huston Smith and Frithjof Schuon both steadfastly claim that reality consists of a great chain of being, *which begins at the Infinite and terminates in the terrestrial.*

---

6. Schoun, *The Transcendent Unity of Religions*, 47.

The Chain of Being

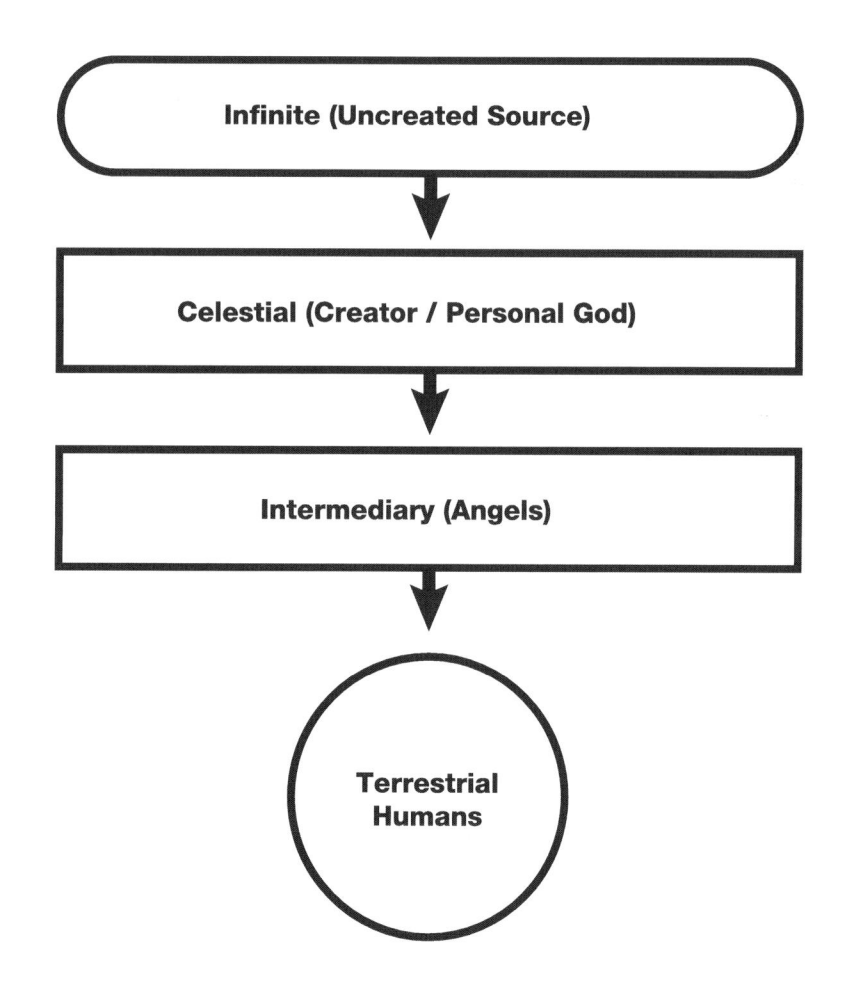

- Infinite (Uncreated Source)
- Celestial (Creator / Personal God)
- Intermediary (Angels)
- Terrestrial Humans

Part I: Five Possible Global Metaphysical Systems for the Twenty-First Century

"Common numbering of the worlds is threefold: terrestrial, intermediary, and celestial. Beyond these three lies a fourth domain that is discontinuous with the others. Not itself a world, it is the Infinite which is their uncreated source."[7] Smith explains that the Infinite can only be described apophatically or through the method of *via negativa*. He points out that, "the Infinite is *nir*-guna (without qualities); in Buddhism it is *nir*-vana (non-drawing, as a fire whose fuel is exhausted has ceased to draw) and Sunyata (emptiness or a void)."[8] He further states, "positive terms apply to the Infinite only analogically."[9] By this Smith means that statements like Brahman is *sat* (being), *chit* (awareness) and *ananda* (bliss) implies only that these terms are more accurate than their opposite meanings.

It is still rather unclear as to how the Infinite, which is without qualities, seems to be described by both Smith and Schuon as having certain abstract qualities, such as—blissfulness, goodness, and wisdom. "This order [the divine order] comprises 'modes': Wisdom, Power, Goodness, that is, the content or the substance of the Supreme Principle consists in these three modes and each of them is at once Absolute, Infinite and Perfect; for each divine mode participates by definition in the nature of the divine Substance and thus comprises absolute Reality."[10] Regardless of the issue of how to understand the Infinite, there is still an important question for our present inquiry and that is how did the process of creation begin?

How did the Infinite give rise to the next level, which is a personal God, and a celestial plane? Schuon informs us that,

> It is Infinitude which so to speak projects the Sovereign Good into relativity, or in other words, which creates relativity, Maya; it is in relativity that the supreme Qualities become differentiated and give rise to the Qualities of the creating, inspiring and acting Divinity, thus to the personal God; it is from Him that are derived all the cosmic qualities with their indefinite gradations and differentiations.[11]

The first hypostasis is the celestial plane and the personal God of the monotheistic faiths. From him, all further derivations are derived and one therefore, gets the intermediate realms of angelic beings and then finally the terrestrial world that we are all-too-familiar with.

What can be mentioned of the celestial plane is that in the final analysis it is not as real or true as the Infinite ground or source. Smith makes this point clear, "Theism is true. It is not the final truth; God's personal mode is not his final mode; it is not the

---

7. Smith, *Forgotten Truth*, 37.
8. Ibid., 55.
9. Ibid.
10. Schuon, *The Essential Frithjof Schuon*, 309.
11. Ibid., 310.

final reality."[12] Nevertheless, this mode "is vastly more real than are the creatures that encounter him in this mode."[13] This idea of a hierarchy or chain of being has been appropriated by other religious studies scholars, most notably John Hick, as a way of understanding religious pluralism. Basically, the idea runs that *each of the different religions is focusing on one of the degrees or levels of reality*.[14] The problem with this approach is rather obvious: it suggests that certain Buddhists, Daoists, and Advaita Vedantists are more correct than all adherents of the monotheistic faiths, because they stress the impersonal Infinite ground, rather than the personal God.

This fact is not shied away from by Schoun who states, "The perspective of Shankara is one of the most adequate expressions possible of the *philosophia perennis* or sapiential esoterism."[15] Perhaps the perennial philosophy is correct, but I am afraid that its usefulness as a paradigm within which to conduct interreligious dialogue is inadequate. Even if the *philosophia perennis* is "true," on a pragmatic level it will most likely not lead to a harmonious globalized religious community *due to its implicit ranking of religions*. Of course Smith and Schuon would strongly reject any arguments suggesting that they are ranking the religions because they will say that on the esoteric level all religions reflect the same structure leading to the "beyond being." I will address this point in my critique in part III, but for now, I wish to return to the actual process of creation in the perennial philosophy.

Point 4: *Creation must of necessity come about because the Absolute is "All Possibility" and the manner of creation is radiation or emanation from the Infinite.*

It is worth looking at one final example of the process of creation because it will serve as a transition into the next contender for a global metaphysical system, while simultaneously tying up any remaining loose ends in one's understanding of the perennial philosophy.

> The Infinite, by its radiation brought about so to speak by the pressure or the overflowing of the innumerable possibilities, transposes the substance of the Absolute, namely the Sovereign Good, into relativity; this transposition gives rise *a priori* to the reflected image of the Good, namely the creating Being. The Good, which coincides with the Absolute, is thus prolonged in the direction of relativity and gives rise first of all to Being, which contains the archetypes, and then to existence, which manifests them in indefinitely varied modes and according to the rhythms of the diverse cosmic cycles.[16]

---

12. Smith, *Forgotten Truth*, 52.
13. Ibid.
14. See Hick, *An Interpretation of Religion*.
15. Schuon, *The Essential Frithjof Schuon*, 90.
16. Ibid., 312.

Part I: Five Possible Global Metaphysical Systems for the Twenty-First Century

One important insight that one can garner from this passage is that creation occurs because the Infinite is "All Possibility" and therefore, *one of these possibilities is to create a spatio-temporal realm*. In other words, the Infinite does not really have a say in the creation of the cosmos, it is borne of the necessity of the Infinite's nature. This nature is pregnant with possibility and so it bursts and overflows, descending into the hypostases or levels of reality discussed earlier. The notion of radiating or emanating, and overflowing under pressure transitions us into the next possibility for a global metaphysical system: emanationism.

Emanationism

The word emanation derives from the Latin term—*emanare*—meaning literally, "to flow from." Given that the perennial philosophy in point four above advocates this precise doctrine, it may seem odd to address emanationism as a separate metaphysical system from the perennial philosophy. However, the perennial philosophy is unique in that it has a very specific view of emanation consisting of only four emanations or levels of reality. In addition, the *philosophia perennis* advocates that all the religions are the same at the esoteric level, a claim not made by other emanation systems. The possibilities for emanation systems are so multifarious, that it would be irresponsible not to recognize that the differences between emanation systems *leads to quite diverse forms of hopes, fears, methods of salvation and implications for the problems of evil, free will and conflicting religious truth claims*. For this reason, I will briefly explore the emanationism of the *DaodeJing*,[17] Hermetic Gnosis, Sethian Gnosticism, and Plotinus because each of these are quite unique and it will be seen *how starting points and other variations lead to radically different conclusions about Ultimate Reality*.

Before delving into the enigmatic text of the *DaodeJing*, I want to list four ways in which emanation systems can differ, so that it will be fresh in one's mind while going over some examples. In this manner, the critical points which lead to differences will be mentally highlighted while reading.

1. *There are different starting points*: the Infinite, the One, the Dyad, the Dao, the Void, the Father, the Mother.

2. *There are different directions of emanating: flowing "in" and flowing "out."* For example, some emanation systems are pantheistic or more accurately, externalizing like the perennial philosophy and Plotinus's system. Other systems are panentheistic or internalizing, like the Hermetism of the *Poimandres* and the creation account of the Christian Gnostic Valentinus.

3. *The number of emanations or levels of reality can vary wildly* from one, two or three emanations as in Simon Magus's system and perhaps the gospel of John, to

---

17. I will utilize the standard Pinyin system of transliteration unless quoting from sources where the older Wade-Giles system is employed.

Four Additional Contenders for a Twenty-First-Century Global Metaphysical System

Valentinus's thirty, to the 365 of Basilidian Gnosticism.

4. Perhaps most importantly, *the path of reunification or the ascent back to the source can range from the most licentious sex acts, to magical and occult techniques, to quiet contemplation and virtue cultivation.*

Daoism

Contrary to the repeated assertions of the perennial philosophy that all of the religions at the esoteric level advocate an emanation doctrine, the historical records suggest that the first emanation doctrine can be found in fifth century B.C.E. China,[18] in the writings of Laozi's *DaodeJing*.[19] Many scholars would likely find even this claim questionable, but given the literal meaning of *emanare* or "flowing from," it can certainly be argued that *at least* two verses of the classic of the Way and its Power promote emanation. The *DaodeJing* is a rich repository of ancient Chinese wisdom and metaphysical/mystical speculation that stands as a direct counter-movement to the predominant Confucian tendencies of the time. In particular, two of the eighty-one cryptic verses *hint at a new metaphysical scheme.*

Verse 42 suggests that all things emanate or to stay true to the Chinese, are begotten or produced from the Dao.

> Tao gives life to the one
> The one gives life to the two
> The two give life to the three
> The three give life to the ten thousand things.[20]

The translation of these lines is actually quite unequivocal, which is a rarity for ancient Chinese, but the clarity of the characters lends more strength to the case that this is not just an example of Westerners taking artistic license with translation. The text reads literally: *Tao* (way or path) *sheng* (begets/produces) *yi* (the one) *yi* (the one) *sheng* (begets/produces) *erh* (the two) *erh* (the two) *sheng* (begets/produces) *san* (the three) *san* (the three) *sheng* (begets/produces) *wan* (the ten thousand/all). This is a classic portrayal of emanation, in this case proceeding from the Dao, which is conceived as nothingness or as an impersonal force. *Notice this is not necessarily the same thing as suggesting that the Dao is "the Infinite" in the sense of all-powerful, all-knowing, wholly good, and all-possibility. The Dao is not an actual entity or an Infinite* endowed with certain characteristics and qualities like knowing and lovingness. This metaphysical picture is therefore,

---

18. It may be possible to argue that in the fifth century BCE in Greece and Sicily that Anaximander's *apeiron* and Empedocles's Love and Strife have some structural similarities to the cosmogonies of emanation systems.

19. Before this time most religions were operating with an *eternal three-story universe* picture of the cosmos with sky or heaven above, earth in the middle, and a subterranean underworld. I will discuss this view and its relation to emanationism and other doctrines later in this chapter and in part III.

20. Lao-tzu, *The Tao-Te-Ching*, 55.

different from the perennial philosophy right from the start, although adherents of the perennial philosophy do attempt to use Daoism to prove their central theses, they cannot do so without distorting the true intentions of many ancient Scriptures.

Daoist Emanation

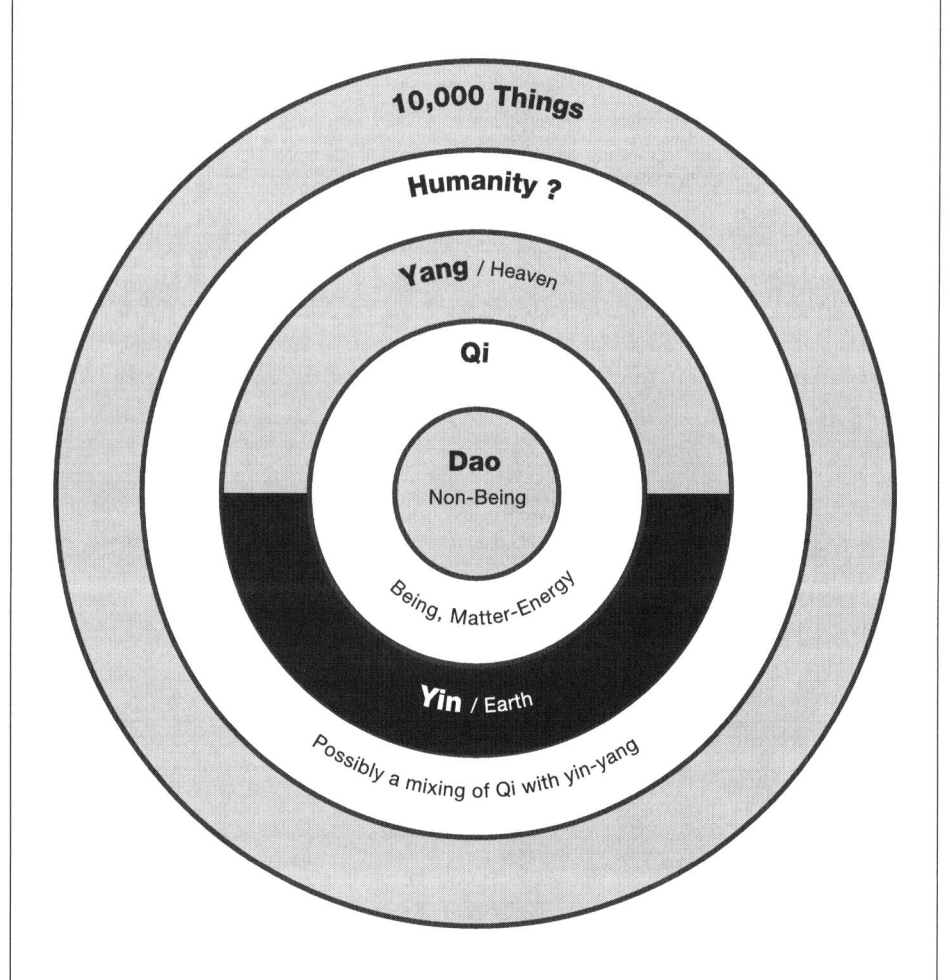

- 10,000 Things
- Humanity ?
- Yang / Heaven
- Qi
- **Dao** — Non-Being
- Being, Matter-Energy
- **Yin** / Earth
- Possibly a mixing of Qi with yin-yang

Part I: Five Possible Global Metaphysical Systems for the Twenty-First Century

One can also learn a great deal about emanation systems when they are described in reverse as sometimes this can clarify what order things emanated if it is still ambiguous. For example, in the above verse it is not exactly clear what the one is or what the two are. However, we learn in verse 40:

> The movement of Tao is to return
> The way of Tao is to yield
> Heaven, Earth, and all things
> Are born of the existent world
> The existent world is born of the nothingness of Tao.[21]

This verse informs us that heaven is *not* the first emanation, rather, it is existence or more accurately Being or the power of Being. This is also a distinction from the perennial philosophy, which states that *the celestial or heavenly realm is the first emanation, the realm of the personal God*. Laozi instead insists that non-being or nothingness, which he calls the *Dao*, produces the power of Being, which we can see from many other verses is known as *De (Te)*. *De* is the term for the power of being, existence or manifestation and hence, the book (*jing*) is called the *DaodeJing*, or the Book of the Way and its Power. *This title aptly describes the ground and the first emanation*. Verse 65 leaves us with no doubts as to this point.

> He who knows the play of Tao and Te
> Knows the nature of the universe
> Tao brings forth Te from its own being
> Te expands in all directions
> Filling every corner of the world
> Becoming the splendor of all creation
> Yet at every moment Te seeks Tao
> This is the movement that guides the universe
> This is the impulse that leads all things back home.[22]

The emanation picture one is presented with here is that of the *Dao giving rise or emanating De or Being and then Being giving rise to heaven and earth and finally heaven and earth giving rise to humanity and from there all the rest of the ten thousand things are derived*. It is a pantheistic or externalizing form of emanation, in that all things spring from the Dao and emanate outwards. The way of ascent or return is through *unlearning what one has learned* and attaining to a state of *pure receptivity* and this receptivity allows one to operate from *wu-wei* or non-calculative action. In other words, action that is in perfect accordance with the Dao at that very moment. This spontaneous form of action is known as *ziran* or naturalness.[23]

---

21. Ibid., 53.
22. Ibid., 78.
23. Cf. ibid. 17, 23, 25, and 51.

Laozi's metaphysical system is rather simple to visualize or graphically represent, but attaining his vision of the ideal lifestyle is extremely difficult for modern humanity. Even Laozi himself says in verse 70, "My teachings are very easy to understand and very easy to practice yet so few in this world understand and so few are able to practice."[24] If Daoism feels impenetrably arcane, then the next classic accounts of emanation will push your reason and imagination past the breaking point.

Hermetic Gnosis

Hermetism sprung onto the scene of early second-century Egypt and it distinguished itself by being a creative pastiche of Jewish, Greek, Roman, and Egyptian ideas. Authorship of the seventeen tractates of Hermetism are ascribed to Hermes Trismegestus or Hermes the Thrice Great. This mythic allusion is to Hermes the Greek messenger of the gods and to Thoth the scribe and master of time of the Egyptian pantheon. Hermetism intricately blends together the new cosmological concept of emanation with Platonic and Jewish themes. The text within the *Corpus Hermeticum* that deals with cosmogony is known as the *Poimandres* and it serves as a sort of foundation text for all the other religious and philosophical works ascribed to Hermes Trismegestus. The *Poimandres* is an account of creation and of the nature of God given by the absolute *nous* or mind of God himself, Poimandres—*peime nte re*, "the knowledge of Re"[25]—to Hermes. The dialogue speaks of a *panentheistic universe,* with God creating within himself nine emanations—for a grand total of ten realms—the Pythagorean perfect number often represented by the tetractys. Ten is a frequently assumed number for emanation systems as it is also found in the *Discourse on the Eighth and Ninth*, a Hermetic text found in the Nag Hammadi corpus, *2 Enoch*, a hugely influential intertestamental text, and the Gnostic *Apocalypse of Paul*.

---

24. Ibid., 83.

25. The meaning of the word *Poimandres* is actually uncertain, but "the knowledge of Re" is a suggestion based upon Coptic and is endorsed by some Gnostic scholars like Birger Pearson.

Hermetic Cosmology

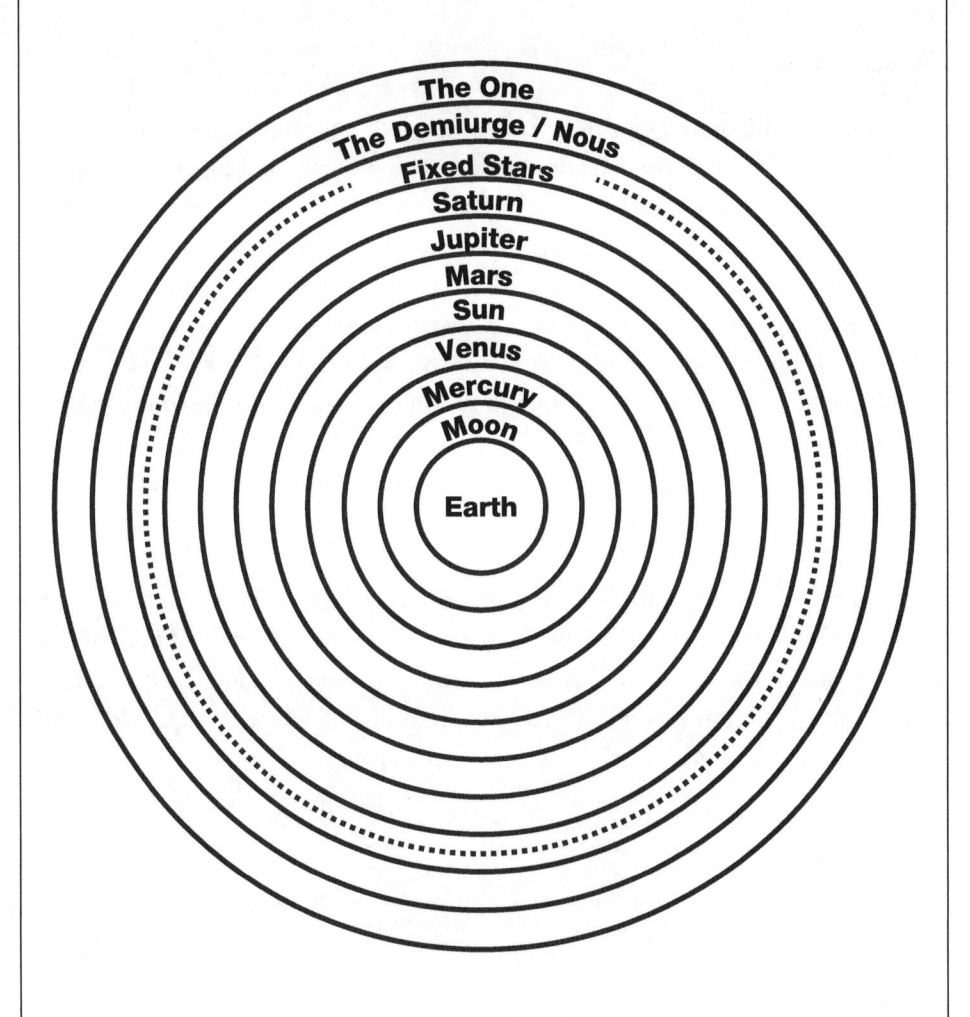

- The One
- The Demiurge / Nous
- Fixed Stars
- Saturn
- Jupiter
- Mars
- Sun
- Venus
- Mercury
- Moon
- Earth

The tractate opens with Poimandres proclaiming, "I am Poimandres, the Intellect of the realm of absolute power."[26] Poimandres is therefore identical with Intellect or *nous*, mind, the source or ground of the totality. Hermes first learns from this divine revelation about the division of light from dark. "All turned into calm and gracious light; and seeing it, I felt a burning desire. And after a little while there was downward-tending darkness,[27] which had come into being in one place; it was frightful and gloomy, and was coiled like a serpent, so far as I could make out."[28] The darkness presumably is heavier and is falling towards the center of the light, if the light is conceived as being a circle the darkness collects at the center. Next Hermes says, "Then the darkness changed into a kind of moist nature, which was unspeakably jumbled and gave off smoke, as from a fire."[29] The notion of a moist nature being unspeakably jumbled is clearly an allusion to Genesis 1:2 with the chaotic waters.

The connection with Genesis is confirmed in the next line.

> Holy reason [or Word] descended upon the natural order. And unmixed fire leaped up out of the moist nature upward into the heights. It was buoyant and bright and at the same time, active. And air being light in weight followed spirit, as it ascended from earth and water to the fire so that it seemed to hang from it . . . and they were in motion because of the spiritual reason [Word] that moved in obedience.[30]

Poimandres explains that the luminous reason or Word that descended upon nature is "a child of God." Reason and intellect however, are not separate from one another and so the Logos should not be viewed as the first emanation; that is reserved for the creation of the craftsman.

The craftsman or demiurge of Plato's *Timaeus* comes on the scene through the interaction of the intellect and his word or reason and it is the craftsman that is responsible for the structured universe. "Now the divine intellect, being androgynous since it existed as life and light, engendered rationally [or through reason/the Word] a second intellect as craftsman; and the latter, being god of fire and spirit, crafted seven controllers, which *encompass* the perceptible world in orbits. And their control is called destiny [or fate]."[31] The craftsman can be seen as the first emanation and then issuing forth from him, there are seven emanations, the seven planets of the ancient world terminating in earth at the center. It is unclear as to whether the eighth, the realm of the fixed stars and the Zodiac, is created by the demiurge or is already there

---

26. Layton, *The Gnostic Scriptures*, 452.
27. No reason is given for why the darkness formed in the first place.
28. Layton, *The Gnostic Scriptures*, 452.
29. Ibid.
30. Ibid., 452–53.
31. Ibid., 453–54.

as the fixed static fire, but in either case, the demiurge can be understood to reside in the ninth realm or inversely, the first emanation.

To reiterate, Hermetic Gnosis represents an early example of a Western emanation theory that is hovering between the old ways typified by the Genesis account, which retains a three story universe and creation out of chaos, and the more philosophical account of creation found within the *Timaeus,* which over time leads to explicit emanation theories like that of Plotinus. It is also unique in that it is panentheistic, as evidenced by the frequent references to the demiurge and to reason and intellect *encompassing* the other realms.[32] "And the intellect that is a craftsman [second intellect/first emanation] together with reason [the Word, one aspect of the bisexual Godhead with intellect being the other aspect of the Ground/Godhead], which encompasses the orbits and spins them with a rush, started its crafted products rotating."[33]

As I will explain below, not all Gnosticisms are the same and Hermetism is no exception, as it is quite different from other popular forms of gnosis in the Mediterranean region. Bentley Layton highlights three key distinctions between Hermetism and other common paths of gnosis.

> (a) The craftsman in Poimandres is neither ignorant nor malicious, unlike Ialdabaoth in the Gnostic myth. (b) Poimandres uses, paraphrases, and adapts the Jewish cosmogony of Genesis, but does not set out to show that Genesis is wrong, as Gnostic myth often does . . . (c) The duty of the Gnostic teacher in Poimandres is not related to a predestined distinction between the saved and the not-to-be-saved; there is no clear delineation of a sect in view, no grand division of humankind, no church of Hermes.[34]

It will be helpful to keep these distinctions in mind while going through the challenging emanation systems of Sethian Gnosis.

Sethian Gnosticism

Anyone who has read through the entire Nag Hammadi Library understands why it is foolish to speak of Gnosticism rather than Gnosticisms. The sheer variety of creation myths is staggering and the complexity of many of the accounts leaves one lost in a labyrinth of emanations, each with a corresponding barbarous name of an archon, or ruler of a particular aeon or realm. Nevertheless, it is possible to make sense of these stories and to classify them according to different kinds of Gnosticism.

I agree with the suggestion of Gnostic scholar Gregory Riley that one should use *an inclusive definition and then a restrictive adjective* to speak about the different Gnosticisms.[35] The inclusive definition would incorporate only two things: a belief in

---

32. The Valentinian system is also panentheistic, but it contains thirty emanations rather than ten.
33. Layton, *The Gnostic Scriptures,* 453–54.
34. Ibid., 449.
35. This suggestion was told to me during a personal correspondence, although I am certain it has

a Monad or Ground of emanation and an insistence that the way of ascent is the same as the way of descent. The only groups that would not fit this basic structure are the Manicheans who believe in two primordial powers one good and the other evil and the Basilidians who posit a primordial dyad.

Beyond this rather austere inclusive definition, one can also reasonably claim that most Gnosticisms advocate *a negative view of the cosmos, a devil figure and some manner of individual gnosis as crucial for salvation*. Aside from these general similarities, the bewildering variety of individual systems necessitates the use of a restrictive adjective, so rather than Gnosticism, one should say Sethian Gnosticism, Valentinian Gnosticism or Thomas Gnosticism.

Although there are such a plethora of Gnostic systems, I will focus on what has been viewed as "Classical Gnosticism" or Sethian Gnosticism. The adjective Sethian refers to the fact that this group, which wrote voluminously, believed themselves to be of the imperishable and unshakeable race of Seth, rather than of Cain. Sethians were an offshoot and counter-movement to Orthodox Judaism, which in the eyes of some Jews was a religion which had failed them time and time again. Perhaps it was this frustration that led to apostasy and polemical writings that reinterpreted the traditions of historical Judaism in a radical and antithetical way to the standard conception.

The classic text of Sethian myth is to be found in the *Apocryphon of John*. Although the *Apocryphon of John* appears to be Christian, it is nearly unanimously agreed upon that the Christian passages are later additions to an original Jewish text. This process of Christianizing Jewish Gnostic texts can also be seen in the text *Eugnostos the Blessed* and the Christian re-adaptation *Sophia of Jesus Christ*. The myth begins its theogony with an account of the invisible Father who emanates Barbelo or the divine mother, who in turn emanates the son Autogenes or self-begotten.

> It is he who gives to all the aeons and in every way, and who gazes upon his image which he sees in the spring of the Spirit. It is he who puts his desire in his water-light which is the spring of the pure light-water which surrounds him. And his thought performed a deed and she came forth, namely she who had appeared before him in the shine of his light. This is the first power which was before all of them and which came forth from his mind . . . The first power, the glory of Barbelo.[36]

The process of emanation begins because the father sees his own reflection on the perimeter of his being. Imagine the Father looking out from the center of a circle with a mellifluously flowing border of light/water and as he gazes, he catches a glimpse of his own image and this inspires a thought and a desire simultaneously. This first thought causes the emanation of the Mother Barbelo or the Mother/Father.

---

been published at some point.

36. *The Nag Hammadi Library in English*, 107. This reference is from the long Greek recension found in NHC II, 1, 4:20–30.

Sethian Myth

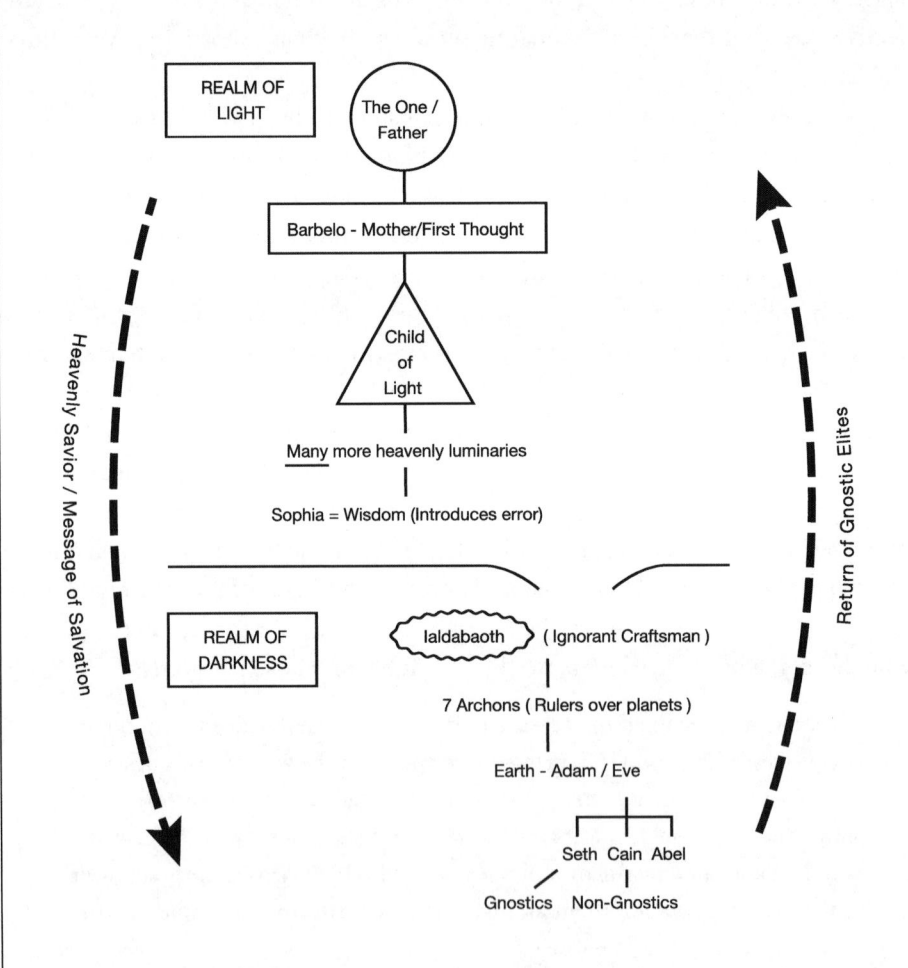

REALM OF LIGHT

The One / Father

Barbelo - Mother/First Thought

Child of Light

Many more heavenly luminaries

Sophia = Wisdom (Introduces error)

REALM OF DARKNESS

Ialdabaoth (Ignorant Craftsman)

7 Archons (Rulers over planets)

Earth - Adam / Eve

Seth   Cain   Abel

Gnostics   Non-Gnostics

Heavenly Savior / Message of Salvation

Return of Gnostic Elites

Next, Barbelo requests certain gifts, like foreknowledge and eternal life from the Father and her requests are granted. Then the next major step happens, which is the birth of the only-begotten son Autogenes. From the son emanate four luminaries and from the four luminaries, further aeons are created *all of which are still within the fullness of the Godhead or the heavenly pleroma*. It is not until the female emanation Sophia, the lowest and last of the heavenly emanations, that a tragic break occurs.

> She wanted to bring forth a likeness out of herself without the consent of the Spirit, he had not approved and without her consort, and without his consideration . . . and she had thought without the consent of the Spirit and the knowledge of her agreement, yet *she brought forth*. And because of the invincible power which is in her, her thought did not remain idle and something came out of her which *was imperfect and different from her appearance* . . . And when she saw the consequences of her desire, it changed into a form of a lion-headed serpent. And its eyes were like lightning, fires which flash. *She cast it away from her, outside that place* . . . And she surrounded it with a luminous cloud and she placed a throne in the middle of the cloud that no one might see it except the holy Spirit who is called mother of the living. And she called his name *Yaltabaoth*.[37]

It is with the birth of Yaltabaoth (alt. Ialdabaoth) that one reaches outside of the *pleroma* (fullness of the stable Godhead) and this is the beginning not of the theogonic account, but of the cosmogonic account. One learns that it is actually from Yaltabaoth *the ignorant and foolish* demiurge that all further creation happens. In the Sethian tradition, *Yaltabaoth is identified with Yahweh the creator God of the Hebrew Bible*. This reversal of the established Jewish tradition is a frequent strategy employed by Sethians as they will also interpret things like the Serpent of Genesis as actually a savior figure, since it entices Adam and Eve to regain true gnosis.

The last point that is worth mentioning is that the cosmogonic account ends with the creation of the seven kings. "And he [Yaltabaoth] placed seven kings each corresponding to the firmaments of heaven, over the seven heavens."[38] In the ancient geocentric cosmology, there is the moon, the sun and then the five planets ending with Saturn. This is important because it explains why so many of the emanation systems have between seven and ten emanations. Beyond the seven planets, there is the realm of the eighth or the fixed stars and then sometimes the ninth, which is either *nous* or the demiurge and then finally, the One.

The Sethian anthropogonic account informs us that poor humans have acquired a sliver of the lost Spirit-Light from the *pleroma* through Yaltabaoth breathing into them. Therefore, it is the duty of the Gnostic to understand the true account of Ultimate Reality and then to make the process of ascent back to the One. The manner of

---

37. Ibid., 110. NHC II, 9, 30-NHC II, 10, 1–20; emphasis mine.
38. Ibid., 111. NHC II, 11, 5.

this ascent or journey of the soul *frequently requires knowledge of the new cosmological map, magic, rituals and passwords.*

In particular, there are two rituals which can be seen in the Sethian tracts: Gnostic baptism and a ritual ascent. An example of a Gnostic baptism can be seen in the *Gospel of the Egyptians.*

> But from now on through the incorruptible man Poimael, and they who are worthy of the invocation, the renunciations of the five seals in the spring baptism, these will know their receivers as they are instructed about them, and they will be known by them. These will by no means taste death. Ieieus eo ou eo oua! Really truly, O Yesseus Mazareus Yessedkeus, O living water, O Child of the child, O glorious name, really truly O existing aeon, iiii eeee eeee oo oo uuuu oooo aaaaa.[39]

This may appear as nonsense at first glance, but in truth it contains what may have been the beginning of a profound initiation involving altered states of consciousness, culminating in a vision of the pleroma or heavenly realm. Notice that the use of vowel chanting could be for one of two reasons, first it could have been a method of invoking certain attendants that presided over the Gnostic baptism or it could represent an encryption of hidden names or meanings through the use of gematria.[40] The latter possibility is intriguing and evidence for it can be seen in that where omicrons are expected next in the list of chanting, there are instead omegas.[41]

Fulfilling the Gnostic baptism meant that the initiate was "worthy of invocation" and therefore, will see and hear the attendants of the pleroma and that in so doing "they will by no means taste death." The initiate has been recognized as a member of the race of Seth the incorruptible one; they are understood as a "child of the Child" meaning a son of Seth. This ritual was likely an individual experience and initiatory, but in *The Three Steles of Seth* there is evidence of a communal ritual of ascent, which was possibly a re-enacting of the initiatory journey of the soul which happened during Gnostic baptism. "For they all bless these individually and together. And afterwards they shall be silent. *And just as they were ordained, they ascend.* After the silence, they descend from the third. They bless the second; after these the first. *The way of ascent is the way of descent.*"[42] This quotation speaks of a communal ritual that likely involved hymnic

---

39. Ibid., 217. NHC III, 2, 66, 1–20.

40. It is worth pointing out that in Ancient Egyptian Religion knowing someone's real name gives one power over that person or even that particular deity. Likewise, eradicating someone's name like what happened to Akhenaton and Nefertiti was symbolic of damning the person and literally erasing them from eternal life. So, many of these Gnostic texts are providing the initiate either *overtly or covertly* with the secret names of the archons, which preside over the various emanations which one must pass by during one's ascent back to the pleroma.

41. Marvin Meyer makes this suggestion in his annotation of the text in *The Gnostic Bible*. If the vowel chanting is meant to encode some secret message one would never be able to figure out the original meaning anyhow, so pursuing this line of reasoning can only go so far.

42. *The Nag Hammadi Library in English*, 401. NHC VII, 5, 127, 10–20.

chanting of the *Steles of Seth* for the purpose of having a mystical experience of union with the source. The three levels described refer to the divine triad that has already been encountered: the Father, the Mother and Geradamas or Autogenes, the Son.

This sort of ritual activity may or may not have included the use of magical paraphernalia as evidenced in *Marsanes,* another Sethian tractate. It is these later Sethian texts, which begin to explicitly incorporate more Platonic motifs. Birger Pearson points out, "Finally, the third-century Platonizing Sethian texts reflect the incorporation of Middle and Neo-Platonic school traditions into the Sethian Gnostic tradition. Adherents of this variety of Gnosticism, which lacks any Christian features, attracted the attention of Plotinus and members of his school in Rome."[43]

Plotinus

Plotinus detested the Gnostics to such an extent that he devoted an entire book, *Against the Gnostics*, to quieting their "sibilant cries." Plotinus abhorred three things: dishonoring the teachings of the illustrious masters of ancient Greece by misrepresenting their true views (*Enn.* II.9.6);[44] proclaiming the creator of the cosmos as evil (II.9.8–9) and the use of ritual magic and licentious acts to affect an ascent back to the source (II.9.14). In contrast, Plotinus considers himself a faithful expositor of Plato (V.1.8), the Creator to be linked with the Good; and the ascent back to the One to consist of *virtue cultivation and quiet contemplation*. Regardless of their differences, the Sethian Gnostics and Plotinus both shared the belief that emanation was the best way of describing the unfolding of the cosmos.

Unlike the Gnostics who unnecessarily set up a "plurality of intellectual essences," Plotinus's system is at first glance quite simple and straightforward. His system consists of at least three, but perhaps as many as five main hypostases: the one or the good, the intellect or divine *nous*/mind, the world-soul or all-soul, nature or *physis* (III.8.4, V.2.1) and then lastly, *hyle* or matter. "There exists a principle which transcends Being; this is the One, whose nature we have sought to establish so far as such matters lend themselves to proof. Upon the One follows immediately the Principle which is at once Being and the Intellectual Principle. Third comes the Principle, Soul" (V.1.10). All the way down the chain of Being one runs into matter or *hyle*, the lowest of all emanations, bordering on complete non-being *because of its distance from the One*, the source of all (III.6.7).

---

43. Pearson, *Ancient Gnosticism*, 99–100.

44. All references to Plotinus are taken from, the *Enneads*, trans. Stephen Mackenna. For the sake of convenience, I will employ the standard in-text abbreviated citations throughout this sub-heading.

Plotinus' Emanation/ Ontological Dependence

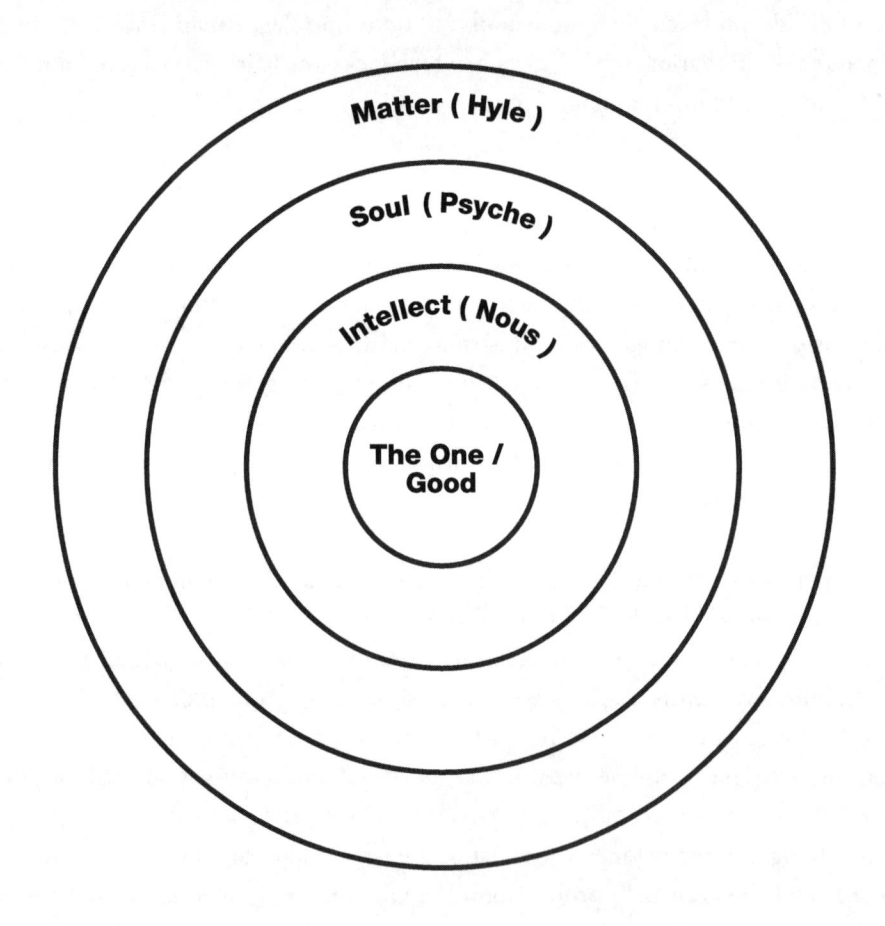

- Matter (Hyle)
- Soul (Psyche)
- Intellect (Nous)
- The One / Good

The One is described as transcendent and beyond Being, and it is unknowable through any normal channels of human cognition. "Certainly this Absolute is none of the things of which it is the source, its nature is that nothing can be affirmed of it, not existence, not essence, not life, since it is that which transcends all these. But possess yourself of it by the very elimination of Being and you hold a marvel" (III.8.10). One can, nonetheless, somehow rest assured that it is the Good. "Once you have uttered The Good, add no further thought: by any addition and in proportion to that addition you introduce deficiency" (III.8.11). Plotinus explains further that the Good lacks nothing and therefore, it strives for nothing; it is a complete unity in eternal repose. However, from this unity the idea of duality must spring forth.

Part of the fullness of the Absolute, which is the One, is the possibility of multiplicity and of thinking, both of which require that there be some degree of separation or duality. Plotinus uses solar imagery as well as the metaphors of a springless spring and an eternal root to explain how the One emanates *Nous* (V.3.9, V.3.12). Just as the sun radiates and illuminates a perfect concentric ring and thereby *externalizes itself through a process that is inherent in its nature*, so too does the One radiate out and *the leading edge of this radiation* is capable of *turning back around* (V.5.5) so to speak and seeing itself; it can have self-vision and self-reflexive thought. This is the function of the intellectual-principle, to have self-vision. What it sees in this vision is the One, *pregnant with the entirety of possibilities and forms*. "It knows the Transcendent in its very essence but, with all its effort to grasp that prior as a pure unity, it goes forth *amassing successive impressions*, so that, to it, the object becomes multiple" (V.3.11). Hence, the realm of the forms are properly to be ascribed to the level of the intellectual-principle.

Aside from the One, which exists in perfect contentment and is wholly self-gathered, and thereby strives for nothing, all later emanations beginning with *Nous*, have a dual character. Therefore, one finds *Nous* striving and turning back around towards the One in eternal contemplation, while at the same time engendering soul. There is always an outward progression and a return or turning back around. Soul as well is engaged in a ceaseless looking or seeing of the intellectual realm of forms and as the vital-principle, it simultaneously is engendering all the lower forms of Being in the visible everyday universe that we are all familiar with. This same pattern of contemplating and then engendering can be seen in all of the creatures, humans included. Only lowly matter is excluded from engendering because it is the end of the sequence; just as the One does not contemplate or strive for anything and only has the out-flowing, so matter conversely only has the capacity to passively receive form.

At the level of the all-soul, which is the third hypostasis and second emanation, this double pattern of looking back and generating forward is explicitly brought out by Plotinus with the terms "celestial soul" or "higher soul," and the "nature-looking soul" or reason principle of the universe. "The total Logos [Soul] with its two distinguishable phases, first, that identified not as Nature but as All-Soul and, next, that operating in Nature and being itself the Nature-Principle" (III.8.3). It is the all-soul's contemplation that produces the lower nature soul and likewise, the nature-soul's contemplation produces beings of the material world; each level of being is a copy of a copy or a vision of a vision. "I gaze and the figures of the material world take being as if they fell from my contemplation. As with my mother the All-Soul and the Beings that begot me so it is with me: they are born of a contemplation and my birth is from them" (III.8.4).

Plotinus's metaphysical system is one of an eternal divine unity with each level of Being contemplating the one above and in its turn, creating copies that are not the same as their originals and act as novel forms of contemplation for still lower levels of Being. What makes the soul unique is that it desired and "contained an unquiet faculty" that insisted upon translating elsewhere what it saw in the authentic realm of the One. It is this desire presumably born of its contemplation, that brought on action and the later creation of the cosmos and with this action and motion, time was also created. Of course, the cosmos and time *eternally exist as possibilities within the fullness of the One* and as ideas within the intellectual principle, but it was not until soul stirred that all of these images that the soul envisaged acquired material existence (III.7.11–13). This is the descent of the soul into nature, that for Plotinus, *one must always keep in mind is not evil*; it is merely a necessary outcome of the act of contemplation.

Emanationism vs. the "Old Paradigm"

What distinguishes the above emanation accounts from earlier myths about the origin of the gods and the cosmos (the eternal three-story universe theories) is that *creation begins from the Monad often conceived as a radically transcendent, depersonalized Source, pure nous/mind or sometimes as that which is beyond Being*. The universe of the ancients had expanded due to technological and scientific achievements and they realized the earth and the cosmos to be much larger places than they originally had thought.[45] Therefore, *the simplistic ideas of a small three-story universe inhabited by actual flesh and blood gods no longer seemed applicable; it lacked any scientific or philosophical subtlety.*

---

45. For example, Aristarchus of Samos (310–230 BCE) and Eratosthenes (276–194 BCE) correctly worked out that the stars are very far away and that the earth was massive in comparison with the current worldview of his time. If the Olympian gods only live on a mountain or somewhere 30,000 feet up in the sky, then who or what is ruling the rest of this vast cosmos?

3 Story Universe vs. Emanation

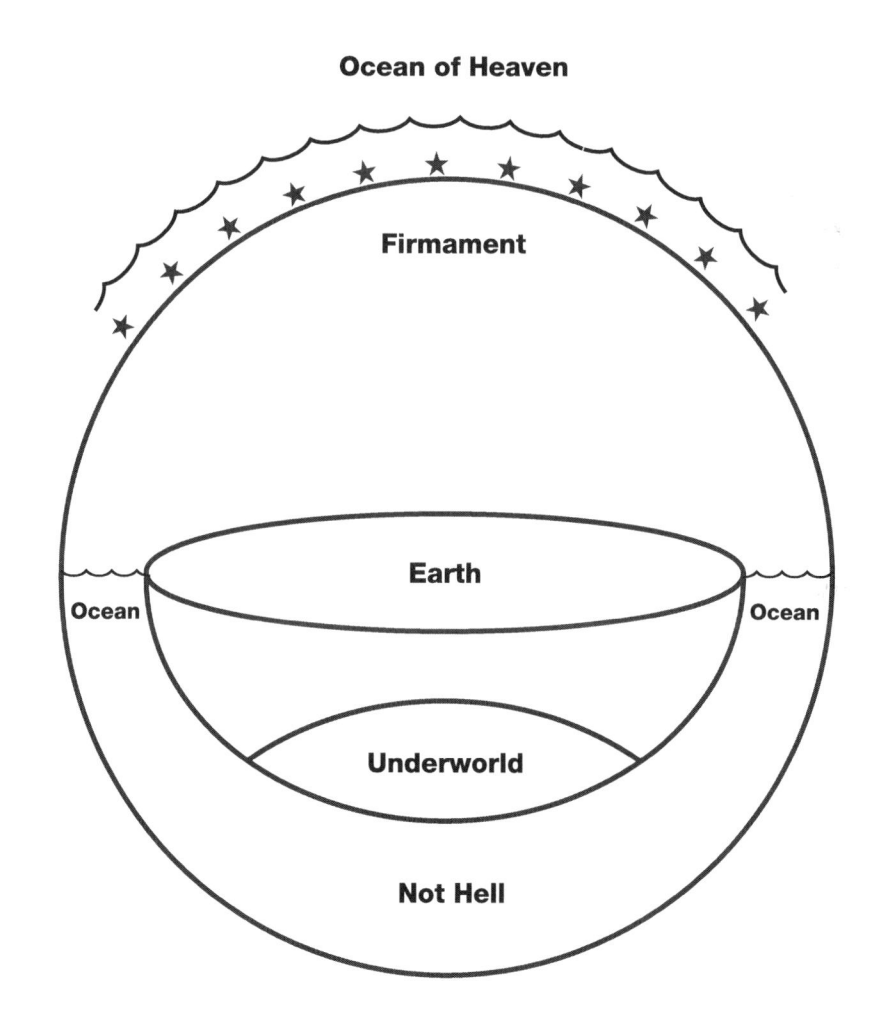

Ocean of Heaven

Firmament

Ocean — **Earth** — **Ocean**

Underworld

Not Hell

Part I: Five Possible Global Metaphysical Systems for the Twenty-First Century

A further difference can be found in the fact that the Monad, the Father, is very intelligent, it is all intelligence, whereas in earlier Greek, Mesopotamian, and Egyptian stories, there is a primordial water and sky universe that is somehow eternal and not the result of emanation. In addition, *this three-story universe is not necessarily endowed or invested with all knowledge and intelligence*; rather, it seems to lack intelligence. Even the ancient Indian and Chinese creation accounts seem to have an eternal three-story universe with certain cyclical changes naturally and automatically taking place over large periods of time, known in the Indian tradition, as *kalpas* and *yugas*.

Another key distinction is that *there is a journey of the soul, which is an implication of the new metaphysics*. For example, in the ancient Greek account of Homer, *there is no journey of the soul because people come from the earth*. There is no "spiritual sliver" that is a remnant of the pleroma or heavenly realm, no "higher aspect of soul" and therefore, *no need of a return journey*. Instead, in Homeric times, one finds a social form of immortality acquired through bravery and heroic deeds. This same pattern can be seen in ancient Hebrew and Mesopotamian accounts. We are just clay or mud vessels filled with air or *ruach* and at death that is basically the end. Virtually everyone goes to Sheol or Hades and only rarely as in Egyptian accounts of the *Aaru* or field of reeds or the Greek Isles of the Blessed, does one see any early visions of paradise or what can be understood as a heavenly plenitude. However, just as emanation theories represented a turning point in the intellectual and religious life of humanity it too was destined to be surpassed by a new contender.

Classical Theism

The term classical theism refers to a certain set of orthodox viewpoints from the Abrahamic religions: Judaism, Christianity, and Islam. These three traditions each share key features concerning their theologies and overall metaphysical paradigms. In this section, I will elucidate these common threads that run through the great monotheistic faiths. However, to say that there are similarities in their theologies is not to give credence to the claims of the adherents of the perennial philosophy. Just to provide a few brief examples on this point, Islam perceives the Trinity as tritheism, the most nefarious heresy, whereas it is a central element of faith for the Christian tradition. Jews do not recognize Jesus as in any way the expected Messiah; whereas, Muslims accept *Isa* or Jesus as one of the prophets, *nabi* or messenger, *rasul*, who brought down a new revelation. Nevertheless, Muslims think Jesus was merely a man and do not accept the incarnation or the resurrection story; instead, they advocate a *docetic view* of Jesus's passion account.

Aside from all their differences at the exoteric and esoteric levels, the Abrahamic faiths do share a set of core beliefs about the nature and function of the one true God. However, before presenting these core beliefs, it will be helpful to explain what classical theism is not and thereby clearly distinguish classical theism from the other two options already encountered: the perennial philosophy and emanationism. The

Four Additional Contenders for a Twenty-First-Century Global Metaphysical System

following is not an exhaustive list of differences, but serves to highlight where and how these three philosophical accounts of religion and metaphysics diverge.

1. The perennial philosophy advocates a great chain of Being that begins with the Infinite, which is described using various metaphors and analogies, but definitively understood as an impersonal Ultimate Reality, with the next level being the celestial or the realm of the personal creator God. *Classical theism places the personal God at the apex of this chain of Being, not as the penultimate element.*

2. Classical theism is distinct from pantheism and the perennial philosophy in that God is separate from and transcends the world; God is not simply immanent.

3. For classical theism, *the creative act unfolds from the will of God and not from a necessity of his infinite nature.* In contrast, both the perennial philosophy and emanationism seem to suggest that the One or the Infinite is compelled out of necessity to create.

4. One critical difference between classical theism and all emanation theories, but especially Christian Gnostic versions, is articulated by St. Augustine. The great doctor of the Catholic Church points out that the fall of humanity through original sin has created an unbridgeable gulf between the human realm and the transcendent and it is only via the grace of God and the redeeming power of Christ that one is justified and one's soul restored to its proper place. Put simply, *the return journey of the soul is impossible without the saving grace of God;* whereas, Gnostics, Neo-Platonists, and Pelagians all believed that either: *meritorious deeds, contemplation or magic could allow one to ascend without the help of Christ.*

5. Classical theism differs from some emanation theories, in that a personal Supreme Being—God—is conceived in classical theism as the *summum bonum* or greatest good. In other words, God is not higher than mind/consciousness or somehow beyond the Good or the One.

6. The Supreme Being of classical theism is also understood as the creator of the world; creation is not delegated to a later emanation or a lower order entity like the demiurge or world-soul as in Plato, Plotinus, Hermetism and Sethian Gnosticism.

The stark contrasts, as well as the subtle nuanced variations between these systems, will become further illuminated by asserting what classical theism is. Due to limitations of space in what is already a verbose chapter, I will only cover three of the central tenets of classical theism. Three of these core beliefs are: (1) There is but *one God* who is understood as a necessarily existing Supreme Being, a personal Ultimate Reality; (2) This God creates the world *ex nihilo* and by divine fiat, rather than a flowing-out (*emanare*); (3) Through reason, one can discern that *God is eternal* and has specific attributes like: immutability, impassibility, aseity, simplicity, omnipotence, omniscience and perfect goodness.

1. The One True God

Judaism, Christianity, and Islam are all united around one foundational and crucially imperative belief: the oneness of God. In Judaism, the oneness of God is so central that the *Shema Yisrael* is to be recited twice a day and is perhaps the most important of the daily *mitzvots*. The *Shema Yisrael* is transliterated from the Hebrew as follows: "*Shema Yisrael Adonai Eloheinu Adonai Echad.*" In English this would read, "Hear O Israel, the Lord is our God, the Lord is One." This creedal profession of faith is taken directly from the pages of the Torah and can be found in Deuteronomy 6:4.[46] The Hebrew Bible provides further examples of the oneness of God from no less of a source than God himself. Yahweh states in Isaiah 44:6, "There is no God beside me."

God's unicity is carried over from Judaism into Christianity. The clearest expression of the oneness of God is in the first and arguably the most relevant creed, the Nicene Creed of 325 CE. The first Nicene Creed of 325 and the revised version of 381 begin with a similar but not identical wording, "We believe in one God, the Father Almighty, Maker of heaven and earth, and of all things visible and invisible." In the case of Christianity, the oneness of God is a little bit trickier, in that Christians adhere to a Trinitarian monotheism of Father, Son, and Holy Spirit. Nonetheless, major interpreters of the Christian faith, such as St. Augustine and St. Thomas Aquinas, have applied the doctrine of divine simplicity to include a Trinitarian conception.[47]

The first pillar of Islam is known as the *Shahadah* or the recitation of the oneness of God. "I testify that, there is no God but Allah, and Muhammad is the messenger of Allah." If the *Shahadah* is professed with sincerity, then it is all that is necessary to be considered a genuine Muslim. As I mentioned earlier, Muslims, in agreement with Jews, do not accept any form of a Trinitarian doctrine. Instead, Islam is considered a religion of radical monotheism. This doctrine of divine oneness is known as *Tawhid*. A verse from the Qur'an that neatly summarizes the Islamic conception of God is Surah 112:1–4. "Say: He is God the Only; God the Indivisible; He gives not birth, nor is He begotten, and He is, in Himself, not dependent on anything."[48] This verse not only draws attention to the radical monotheism of Islam, but also to the necessary existence of God and the utterly transcendent nature of God from the created world.

---

46. All the references from the Hebrew Bible and the New Testament are taken from the NRSV Bible. I will employ the standard abbreviated in-text citations.

47. A simplified defense of the Trinity can be found in St. Thomas Aquinas' *Compendium Theologiae* and a more rigorous defense can of course be found in many places throughout the *Summa Theologiae*. Cf. also St. Augustine's *De Trinitate*.

48. All references to the Qur'an are taken from, the *Qur'an*, trans. M. H. Shakir. I will employ the standard in-text abbreviated citations.

Even though God is indivisible, and independent of anything else other than God's self, God nonetheless ushers in the creation of the world as we know it.

2. *Creatio ex Nihilo*

Scholars have yet to be able to state with certitude when the doctrine known as *creatio ex nihilo* first sprang up. Some believe that it is biblical and that the opening lines of Genesis prove this. "In the beginning God created the heavens and the earth" (Genesis 1:1). However, others like Thomas Jay Oord, Gerhard May, and Jon Levenson, have shown that this is an untenable hypothesis and that the Genesis account is actually *creatio ex materia*, which seems far more likely to me given the antiquity of the Hebrew creation story. It is possible that the first major proponent of creation *ex nihilo* was either Theophilus of Antioch or the Gnostic Basilides, as can be gleaned from the refutations of the Ante-Nicene Fathers like Hippolytus. Regardless of who originated the concept or when it first came on the scene, throughout most of the last two thousand years it has reigned supreme among the orthodox leaders and philosophers of all three of the great monotheistic faiths. In the Jewish tradition, there is a scarcity of scriptural evidence, but there are a couple of verses that have been pointed to in support of *creatio ex nihilo* in Judaism. Aside from Genesis 1:1 mentioned above, the Torah provides another brief clue in Deuteronomy 33:27: "God who preceded [all existence] is a refuge." The other major citation that is far more explicit about the act of creation coming from nothing comes hundreds of years later in the non-canonical intertestamental literature of 2 Maccabees 7:28. "I beg you, my child, to look at the heaven and the earth and see everything that is in them, and recognize that God did not make them out of things that existed." Even though there is a paucity of evidence for creation *ex nihilo* in the Hebrew Bible, the towering figures in Jewish philosophy like Moses ben Maimon or Maimonides as he is better known, are insistent that the orthodox Jewish position is that God created the world out of nothing. In the *Guide for the Perplexed* 2.13, Maimonides states,

> Those who follow the Law of Moses, our Teacher, hold that the whole universe, i.e., everything except God, has been brought by Him into existence out of non-existence. In the beginning God alone existed, and nothing else, neither angels nor spheres, nor the things that are contained within the spheres existed. He then *produced from nothing all existing things* such as they are, by His will and desire.[49]

Maimonides's whole system can be ascertained from this one statement. It is clear that God existed first and then he created the angels and then the spheres and it is possible that the spheres or heavenly bodies could from that point on regulate the created world allowing God to remain that much farther removed and wholly

---

49. Maimon, *The Guide for the Perplexed*, sec. II, ch. XIII.

transcendent from creation. At the dawn of Christianity in the first century, the idea of *creatio ex nihilo* was still in its infancy and so there are few biblical references from the New Testament to support the doctrine. However, some have cited John 1:3, "All things came into being through him, and without him not one thing came into being." Hebrews 11:3 has also been employed in support of *creatio ex nihilo*. "By faith we understand that the worlds were prepared by the word of God, so that what is seen was made from things that are not visible."

In addition to this meager evidence from the New Testament, one finds additional support from early second century writers like Tatian in his *Address to the Greeks* and from the revelation known as the *Shepherd of Hermas* once considered canonical by the early church fathers Irenaus and Tertullian. The unknown author of the *Shepherd* writes in the early second century, "God, who dwells in the heavens, and made out of nothing the things that exist."[50] Tatian, attempting to prove the superiority of Christianity to the dominant paganism of the era proclaims, "For matter is not, like God, without beginning, nor, as having no beginning, is of equal power with God; it is begotten, and not produced by any other being, but brought into existence by the Framer of all things alone."[51] Tatian belabors his point as *creatio ex materia* is central to the Greek conception of creation and he must make it definitively clear that the Christian position is different. "The case stands thus: we can see that the whole structure of the world, and the whole creation, has been produced from matter, and the matter itself brought into existence by God."[52]

By the third and fourth centuries, the doctrine of *creatio ex nihilo* was firmly established in the Christian tradition and St. Augustine can be found vehemently defending it in the face of continued pagan opposition, this time from his former brothers the Manicheans. "There are people [Manichees] who are displeased at your works. They say you made many of them, such as the fabric of the heavens and the constellations of the stars, under compulsion of necessity. They say you did not produce the creation from your own matter, but that its elements were already created elsewhere by another power."[53] In contrast to this Manichean dualism, Augustine makes clear that the Christian position is one of a creation from absolute nothingness. "They are made out of nothing by you, *not from you*,[54] not from some matter not of your making

---

50. See *The Shepherd of Hermas*.
51. Tatian, *Address to the Greeks*, 5.
52. Ibid., 12.
53. St. Augustine, *Confessions*, 300.

54. This is a key distinction and has major implications for Augustine's theodicy. For example, if humans were created of the same substance as God, then they would be simple and incapable of change and basically they would be God, like Jesus and the Holy Spirit. The difference is between being *begotten*, which means of the same substance as God, like Jesus, and being *created out of nothing*, which allows for the possibility of change, choice, free will, and therefore, the potential for evil to arise.

or previously existing, but from matter created by you together with its form—that is simultaneously . . . You made the matter from absolutely nothing."[55]

St. Augustine is consistent in his belief that the true Christian position is *creatio ex nihilo* because it is addressed numerous times in the *Confessions*,[56] but also comes up in his other masterwork—the *City of God*. While discussing the fact that God needs no help in the act of creation from any other beings such as angels, Augustine succinctly asserts, "He needed no material from the world, nor help from the angels, when he made the world itself, and created the angels."[57] Augustine's account is actually quite similar to Maimonides in that God creates the angels and the world. Augustine is also the first to make an even bolder claim, which I will address below and that later philosophers pick up on, and that is *that God creates time itself*. For the sake of space in an already wordy chapter, I will not address the thoughts of St. Thomas Aquinas or those of Luther and Calvin on the subject, but suffice it to say, they all share the belief in creation out of nothingness. Roughly two hundred years after Augustine, a new religion explodes onto the religious landscape, but once again, the burgeoning notion of *creatio ex nihilo* can be found.

In the religion of Islam, one can find a more explicit adherence to *creatio ex nihilo*. It is not surprising that the Islamic tradition would have more scriptural references to *creatio ex nihilo* because it is the most recent of the monotheistic faiths and Muhammad openly states that the prophets of Israel as well as Jesus can be seen as early messengers of which, Muhammad is the seal or paraclete. Muhammad's primary goal was to uncover and reinstate the *din Ibrahim* or true religion of Abraham. He was in contact with many Jews during the Medina period and during the Meccan period even one famous Christian, his uncle-in-law Waraqa Naufal. Perhaps his association with members of the other Abrahamic faiths gave him the opportunity to come into contact with the concept of *creatio ex nihilo*.

It is probable that the Qur'anic position is one of creation out of nothingness. Whereas Judaism and Christianity struggled to find support from scripture, Muslims can cite at least eight verses that appear to advocate *creatio ex nihilo*. Here are the first four verses: "Wonderful *Originator of the heavens and the earth*, and when he decrees an affair, He only says to it, Be, so there it is."[58] This verse informs us that God is the Originator of the heavens and the earth not merely a being that brings order to chaos. "Surely your Lord is Allah, Who created the heavens and the earth in six periods of time, and He is firm in power; He throws the veil of night over the day, which it pursues incessantly; and *He created the sun and the moon and the stars*" (Q 7:54). It is important to remember that most ancient cosmologies either understood the stars as

---

55. St. Augustine, *Confessions*, 302.
56. Ibid. Cf. XII.7; XII.24–25; and XIII.1–3.
57. St. Augustine, *City of God*, 505.
58. Qur'an 2:117. All further references to the Qur'an will be in the standard form of Q followed by the verse number.

eternal, or they understood God as existing in the realm just beyond the fixed stars or the firmament and therefore, God would have created the stars out of nothing and the chain of causes would end with God. The Qur'an is therefore telling us that the stars are not eternal and that God is even more powerful than the fixed stars, which were often believed to control the fates of men and women.

The fact that Allah has created the sun and stars does not necessarily rule out the possibility that he is not alone before the creation of the firmament, but this possibility is also extinguished by the Qur'an. "Say: Who is the Lord of the heavens and the earth? Say: Allah . . . *Or have they set up with Allah associates who have created creation like His*, so that what is created became confused to them? Say: *Allah is the Creator of all things*, and He is the One, the Supreme" (Qur'an 13:16). "Your Lord says: It is easy to Me, and *indeed I created you before, when you were nothing*" (Qur'an 19:9). Qur'an 19:9 is admittedly the only verse that actually uses the word for nothing when discussing creation, but it is fairly clear that Muhammad's message was that God is alone the Supreme Being unlimited in power and creative ability and not restrained by any pre-existing materials. In addition to these four verses, there are at least four more references from the Qur'an and one from a reputable Hadith suggesting that God is unlimited in power and creative ability and is therefore, helped by no one, nor is he in need of any material.[59]

The meteoric rise of Islam in its first hundred years resulted in an intermingling of Islamic religion with ancient Greek ideals. Islam was in control of some of the last great bastions of Greek philosophy like the cities of Harran and Alexandria. This close contact with philosophy led to the rise of alternative Islamic views of creation. Philosophers like Avicenna and Averroes began to inject Neo-Platonic emanationist views into Islam. However, the orthodox view of Islam was still unequivocally that of *creatio ex nihilo*. The famous Sunni jurist and theologian Abu Hamid Al-Ghazali writes in his *The Revival of the Religious Sciences* that Allah is the source of all things and He created them out of nothingness.

> Everything besides Him, men and jinn, angel and devils, Heaven and earth, animals, plants, and inanimates, substance and accident, as well as things perceived and things felt, are all originated things which He created by His power from nothing and made from nought, since He existed in eternity by Himself and there was not along with Him any other.[60]

Throughout the Middle Ages, jurists like Sahih Bukhari and Al-Ghazali secured the widespread belief among the Abrahamic faiths that God's creation of the universe was of his own will and was brought about without any pre-existing materials. This belief continues until today in all three of the monotheistic faiths.

59. Cf. Qur'an 19:67; 21:56; 35:1; and 51: 47. Sahih Bukhari Hadith vol. 4, book 54, #414. "The prophet said: *first of all there was nothing but Allah* and then he created His throne"; emphasis mine.

60. Al-Ghazali, *The Revival of the Religious Sciences*, 7.

3. God's Attributes

God has been conceived by most adherents of the monotheistic religions as the superlative Being in all ways. God's perfection entails that God has certain attributes, which are unique to him such as: atemporality, omnipotence and omniscience to name but a few. The necessity for God's existing outside of the spatio-temporal matrix is related to other attributes predicated of God—simplicity, immutability and aseity. I will not cover all the details here, but the basic idea runs that God, being perfect, is therefore immutable because what could he possibly gain? Being the one and only God and the source of all Being and life, how could God have had a predecessor or progenitor? Therefore, God must have aseity or *a se esse,* self-existence. The perfection of God's nature requires that God also be outside of time, since time is the realm of becoming, change and perishing and God does not change, become or perish. God, out of his love and effluent nature, creates not only the universe, but time itself.

> Since God in whose eternity there is no change at all, is the creator and director of time, I cannot see how it can be said that he created the world after a lapse of ages, unless it is asserted that there was some creation before this world existed, whose movements would make possible the course of time. The Bible says and the Bible never lies: 'In the beginning God made heaven and earth.' It must be inferred that God had created nothing before that; 'in the beginning' must refer to whatever he made before all his works. Thus there can be no doubt that the world was not created *in* time but *with* time.[61]

The belief in God's transcending time and space is not limited to Christianity, but can also be found in the other two major monotheistic faiths. In Judaism, one can find scriptural references to God's eternality. Psalm 90:2 states, "Before the mountains were brought forth, or ever you had formed the earth and the world, from everlasting to everlasting you are God." From Isaiah 57:15 it is clear that God's home is eternity. "For thus says the high and lofty one who inhabits eternity, whose name is Holy." A final reference in the Hebrew Bible to God's eternal and unchanging nature comes from Malachi 3:6. "For I the Lord do not change." This belief in the eternality and atemporal nature of God in Judaism can also be found in areas of the Mishnah as well as later Jewish philosophers of the Middle Ages. The Qur'an in Surah 57 has a wonderfully concise account of not only God's eternality but of all his other major attributes to be discussed below.

> Whatever is in the heavens and the earth declares the glory of Allah, and He is mighty and Wise. His is the kingdom of the heavens and the earth; He gives life and causes death; and He has power over all things. He is the first and the last and the Ascendant over all and the knower of hidden things, and he is cognizant of all things. He it is who created the heavens and the earth in six

---

61. St. Augustine, *City of God*, 435.

periods, and He is firm in power; He knows that which goes deep down into the earth and that which comes forth out of it, and that which comes down from the heaven and that which goes up into it, and He is with you wherever you are; and Allah sees what you do. (Qur'an 57:1–4)

This is without doubt the most succinct statement one can find anywhere expressing all of the major tenets of what comes to be called classical theism. In this one Surah, one learns that God is eternal, transcendent, omnipotent, omniscient, creator of all, and omnipresent.

Nowhere in Jewish or Christian Scripture does one find so much information about God compiled into such a short statement as is found in the above Surah. Nevertheless, the same picture of God's other attributes like omnipotence and omniscience can still be seen reflected time and time again throughout both the Scriptures and the major philosophers of both Jewish and Christian history. As far back as Genesis, the notion that the Hebrew God is at least *the most powerful* can arguably be found. "When Abram was ninety nine years old, the Lord appeared to Abram, and said to him, 'I am God almighty; walk before me and be blameless.'" Although this may be a reference to God as the most powerful of all deities and therefore represent some sort of early henotheism, the reference can also be taken to reflect the early God of Israel as being omnipotent. Another possible reference to God's omnipotence can be found in Jeremiah 32:27. "See, I am the LORD, the God of all flesh; is anything too hard for me?" From Revelation 19:6 one finds a more straightforward statement of God's omnipotence. "For the Lord our God the almighty [or omnipotent as in the King James version] reigns."

Omnipotence is not as obviously evident in the Jewish and Christian scriptures as some of the other attributes later attributed to God like omniscience.[62] For example in Psalms 33:15 it is stated, "From where he sits enthroned he watches all the inhabitants of the earth, he who fashions the hearts of them all, and observes/comprehends all their deeds." Maimonides alludes to this Psalm as implying that God knows and sees all things. In fact this reference was a major contributing factor to Maimonides 10th principle of faith. "I believe with perfect faith that the Creator, Blessed be His name, knows all the deeds of human beings and all their thoughts." Another straightforward reference to divine omniscience in the Hebrew Bible is to be found in Isaiah 46:9–10. "For I am God, and there is no other; I am God, and there is no one like me, declaring the end from the beginning and from ancient times things not yet done." Unlike divine omnipotence, the idea that God knows all things is well grounded in Jewish Scripture.

Turning to Christianity, the belief in God's omniscience can also be seen more frequently. Directly preceding the famous Lord's Prayer, Matthew has Jesus saying, "Do not be like them [Gentiles] for your Father knows what you need before you ask him" (Matthew 6:8). This belief in God's all-knowing abilities is echoed later in Matthew 6:32 and 10:30. Outside of the Gospels, the book of Acts 2:23 states, "this man handed over

---

62. I will return to this intriguing fact later in part III when discussing the merits of Cosmosyntheism over against the other rival systems.

to you according to the definite plan and foreknowledge of God." Finally, in Revelation 2:23 God is speaking and says, "And all the churches will know that I am the one who searches minds and hearts, and I will give to each of you as your works deserve."

St. Augustine and St. Aquinas refine the notion of omnipotence and omniscience. Recognizing what has become known as the problem of theological fatalism or the conflict between divine omniscience and free will, Augustine and Aquinas claim that God's power and knowledge are infinite, *but that does not entail that God can do or know the logically impossible in the sense of violating the most fundamental axiom of the law of non-contradiction.* God knows all things because he is outside of time and has a holistic and transcendent perspective from which to comprehend the whole linear progression that unfolds within the realm of space and time.

The last attribute of God that will be of immense importance in part III is God's omnibenevolence. The centrality of God's goodness is stressed as the most significant aspect of God because it is due to his goodness that he can be trusted without any doubt. In Genesis 1:4, 10, 14, 18, 21 and 25, one finds the words, "And God saw that it was good." These lines allude to all aspects of God's creation, so one is to understand all of creation as good and as the result of a good God. This is reiterated at the end of the creation account in Genesis 1:31: "And God saw everything that he had made, and indeed, it was very good." This inclusion of "very" should leave no ambiguity as to the status of creation and its creator.

In the New Testament, the most striking verse concerning God's goodness comes from 1 John 4:8, "Whoever does not love does not know God, for God is love." Perhaps the most famous of all biblical verses, John 3:16 says, "For God so loved the world that he gave his only Son, so that everyone who believes in him may not perish but may have eternal life." Finally, in the opening of the Qur'an and preceding each Surah, one finds these simple yet telling words, "In the name of Allah the beneficent, the merciful."

Emergent Theism

In the early twentieth century, the last great metaphysicians attempted to reconcile the radical breakthroughs in science with our persistent feeling that God still somehow mattered; the story was not yet complete. One of the more brilliant attempts at wedding scientific theories like evolution with a prevailing religious sentiment became known as emergent theism. The most influential proponent of this view was Samuel Alexander, a little known and oft-overlooked philosopher. Samuel Alexander put forth his grand metaphysical scheme in his Gifford lectures of 1916–1918. These lectures were later compiled into what is now his magnum opus—*Space, Time and Deity*.

In a nutshell, emergent theism, especially as portrayed in *Space, Time and Deity*, turns classical theism upside down. Against the classical tradition, emergent theism holds that there is no omnipotent and omniscient God at the beginning of all time creating the world by divine fiat; instead, there is simply space-time. Emergent theism

Part I: Five Possible Global Metaphysical Systems for the Twenty-First Century

is therefore in line with mainstream cosmology and biology, in discussing the primordial beginning as arising out of the matrix of space-time. "But in any case the universe at the stage of simplicity represented by mere Time and Space has no place for so complex an idea as creation, *still less for that of a supreme Creator. Time and Space are on our hypothesis the simplest characters of the world*, and the idea of a Creator lies miles in front."[63] This quote nicely summarizes the distinction between Alexander and classical theism. He states plainly that his hypothesis is that time and space are all that is needed and he alludes to what will be one of his most progressive/contentious ideas, that the concept of a creator or one could say God, lies miles in front. God is in the distant future, many emergent levels beyond rudimentary space-time, but "deity" is not, an issue I will address below.

Naturally, one is tempted to ask what comes after space-time, what levels of being are there between the simplest and the most complex, such as human minds? This question would be premature because in order to comprehend Alexander's entire system, one must understand his view that "Time is the mind of Space and Space the body of Time."[64] Alexander stresses repeatedly that space needs time and likewise time needs space because without time, space would be a blank, *it could not be divided* and without space, time would be a "mere now." This may seem quite odd, but one must become aware of the fact that for Alexander, time plays a role analogous to the mind or soul within the space-time matrix. "There must therefore be some form of existence, some entity not itself spatial which distinguishes and separates the parts of Space. This other form of existence is Time."[65] Space-time once broken down or separated can be viewed as "point-instants." "I shall call these parts points and instants . . . and meaning by their connectedness or continuity at any rate that between any two points or instants another can be found . . . this is a way of saying that the points and instants are not isolated."[66] The idea of point-instants share similarities with Whitehead's notion of actual occasions or occasions of experience and Leibniz's monads.

Time achieves this act of breaking up the entirety of space-time because its nature is motion, or as Alexander says, time is "restless." It is this restlessness that is later described as a "nisus" or creative urge towards complexity. Time's ceaseless motion or the nisus, allows for the creation of the empirical things higher than space-time, the first of which is materiality.[67] However, all empirical things are endowed with the categories, which precede, so to speak, the rise of the empirical objects. "All things come

---

63. Alexander, *Space, Time and Deity*, vol. 1, 45.
64. Ibid., vol. 2, 38.
65. Ibid., vol. 1, 47.
66. Ibid., 43–44.
67. This is interesting because Alexander is suggesting that space-time may be something like a Higgs field that gives mass to the most simple of subatomic particles. This idea of a Higgs field and the long sought after God-particle has recently been confirmed by the Large Hadron Collider.

Four Additional Contenders for a Twenty-First-Century Global Metaphysical System

into being endowed with the categories and with all of them."[68] "The major categories are the first four—existence, universality, relation, and order . . . The next group of categories are—substance, quantity, number . . . Motion forms the last or third group of the categories. It presupposes the other categories and communicates with them."[69]

So the picture unfolding is that space-time endows all finite empirical entities with the categories and time as the mind of space, breaks up space into point-instants. "In any point-instant the instant is the mind or soul of its point; in a group of points there is a mind of those points, which upon the primary level of Space-Time itself is the corresponding time of that complex. Qualities will be seen to be the special form which on each successive level of existence the mind element assumes."[70] Space-time, as permeated by a nisus towards higher perfection, creates groupings of these point-instants, which are progressively more complex and create "whirlpools" or "crystals" within the matrix of space-time, with matter being the first empirical emergent quality and the closest to pure space-time.[71]

After matter, there are three additional levels before one arrives at mind, the highest level known to humanity. From the highest level known to us to the simplest, each emerged from the more basic as follows: "mind in terms of living process, life in terms of physico-chemical process, sense-quality like colour in terms of matter with its movements, matter itself in terms of motion."[72] It is a character of emergence theory that as each new empirical quality is created the lower levels although composing "the body" of the next level, cannot speculate what the higher level is or what it would be like to exist as or on this higher plane. Another peculiar feature of *strong emergence theories*[73] in general is that the higher levels can exert downward causation, but the lower levels can also exert upward causation, so there is a feedback loop created and a symbiosis. However, Alexander's position is one of *weak emergence* that does not necessarily allow for downward causation.

---

68. Alexander, *Space, Time and Deity*, vol. 1, 188.

69. Ibid., 322–23.

70. Ibid., vol. 2, 39.

71. Alexander actually states that motion is "the meeting point between the categories and the first qualities" and so in a sense it is actually the first quality, but it did not emerge for it always has been.

72. Alexander, *Space, Time and Deity*, vol. 2, 67.

73. Some of the best examples of strong emergence proposals can be found in the work of C. D. Broad, C. L. Morgan, Michael Polanyi, Roger Sperry, and Philip Clayton. For examples of weak emergence interpretations that still employ "God-language" see in addition to Alexander, Michael Arbib, and Mary Hesse.

Key Emergent Levels

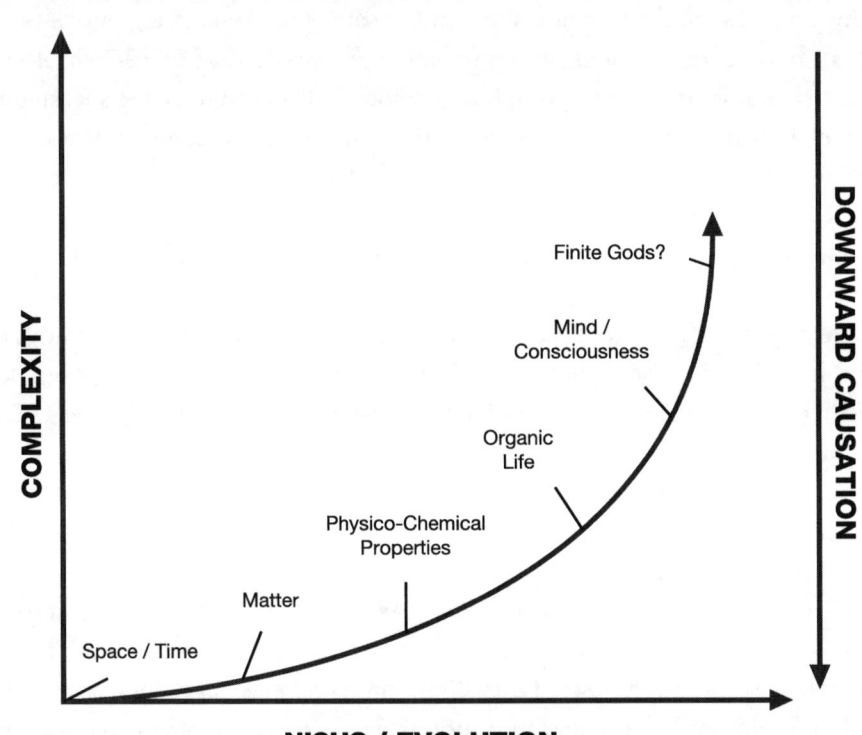

```
         ↑
         │                                        Finite Gods?  ↗
         │                                                    ╱       ↑
         │                                   Mind /         ╱         │
         │                                Consciousness  ╱            │
COMPLEXITY                                            ╱                │  DOWNWARD
         │                            Organic      ╱                   │  CAUSATION
         │                             Life     ╱                      │
         │                                   ╱                         │
         │               Physico-Chemical ╱                            │
         │                 Properties  ╱                               │
         │                          ╱                                  │
         │              Matter  ╱                                      ↓
         │         Space/Time╱
         └──────────────────────────────────────→
                      NISUS / EVOLUTION
```

Four Additional Contenders for a Twenty-First-Century Global Metaphysical System

Where Alexander's metaphysics becomes particularly important for the present study is in his belief that mind, what we think to be the highest level, may actually be "the body" of a yet higher level. It is at this intriguing juncture that it begins to be quite difficult to discern his intended meaning. What is certain is that the next level after mind is the quality deity. "Deity is the next higher empirical quality to the highest we know."[74] However, it is unclear as to whether that level exists currently but unbeknownst to humanity or whether deity understood as the infinite God is merely an ideal.

One can infer three possible usages for the term deity and it is this ambiguous employment of the term that makes deity so difficult to comprehend. Deity can mean: (1) the next higher empirical quality after mind. This next level may or may not already exist and if it does, we can call the bearers of this quality as actualized, "finite gods" or angels. (2) Deity is sometimes referred to as infinite deity and in this usage, deity is referring to something similar to the standard usage of the word God, an all-powerful all-encompassing object of worship and reverence. (3) Lastly, deity can stand for the nisus of space-time where the restlessness of time pushes the world ever onward straining to realize new forms of deity or ever-higher levels of emergent empirical qualities. Thus, deity for the level of physico-chemical processes would be life and deity for life would be mind; deity is just a word signifying the next higher stage from the stage one currently resides in.[75]

Alexander first explores the possibility of deity–1 and it is at this point that he states there may be an actual emergent level of "finite gods" containing the quality of deity, whatever that may be. As Alexander says, "What that quality is we cannot know; for we can neither enjoy nor still less contemplate it . . . What we know of it is but its relation to the other empirical qualities which precede it in time."[76] Nevertheless, Alexander reminds his readers of an early image of angelic beings contemplating the level of mind, which he says he formerly used "half-playfully," "but we now can see it is a serious conception."[77] This statement suggests to me that he believes the quality of deity to be instantiated in finite gods or angelic-like beings.

There is additional evidence to bolster the assumption that Alexander believed angels represented the quality of deity actualized in the real world. "For the angelic quality the possession of which enables such beings to contemplate minds is this next higher empirical quality of deity and our supposed angels are finite beings with this quality. We shall have to ask how such finite deities are related to the infinite God, for they themselves are finite gods."[78] Later in the same chapter in reply to the question of whether finite gods actually exist he, not surprisingly, responds we do not know (because we cannot know the higher level with certainty but only through a feeling or sentiment).

---

74. Alexander, *Space, Time and Deity*, vol. 2, 345.
75. See p. 348 for this understanding of the term deity.
76. Alexander, *Space, Time and Deity*, vol. 2, 347.
77. Ibid., 346.
78. Ibid.

The second aspect of Alexander's conception of deity, or deity-2, is whether or not an infinite deity or God actually exists. To this possibility, he is compelled to answer: no. "Does infinite deity exist? The answer is that the world in its infinity tends towards infinite deity, or is pregnant with it, but that infinite deity does not exist."[79] If infinite deity was fully realized or achieved, then "God, the actual world possessing infinite deity, would cease to be infinite God and break up into a multiplicity of finite Gods, which would be merely a higher race of creatures than ourselves with a God beyond."[80] The problem is that infinite God or deity would conflict with the categories, which apply to all existent empirical entities. God's body, space-time, created the categories but could never be subject to them. For example, as infinite, God could not fulfill the category of universality because a universal or Form is meant to be repeatable, but infinite deity understood as the whole could admit of no repetition. Furthermore, infinite deity or God could not be a substance because as the whole, it could not be related to any other substances and relatedness is a categorical imperative for substances.

For these reasons and others, Alexander is led to state that, "Infinite deity then embodies the conception of the infinite world in its straining after deity."[81] This straining after deity brings us to the third and final element of the term deity or deity-3. "Deity is a nisus and not an accomplishment."[82] In other words, deity is a combination of the restlessness of time with the idealized level yet to emerge. The actual God of our religious sentiment is an ideal, an image of the hoped for attainment of higher possibilities yet to come. "God as an actual existent is always becoming deity but never attains it. He is the ideal God in embryo."[83]

Samuel Alexander's emergent theism bridges the gap between the metaphysical systems which unequivocally argue for one religious ultimate and the positions of Whitehead, Cobb and Griffin who insist that there are multiple religious ultimates. Alexander's metaphysics could be argued to have one religious ultimate—space-time—but as he himself says, space-time is no religious object of worship. It could be that time or the nisus towards deity is the one ultimate, perhaps space and time are two ultimates, or it could be that Ultimate Reality is the totality of the empirical existents within space-time. The point is that it is uncertain how many ultimates there are and therefore, Alexander's philosophy provides a nice transition from theories of a single religious ultimate—either a creator or a creative force—to the central thesis of this book: that there are multiple religious ultimates. In the subsequent part, I will be expounding my own hypothesis that there may actually be *five mutually grounding ultimates*.

79. Ibid., 365.
80. Ibid.
81. Ibid.
82. Ibid., 364.
83. Ibid., 365.

Four Additional Contenders for a Twenty-First-Century Global Metaphysical System

Summary

- The perennial philosophy, emanationism, classical theism, and emergent theism adequately reflect a wide range of the spectrum of live and viable options for metaphysical systems in the twenty-first century.

- The perennial philosophy believes that all religions are the same on the esoteric level.

- Emanationism suggests that the universe is hierarchical and all things flowed out from the One or the ground. The closer something is to the source, the greater the share it will have of the Good and of Being in general.

- Classical theism differs from emanationism because it states that God created from divine fiat rather than by any internal or external necessity.

- Classical theism also suggests that the return to God requires the redeeming power of Christ as intermediary between the fallen soul and God.

- Emergent theism reverses the traditional picture found in classical theism and puts the idea of God or finite gods as the most recent emergent phenomenon in the universe, rather than as an all-powerful, all-knowing entity at the beginning of the evolutionary process.

- Deity can be understood in three ways for Alexander, but none of the three ways suggests that an actual infinite Being resembling the classical God has ever or could ever exist.

PART II

Cosmosyntheism: A New Option

CHAPTER 3

The Five Mutually Grounding Ultimates and Cosmosyntheism's Nine Key Advancements

The pure conservative is fighting against the essence of the universe.

—ALFRED WHITEHEAD, *ADVENTURES OF IDEAS*

Jesus said, "Blessed is he who came into being before he came into being. If you become my disciples and listen to my words, these stones will minister to you. For there are five trees for you in Paradise which remain undisturbed summer and winter and whose leaves do not fall. Whoever becomes acquainted with them will not experience death.

—*THE GOSPEL OF THOMAS*, LOGION 19

IN PART I, I presented the core beliefs of what I consider to be the five most viable options for a global metaphysical system in the twenty-first century. In chapter 1, I described the positions of John Cobb and David Griffin, both of whom advocate a pluralistic metaphysics based upon the philosophy of Alfred Whitehead. I further showed how this pluralistic metaphysics that consists of Creativity, God, and a World can be invoked to explain the differences in the accounts of religious experience from around the world. The idea being that each religious tradition is *primarily* focused on one of the three elements that comprise Ultimate Reality and therefore, they have differing accounts of their experiences of the sacred.

In chapter 2, I provided a cursory overview of the other four live options for a global system: the perennial philosophy, emanationism, classical theism and emergent

Part II: Cosmosyntheism: A New Option

theism. The main objective of that chapter was to layout the primary beliefs and guiding principles of those four systems, so that the similarities and differences between them could be clearly seen. One of the common underlying threads that unite these four options is the belief in only one truly ultimate element composing Reality, although each of the four systems came up with ingenious ways of accommodating plurality within their metaphysical scheme. However, in chapters 10 through 13, I will systematically argue for the strengths of Cosmosyntheism over these four options. Whereas chapters 1 and 2 were merely *descriptive*, the remainder of the work will be *both descriptive and argumentative*.

The current chapter provides an introduction to the five elements that comprise religious ultimacy—the Forms, God, a World, Creativity/Eros, and the Receptacle—and a brief explanation of why all five are necessary, co-eternal and mutually grounding. The other major purpose of this chapter is to list the specific modifications Cosmosyntheism has made over other contemporary theologies and the Cobb/Griffin family of process theology in particular. There are nine key advancements. The details of all of the advances will be delineated thematically in the succeeding chapters.

The Nine Advancements

1. Five mutually grounding ultimates instead of three or two (chapter 3).
2. A new interpretation of the ontological principle that allows for ingression and exgression of Forms (chapters 3 and 6).
3. The possibility that all five elements of Ultimate Reality operating as one complex adaptive system could give rise to an even higher emergent level of reality over time, *even higher than what most people now call God and I would call reality as a whole* (chapters 3 and 5).
4. An expanded notion of free-will based upon my revised ontological principle (chapter 10).
5. A long overdue reversal of the demonization of the roles of chaos and randomness and the removal of their unfortunate association throughout history with women, primitive indigenous groups, and anything foreign. Put differently, a call for the sanctification of the roles of chaos and randomness (chapter 6).
6. Artificial Intelligence and cyborgs as a new analogy for understanding panentheism (chapter 5).
7. A new type of categorical imperative designed to mediate between conflicting ethical views or systems (chapter 14).
8. A complete system of self-cultivation, which is derived from the principles of Cosmosyntheism (chapter 14).

9. A novel conception of worship and religious experience for the twenty-first century (appendix).

The Five Mutually Grounding or Presupposing Ultimates

Why is it more rational or logical for there to be only one ultimate? The universal question will still remain—where did that One come from? If we must eventually stop our chain of regression at some terminal point or first cause that is somehow necessary, *then why can't we just as coherently state that we must stop at five rather than one*? It is just as perplexing and vexing a problem to answer where did the One come from as, where did the five come from? For millennia, philosophers have grappled with the problems that unfold from a chain of regression terminating in one necessary ultimate. Doesn't it make more sense to assume a set of initial conditions or elements that when properly described, *more adequately explain the universe as we currently know it . . . sense it . . . feel it . . . intuit it to be like?*

The ancient Greek ideal of perfection still haunts us today and we feel somehow entranced by the belief that one ultimate is always somehow better or more rational than two, three or five. Perhaps we owe it to ourselves to at least entertain the possibility that perfection need not be found in a tracing back or simplification down to the numbers one or zero. I argue that this fundamental paradigm shift—which could become one hallmark of this century—will be a move towards plurality, complexity and interrelatedness.

It should be pointed out that ancient philosophers and theologians did toy with the idea of a metaphysical dualism or even with a dialectical or triadic structure. However, to my knowledge few, if any, explicitly stated a belief in five ultimates.[1] Nevertheless, there are at least four reasons why I have made the transition to five ultimates rather than one, two, three, six, or more.

1. The first reason, I have already addressed above and that is that there is no logical rule whereby one must be confined to a regression back to a single ultimate. In fact, I will argue later that it is more logical or at least more practical to adopt five ultimates.

2. The second reason has to do with the Cobbian/Griffian school or family within which I find myself closely aligned. Cobb focused on three ultimates, but Griffin has most recently hinted in passing at four, so it is a short step to adding one more.

3. A third reason stems exclusively from problems of theodicy that arise within

---

1. Of course, there is the idea of Five Element Theory in Chinese medicine and philosophy as well as a post-Aristotelian Five Element Theory in the Western world. Neither of these systems, however, are really suggesting that these five are religious ultimates or that they have the nature or functions that I am ascribing to the five ultimates I have identified. Instead, Five Element Theories describe physical reality, phenomena, the natural world and its changes, *not metaphysical reality.*

Part II: Cosmosyntheism: A New Option

all philosophical forms of monism (e.g., in the end, all evils eventually trace back to the one source).

4. In regard to why not more than five, I rely on a combination of both *religious experience and philosophical analysis*. Upon a thorough examination of religious Scriptures and accounts of religious experience, there does not appear to be more than five ultimates being dealt with. In addition, philosophically, you do not need to posit more than five ultimates in the beginning, in order to adequately explain what our common-sense reasoning tells us about the present state of affairs.

I will not directly go into the four reasons in any more depth at this point but each one will come up time and again throughout the rest of this work and thus, my reasoning for all four points will become clear if it currently seems to remain rather obscure. I now return to the issue of interrelatedness and complexity.

Within the sciences, one can already see a trend away from Occam's vicious razor and its corresponding reductionism, towards a science of systems and complexity. The sciences of emergent complexity, systems biology, chaos theory and quantum mechanics are but a few areas where the strict determinism of older scientific theories appears to fall short. Metaphysics and theology, if they are to have any relevant future in the twenty-first century, must adapt and evolve with the advances in the scientific community. Cosmosyntheism incorporates complexity, interrelatedness, chaos and indeterminacy into the groundwork of its system. However, in this chapter I will restrict my focus to explaining how Cosmosyntheism involves complexity and interrelatedness. I will employ examples from cutting-edge science in order to help clarify certain claims that are made.

At the heart of Cosmosyntheism lies a pluralistic metaphysics. This pluralistic metaphysics is comprised of five mutually grounding or pre-supposing elements: the Forms, God, Creativity, a World and the Receptacle. By mutually grounding or pre-supposing, I mean that if you were to take away even one of the elements, then inconsistencies would arise or incoherence would ensue. In other words, *the five elements are interrelated, co-necessary and co-eternal*. One must also keep in mind that my hypothesis *is that each of the world's religions primarily focuses on one or more of these five elements of Ultimate Reality and hence, their descriptions of religious experience may differ.*

Definitions of the Five Ultimates

It is the goal of the subsequent five chapters to elucidate *the nature and functions* of each of the five ultimates individually and in detail; however, in order to explain the complexity and interrelatedness of each of the five, some preliminary definitions are in order.

1. *The Forms*: The Forms are possibilities,[2] ideas, concepts or images that are *mainly,*

---

2. A critical distinction must be raised here between the classical view of the Forms as typified in Plato's works and the way that the term Forms is used today by both process theologians and the

The Five Mutually Grounding Ultimates and Cosmosyntheism's Nine Key Advancements

but not solely, envisaged or entertained by God *primordially* in a theoretical, not-yet-actual and therefore, in a longing manner. However, some of the more abstract Forms, such as, order, chaos and process *have always been instantiated or actualized eternally*. The Forms must reside in something actual, as that which is ideal must be related to an actuality per Whitehead's ontological principle and Aristotle's *Metaphysics*. Some Forms are instantiated in a primordial world and through the reciprocal process of the God-World interaction, *new Forms, i.e., possibilities, arise for both God and the World*.

2. **God**: By God I do not mean anything similar to the classical theistic position. I envision a new list of divine attributes—maxipotent (maximally powerful), maxiniscient (maximally knowing), omnipresent, omnibenevolent and the source of moral norms and values. In other words, God is not *all powerful, but maximally powerful and not all knowing but maximally knowing*. God is also actual, a real entity or more accurately, *a serially ordered society of occasions of experience* just as you and I are. However, God is also much more than you or I, in that God is a higher-order being, with a unique set of functions in at least a few ways distinct from our own roles and functions. Also, I accept the doctrine of *panentheism* implying that all things are in God, but not numerically identical with God. Everything may be *in* God, but not necessarily *of* God in the sense of either materially, formally, finally or efficiently derived from God. Therefore, God is the source of *many* of the novel Forms presented to the World, *but not all of them*. This gives way to my definition of a World.

3. **A World**: There is always some world or other consisting of numerous actual entities possibly "strings" presumably of an ultra-simplistic indeterminate nature at the beginning of any new universe or cosmic epoch. *Our particular universe may not be necessary, but a World is*. The fact that God is not alone at the beginning means that power is shared among all the various actualities and thus, God does not have unilateral coercive power over the rest of the entities. Instead, power, *at least among actualities*, is always relative and persuasive rather than coercive and absolute.

4. **Creativity**: Creativity is the fundamental metaphysical principle or objective. Both God and the World are subject to this utmost law or *principle of oscillation,* whereby all things are brought together and then pulled apart, again and again. *It is a single energizing power that has two directions of movement*; when it pulls things together it is called Eros and when it pulls things apart and entices them onwards, it is known as Creativity. As Eros, it attracts like-to-like via resonance and then as Creativity it pulls them apart in order to allow for a creative

---

perennial philosophy. The classical view did not necessarily understand the realm of Forms to consist of all the possibilities that could ever come up, but instead as universals or blueprints, of which, things on earth were particular instantiations and conglomerations of Forms and matter. Process theists and perennialists however, use the term Forms to refer to possibilities, ideals, as well as universals. I will primarily be employing the term Forms under the contemporary usage.

Part II: Cosmosyntheism: A New Option

self-transcendence and genuine novelty within the world.

5. *The Receptacle*: This is a complex notion best understood as either a plane, membrane, space, or sub-space of mutual immanence. *It is the place before and after emplacement within the phenomenal world; yet, it is also the space in which all things come to be.* It is the realm where all things come together and intermingle and share in togetherness and communion. As the term "receptacle" suggests, it also passively receives all the data that comes into it. Additionally, *it retains this information forever* as if each moment in time is emblazoned onto a piece of film or a piece of "holofilm" comprised of encoded interference wave patterns always available from that point on to be drawn from as data.

How They Ground One Another

Now that we have some working definitions of the five ultimates, we can explore how they are interconnected and mutually grounding. I will start with the Forms. The Forms ground both God and the World by providing possibilities for actualization or realization in the material world. Without this formal ground, what would be the need for Creativity and what would there be to retain and record in the Receptacle? The Forms are raw ideas, concepts, ideals or imaginative possibilities that are available to become instantiated by any actual entity. God and the World primordially exemplify *some* Forms and so *some* Forms have been eternally actualized, such as the abstract notions of order and chaos, love and beauty and the Good. However, most of the Forms are as yet still ideals and non-actual, awaiting to be manifested within the World. It should be pointed out here that many constructive theologies even within the emergence and process communities would disagree with me on the notion that only a small set of initial Forms were within God and a World at the beginning.[3]

The main point concerning the Forms is that *there needs to be a primordial set of data*, ideas or concepts that the actual things, God and a World of simple finite entities can draw from in order to set the process of experience and creation into motion. This is the primary role of the Forms or Ideas, *they are the raw ingredients, the food for thought and imagination and hence, they provide a ground for both God and the World and a need and purpose for both Creativity and the Receptacle*.

The Forms are nevertheless, nothing without God and a World. This is because God and the World provide an ontological grounding for the Forms to reside in. There

---

3. Cf. Philip Clayton's recent work, *Adventures in the Spirit*. Clayton argues for a synthesis of emergence theory with classical Trinitarian thought and thus proposes that God at the beginning was in a sense infinite. The work of Stuart Kauffman, *Reinventing the Sacred: A New View of Science, Religion and the Sacred*, proposes a non-theistic or modified pantheistic version of emergence theory that nevertheless has a role for spirituality to play, namely through creativity as an ultimate. In addition, I have already discussed how most Whiteheadians and process thinkers believe that the primordial nature of God contains all the Forms.

can be no Forms, ideas, or possibilities without something actual to contain, envisage and act upon these ideas or Forms. So God and the World also provide a ground for the Forms. This is Whitehead's ontological principle.

> Everything must be somewhere, and here "somewhere" means "some actual entity"... This "somewhere" is the non-temporal actual entity [the Primordial Nature of God]... It is a contradiction in terms to assume that some explanatory fact can float into the actual world out of nonentity. Nonentity is nothingness. Every explanatory fact refers to the decision and to the efficacy of an actual thing.[4]

God helps to order and provide pertinent Forms to each of the actual entities that make up the World and so God attempts to set relevant limitations on possibilities at any given moment. God is the primordial higher-order being that has always existed, but God needs the Forms just as much as God needs the World.

God needs the World because the World has its own real power, indeterminacy, randomness and its own Form(s). The world helps God to play out progressively more sophisticated Forms and through the feedback loop that is inherent in their interconnectivity, God gains a new form of knowledge: *experiential or existential*. So, the World provides loci of experience, but it also is the ground of randomness, which results in *unforeseen transmutations and possibilities* for God and future worldly occasions of experience. The World is *a genuine ground of primordial otherness* that allows for an authentic primordial community and *an eternal form of love and care between God and the World*. However, this community would be a prison full of nothing but solitary confinements if it were not for Creativity/Eros and the Receptacle or Storehouse. Creativity/Eros grounds God, the World and the Forms because it is the original force or metaphysical principle of oscillation. Creativity brings the individual entities or members together into a communion of mutual immanence. Creativity is the ground of both process and growth in that it is the raw power that drives the entire system upwards and onwards. Without this ground, *reality would be lifeless, static and inert*. This oscillating power shifts all entities from a particle-like state to a wave-like state. *It brings all things into and out of the Receptacle*.

The Receptacle provides the stage or the place for mutual immanence or togetherness to occur. If Creativity is the how, the Receptacle is the where. It is passive in its reception of entities and data. However, like a giant piece of holographic film, it retains an image, a memory of all that comes within it *at every moment*, permanently recording it. *It is the ground for commingling, sharing and immanence*.

Without the Forms there would be little to no possibilities, merely vacuous or impoverished entities. Without God, there would be no primordial ordering of relevant possibilities. Without the World, there would merely be the imaginative playing out of God's original plan lacking actuality and any continued, spontaneous novelty; that

---

4. Whitehead, *Process and Reality*, 46.

Part II: Cosmosyntheism: A New Option

is if there could still even be a God. Without Creativity, there would be no progress or interrelation. Without the Receptacle there would be no mutual immanence and no record of what has happened. Without God, a World, Creativity, and the Forms, the Receptacle would permanently remain empty and incapable of achieving its primary function, which is to receive. The mutually grounding interconnections go on and on, but I must move forward since the general idea has been sufficiently illustrated.

Cosmosyntheism's
5 Mutually Grounding Ultimates

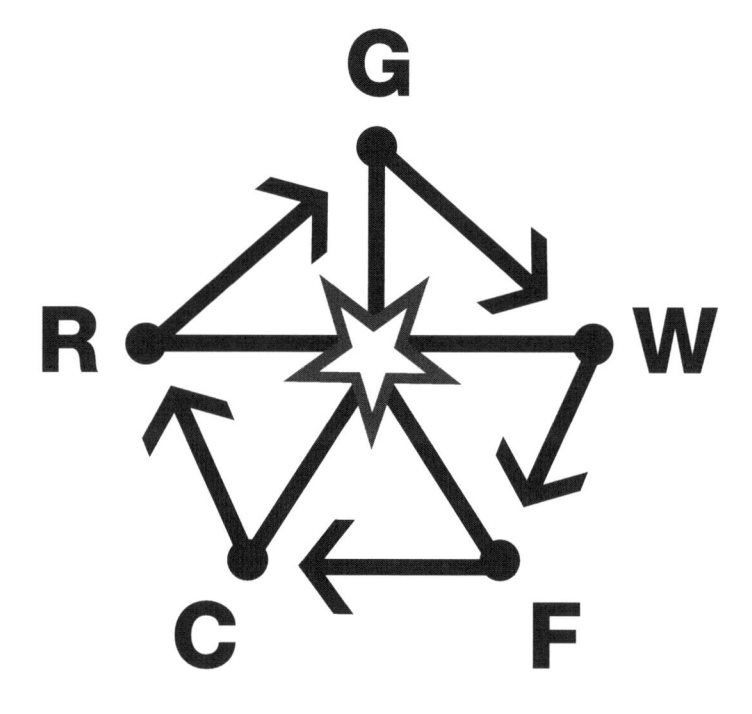

Part II: Cosmosyntheism: A New Option

Reality: A Complex Adaptive System?

What if reality is a complex adaptive system dwelling at the edge of chaos? This is exactly what I am striving to put forward, the notion that reality is not simple, but has emerged out of a complex web of interconnections and mutually supporting relationships among numerous primordial elements. Interestingly, many contemporary sciences, such as complexity science, systems biology, artificial systems, and chaos theory are drawn towards models of nature as a complex adaptive system. *By complex it is meant that there are multiple elements involved and by adaptive it means that the system grows and learns from the interactions of its members.*

In terms of Cosmosyntheism, the system is complex in that it has five primordial elements and it is adaptive in that it is processive, constantly changing and growing, learning from the past. Cosmosyntheism in particular finds a strong parallel with the notion of "self-organized criticality" found within the fields of chaos theory and complexity science. Self-organized criticality is just a fancy way of saying existing at the edge of chaos. It has been proven at various levels—which demonstrates the scale invariance of this apparent fact of nature—that *the most efficient and useful state of being for any actuality is at the brink of lapsing into complete chaos.* By having a degree of order and a degree of disorder within a system, the processing speed is greatly enhanced and it allows for the quickest way to try out possibilities and to actualize various ideas or forms.

Another major cutting-edge scientific concept that resonates well with Cosmosyntheism is the idea of emergence, which was briefly encountered in the previous chapter. As a quick summary, what separates emergence from reductionist science is that emergence thinkers have shown that higher-order systems cannot be fully or adequately explained using the tools and methodology that was applicable to the lower-order level. Complex systems are more than the sum of their parts. Put differently, psychology is more than applied biology, just as biology is more than applied chemistry and chemistry is more than applied physics. What follows below is one hypothetical scenario, which highlights Cosmosyntheism's answer to the mystery of creation. By providing this creation account, it will become clearer how self-organized criticality and emergence fits into my system.

Cosmosyntheism and Creation

In the beginning, there were the Forms, God, a World, Creativity and the Receptacle. As the dynamic power of Creativity brought God and the World together for the first time, order encountered chaos. In this initial encounter, God provided the forms of order and stability, but a radical inflationary expansion spontaneously ensued due to the explosive meeting of order and chaos. This inflation took place within God and within the Receptacle as God encapsulated both the space-time of our universe, but also the higher-dimensional space of the Receptacle. However, the chaotic world of simplistic entities had a profound reservoir of power and so in their initial meeting, these two ultimate powers merged and a system that contained the greatness of both resulted.

To assume that our particular world was the first to be born is naïve. As order struggled with chaos, a multiverse more than likely resulted. God was not omnipotent, far from it in fact, and so it took time, trial and error to carve out a hospitable universe for advanced life. Nevertheless, with each new universe, knowledge was gained. Eventually our universe was born with precisely the right initial conditions to sustain complex life. But once again, why assume we are so privileged? Perhaps the other universes are equally as important, especially those harboring intelligent life. If what matters most is the creation of novel forms of value and the knowledge and enjoyment derived thereof, then a multiverse was merely the most expedient means to attain this goal. In fact, *a multiverse was the most logical outcome of an order constantly grappling with a random chaotic power.*

This combination of a degree of order and a degree of chaos led to the most productive means to actualize new Forms both within the emerging worlds and within an emerging God. God's ordering allowed for more complex Forms to arise, but the randomness inherent in the primordial World insured that spontaneous Forms, ideas and concepts would emerge for the worlds and for God. This uncertainty deeply enriched God's imaginative or theoretical possibilities and allowed the unfolding process to go on *ad infinitum* with new Forms being actualized, realized and in turn, enjoyed.

This was now a complex adaptive system. As each moment of time gave way to the next in our emerging universe, the Receptacle was being filled with more and more information. As creation progressed, emergent levels of complexity formed within the system, and evolution, spurred on by the power of Eros/Creativity, took place continuously at all levels. Even God evolved. *This implied that over time, God in combination with the rest of the evolving system might give way to an even higher emergent level of reality.* The original set of Forms or possibilities appeared to be growing at an exponential rate approaching infinity. Perhaps there is no end to the process, no distant omega point, just an increasing storehouse of prior beginnings, endings and new beginnings.

Summary

- Cosmosyntheism is a new paradigm that is based upon the belief in the following five, co-equal and co-eternal ultimates: Forms, God, a World, Creativity, and the Receptacle.

- The five ultimates are mutually pre-supposing and ground one another. In addition, Ultimate Reality may act as a complex adaptive system.

- It is just as reasonable to assert that there are multiple ultimates as it is to assert only one, especially if by doing so more criteria for a successful metaphysical system can be accommodated.

Part II: Cosmosyntheism: A New Option

- In addition to the above point, there are two other major reasons for adopting five rather than three or six ultimates. First, religious experience and current evidence from religious studies suggests that different religions are describing distinct religious ultimates; five religious ultimates seem to be implicated. The second reason is that by advocating five ultimates rather than just one, say, God, many of the insights from contemporary science can be included within the paradigm.

Chapter 4

The Forms

But this is how I see it: In the knowable realm, the Form of the Good is the last thing to be seen and it is reached only with difficulty. Once one has seen it, however, one must conclude that it is the cause of all that is correct and beautiful in anything.

—PLATO, *REPUBLIC* BOOK VII

This then is how it has come to be: it is a work of craft, modeled after that which is changeless and is grasped by a rational account, that is, by wisdom.

—PLATO, *TIMAEUS*

IN THE LAST CHAPTER, I briefly examined Ultimate Reality as it is portrayed in Cosmosyntheism. In this chapter, I take a much closer look at one of the five constitutive components: the Forms. My account of the Forms is different from both Plato and Whitehead, but overlaps on certain points. For example, Plato wrestles with whether or not there are Forms for all things, both good and bad, whereas, process theists use the term Forms to refer to possibilities, without restricting those possibilities to good and beautiful ideas. Therefore, it is necessary to first provide an historical overview of the Forms as understood by Plato and Whitehead before I present the Forms as employed by Cosmosyntheism's metaphysics. Before the historical descriptions, however, I lead off with a simple, yet pertinent question, which will be the format that I utilize at the beginning and end of the next five chapters.

Why the Forms?

The Forms are necessary because there needs to be at least some universal notions or ideas—initial data—that act as a blueprint for the unfolding process of becoming. However, before expounding upon this important point within Cosmosyntheism's metaphysics, it is mandatory that one takes a look at two famous conceptions of the Forms so that the advancements of Cosmosyntheism can be better appreciated.

Plato and the Theory of the Forms

Plato's Theory of the Forms is simultaneously one of the most interesting and most confusing aspects of his metaphysics. The Forms (*eidos, idea*) are brought up throughout numerous dialogues, sometimes receiving a sustained treatment, but often only as a secondary or tertiary topic to help explain the central theme of the dialogue. For Plato, the Forms are that which is most real. Almost everything—humans, houses and chairs has a Form.[1] Even abstract concepts like justice, order and goodness have a Form. Furthermore, there is a chain of being or hierarchy of Reality, which is best described by the well-known "divided line" metaphor in Book VI of the *Republic*.

> It is like a line divided into two unequal sections. Then divide each section—namely, that of the visible and that of the intelligible—in the same ratio as the line. In terms now of relative clarity and opacity, one subsection of the visible consists of images. And by images I mean, first, shadows, then reflections in water and in all close-packed, smooth, shiny materials, and everything of that sort, if you understand. I do. In the other subsection of the visible, put the originals of these images, namely, the animals around us, all the plants, and the whole class of manufactured things. Consider them put. Would you be willing to say that, as regards truth and untruth, the division is in this proportion: As the opinable is to the knowable, so the likeness is to the thing that it is like? Certainly. Consider how the section of the intelligible is to be divided. How? As follows: In one subsection, the soul, using as images the things that were imitated before, is forced to investigate from hypotheses, proceeding not to a first principle but to a conclusion. In the other subsection, however, it makes its way to a first principle that is not a hypothesis, proceeding from a hypothesis, but *without the images used in the previous subsection, using Forms themselves and making its investigation through them.*[2]

---

1. In the *Parmenides*, Plato debates whether or not there is a Form for bad, ugly, and evil things such as dirt or filth.
2. Plato, *Complete Works*, 1130–31; emphasis mine.

Plato's Divided Line

	Mental States	**Objects**
Intelligible World	Intelligence (noesis)	The Good Forms
	Thought (dianoia)	Geometrical Objects
World of Becoming Appearance	Belief (Pistis)	All Visible Entities
	Imagination (eikasia)	Shadows / Reflections

Part II: Cosmosyntheism: A New Option

What Plato is suggesting above is that "knowledge" derived from the world of becoming—which is our everyday reality—is not true knowledge; it is rather opinion and belief. One must rise beyond empiricism and sense-perception in order to either intuit, remember or dialectically come to understand, the Forms in their pure state. It is only then that one can approach genuine understanding or (*noesis*). Therefore, "there are four such conditions in the soul, corresponding to the four subsections of our line: Understanding for the highest, thought for the second, belief for the third, and imaging for the last. Arrange them in a ratio, and consider that each shares in clarity to the degree that the subsection it is set over shares in truth."[3] What this implies is that the realm of the intelligible, which is synonymous with the realm of the Forms, is above the world of imagination and belief. Furthermore, the realm of the intelligible has a lower level comprised of archetypes of ordinary objects and even purer and higher concepts like order, beauty, justice and goodness.

The famous *Allegory of the Cave* expounds upon the metaphor of the divided line and helps to clarify the differences between the intelligible realm of Forms and the visible realm of appearances. Here Plato suggests that what we see on earth is analogous to a shadow puppet show unfolding within a deep cave. Many people are certainly familiar with Plato's iconic imagery of fettered prisoners forced to look forward at this puppet show that is being lit from a fire behind them. Eventually, one of the prisoners is released and forcibly dragged out of the cave into the sunlight where he dwells for awhile before returning to the cave in an attempt to enlighten his former brethren. The interpretation of this story is recounted by Plato to Glaucon.

> The visible realm should be likened to the prison dwelling, and the light of the fire inside it to the power of the sun. And if you interpret the upward journey and the study of things above as the upward journey of the soul to the intelligible realm, you'll grasp what I hope to convey. . .In the knowable realm, the form of the good is the last thing to be seen, and it is reached only with difficulty. Once one has seen it, however, one must conclude that it is the cause of all that is correct and beautiful in anything, that it produces both light and its source in the visible realm, and that in the intelligible realm it controls and provides truth and understanding.[4]

In other words, our world of substance mimics reality, which is the realm of the Forms and true education requires an ascent to the Good and then the return to benefit others within society.

As one saw above, the pinnacle of the hierarchy of Forms is "the Good," (*to Agathon*) which is metaphorically related by Plato to the Sun. "What the Good itself is in the intelligible realm, in relation to understanding and intelligible things, the sun is in

---

3. Ibid., 1132.
4. Ibid., 1135.

the visible realm, in relation to sight and visible things."[5] The sun or the Good enlightens all the lower Forms and casts their opaque shadows into the human realm, just as the actual sun illuminates terrestrial objects for sight and the eyes. However, one learns from Plato that one must not dwell on the realm of shadows because Plato's epistemology explains that doing so will result in an utter lack of true understanding. "Well understand the soul in the same way: When it focuses on something illuminated by truth and what is, it understands, knows and apparently possesses understanding, but when it focuses on what is mixed with obscurity, on what comes to be and passes away, it opines and is dimmed, changes its opinions this way and that, and seems bereft of understanding."[6]

In the terrestrial world of ephemeral appearances, there is constant change, imagination, opinion and belief, the lowest and most obscure forms of knowledge, but underlying all this change is prime matter or substance. Prime matter passively receives new Forms from the heavenly intelligible realm into nature. This is the basic dualistic structure of Reality known as *hylomorphism* that one finds in Plato's metaphysics. This dualism between matter and Form also allows for a source of evil that is far from the Form of the Good: matter. This is how one gets pessimistic and world-negating phrases like "the soul imprisoned within matter" or "the soul is weighed down by matter" and hence, one has the Platonic goal of ascending the ladder of truth and love back to the One; the source of beauty and truth, which is the Good.[7]

All of the above material on the Forms has been derived from only one of Plato's dialogues, but throughout the rest of his thirty-four dialogues, one learns some additional pieces of information. For example, one learns that the Forms are *immaterial, aspatial, atemporal, unchanging and the objects of higher knowledge*. First, they are immaterial[8] because they are purged of matter and are therefore, in a state of perpetual purity untainted by the adulterated physical matter that comprises the terrestrial world. The Forms also transcend both space and time[9] and thus are unchanging[10] and these unique features of the Forms are what make them the proper objects of higher study.

Whitehead's Eternal Objects

Whitehead alters the Platonic Forms into what he calls "eternal objects." "I use the phrase eternal object for what in the preceding paragraph of this section I have termed a Platonic Form. *Any entity whose conceptual recognition does not involve a necessary*

---

5. Ibid., 1129.

6. Ibid.

7. See for example *Republic* VII, 519 b on the imprisoning effects of matter and Socrates's speech in the *Symposium* 201d–212c on ascending the ladder of love.

8. See *Sophist* 246b+, 248a+ and 254c.

9. See *Phaedrus* 247c; *Phaedo* 109a–111c; and *Symposium* 211b.

10. See *Cratylus* 389+ and especially 439d–440d.

Part II: Cosmosyntheism: A New Option

reference to any definite actual entities of the temporal world is called an eternal object."[11] And again, "An eternal object is always *a potentiality* for actual entities; but in itself, as conceptually felt, it is neutral as to the fact of its physical ingression in any particular actual entity of the temporal world."[12] For Whitehead there are two main things that can contribute to an emerging moment of experience within a person: another actual entity, say another person, and pure potentials or Forms which do not refer to a particular individual. Thus, an eternal object merely means that an emerging moment of human experience recognizes an element of the data as not referring to another actual entity like another person, but from the realm of the multiplicity of Forms.

In many ways eternal objects are similar to the Platonic Forms. For example, "There are eight Categories of Existence: (i) Actual Entities (also termed actual occasions), or Final Realities, or *Res Verae* . . . (v) Eternal Objects, or Pure Potentials for the Specific Determination of Fact, or Forms of Definiteness."[13] This sounds strikingly similar to the notion of *hylomorphism* or prime substance and a realm of Forms. Also like Plato, Whitehead sees the Forms as possibilities for what Whitehead calls "ingression" into the actual world. The notion of ingression invokes similar images to Plato's architect or Demiurge in the *Timaeus* combining the Forms with prime matter as if pressing them into clay or dipping the Forms into gold.

Another similarity between both Plato and Whitehead is that they both have Forms for what appear to us as solid objects, like chairs and rocks as well as for abstract principles and concepts, like beauty and goodness. Whitehead further distinguishes between what he calls "eternal objects of the objective species" and "eternal objects of the subjective species." The objective species refer to things like numbers, mathematical and logical ideas, whereas the subjective species allude to more qualitative values and concepts like moral ideals. However, the similarities begin to diverge when Whitehead discusses not so much what the Forms are, *but where they are and their two modes of ingression.*

Both Whitehead and Plato share the belief that the class (Plato) or multiplicity (Whitehead) of Forms contains *nearly* all possibilities, eternally for Whitehead, or for Plato, atemporally. However, one hears Whitehead explaining that all of the eternal objects or the multiplicity of Platonic Forms *require a primordial nature of God that unifies and orders these possibilities.* For Whitehead a multiplicity is a "pure disjunction of diverse entities"[14] and therefore, it requires some ordering by a primordial actual entity: God. "The primordial created fact is the unconditioned conceptual valuation of the entire multiplicity of eternal objects. This is the primordial nature of God."[15] Whitehead's ontological principle marks the major separation from Plato's thought.

11. Whitehead, *Process and Reality*, 44.
12. Ibid.
13. Ibid., 22.
14. Ibid.
15. Ibid., 31.

The eternal objects reside within the primordial nature of God. In other words, *they are always in an actual entity.*

Whitehead's ontological principle allows him to avoid one of the major criticisms against Plato's Theory of the Forms: where are they exactly? How can they be free-floating, devoid of an actuality containing or envisaging them? It is inconceivable how concepts like order, justice and goodness could simply be existing in a pure land or realm that is extra-mental and outside space, time and materiality. One cannot reasonably divorce ideas and concepts from mentality and actuality. This is why Whitehead's ontological principle provides *the where* for the Forms: inside God. The doctrine of panentheism states that all things are within God, including the Forms.

The final point of departure between Plato and Whitehead concerns Whitehead's doctrines of internal relations or universal relativity.

> The antithetical terms "universals" and "particulars" are the usual words employed to denote respectively entities which nearly, though not quite, correspond to the entities here termed "eternal objects," and "actual entities." These terms, "universals" and "particulars," both in the suggestiveness of the two words and in their current philosophical use, are somewhat misleading. The ontological principle, and the wider doctrine of universal relativity, on which the present metaphysical discussion is founded, blur the sharp distinction between what is universal and what is particular. The notion of a universal is of that which can enter into the description of many particulars; whereas the notion of a particular is that it is described by universals, and does not itself enter into the description of any other particular. According to the doctrine of relativity which is the basis of the present lectures, both these notions involve a misconception. An actual entity cannot be described, even inadequately, by universals; *because other actual entities do enter into the description of any one actual entity.* Thus every so-called 'universal' is particular in the sense of being just what it is, diverse from everything else; and *every so-called 'particular' is universal in the sense of entering into the constitutions of other actual entities.*[16] [Italics mine]

What this lengthy quotation means is that in the process of change and becoming there are Forms which enter into a new moment of experience from two vectors or routes: *other prior actual entities and the primordial nature of God.* Any entity receives possibilities from an impure Form or set of Forms received as mediated through a *physical prehension* of other prior entities and from a *conceptual prehension* of the pure, unalloyed realm of Forms within God's primordial nature. This is a radical doctrine that introduces a tremendous amount of complexity in explaining and understanding the world around us and the process of becoming and change. Nonetheless, even Whitehead's more sophisticated explanation of the Forms is not without serious problems.

---

16. Ibid., 48.

Part II: Cosmosyntheism: A New Option

Cosmosyntheism's Expanding Set of Forms

Cosmosyntheism diverges from Plato and Whitehead on two points. As far as Plato is concerned, it seems unsustainable and irresponsible to propose that all of the universals are somehow, "out there," devoid of any actual entity containing them, thinking them or envisioning them. Granted, Plato has notions like the demiurge and the world-soul, but neither of these fully contain the Forms, they just use them or are affected by them in some way. This is where I partially agree with Whitehead by accepting the ontological principle in that "if one is searching for a reason it must refer to some actuality" and "that all things must be somewhere and here somewhere refers to the non-temporal actual entity."[17]

The second issue I have with Plato is also the first problem that is shared with Whitehead. Why do *all of the Forms or possibilities* have to exist eternally or atemporally? A second aspect arises in Whitehead's case and that is: how can all of the possibilities *be ordered for relevance primordially* when God is not omnipotent or omniscient and therefore, cannot know what Forms will be relevant for each given actuality at any given moment during the historical process? By leveling this criticism against Whitehead, I am following the Cobbian/Griffian school of interpretation of Whitehead.[18] However, the following propositions within this chapter break away from the Cobbian/Griffian family of process thought.

I will begin with the first issue of the supposed necessity that all of the Forms exist primordially. It seems strange to say the least to suggest that there have always been Forms of such complex things as spaceships, robots or computers. The problem is actually less acute for Plato than for Whitehead, in that Plato does not believe that the Forms, once instantiated, are brought back into the constitution of the Demiurge or the Form of the Good to be enjoyed.[19] Whitehead's doctrine of the consequent nature of God suggests that God in turn prehends the experiences of the entire world of actual entities and it therefore becomes data for God, a new type of data: experiential knowledge. My main issue is *how does the experiential knowledge gained from the world not affect God in such a way that new Forms or possibilities arise in the mind of God*? If it is really as true to say that God creates the World as that the World creates God, then how is it that God could have known all the possibilities that could only have arisen from long periods of experience, trial-and-error and then refinement?

To Plato, I must ask, if the purpose of life is to bring novel Forms into the realm of appearances, *what is the point if nothing is gained therein for the Good or the Demiurge*? To Whitehead, who accepts that God is literally affected by the decisions of the other actual entities throughout time, I must ask, how is it that both experiential

---

17. Ibid., 46. I disagree, however, with Whitehead that all of the Forms must be in the non-temporal actual entity.

18. See chapter 5 of *Reenchantment without Supernaturalism* for a sustained treatment of this issue by Griffin.

19. For example, see Plato's *Republic* VI 509 b.

knowledge gained *and an eternal struggle with chaotic forces doesn't result in unforeseen possibilities*? If God somehow always knew what the chaotic world was going to do or knew how the experiential knowledge would affect him, then it seems we are returning to a God of omnipotence and omniscience, which Whitehead, Hartshorne, Cobb, Griffin and I reject.

Another problem is the issue of prime matter or substance, for Plato, or "a World" for Whitehead. Does the primordial realm of actual entities that co-exists with God have any Forms, or does prime matter have a Form? Plato seems to believe that it does not, *but that is impossible*. I would imagine that the primordial world had at least the Form of chaos or randomness. Wouldn't the Demiurge or craftsman who is using the Forms as a blueprint have trouble impressing them into a chaotic world? *Wouldn't the chaos alter the original intention or plan*? More importantly, randomness and spontaneity are essentially unknowable and so with each encounter between the world and God, I would assume that the chaos injects some huge variables into the initial equation or plan of God or the Demiurge.

As an alternative to both Plato's Theory of the Forms and Whitehead's eternal objects, Cosmosyntheism posits the following revisions:

1. The primordial "World" or substance does have some Forms, such as chaos, randomness and spontaneity, *which are fully allowed by Whitehead's own ontological principle*. In fact, this appears to be a completely neglected implication of the principle.

2. The primordial World can have these Forms because it is comprised of simplistic non-enduring actual entities that are random, but actual entities nonetheless and actual entities by definition can contain Forms.

3. There are only a *limited set of initial Forms* which God entertains at the beginning of time and it is through the reciprocal God-World relationship that more complex Forms arise for the World and God.

4. No one—not even God—can have complete foreknowledge of all the possible outcomes of even a minute into the future. However, God, in knowing all that has happened, is in a better position to conjecture what the future might be like since a large portion of what will come to comprise the future are the past objectified actualities.

5. The true process of reality is this interplay between the ordering effect of God and the chaotic disruption inherent in the indeterminacy of the World.

6. This epic struggle provides novelty for God and the world in two ways: through experiential knowledge gained from actualizing Forms within the World and by way of the chaotic indeterminacy that permeates the universe.

7. The meaning of life is to instantiate new Forms in the realm of appearances for the sake of immediate enjoyment and for enhancing the possibilities of future

actualizations, satisfactions *and knowledge* (theoretical and experiential).

Why Not Just the Forms?

If Ultimate Reality consisted of merely the Forms, what would be wrong with this picture? The problems with just having the Forms are legion. I will address only the most glaringly obvious issues. The first problem that comes to mind is how can there be any ideas and Forms without an actual entity to contain them. I have discussed this problem above and it is essentially just a restatement of what Whitehead realized and defined as his ontological principle, whereby everything must be somewhere, and here somewhere refers to some actual entity. In other words, the Forms cannot be free-floating patterns or blueprints if there is nothing actual to conceive, contain, envisage or work with them.

Another related problem is where is the prime matter going to come from? If you just had the Forms then somehow the Forms would have to generate substance or matter in order for them to take concrete shape. *How can things that are by definition not actual exert a causal efficacy capable of producing something concrete and actual*? Who or what would be ordering the relevance of each particular Form to each particular unfolding concrete scenario? Even assuming all of the above could somehow take place, if the realm of the Forms is perfect, complete and unchanging, *then why would there ever be a realm of appearances and becoming at all*? It seems there would just be a static, inert heaven of ideal perfection. There would be no world the likes of which one participates in daily and knows to be existent. This is the greatest reason to abandon this line of inquiry, because if it were true, then everything one holds most dear and sacred would be a lie. All of our common sense intuitions, our experiences, everything associated with the actual substantial world, would be an illusion, the ultimate chimera.

To put it bluntly, this option is just too preposterous to be imagined as true or even possible. A reality of this kind would certainly be the mystery of all mysteries. Most of the problems with this option revolve around one key factor: there is no primordial or necessary Being or beings. It is for this reason that we must move on to the next crucial ingredient in the burgeoning metaphysics of Cosmosyntheism: God. Perhaps a reality comprised of God alone will lead us to a comprehensible and compelling metaphysics.

Summary

- Plato was the first to suggest the eternal Forms.
- For Plato, the Forms were immaterial and unchanging blueprints from which the demiurge could look to in order to create the material world.

The Forms

- Plato seems willing to restrict which particulars can have a universal; e.g., is there a Form of dirt or excrement? Cosmosyntheism, Whitehead and Perennialists view the Forms as possibilities, rather than intelligibles, as in the classical tradition.

- Whitehead agrees with Plato about the nature of the Forms on most accounts but he diverges from Plato when he suggests that all the Forms reside within the primordial nature of God.

- Cosmosyntheism also accepts the reality of the Forms with Whitehead's insistence that the Forms must reside in an actual entity. However, unlike Whitehead, Cosmosyntheism claims that God does not have or entertain *all* the Forms within his primordial nature; instead, *some* Forms reside in a co-eternal World of finite actual entities.

CHAPTER 5

The Dipolar Deity

Thus, analogously to all actual entities, the nature of God is dipolar. He has a primordial nature and a consequent nature.

—ALFRED WHITEHEAD, *PROCESS AND REALITY*

God is the great companion—the fellow-sufferer who understands.

—ALFRED WHITEHEAD, *PROCESS AND REALITY*

IN THE PREVIOUS PAGES, I discussed the nature and function of the Forms for both Plato and Whitehead. I next explained how Cosmosyntheism differs from both Plato and Whitehead by portraying the Forms as being primordially instantiated in both a World and in a God. I also argued that experiential knowledge and a chaotic primordial world would lead to the emergence of new Forms over time. In this chapter, I shift my attention to God. However, the God of Cosmosyntheism is so different from any classical versions of God that, I once again, will have to provide a brief historical overview of process theism, which Cosmosyntheism is highly indebted to. To this end, I will outline the main tenets of process theism as presented by Alfred Whitehead, Charles Hartshorne and David Ray Griffin. Following these descriptions of a process God, I will then lay out the two major ways in which Cosmosyntheism builds upon and differs from its process predecessors.

Why a God?

A God is necessary because there needs to be an ordering principle or agent and a primordial actuality within which a certain set of initial possibilities can reside. There must be a powerful entity driven in its very nature to seek greater complexity, which in turn requires a degree of stability from which to build upon. What *is not necessary* is that this God have all of the attributes—omnipotence, infinite perfection, impassibility and omniscience—that have classically been attributed *to him* . . . another unfortunate and unnecessary aspect.[1]

The next frequently asked question is: what evidence is there for believing in a God? The evidence that has been amassed in response to this question has usually taken the form of six main arguments: cosmological, ontological, teleological, moral, anthropic and experiential. Briefly stated, the cosmological argument points to the fact that there is change, motion, causes and effects and so at the end of a chain of regressing causes, there must be a necessary first cause (*Primum Movens*) or prime mover (*Primum Mobile*) that started the process: God.

The ontological argument posed by St. Anselm of Canterbury in his *Proslogion* first asserts that God is to be understood as, "a being than which nothing greater can be conceived."[2] He then proceeds to show that if we can conceive of such a perfect being in our mind only, then there is actually something greater than that, and that would be this most perfect being *truly, actually existing in reality, not merely our minds.* "If then that than which a greater *cannot* be thought exists in the mind alone, this same that than which a greater cannot be thought is that than which a greater *can* be thought."[3] Anselm's point although apparently confusing is actually quite simple; if it (this perfect Being) exists only in your mind then it could be more perfect; i.e., God could also exist in reality; therefore, God does actually exist in reality. A different form of ontological argument is Whitehead's ontological principle whereby, "all things must be somewhere and here somewhere refers to some actual entity"[4] *so that the potentiality of the universe itself* must be somewhere, mainly, in God. The teleological argument is most famously known through the version put forth by William Paley. Paley uses the example of stumbling across a watch in a desert.

> Suppose that while walking in a desert place I see a rock lying on the ground and ask myself how this object came to exist. I can properly attribute its presence to chance, meaning in this case the operation of such natural forces as wind, rain, heat, frost and volcanic action. However, if I see a watch lying on the ground I cannot reasonably account for it in a similar way. A watch consists of complex arrangements of wheels, cogs, axles, springs, and balances, all operating accurately together to provide a regular measurement of time. It would be utterly implausible to attribute the formation and assembling of these metal parts into a functioning machine to the chance operation of such

---

1. One may have noticed that I have referred to God as "he" up until this point. My use of "he" and "him" is solely for the purpose of aiding the fluidity of the prose; I would be more than happy to replace all the masculine attributions with female or neutral ones. In other words, I am in no way assuming that God is male or female for that matter.

2. St. Anselm, *Proslogion*, chap. 2.

3. Ibid.

4. Whitehead, *Process and Reality*, 46.

Part II: Cosmosyntheism: A New Option

factors as wind and rain. We are obliged to postulate an intelligent mind which is responsible for the phenomenon.[5]

Paley's argument compares the complexity of the watch to the complexity one sees in the natural world, where it would be difficult to attribute all of the sophistication and fine-tuning to chance.

The moral argument is most famously proposed by the great Enlightenment philosopher Immanuel Kant. Kant asserted that our feeling of an inalienable obligation to other people as free human beings in their own right alludes to the fact of an underlying ground or source for these moral intuitions. This moral ground is God. To recognize moral values as somehow taking precedence over other concerns in life seems to suggest a move towards a reality that is beyond the empirical and therefore, possibly aiming at or derived from a divine source. Next, the argument from religious experience simply runs that people report having religious experiences in all cultures all over the world and this seems to suggest that there may be a higher power of some kind.

One of the most recent arguments for the existence of God is of special importance to this current project: the anthropic principle. The anthropic principle claims that the universe appears to have been fine-tuned to such minute precision that if even one of the fundamental cosmological constants or laws of physics had been even slightly tweaked differently, no life could have evolved anywhere in our universe. This is very similar to the teleological argument above, but on a grander scale and it is in fact true that if these initial conditions were any different, life would not have existed because star formation would not have been possible. This is a compelling argument, but like all the arguments posed above, an effective counter-argument has arisen to cast sufficient doubt on the hypothesis. In this case, the counter-argument is known as the many worlds hypothesis or multiverse theory, which I will return to at the end of this chapter.

One question that arises is, are all of the above arguments useless since there appear to be equally as compelling counter-points? David Griffin wisely says yes and no. Yes, they are useless, if the arguments are trying to prove a God that is similar to that of classical theism, with all of its attributes of perfection, but no if they are applied to a different conception of deity, such as, the version that process theism suggests. The problem as David Griffin explains is that "the main reason for the failure of traditional natural theology was not the weakness of its arguments against atheism but the fact that traditional theism's concept of God was inconsistent with the world as we know it and in its classical form, incoherent."[6] I agree with this assessment and believe that taken together as a cumulative argument the traditional arguments become far more plausible if used to prove the existence of a God like that found in process thought. However, even if these arguments were valid and sound, most of them do not tell us much about the *nature* of this God, so that many of the classically attributed predicates

---

5. Hick, *Philosophy of Religion*, 23.
6. Griffin, *Reenchantment without Supernaturalism*, 202.

would not necessarily follow from the conclusions of these arguments. Perhaps this should cause us to take pause and reassess the nature of deity and propose a more responsible notion of God. This is exactly what Whitehead attempted to do.

Whitehead's Dipolar Process Theism

Whitehead was essentially one of the first to radically rethink the notion of deity in a way that stood strongly at odds with all versions of classical theism. He was not satisfied by classical theism, pantheism, deism or atheism. This led him into uncharted territory, where he was left to his own devices to contemplate the divine mystery in profoundly original ways. What resulted from this sustained meditation on the nature of God were some intriguing notions. Some of his major modifications are as follows: God *is not* omnipotent, omniscient, impassible, immutable, monopolar or the necessary efficient cause of all things. Not all of these changes occurred at one moment in time or even during one phase of Whitehead's intellectual development; rather, Whitehead's position on the nature and function of God evolved throughout his life.

The earliest notions of God one finds systematically outlined by Whitehead are to be found in his *Religion in the Making*. It is here that he says, "The actual but non-temporal entity whereby the indetermination of mere creativity is transmuted into a determinate freedom. This non-temporal actual entity is what men call God, the supreme God of rationalized religion."[7] God's major function is as an ordering agent, or entity, who provides relevant ideal Forms to the actual world in each moment, for the sake of issuing in novelty. "The purpose of God is the attainment of value in the temporal world."[8]

Now, the attainment of this value requires that there be both an ordering element *and an actual world*. "There is an actual world because there is an order in nature. If there were no order, there would be no world. Also since there is a world, we know that there is an order. The ordering entity [God] is a necessary element in the metaphysical situation presented by the actual world."[9] So, God provides an ordered relevance of possibilities in the way of Forms and the world then instantiates these possibilities. "The actual world is the outcome of the aesthetic order, and the aesthetic order is derived from the immanence of God."[10] This aesthetic order is regrettably viewed as an already completed ideal harmony within the non-temporal deity and the world is just playing out these different possibilities as time and history progress. Whitehead says, "God is the completed ideal harmony."[11]

---

7. Whitehead, *Religion in the Making*, 90.
8. Ibid., 100.
9. Ibid., 104.
10. Ibid., 105.
11. Ibid., 120.

Part II: Cosmosyntheism: A New Option

These first intuitions are refined in Whitehead's magnum opus *Process and Reality*. In this work, one finds Whitehead stressing *the receptive aspect of a dipolar deity*. The notion of dipolarity refers to the fact that each moment of experience has a receptive physical side and a mental self-determining side. This structure was already developed in *Religion in the Making*, but in *Process and Reality* there is an emphasis placed on the receptive aspect of God known as the *consequent nature of God*.

> But God as well as being primordial, is also consequent. He shares with every new creation its actual world; and the concrescent creature is objectified in God as a novel element in God's objectification of that actual world *God's conceptual nature is unchanged, by reason of its final completeness*. But his derivative nature is consequent upon the creative advance of the world. Thus analogously to all actual entities, the nature of God is dipolar. He has a primordial nature and a consequent nature. *The consequent nature of God is conscious;* and it is the realization of the actual world in the unity of his nature, and through the transformation of his wisdom. The primordial nature is conceptual, *the consequent nature is the weaving of God's physical feelings upon his primordial concepts.*[12] (emphasis mine)

This passage is so rich in that it contains some of Whitehead's greatest ideas *and also his largest error*. Two major problems arise from the above passage. The first problem is *how God as an actual entity in eternal concrescence, rather than as a serially-ordered society, can provide relevant initial aims to truly free, partially self-determining creatures?* In technical language, God is always in concrescence but never in a transition, which is the other type of process for Whitehead. Transition is where the past moment "transitions" from its moment of subjective immediacy to being an objectified fact available as data for the next moment of concrescence. This problem is taken up below under the heading of Hartshorne and Griffin. The second problem is *how can the consequent nature of God as "the weaving of God's physical feelings upon his primordial concepts," not alter the original set of primordial concepts?*

Before diving into these two problems, I must address two more unique beliefs that Whitehead held concerning God. First, he believed that God saved all the information derived from the prior actual entities and that they achieved what he called "objective immortality." In at least this one sense there is not a perpetual perishing of achieved value and subjectivity. "He saves the world as it passes into the immediacy of his own life. It is the judgment of a tenderness which loses nothing that can be saved."[13] The second realization he had, I have already touched on: *God needs a World*. This point is explicitly recognized at least as far back as *Religion in the Making* where Whitehead says, "There is no entity, not even God, which requires nothing but itself

---

12. Whitehead, *Process and Reality*, 345.
13. Ibid., 346.

in order to exist."[14] However, in *Process and Reality* and his later *Adventures of Ideas* this point seems ubiquitous. *Both the notion of objective immortality and the necessity of both God and a World are shared by Cosmosyntheism's metaphysics.* However, when it comes to the issue of God as one actual entity in eternal concrescence, Cosmosyntheism strongly opposes this view and sides instead with the insightful revisions of Charles Hartshorne and David Ray Griffin.

Hartshorne and Griffin's Dipolar God as a Serially Ordered Society of Actual Occasions

In contrast to Whitehead's portrayal of God as a single actual entity in one eternal concrescence, Charles Hartshorne and David Ray Griffin have correctly surmised that this is not a viable option. There are numerous reasons why God cannot be conceived as one single entity, but the main concern is how God's primordial nature, which is deficient in actuality, can supply reasons or aims for the creatures from moment-to-moment. Whitehead's own ontological principle states that only actual entities can supply reasons and exert influence on other actual entities, so it is unclear how the primordial nature would be exempt from this metaphysical principle. This problem is especially acute since Whitehead himself states that God, "is not to be treated as an exception to metaphysical principles; he is their chief exemplification."[15] The concern over the primordial nature's ability to provide pertinent aims is only the tip of the iceberg.

More problems seem to crop up due to this one issue. How could God's unchanging primordial nature have foreknown which initial aims would be relevant for each entity at each specific moment in time if the world is truly comprised of free or at least partially-determining agents? This would imply that God is actually somehow omniscient. Furthermore, Whitehead states that all enduring things are in truth, temporally ordered societies of actual entities. "The real actual things that endure are societies."[16] Yet, for some reason Whitehead's God endures forever, but is not a serially-ordered society.[17] For these reasons and others, Charles Hartshorne and David Griffin were led to assert the obvious: *God is a serially-ordered society of occasions of experience.* "These problems point to the necessity of saying that the act of providing initial aims is an act of God as a whole at that moment, not simply of God's primordial nature. These problems can be handled in the following way: God is, analogously to a human soul, a serially-ordered society of occasions of experience."[18]

The picture that emerges from Hartshorne and Griffin is one of God as a chain of momentary events, each of which prehends all of the pre-existing worldly and divine

---

14. Whitehead, *Religion in the Making*, 108.
15. Whitehead, *Process and Reality*, 343.
16. Ibid., 34–35.
17. For an interesting discussion of God as a society, see Bracken, *The Divine Matrix*.
18. Griffin, *Reenchantment without Supernaturalism*, 156–60.

occasions and then provides a relevant aim for the new occasions based upon their prior decisions. Hartshorne and Griffin have reconceived God as a living person who operates analogously to how the soul and the body interact. God as "soul of the universe" is the "dominant member" of the universe, meaning that God includes within God's self the subordinate regions or members of the universe, like humans, animals, plants etc. This is the philosophical doctrine of *panentheism* that I touched on earlier and it is crucial to both Hartshorne and Griffin's conception of God. It implies that all finite things are within God or that God includes all of the lower members analogously to how the soul includes all the mental states associated with our personality and our body. As Griffin says, "Just as the brain is in the soul, the universe is in God."[19] In Hartshorne's words, "The world as an integrated individual is not a 'world' as this term is normally and properly used, but 'God.' God, the World Soul, is the individual integrity of the world, which otherwise is just the myriad creatures."[20]

The God of Cosmosyntheism

The God of Cosmosyntheism is in many respects quite similar to former conceptions put forth by process theists. For example, reconceiving God as a living person who is the dominant member of the universe in the sense of including the entire universe within God's own internal experiences moment-by-moment is a move that is totally accepted by Cosmosyntheism. Panentheism is the most adequate philosophical term to describe Whitehead's, Hartshorne's, Griffin's and my own metaphysics. However, I begin to part ways with all of these thinkers in that they all seem to find it necessary for God to have an aspect that is permanently unchanging.[21]

Hartshorne calls the unchanging element of God's nature, his "abstract essence" and Whitehead calls it the primordial nature. I agree that there are certain elements of God's character that endure with little or no change, like the attempt to instill order and stability on the universe and to provide new aims for each actual occasion, but it is unclear as to whether these extremely long-lasting attributes will continue unperturbed forever. Perhaps, through gaining enough experiential knowledge and consciousness, God will have a change of heart, so to speak. It is not abundantly clear to me as to why God would be unable to do this if God is constantly changing with the shifting tides of the world. Granted, God is bound by the metaphysical law of Creativity to interact with other actual entities, but there is no guarantee that God will always seek to promote continued order or will actively attempt to provide relevant initial aims leading to greater complexity and beauty.

---

19. Ibid., 141.
20. Hartshorne, *Omnipotence and Other Theological Mistakes*, 59.
21. In fairness to Charles Hartshorne, he is reluctant to accept Whitehead's eternal objects of the subjective species and so his position is at least closer to my own view.

Eventually, Cosmosyntheism irreparably parts ways with most of the above thinkers because they believe that God contains *all possibilities eternally* in either the primordial nature or the abstract essence. An exception might be found in the apparent fact that Hartshorne only believed that God's abstract essence contained the eternal objects of the objective species, but not the subjective species.[22] This seems to be more likely to me, but that would depend upon a more specific description of exactly which eternal objects of the subjective species are being denied.

As an example of the confusion surrounding the notion of God having all possibilities, one can look at the wheel and its many applications. If we are to assume that God has no experiential knowledge or consciousness in his primordial nature, then how could it be that there is the possibility of the wheel alone, plus a wheel used for a cart, and for a chariot and then for an automobile. If primordially God had no experiential knowledge of how a wheel would operate on say, an ox-cart, *then how could God have also primordially envisaged the workings of wheels on an advanced automobile?*

It is only through trial-and-error in the real world that the experience could have been gained that would have taught one that you need an axle and brakes and then later, an engine with all its complex components to have an automobile. The limits of credulity reach a breaking point when God is said to have all possibilities primordially, yet also *is deficient in consciousness*. Add to this the fact that God requires a union with a World that has its own real power, and it becomes truly inconceivable that God could have had all possibilities eternally stored away in a primordial nature. *The indeterminacy of the actual world alone would make it impossible for a primordial entity to envisage all possibilities non-temporally.*

Another area of resemblance between Cosmosyntheism and prior process theisms is to be found in the shared philosophic belief known as panentheism. However, the analogy employed to understand panentheism is quite different.[23] Whereas Hartshorne and Griffin use the analogy of God as the soul of the universe and see God as a living person, Cosmosyntheism opts for a more contemporary analogy: *Artificial Intelligence/Cyborgs* (A.I.). This may come as somewhat of a shock or a leap, but it actually makes sense in that humans frequently employ analogies for God based on *the highest or most sophisticated life forms we know of*. Hence, over the millennia we have had many trends towards anthropocentric accounts of the divine nature, but now we have a new, higher form of life poised to take its rightful place as heir to humankind.

What makes A.I. a superior analogy to the body/soul analogy is that it draws attention to the fact of *top-down and bottom-up learning*. What I mean here is that in contemporary artificial intelligence, robots do not simply come pre-programmed with a massive amount of coded rules (top-down). Instead, A.I. comes with a minimal

---

22. Hartshorne's philosophy is best captured in his magnum opus *Creative Synthesis and Philosophic Method*, which outlines his unique version of process thought.

23. See *In Whom We Live and Move and Have Our Being* for some suggested analogies for panentheism.

set of initial data and possibilities and through interacting and bumping into its environment, the A.I. unit learns and evolves in a very organic fashion (bottom up). It is this combination of top-down and bottom-up programming that makes it the best available analogy for understanding God and the God/World relationship.

In Cosmosyntheism, God begins with only a limited set of initial data or "programming" and through God's interaction with the chaotic world new Forms and possibilities arise *for God and for the World*. This is precisely analogous to how an A.I. unit works. Cyborgs, with their combination of amazing machine-like computational skills plus their organic abilities at pattern recognition make for an ideal combination of the best of both worlds and also provide another possible analogue for the God/World relationship. The advantage of the cyborg analogy is that it highlights the aspect of a complex adaptive system. This provides an analogy not just for God, but for my entire metaphysics, where the five mutually grounding ultimates act as one complex adaptive system.

The issue of an adaptive system combined with constant process and *my belief that God is truly changing and growing in knowledge in every moment, i.e. not yet infinite*, leads to a third hypothesis that distinguishes Cosmosyntheism from prior process theologies: *God could give way to an even higher emergent level of reality*. This particular claim is highly speculative, but it is within the realm of possible implications given the metaphysics that has been suggested thus far. Unfortunately, what this higher level's nature and function would be is completely outside my ability to speculate on. Any theories provided would be merely that, pure conjecture. Nevertheless, it may be possible that an incomplete non-infinite God through the numerous interactions with the World and the other five ultimates, could give rise to something radically new and more complex.

The final advance made by Cosmosyntheism is its upheaval of the traditional implication of multiverse theories. Many atheistic scientists have invoked the multiverse as an effective counter-argument to the anthropic principle. Whereas, the anthropic principle states that the apparent fine-tuning of the cosmological constants that started this universe implies a designer who tweaked the laws of physics to just the right initial conditions, the multiverse theory counters by saying that our universe is not unique. Instead, our universe is but one in a perhaps infinite set of universes floating in a "bulk" comprised of numerous other universes. The argument goes that the reason for the apparent fine-tuning is simply that one of the billions of universes was bound to have these initial parameters that allow for star formation and then the rise of life. In short, the creation of our particular universe was random and not planned. This idea is somewhat similar to the old Epicurean and Democritean idea of a finite set of particles moving around that eventually go through all the possible forms and combinations.

Cosmosyntheism's metaphysics anticipates a multiverse as well, but posits that the reason for our universe being unique is that after many trials and experiments with other universes, God hit upon the right combination to allow for continued stability over time. Remember, I am suggesting that God as an ordering principle primordially interacted with a chaotic World and this indeterminacy that infected God's original plan would likely have led to a branching multiverse. Perhaps it could have even been a part of the initial plan because Cosmosyntheism also accepts that the purpose of life is to issue in novelty of ever increasing complexity and so *the most efficient mechanism by which to do this would be a multiverse because you could allow for an exponentially larger set of possibilities to play out much quicker than through one gradually evolving universe.*

Whereas critics of the anthropic principle polemically use the multiverse argument to disprove God, Cosmosyntheism turns this on its head and argues that a multiverse is a likely outcome of one of two scenarios: God intentionally using a multiverse to allow for more probabilities to emerge and play out, or of the fact that order encountered chaos and the indeterminacy led to many failed beginnings, which nonetheless, revealed some degree of experiential knowledge from which God could have learned to adjust the initial parameters until getting it right in our universe. *The question still remains though as to precisely what role a primordial world would have played in this unfolding picture of Ultimate Reality?* To answer this question, I must now move on to the ultimate: a World.

Summary

- Over the millennia, there have been numerous arguments put forth to prove the existence of God; however, the arguments all seem to be inconclusive. The arguments do, nonetheless, become quite effective if taken as a *cumulative argument*, which tries to prove a *reconceived* notion of deity.

- Whitehead's dipolar God represents one promising step towards a reconceived understanding of deity.

- Charles Hartshorne and David Griffin take Whitehead's early intuitions one step further by describing God as a serially ordered society of occasions of experience.

- Cosmosyntheism differs from Whitehead, Hartshorne, and Griffin by asserting that God *does not* contain all possibilities primordially.

- Cosmosyntheism also utilizes A.I. and ALife as an alternative model for explaining panentheism and the God/World relationship.

Chapter 6

A World/Cosmos

Chaos in the world brings uneasiness, but it also allows the opportunity for creativity and growth.
—TOM BARRETT

Chaos often breeds life, when order breeds habit.
—HENRY ADAMS

Chaos is the score upon which reality is written.
—HENRY MILLER

IF EVER THERE WAS a true perennial philosophy, it consisted of only this one belief: the primeval truth of the duality of order and chaos. In the preceding pages, I addressed the first member of this pair and in this chapter, I will explain the nature and function of the latter member of this genuinely archaic and ubiquitous duality. I will begin with a brief survey of the world's myths, which provide support by way of tradition for my central thesis that there are and always have been multiple religious ultimates. Two of these ultimates can be described as order and chaos, with chaos referring to some pre-existing world of raw material. Next, I will explore how Aristotle refined this idea of raw matter and made coherent arguments for its necessity as a prime material cause. After reviewing Aristotle's position, I jump through time up to the present day with a look at how membrane theory and the various string theories can provide a helpful framework from which to understand the nature and function of this original chaotic world. I conclude the chapter with a description of Cosmosyntheism's advances over the former ways of understanding a primordial world.

Creation out of Chaos

The existence of a primeval chaotic world persisting alongside an ordering deity or deities can be found in nearly all of the world's most ancient myths. Throughout Egypt, one reads numerous variations on one central theme. The theme is the protrusion of a stable order represented by a primeval mound of earth personified as Tatjenen out of a chaotic watery world. Each major city in Ancient Egypt had their own version of exactly how order was first brought to chaos through the mound, but in all of the versions creation consisted of an ordering principle and a principle of disorder.[1]

For the Heliopolitans of Lower Egypt, Atum was the first God to rise from the mound. Atum then created the Ennead or "group of nine gods" that comprised the Heliopolitan pantheon. As one learns from the Pyramid Texts,[2] Atum's creation was enacted through a masturbatory process of procreation. In the city of Memphis, Ptah's role as creator was stressed. However, Ptah's creation was through thought and speech, rather than the more physical account of creation on finds with Atum. What is interesting for us is that both of these stories co-existed and so there is the physical element of creation of a god of order dealing with chaos and fashioning it in an active manner. There is also the idea of Ptah envisaging the Forms as possibilities, one could say, and creating from this divine blueprint. Ptah's function is similar to Whitehead's primordial nature of God and Atum's to what is known as the superjective nature of God or God as providing aims and possibilities to the world by actually interacting with the rest of reality.

The pair of opposites identified as order and chaos were not limited to an account of creation. There is also the order of the cosmos that is visible in the fixed stars above and during the New Kingdom period, the uncertainty of the Duat or underworld, through which the sun God Re's solar barge must journey each night in order to rise again in the morning. A more common representation of the continuing struggle between the forces of order and chaos are the two gods Horus and Seth.[3] Horus, as the son of Osiris and Isis, signifies order but his uncle, Seth, rules over the wastelands of the desert outside of the confines of the ordered city and empire of the pharaoh. The epic battles between these two gods are some of the most interesting tales derived from ancient Egypt, but what they purport to tell us is that the tension between order and chaos is ongoing and the order we do have is a tenuous stability. Maintenance of order requires rituals that symbolically re-enact the way of the gods and a social structure that mimics their cosmology.

---

1. *The Masks of God,* a four-volume work by Joseph Campbell, remains one of the best sources for information regarding mythology and hence, a good portion of my discussion in this section relies on this series.

2. A recent translation of the Pyramid Texts can be found in the SBL series Writings from the Ancient World. See *The Ancient Egyptian Pyramid Texts.*

3. Cf. the articles on Horus and Seth in *The Ancient Gods Speak,* edited by Donald Redford, for a good overview of these two major Egyptian deities.

Part II: Cosmosyntheism: A New Option

This same pattern of creation out of chaos is apparent in the Sumerian and Akkadian creation epic the Enuma Elish.[4] In this myth, one first reads that the fresh waters known as Apsu meet and commingle with salt water, Tiamat, and thus the creation of the gods begins to take place out of these two primordial powers. However, it is not until later that one finds out that it is the power of order personified in the God/king Marduk, which results in the creation of the cosmos out of the chaotic forces of the raging sea goddess Tiamat. Marduk, as the ordering principle, kills Tiamat and "splits her in two like a dried fish" and makes the heavens above out of one half and the earth below out of the other half. Just as in the Horus story in Egypt, it is Marduk, a later God that becomes associated with the kingship and political authority as it becomes bestowed upon him by a sort of voting of the assemblage or pantheon of other gods.

In China, the legend of Pan Gu states that in the beginning there was a cosmic egg with a man gestating inside of this formless chaos.[5] After eighteen thousand years, he awoke and broke the egg open with a hammer and chisel causing the yang aspects of this primordial chaos to ascend and create heaven and the yin element to descend and create the earth. After more hard work and toil, Pan Gu died and his body falling upon the earth provided a plethora of new and beautiful Forms for the world to experience. In an alternative creation account given by the famous Daoist philosopher Zhuangzi, Hundun or chaos plays host to the two forces of the southern sea—Shu—and the northern sea—Hu. To repay Hundun's hospitality Shu and Hu decide to drill holes in his head so that he can see and hear, but instead they only end up killing and destroying chaos and thereby bringing order and an end to indeterminacy.

In India, there is a similar story to that of Pan Gu found in the Rig Veda.[6] In this account, Visvakarman "the maker of all" ritually sacrifices himself for the sake of bringing order out of chaos and thereby achieving his goal of separating the heavens and the earth. The Purusha tale, which is more popular, is really just a refinement of the older Visvakarman tale with Purusha's various body parts representing aspects of the world as we know it today. The tale is used to help explain the caste system with brahmins issuing from his mouth, kshatriya or warriors from his arms, vaishya or merchants and farmers from his legs, and shudra or servants from his feet. A later tale from the Laws of Manu has Brahman or universal consciousness desiring to create living beings and so he wills into being the waters and a golden egg, which hatches Brahma or the personified aspect of Brahman. Brahma brings order to the chaotic waters. One day for Brahma lasts 4,320 million Earth years and during this time there is order, but when he sleeps for the same length of time the cosmos lapses back into chaos and then the next day 4,320 million years later, the order is restored in a cyclical fashion.

4. For a good reference of Mesopotamian myths, see *Myths from Mesopotamia*, translated by Stephanie Dalley. All of the above information is drawn from *Myths from Mesopotamia*.

5. A fine collection of Chinese mythology can be found in *Handbook of Chinese Mythology* by Lihui Yang and Deming An.

6. See Zaehner, *Hindu Scriptures*.

The last two mythical accounts of creation worth mentioning are that of the Hebrews and Greeks. In the Hebrew version, one finds that the Biblical account of creation is actually creation out of chaos not creation ex nihilo. For example, the opening lines of Genesis can be translated in one of two ways, both of which are mentioned in the NRSV Bible. The first way is the most familiar, "In the beginning when God created the heavens and the earth, the earth was a formless void."[7] However, many contemporary scholars of the Hebrew Bible[8] correctly point out that a better translation is "When God began to create the heaven and the earth the world was without form and void."[9] The second position is actually far more likely for two reasons: (1) because it says later in Genesis 1:6–13 that heaven and earth were created on the second and third days respectively and (2) because there is never any mention that "the waters" in Genesis 1 were created, instead they appear to be pre-existent. Given the general cosmologies that pervaded the cultural milieu of the early Hebrews it is far more likely that Genesis is advocating creation out of chaos.

The Greek accounts are similar to the above myths with Homer describing creation as beginning in the waters of Oceanus and the Orphic mystery tradition describing the birth of Phanes from an egg fashioned by Chronos. Phanes was also viewed as Eros and Eros or love mated with his daughter, night, to bring about all of creation. However, the most interesting account comes from Hesiod's *Theogony*.[10] Hesiod tells us that in the beginning there was chaos, but chaos begot five elemental powers: Gaia or Earth, Tartarus, the underworld, Erebus the gloom of Tartarus, Eros or love and Nyx or night, the power of darkness. It is the interplay of these five powers that results in all of the rest of creation. This ancient idea is somewhat akin to Cosmosyntheism's view of Ultimate Reality as a complex adaptive system.

The main point that I have belabored to prove here through so many examples is that God creates order, not the raw material out of which all things are then made. All of the above myths show that there was some sort of pre-existing material, often in the guise of water, mist or clay/earth that is available for creating with, but it must first be tamed and ordered. God does not create the world out of absolute nothingness in most of the ancient myths. It is this supremely ancient wisdom that I feel must be reapplied in modern times. It is still very unclear exactly how each of these cultures understood the role of chaos or pre-existing matter. Nevertheless, the myths or mythos, were stories that helped the average person orient him or herself in an uncertain world. It was up to the later philosophers to provide a more precise statement through logos or reason of exactly why one needed this matter and how it was

---

7. This is the first possibility suggested by the third edition of the NRSV Bible published by Oxford Press.

8. Most notably in Levenson, *Creation and the Persistence of Evil*, and May, *Creatio ex Nihilo*.

9. This second possible translation is indicated in the NRSV in n. 7.

10. My information concerning the *Theogony* is derived from the *Theogony*, translated Apostolos N. Athanassakis.

utilized by a primordial principle or agent of order. This is where Aristotle comes into play, because he provides the sort of sustained philosophical inquiry that can point to exactly why one needs a primordial world or prime matter.

Aristotle and Prime Matter

Throughout Aristotle's massive corpus of work, there is one book that has a particular relevance for the present study: *Metaphysics*. It is here that Aristotle describes what has come to be known as prime matter. Aristotle believed that in order to explain the nature and function of things, one must look to four distinct types of causes: material (what something is made of), formal (its essence), efficient (what brought it to be what it currently is) and final (its purpose, function or end). What concerns us right now are the first two. In *Metaphysics* book VII Z3, one encounters Aristotle struggling to understand what it means to be the ultimate substance of anything. It is here that one finds the beginning of his discussion on prime matter. "Now the substratum is that of which other things are predicated, while it is itself not predicated of anything else. And so we must first determine the nature of this; for that which underlies a thing primarily is thought to be in the truest sense its substance. And in one sense matter is said to be of the nature of substratum."[11]

Aristotle continues on to contemplate the possibility of matter that has been expunged of all Forms and thereby acts as the ultimate substratum.

> When all else is taken away evidently nothing but matter remains . . . But when length and breadth and depth are taken away we see nothing left except that which is bounded by these, whatever it be; so that to those who consider the question thus matter alone must seem to be substance. By matter I mean that which in itself is neither a particular thing nor of a certain quantity nor assigned to any other of the categories by which being is determined. For there is something of which each of these is predicated, so that its being is different from that of each of the predicates; for the predicates other than substance are predicated of substance, while substance is predicated of matter. Therefore the ultimate substratum is of itself neither a particular thing nor of a particular quantity nor otherwise positively characterized; nor yet negatively, for negations also will belong to it only by accident.[12]

But Aristotle says himself that such a prime matter expunged of all Forms and predicates is impossible to conceive. I would have to agree that prime matter as somehow devoid of any Forms and any actuality makes no sense. Nevertheless, in the final analysis, it is the compound of both matter and Form and the unity of potentiality and actuality that makes anything concrete and sensible. "The substratum is substance and

---

11. Aristotle, "*Metaphysics* Book VII Z3," 1028B35–1029A1–3.
12. Ibid., 1029A10–25.

this is in one sense the matter (and by matter I mean that which, not being a 'this' actually, is potentially a 'this'), and in another sense the formula or form (which being a 'this' can be separately formulated), and thirdly the complex of matter and form."[13] This is the doctrine of hylomorphism, which shares some similarities with its Platonic counterpart.

Aristotle's matter, however it is to be understood, is clearly passive in its reception of Forms, meaning that the matter is inert and doesn't play an active role in the process of combination and becoming. However, towards the end of his *Metaphysics*, Aristotle suggests that there could be as many as fifty-five prime movers, one for each type of motion and perhaps in this caveat, one can find a place for the role of chaos within his system. Regardless of this possibility, Cosmosyntheism's view of primeval matter differs markedly from Aristotle's prime matter. Most importantly, the principles of Cosmosyntheism result in a denial that prime matter is passive, vacuous and devoid of all Forms. What I refer to as "a World" is rather, a group of ultra-simplistic entities that flick in and out of existence at the lowest quantum level. However, these simple entities are actual, in contradistinction to Aristotle's prime matter or matter. In order to get a more straightforward account of what I mean, one must fast-forward in time to the present day and take a look at cutting-edge theories in theoretical physics.

A World of Strings

I explained above that Aristotle's philosophy of hylomorphism requires the combination of both matter and form in order to make something actual and concrete. I also showed that Aristotle was toying with the notion that there may be an ultimate or primary type of matter, but he does not commit one way or another on this issue. He does tell us that it would seem to be impossible for such utterly formless matter to exist, but in contemporary physics one encounters something that sounds strikingly reminiscent of Aristotle's prime matter: strings.[14]

String theory or more accurately, string theories as there are five main versions of the theory, all suggest that the ultimate matter making up the universe are infinitesimally small strings and membranes. Quantum physicists came to this insight after centuries of assuming that atomic and sub-atomic structures were actually point particles. However, after decades of employing atom-smashers, physicists were beginning to become disillusioned by the staggering variety of sub-atomic particles like: quarks, neutrinos, leptons, bosons, gluons etc. Eventually a new solution was proposed and that is that all of these sub-atomic particles are actually composed of the same "stuff," strings. What makes a neutrino different from a proton is the way or the rate at which the string vibrates.

---

13. Ibid., Book VIII H1, 1041B25–32.

14. In the last decade, string theory has been popularized and thus reached a broader audience than just the theoretical physics community, partially via the works: *The Elegant Universe* and *The Fabric of the Cosmos* by Brian Greene, and Michio Kaku's *Parallel Worlds*.

Part II: Cosmosyntheism: A New Option

Another intriguing feature of string theory is that it operates in ten or eleven dimensions and it cannot work in less than this. This suggests that perhaps our universe is floating within hyperspace or the "bulk" and that our universe is one massive membrane with other membrane universes floating around us in higher-dimensional space. The idea of multiple higher dimensions will be relevant for the present study when we reach the chapter on the Receptacle. However, what concerns us presently is that this idea of a prime matter composed of vibrating strings is very much in line with what I am suggesting for Cosmosyntheism's notion of "a primordial World." Even Whitehead discusses the fundamental vibratory nature of the universe, which is possibly a vague intuition on his part of the things to come. "But so far there has been no reference to the ultimate vibratory characters of organisms and to the potential element in nature."[15]

Cosmosyntheism's Primordial World

What does all of this mean for my system? I propose that there are seven implications of this reconceived notion of the God-World relationship.

1. God is not alone and has always been related to a World of some kind.
2. The interrelatedness of God and a World suggests that God is now capable of genuine love, sharing and compassion because there is an "authentic primordial other."
3. The primordial world is composed of actual entities that are indeterminate as to their potential future essences.
4. Order and chaos are fundamental and need one another.
5. This primordial world "holds" or "embodies" at least the Forms of chaos, randomness and indeterminacy.
6. Through the God-World interaction, new non-primordially envisaged Forms pop into existence through experiential knowledge, which is "exgressed" from the world back into God and other entities; plus, new Forms arise via a pervasive semi-restrained degree of systemic chaos.
7. There has always been time because there have always been experiencing entities.

What follows is some added context, which hopefully, will serve to illuminate many of the above claims and help to make clear the implications that result from accepting them.

What one learns from the ancient myths is that there is something crucial about the ultimate abstract duality of order and chaos and that somehow these two forces are at work within creation. An unfortunate aspect of many of the ancient ways was

---

15. Whitehead, *Process and Reality*, 239.

that the powers of chaos became linked to all things mysterious: women, foreigners, uncharted territories, destruction and death. Chaos instilled fear, and rightfully so, but this terror of the ancients was balanced with a healthy respect for the role of chaos in the creation and proper balancing of our everyday reality. It can be traced that over time, this initial healthy respect for the forces of chaos devolved, via the monotheistic faiths, into a complete hatred and demonization of chaos as something that completely works against the creation of an all-powerful and good deity. Therefore, chaos is wholly evil and should be avoided at all costs.

The combination of linking chaos with women and foreigners, plus the resulting purging of the importance of chaos to the point of totally eliminating its necessary role, represents religion's darkest turn. This colossal mistake still plagues and haunts many of the various world religions and is one reason for the great disdain that some groups have for anything religious. Cosmosyntheism does away with the longstanding notion that chaos is, one, something to be avoided and, two, evil by nature. In fact, as one learns from complexity science and chaos theory, existing at the edge of chaos is the most efficient means for issuing in novelty within a system. For this reason, Cosmosyntheism goes so far as to suggest a sanctification of the role of chaos within Ultimate Reality.

Concerning Aristotle's hylomorphism, Cosmosyntheism proposes a different picture. Perhaps it is true that all that we see around us is the result of various combinations of matter and Form, but what exactly is the role of matter regarding formal, efficient and final causation? Aristotle seems to suggest that matter has a rather "unessential" role to play concerning the makeup and substance of a thing. He believes that the essence of a thing is derived from its Form not its material substrate, but if the material substrate is the repository of the Form of indeterminacy, randomness and chaos, then it seems that it would have a major impact on the unfolding essence of any specific thing.

Cosmosyntheism emphasizes the power of a primordial world of strings as they operate by different quantum mechanical laws and they act as the "joker" or "wild cards" in a cosmic game of poker, always injecting a new spin or angle on the unfolding process. This quantum randomness inherent in the primordial world altered the original plan: formally, by suggesting new Forms through semi-chaotic interaction with the ordering principle and the existential knowledge gained by way of actualizing whatever was previously only potential; finally, by exercising its own self-determination—as is the right of all actual entities—no matter how simple and how trivial the freedom and efficiently, by interacting with other sub-atomic particles and elements.

Although Aristotle is unclear as to whether or not he believes prime matter actually exists, Cosmosyntheism states that it does exist as infinitesimally small strings that are actual, but indefinite or indeterminate. Indeterminate of what one might ask? Indeterminate of any particular Forms that it is capable of instantiating. As prime or ultimate, these actualities do not endure like serially-ordered societies do, but they are momentary actual entities and therefore, they are capable of "holding" or "exhibiting" Forms and then passing them on the next moment.

Part II: Cosmosyntheism: A New Option

As I stated in the previous chapter on God, these Forms within the primordial world are in some sense foreign to God. All things are in God as panentheism demands, but that does not mean all things are of or from God. The World is, in other words, capable of surprising God through spontaneity and through experiential knowledge gained through the process of hylomorphism or Forms ingressing into matter and then being brought back up into God and thereby understood or known in a different manner. In distinction from Whitehead and the Cobbian/Griffian school of thought, Cosmosyntheism says that there is both ingression of new Forms from God and "exgression" of new Forms back into God. As the saying goes, there is a difference between knowing the path and walking it. The real point of this saying is that what you thought you knew turns out to be wrong or at least incomplete until you begin the journey—and so it was for God.

Why Not Just a World/Cosmos?

This is a very important question because mainstream science—as well as some forms of emergent theism—begin from the premise that in the beginning, all that existed was some collection of ultra-simplistic particles. The typical cosmological picture of creation begins with a quantum fluctuation in the void of space set off perhaps by a tachyon and this initiated the breaking apart of a primordial singularity resulting in an inflationary big-bang scenario. This is clearly one viable option for understanding Reality, but the standard cosmological models are not without their own flaws.

I do not intend for this section to be an exhaustive account of problems plaguing modern scientific disciplines; however, it is worth briefly mentioning some of these issues as they serve to cast significant doubts on the status of science as the sole arbiter of truth and of what is possible when it comes to describing reality. I will address some of the problems by moving from the specific to the more abstract. One specific problem arises within cosmology for the idea of reality as being simply a cosmos, and that is the horizon problem. The horizon problem asks the question, how can the opposite corners of the universe have a uniform temperature if they are 28 billion light years apart and the universe is only 13.7 billion years old? Cosmologists have patched the big-bang theory with inflation to resolve this paradox, with inflation causing a brief, yet extremely rapid period of expansion in the early universe that allowed for the uniformity to be created. But, one must ask, what caused this rapid inflation in the first place? Furthermore, what gave mass to the subatomic particles in the first place? Supposedly, the answer to this question is the breaking of the electroweak force, but we do not know how this occurred either.

A more general concern is how any universe could have evolved to the degree that ours has in complexity without some principle of order. I allude here to the apparent fine-tuning issue invoked by the anthropic principle, because even if there is a multiverse to account for the fine-tuning of cosmological constants, there is still no adequate explanation of how the completely vacuous entities of particle physics could possibly give rise to experiencing agents with consciousness. If the simpler particles are devoid of any experience, then how would arranging even larger aggregates of "nothing" together account for emergent complexity? How did life emerge out of totally inorganic compounds? What mechanism was it that supplied some of the earliest Forms? How can there be any progress or information transfer if there are no internal relations between entities? Where and how is the information stored that is gained at the early stages of the process of evolution? What force is it that brings the entities together and guides them, goading them onwards to greater complexity? It is this last question that transitions us into the next chapter on Creativity/Eros as the metaphysical principle and power that performs precisely this function of bringing the entities together and driving progress forward.

Summary

- Nearly all of the ancient civilizations contain a creation myth that describes a God bringing order out of a pre-existing chaos, thus suggesting at least two ultimates.

- The early Greek philosophers also contemplated a hypothetical prime matter that acted as the substrate for all material things.

- Contemporary theoretical physics suggests that string theory is the most promising theory for explaining reality. These strings are infinitesimally small and operate via quantum laws.

- Cosmosyntheism states that this co-existing quantum world holds or embodies its own Forms.

- By having a genuine other, God is capable of real love and interaction. Plus, by interacting with the unpredictable power embodied in this quantum world, radically new Forms may arise for God and the World.

Chapter 7

Creativity/Eros

The ultimate metaphysical principle is the advance from disjunction to conjunction, creating a novel entity other than the entities given in disjunction. The novel entity is at once the togetherness of the many which it finds, and also it is one among the disjunctive many which it leaves . . . The many become one and are increased by one.

—ALFRED WHITEHEAD, *PROCESS AND REALITY*

IN CHAPTER 6, I discussed the nature and function of a primordial world. However, it remains to be shown just how and why the two ultimate elements, God and a World, interact. Enter Creativity/Eros. The purpose of this brief chapter is to explain the role of this critical fourth element within the emerging metaphysics of Cosmosyntheism. I will begin as always with the abridged answer as to why this particular metaphysical element is indispensable. Next, it is necessary to first explain Creativity's similarities and key differences from Aristotle's prime matter, as this could be a cause of great confusion, due to the fact that I discussed prime matter in the last chapter in relation to a World of actual entities, but Whitehead and others seem to equate prime matter with Creativity. Then I will address Whitehead's definitions of Creativity and finally, I will put forth my own interpretation and slight variations in a heading on the role of Creativity/Eros in Cosmosyntheism's metaphysics.

Why Creativity?

Eros/Creativity is that basic element which draws the many entities together into a sharing community and then pulls them back apart into the mode of individuality, free-will and creative self-transcendence. This process happens over and over again. It is the pendulum-like swing of the totality, the oscillatory force that drives the system onward and upward. Creativity is the ultimate metaphysical principle; it holds and is reflected at all levels of reality.

Creativity, What It Is and What It Isn't

Creativity/Eros may seem to be a vague and ambiguous notion, but it is nonetheless a critical element in some metaphysical frameworks. For Whitehead it is often compared with Aristotle's hypothetical prime matter, which is only actual in virtue of its accidents. "In all philosophic theory there is an ultimate which is actual in virtue of its accidents. It is only then capable of characterization through its accidental embodiments, and apart from these accidents is devoid of actuality. In the philosophy of organism this ultimate is termed Creativity."[1] Whitehead says later, "Creativity is without a character of its own in exactly the same sense in which the Aristotelian "matter" is without a character of its own. It is that ultimate notion of the highest generality at the base of actuality."[2]

This equating of prime matter and Creativity may be confusing seeing as how I discussed prime matter in the last chapter and suggested that it corresponded more with a primordial world of simplistic actual entities. However, I was attempting to explain what this primordial actual world consisted of in actuality, what it was comprised of substantially, e.g., strings. I was examining the simplest, actually real things, primordially in existence. Creativity and prime matter differ from a primordial world of simple entities in that Creativity is *not actual, it is not an "actual entity."* Creativity is without or as Whitehead says, "behind all Forms." Remember, there must be a many or a multiplicity at the beginning, I have described the actual members of this multiplicity as God and a World, with a World being comprised of the simplest actual entities or strings. Hence, the last chapter was aimed at elucidating the nature and function of this most elementary and fundamental type of actual matter, which I likened to the strings or sub-atomic particles of contemporary physics.

The burning question still exists, what is Creativity exactly and precisely how is it different from the Forms, God, and the World of simple entities? The most concise answer is that *it is that which is instantiated in all actualities unlike the specific Forms, which serve to differentiate one thing from another and are only instantiated in one or a limited set of actual things.* As David Griffin says, "it is that which makes something a concrete thing rather than a mere possibility."[3] This making a potential into a concrete thing happens because Creativity is *the power of togetherness generated by an existing multiplicity*; it is what draws God towards the world again and again. It is *the power of Being*, a power that oscillates between drawing beings or a multiplicity together and then pulling them apart again. This energizing force drives the whole system forward and upward; it is the engine of progress, the contemporary Hermes/Mercury mediating between God and man. However, *in itself, it is nothing; it is empty, in the sense of lacking either actuality or Forms*. One may ask, how can this be?

1. Whitehead, *Process and Reality*, 7.
2. Ibid., 31.
3. Griffin, *Reenchantment without Supernaturalism*, 262.

Part II: Cosmosyntheism: A New Option

As an analogy, try to picture the workings of gravity within space-time. Imagine an empty area of space-time with no objects in it, one would say that it is empty, one would not talk about forces or about mass or any matter; one would simply say it is a void. However, if one suddenly placed two large objects in close proximity to one another in that empty space, all of a sudden they will exert a pull on one another and draw the other in. Was a third object added, an object that is pulling the two together? Of course not, the third element is a latent force that is present as soon as beings or matter are present and so it is with Creativity, it does not come later in time than Being, it is always there instantiated in Being wherever and whenever there are beings.

The analogy breaks down eventually because gravity is a *physical law* of our universe, whereas Creativity is a *metaphysical law,* the metaphysical law or principle, meaning that both God and the other entities are subject to its power and effects no matter which universe of a larger multiverse you happened to be in. This metaphysical law actively unites God and a World into a complex communion and then returns them to a state of individual creative freedom. This oscillatory process is repeated constantly and indefinitely. With each new cycle of the oscillation, "the many become one and are increased by one."[4] And hence, the whole system progresses to a greater degree of depth, subtlety and frequently, complexity.

Creativity/Eros in Cosmosyntheism

In the previous pages, I have shown ways in which Cosmosyntheism differs from Whitehead and other process theologies, with most of the differences stemming from my assertion that *God does not have all the Forms primordially and that a World holds or embodies its own Forms*, but on the topic of Creativity, Cosmosyntheism is more in line with mainstream process theology. That said, Whitehead was not always clear about the relationship between Creativity, God and the World. I will first provide a brief synopsis that encompasses all the major points concerning the nature and function of Creativity including any refinements made by Cosmosyntheism and then I will discuss the proper relationship between these three elements of Ultimate Reality.

Creativity is by nature non-actual in the sense that it is not an actual thing or entity in its own right. Instead, it is non-actual just like an eternal Form, but also like all other Forms, it must be instantiated in an actual being. However, unlike other Forms it is instantiated in all beings. Its essential function is as a single energizing power with two directions of movement, pulling together and pulling apart over and over again. When Creativity/Eros is discussed in its function as drawing in or together, it is known as Eros, and it is a bringing together of entities in an experiential sharing and commingling. In some respects, the Greek word *agape* is more adequate in that it is an unconditional type

---

4. Whitehead, *Process and Reality*, 21.

of love in that it brings together all things, but it is more precisely—*Eros*—in that it is never fully satisfied and it also draws like-to-like via resonance.

The notion of resonance ties in with Whitehead's intuition of the ultimately vibratory character of all things and with the previous discussion of string theory. Perhaps, and this is admittedly highly speculative, all things are vibrating or oscillating between two states, one particle-like state that we are familiar with and would define as normal reality, and another wave-like state where our experiences, feelings and data are shared with other parts of the overall universe or system and this sharing would be Eros. As Eros gives way to Creativity, we have our more familiar individualized, subjective experience of self-determination and creative response/experience/transcendence. This is the oscillatory motion of Eros/Creativity, bringing the many together into an experiential unity and then pulling them apart again, in order to increase the range of possibilities, experiences and enjoyments.

Maybe the Hermetic axiom emblazoned on the Emerald Tablet "As above so below" is true, in that the function of this metaphysical principle also reveals itself at the level of our everyday world. We see the effects of Creativity on the sensible scale in the apparent need for societies, for sharing, for companionship. When we are utterly alone we often fall into despair. Perhaps this is because we have been severed from the ultimate purpose and meaning of the universe and we at least feel this on a subconscious level and it results in a debilitating melancholy.

Why Not Just Creativity?

It would be impossible to conceive of ultimate reality as merely consisting of Creativity because Creativity is nothing and cannot function without some actual entities. Creativity's primary function is to oscillate all the actual entities between two states and if there are no actual entities there is no need for Creativity. Given the previous statements, it seems bordering on impossible that reality would consist solely of this metaphysical principle.

Assuming that all of the above is at least in principal possible, there is still one looming question. *Where or what is Eros pulling the entities to or into and then where or what is Creativity emptying them from?* This question is not an easy one to solve, but it brings us to the final challenging element of the metaphysics: the Receptacle or the Place.

Summary

- Creativity/Eros is *not an actual entity* like God or a person; instead, it is an invisible force somewhat akin to gravity.

- Creativity/Eros is a single energizing power that has two directions of movement.

Part II: Cosmosyntheism: A New Option

When pulling all things together it is known as Eros, when pulling them apart again it is better understood as Creativity.

- Creativity/Eros is a *metaphysical* law meaning that it will be operative at all levels of reality even within other universes if any actually exist.

Chapter 8

The Plane of Mutual Immanence

There are being, space, and becoming, three distinct things which existed even before the universe came to be.

—PLATO, *TIMAEUS*

The Receptacle, as discussed in the *Timaeus*, is the way in which Plato conceived the many actualities of the physical world as components in each other's natures. It is the doctrine of the immanence of Law, derived from *the mutual immanence of actualities*. It is Plato's doctrine of *the medium of intercommunication*.

—ALFRED WHITEHEAD, *ADVENTURES OF IDEAS*

IT WAS SHOWN ABOVE that Creativity is an oscillating power that brings all of the actualities together and pulls them apart again. In this chapter, I will cover the Receptacle, Locus or Storehouse, which is the "where," or the "what," that entities are drawn into and out of. In order to grasp this obscure topic, it will be necessary to evaluate some of Plato's and Whitehead's descriptions before expressing precisely how the Receptacle is to be understood in Cosmosyntheism. There are similarities between Plato's and Whitehead's understandings of the Receptacle and my own; however, I have the advantage of new conceptual frameworks that can be employed in order to ascertain a more perspicacious account of what the Receptacle's nature and function actually is. For example, I will utilize the concepts of higher-dimensional space and holography to clarify this critical element of Ultimate Reality.

Why a Receptacle or Plane of Mutual Immanence?

A Receptacle is necessary for at least two reasons. First, there must be a place of mutual immanence where the *information, affective tones, experiences and future possibilities can*

Part II: Cosmosyntheism: A New Option

be shared from entity to entity nearly instantly. Second, there must be a precise record of all that has happened and of *the possibilities which are known now, but not yet fully actualized*. In other words, there must be *a cosmic memory or hard drive* that records forever all things that have ever come into it. It must retain and provide a unity of all the things which enter into it, but this second aspect of imposing unity is actually a function of *God as a whole*, whereas the Receptacle can be understood as *the memory bank of the totality*. As we will see below, Plato explains that the Receptacle is a "Necessity" because there is Being and Becoming, but there also must be *that in which things become*.

Plato's *Timaeus*

The *Timaeus* is a lengthy dialogue about cosmology, metaphysics and physics. In some sense, it is Plato's attempt at uniting many of the ideas he has discussed in the early and middle period dialogues. Within the *Timaeus* however, Plato reveals a new concept—a third kind or *triton genos*—that he defines as the Receptacle or Container (υποδοχη, *upodoche*). He says right from the start, "it appears that our account compels us to attempt to illuminate in words a kind that is difficult and vague."[1] He asks what we are to suppose that it does and is. To this preliminary question he gives his first simple description of the Receptacle. "This above all: it is a receptacle of all becoming, its wetnurse, as it were."[2] What one learns from this initial account are some of the functions of the Receptacle. The Receptacle somehow plays a critical role in the process of change, growth and all becoming. However, Plato provides more details as to the Receptacle's functions and its overall role in the picture of Ultimate Reality.

Plato later says of the Receptacle's nature and functions,

> Not only does it always receive all things, it has never in any way whatever taken on any characteristic similar to any of the things that enter it. Its nature is to be available for anything to make its impression upon, and it is modified, shaped and reshaped by the things that enter it. These are the things that make it appear different at different times. The things that enter and leave it are imitations of those things that always are, imprinted after their likeness in a marvelous way that is hard to describe.[3]

The Receptacle in other words, *takes in* all of the matter and energy in the world, all of the things or beings into itself, and all of these things *make an impression upon* the Receptacle, modifying it in a way similar to how a piece of photographic film is modified by all that it encounters. After this impression is made, one learns that *the things leave the Receptacle* after having presumably intermingled there with other entities and with other Ideas/Forms, which the things then *imitate in the material world* once

---

1. Plato, "Timaeus," in *Complete Works*, 49a, 1251.
2. Ibid.
3. Ibid., 50c, 1253.

they leave the Receptacle. It is not quite clear how the material world or the realm of becoming is distinct from the Receptacle. How do things leave it if it is that in which all things come to be? We will return to this issue later.

An outline of the essential ingredients for reality is now in place and Plato gives us a concise synopsis of the key elements. "For the moment we need to keep in mind three types of things: that which comes to be, that in which it comes to be, and that after which the things coming to be is modeled, and which is the source of its coming to be. It is in fact appropriate to compare the receiving thing to a mother, the source to a father, and the nature between them to their offspring."[4] The Receptacle is of course "that in which it comes to be," and is the mother of all creation. If we think of motherliness, a few qualities immediately present themselves: receptive, protective, caring and sharing. These are the qualities of the Receptacle, *it receives all the things or entities within it and it protects all that has come within it by saving an impression or snapshot of that particular moment in time*. Regarding its all-receptive nature, Plato provides three analogies: shapes being dipped into gold, a neutral base from which one makes perfumes and unformed clay awaiting impressions.[5]

Concerning the qualities of caring and sharing, the Receptacle can be viewed as space (*khora*), in that it provides the space for things to both be what they are and also a type of space/place where they can intermingle with one another and transform into one another. Plato is led to say, "There are being, space and becoming, three distinct things which existed even before the universe came to be."[6] This picture is somewhat similar to my own, in that I have: a maximally powerful being, God; other simple beings or entities; the Forms; space, or the Receptacle; and becoming or Creativity/Eros.

Before concluding this examination of Plato's Receptacle one last function must be highlighted: *sorting/sharing*. Since all things enter into the Receptacle and share their natures with it, Plato says that it is:

> filled with powers that are neither similar nor evenly balanced . . . it sways irregularly in every direction as it is shaken by those things, and being set in motion it in turn shakes them . . . That is how at that time the four kinds [traces of the four elements: earth, air, fire and water] were being shaken by the receiver, which was itself agitating like a shaking machine, separating the kinds most unlike each other furthest apart and pushing those most like each other closest together into the same region.[7]

All of the things appear to intermingle to some degree, but in the end, like is attracted to like and all things are sifted as if by winnowing sieves as Plato says. So, the Receptacle also *imposes some degree of unity as well as a degree of interpenetration of all things*

---

4. Ibid., 50d, 1253.
5. Ibid., 50e–51a, 1253–1254.
6. Ibid., 52d, 1255.
7. Ibid., 52e–53a, 1255.

and in the end it spits all things back out into a well-defined region or locus of space-time. But one may still be left wondering, what is it in its own nature and where is it?

Plato gives no concrete answer as to where the Receptacle is. However, we have seen enough to understand that the answer is that *it is everywhere and nowhere in particular.* All of ordinary space-time is in a sense the Receptacle in that it receives all the things back into their specific localized regions of space and time, but there is the other aspect of the Receptacle, which can be understood as higher-dimensional space. This higher-dimensional space can be viewed as the place where all things interact and a record of each moment is kept. This account is not Plato's however, and for Plato the Receptacle can be understood primarily as ordinary space-time (or more properly just space, as time has a Form/archetype whereas space does not).[8]

Even as ordinary space-time, each region of space contains data of the impressions made upon the whole of space-time. As an example, think of how the Internet stores data non-locally and shares it across a vast network of interconnected computers. This network is known as "the cloud," and so it is with the Receptacle, it utilizes all of space-time as a sort of cosmic memory bank, *with each region containing traces of the entirety*. In short, the Receptacle stores data non-locally and holographically. Therefore, the Receptacle truly is nowhere and everywhere simultaneously. I turn now to Whitehead, who provides us with some further clarity on this topic of the Receptacle and its relation to space-time.

The Receptacle in Whitehead's *Adventures of Ideas*

The notion of a Receptacle cannot be seen in Whitehead's thought until at least Part IV of *Process and Reality,* where he discusses the "extensive continuum" and "actual worlds." However, he does not actually use the word Receptacle until *Adventures of Ideas*, and his earlier discussions on the topic were merely the germination of what comes to full fruition throughout *Adventures of Ideas*. Whitehead explicitly gives credit to Plato for the concept, but he wants to attempt to understand what this term referred to and what role it played in the larger metaphysics of Plato's *Timaeus*. Whitehead begins his exposition of the Receptacle with some initial statements that help to narrow the possibilities as to its nature and function.

> This community of the world, which is the matrix for all begetting, and whose essence is process with retention of connectedness, this community is what Plato terms the Receptacle. In our effort to divine his meaning, we must remember that Plato says that it is an obscure and difficult concept, and that in its own essence the Receptacle is devoid of all forms. It is thus certainly not the

---

8. For the distinction between space and time in Plato, see Cornford's *Plato's Cosmology,* especially page 193. John Sallis has suggested in his *Chorology*, that *khora* is untranslatable and that Plato intended to use an inherently ambiguous term. Sallis points out the problems with using: space, place, void or locus to translate *khora* on pp. 115–19.

> ordinary geometrical space with its mathematical relations . . . The Receptacle imposes a common relationship on all that happens, but does not impose what that relationship shall be.[9]

One learns a great deal in this first paragraph explaining the Receptacle. First, one learns that its essence is process with retention of connectedness. Presumably this refers to the fact that the Receptacle is a place of mutual immanence for all the actual entities and that as each moment passes into the next, there is a retention of the data that preceded the present moment. Whitehead next repeats what we encountered earlier, which is that the Receptacle is in its own essence devoid of all Forms—even common geometrical/mathematical relations. To me this suggests that Whitehead believes that the Receptacle is more than simple space-time. I fully agree with this assessment. Instead, the Receptacle may be *a place between spaces or below/above normal geometrical space*, although this attempt at fixing its coordinate location is still misleading. The point is that it is a plane where all things are interconnected and in its own essence, it is passive and receptive rather than actively imposing Forms or ideas onto those that enter into it.

Before continuing his description of the Receptacle in a later chapter, Whitehead forays into a discussion on how to locate objects within space-time. This discussion is relevant because it ties in directly with the notion of interconnectedness. Whitehead denies that one can precisely identify a thing's location in space-time because each thing is a modification of conditions within space-time, extending throughout its whole range. He goes on to say, "There is a focal region, which in common speech is where the thing is. But its influence streams away from it with finite velocity throughout the utmost recesses of space and time . . . For physics, the thing itself is what it does, and what it does is this divergent stream of influence."[10] Explaining this fact of interrelatedness and interconnectedness among all entities within the universe, Whitehead says, "Again, with the denial of simple location we must admit that within any region of space-time the innumerable multitude of these physical things are in a sense superposed. Thus the physical fact at each region of space-time is a composition of what the physical entities throughout the Universe mean for that region."[11] The ideas of "superposition," "mutual immanence" and "extended streams of influence" are helpful ways of understanding what all of the things or entities themselves look like and how they operate within the Receptacle.

Whitehead picks back up the topic of the Receptacle, this time quoting Plato at length, but with a few key modifications where he inserts his own technical terminology in place of some of Plato's phrases.

> In addition to the welter of events and of the forms which they illustrate, we require a third term, personal unity. It is a perplexed and obscure concept. We

---

9. Whitehead, *Adventures of Ideas*, 150.
10. Ibid., 157.
11. Ibid., 158.

> must conceive it the receptacle, the foster mother as I might say, of the becoming of our occasions of experience. This personal identity is the thing which receives all occasions of the man's existence. It is there as a natural matrix for all transitions of life, and is changed and variously figured by the things that enter it; so that it differs in its character at different times. Since it receives all manner of experiences into its own unity, it must itself be bare of all forms. We shall not be far wrong if we describe it as invisible, formless and all-receptive. It is a locus which persists, and provides an emplacement for all the occasions of experience. That which happens in it is conditioned by the compulsion of its own past, and by the persuasion of its immanent ideals.[12]

What must be taken away from this description is that for Whitehead the Receptacle allows for there to be *a continuity of experience*. The Receptacle achieves this goal by retaining our past experiences and giving us the sensation of our lives being that of one enduring soul substance, when in truth, *our lives consist of societies of events held together by certain distinguishing characteristics*. "The conclusion follows that our consciousness of the self-identity pervading our life-thread of occasions, is nothing other than knowledge of a special strand of unity within the general unity of nature."[13]

The sole function of the Receptacle then is the imposition of a unity upon all the events of nature. It performs this function in the transition from one occasion of experience to another, or put differently, when there is a shift from the subject structure of experience to the object structure of experience. Whitehead explains this fundamental structure of reality. "This general principle is the object-to-subject structure of experience. It can otherwise be stated as the vector-structure of nature. Or otherwise, it can be conceived as the doctrine of *the immanence of the past energizing in the present.*"[14] That which retains this connectedness, allows for mutual immanence and provides a semblance of order and unity to all of life and experience is the Receptacle. *The Receptacle maintains and unifies the past, but it also provides the stage for the present; God aims to harmonize, intensify and order both the present and the future by providing novel Forms (possibilities) and enriching avenues for experience and enjoyment.* It is always in the present where all five of the ultimates combine.

Since Whitehead's time a few other famous philosophers have mentioned the Receptacle. Martin Heidegger mentions the *khora* in relation to his central concept of a "clearing" for being to take place. Jacques Derrida has provided an even more detailed account where he views the *khora* as "radical otherness," which similar to Heidegger, provides a place for being and action to unfold.[15] Derrida even goes so far as to call himself an Ankhorite (An-khora-ite) or a devotee of this *atheological*

---

12. Ibid., 187.
13. Ibid.
14. Ibid., 188.
15. Derrida, *On the Name*.

religious ultimate that is below being (*hypoousias*). "God is ineffable the way Plato's *agathon* is ineffable, beyond being, whereas différance is like the atheological ineffability of Plato's khora, beneath being."[16] In two influential essays—"Khora" and "How Not To Speak"—Derrida masterfully points out the difference between *khora* as a religious ultimate and God, the hyper-being (*hyperousias*) of Christian monasticism and mysticism. John Caputo, a Heideggerian scholar, follows Derrida in believing that *khora* or the Receptacle is "*toute autre*" or wholly other.[17] Of course, for Derrida and Caputo, the primary concern is with *khora* and its relation to the limitations of language.

Gilles Deleuze writes in his *Pure Immanence*, "it is only when immanence is no longer immanence to anything other than itself that we can speak of a plane of immanence."[18] While I agree with Deleuze in shifting ontology and metaphysics away from the talk of transcendence or a transcendent Being, I differ as will be seen below because I find his discussions confusing and ambiguous when it comes to real multiplicities and how they come to be. Also, when it comes to the issue of possibilities and potentialities, I believe that truly novel possibilities or Forms arise within or for the plane of immanence. In other words, there is a sense in which even the purely immanent space can be transcendent, *in the sense that it constantly transcends itself*.

The Plane of Mutual Immanence in Cosmosyntheism

As I explained at the outset of this chapter and in prior chapters, there are new conceptual models that can serve as illuminating analogies and metaphors for understanding the nature and function of both Creativity and the Receptacle. I will be making use of many of these analogies in the following pages, as I believe it is the best way to paint a lucid picture about the nature and function of the Receptacle. The first model is that of the wave/particle duality operating within nature and this serves to tie us back to the previous chapter on Creativity, while simultaneously setting the stage for further comprehending the Receptacle.

Contemporary physics has shown that matter exhibits the strange property of having two modes of existence, as a wave and as a point-particle. I briefly introduced this analogy earlier to explain the oscillatory power of Creativity, which by hypothesis, shifts us from between these two different modes. I proposed that perhaps all things are vibrating at different rates and that they transition from a solid everyday reality, *which we are conscious of*, and a subconscious or *pre-conscious* reality that is akin to a wave state, where there is interaction and a sharing of information between all the various actualities.

I also suggested, along with Whitehead, that one must look into the ultimately vibratory nature of things, as differing rates of vibration could be what acts as a marker

---

16. Caputo, *The Prayers and Tears of Jacques Derrida*, 10.
17. Caputo, "Love among the Deconstructibles," 37.
18. Deleuze, *Pure Immanence*.

of personal identity of either a single actual entity or a serially-ordered society of occasions of experience. It would be these differing frequencies or rates of vibration that carve out what becomes the emerging actual world for the next occasion of experience. *Like would be drawn to like through principles of resonance and the other data would merely be noise and therefore, eliminated from the emerging actual world.* However, it is within the Receptacle, which is the "where" or the medium of intercommunication, that all things first enter before being swept back out into an emerging actual world. This medium is a plane of mutual immanence where *all* the experiential data from *all* things is *exchanged, shared and stored holographically*.

The hologram is another useful model because it allows one to accept the possibility that there could be a true mutual immanence, where even a small part of an entire system or network could contain the data of the whole system, *albeit in a corrupted and distorted form*.[19] I suggest that the hologram or more accurately, a holofilm or movie, explains the nature of the Receptacle. It is passive and devoid of any imposition of Forms in its own nature, but it is the "space" where all things intermingle and cross one another's path so to speak. A hologram stores its data as a collection of interference wave patterns on a plate or film and it is this style of memory or data retention that is analogous to the Receptacle. All of the data moment-by-moment is shared and stored holographically, meaning that everything is superpositioned and is potentially available as future data for any other entity. However, as I hypothesized above, it is the vibratory nature of things that draws like-to-like via resonance. Thus, most of the available data for the emerging occasions of experience is eliminated due to *destructive interference*, whereas things that are similar and may be useful to the emerging occasion resonate to a degree and are brought to the forefront by *constructive interference*, which amplifies the intensity of that set of data.

It still is ambiguous as to "where" this receptacle is. It might be that it is the eleventh dimension, the dimension that supposedly all other universes are floating within according to Membrane Theory. It is likely to be higher-dimensional space of some kind, as the speed with which all this sharing would have to unfold would need to be next to instantaneous. My point here is that the Receptacle is not a localized region somewhere in our galaxy or even our universe. It is beyond our own universe, but our universe participates in it and helps to continually shape it. It would be more accurate to say that all space and matter are in some sense the Receptacle, in that they allow for pieces of information or data to be stored within themselves and by their own energy. To return to the analogy of the Internet, one can view each person or entity as one computer connected to a vast neural network spanning the entire multiverse and each universe being

---

19. In fact, some scientists and authors have suggested the idea that the entire universe is one gigantic hologram. For example, physicist David Bohm and author Michael Talbot in their respective books *Wholeness and the Implicate Order* and *The Holographic Universe*. Some recent experiments have also yielded data that may support this hypothesis. Note the article in the January 2009 issue of the *New Scientist* magazine entitled: "You Are a Hologram." Most recently, Brian Greene's *Hidden Reality* examines the possibility that our universe is actually a holographic projection.

a central hub or router and taken as a whole, the sum of the energy and matter within this network represents the seemingly infinite data storage possible for the Receptacle.

One final intriguing aspect of the Receptacle needs to be mentioned—the expansion of space itself. We now know that space itself is expanding and that there is a mysterious "*dark energy*" driving this process. Perhaps more space is being created because there is a greater need for data storage and thus more memory/space is necessary. I only bring this up as food for thought, but the Receptacle could be growing due to the process of reality itself, the interplay of the five ultimates and the cosmic aim of life. Since the Receptacle or Container is such a vague notion, I provide below the most concise descriptions of its nature and functions as is possible given the limitations of language and reason.

1. It is not a unique "thing" or "entity" in its own right and it is *not outside of God*. Rather, it is the circumference, periphery and all spaces in between, whose primary function is *to be a stage for mutual immanence and internal relations* and the *sharing of new and old theoretical data and already achieved experiential knowledge*.

2. A certain region of it (higher dimensional space?) is the place *before and after emplacement within the everyday world*.

3. *In its essence it is empty*, yet it is constantly being filled. It becomes full and then empties itself again and again. Think of a strip of film, its essence is to be empty and impressionable, but each slide is filled in its turn. Nonetheless, each slide is capable of being emptied again if illuminated. *Some of the film has been exposed and some remains to be exposed*. In a reciprocal process it empties itself and then is filled or exposed again.

4. It is *the memory of the totality* and it never forgets or excludes anything which enters into it or goes out of it.

5. It allows for a perceived *continuity of experience over time* and for a sense of *personal identity*.

6. Each thing that enters into it is distinguished from everything else, perhaps by a rate of vibration or a frequency. *Varying rates of vibration mark off differing "regions," "vectors" and emerging "actual worlds."*

7. Novelty and new experiences *are not simply derived from God imposing new Forms*. Instead, *it is a combination of new Forms from God, the power of the past experiences stored in the Receptacle and the uncertainty or chaos inherent in any emerging actual entity*.

Part II: Cosmosyntheism: A New Option

Why Not Just the Receptacle?

If Ultimate Reality consisted solely of the Receptacle, then there would truly be nothingness or a void. Some religions, like Daoism, suggest that there may have been an emanation from a primeval void, but it is completely unclear as to how anything actual could ever come about from a *genuine* void. How could nothingness act, move or make initial decisions? This possibility is certainly difficult to uphold. Some modern cosmologists suggest that a quantum fluctuation in the *apparent void* of empty space could have started the Big Bang, but even assuming that this hypothesis were true, *the emptiness of space-time is not truly empty as we now know, but instead is comprised of ultra-simplistic quantum particles, whereas the Receptacle is truly empty*. Furthermore, the Receptacle is always said to be completely passive rather than active, so *it is inconceivable that it could have ever initiated a type of creation*. As Whitehead says, "If we omit the Psyche and the Eros, we should obtain a static world."[20]

Summary

- Plato is the first to express the notion of a Receptacle that functions as the "wet nurse" of all becoming, receiving all things and retaining the impression that they make.

- Plato further suggests that the Receptacle sifts or sorts things that come into it, pushing those most like each other closest together.

- Whitehead believes that the Receptacle's primary function is to impose an order and unity within nature.

- For Whitehead, the Receptacle also allows for there to be a sense of continuity and personal identity over time.

- Cosmosyntheism modernizes the above accounts of the Receptacle by employing contemporary analogies from quantum physics and holography.

---

20. Whitehead, *Adventures of Ideas*, 275.

CHAPTER 9

The Logical Inconsistencies of All Other Possible Combinations

Innovation is not the product of logical thought, although the result is tied to a logical structure.

—ALBERT EINSTEIN

THE PREVIOUS SIX CHAPTERS shed light on the nature and functions of the five ultimates that make up Cosmosyntheism's metaphysics. However, there is still one major point that remains to be argued: why *these* five ultimates and *only* these five? In this chapter, I will cover all of the remaining twenty-six possible combinations of the five elements of Ultimate Reality that I have suggested: the Forms, Creativity, God, a World and the Receptacle.

The objective of this chapter is *to meet my third criterion for any successful constructive theology in the twenty-first century,* which was discussed on page eight of the introduction. The third criterion is *logical consistency,* but in addition, this chapter in taking a strictly philosophical, rather than a religious approach, also serves to *partially fulfill criterion two, which is to be interdisciplinary.* Criterion two is also fulfilled in that a few of the below combinations reflect typical *scientific views of creation.* I will argue for the logical consistency of Cosmosyntheism's five mutually grounding ultimates by demonstrating how all other potential combinations of the five ultimates results in inherent flaws, ambiguities and inconsistencies. In order to place this task into a clearer perspective, the table below presents all of the possible combinations of the five elements. An "X" in a column suggests that that ultimate is present, whereas blank space represents the absence of that ultimate.

Part II: Cosmosyntheism: A New Option

#	Forms	Creativity	God	World	Receptacle	Feasibility
1	X					0
2		X				0
3			X			0
4				X		0
5					X	0
6	X	X				0
7	X		X			8
8	X			X		2
9	X				X	0
10		X	X			0
11		X		X		0
12		X			X	0
13			X	X		0
14			X		X	0
15				X	X	0
16	X	X	X			6
17	X	X		X		8
18	X	X			X	5
19	X		X	X		4
20	X		X		X	2
21	X			X	X	6
22		X	X	X		0
23		X		X	X	0
24		X	X		X	0
25			X	X	X	0
26	X	X	X	X		8
27	X	X	X		X	6
28	X	X		X	X	8
29	X		X	X	X	3
30		X	X	X	X	0
31	X	X	X	X	X	9

Before proceeding, a couple of features concerning the above table must be noted. First off, I have included a column entitled: feasibility. The purpose of the feasibility column is to draw one's attention to the other metaphysical schemes that are *minimally, somewhat*, or perhaps, even *highly consistent* and therefore, *possibly* true. A numerical score of 0–3 qualifies a system as minimally consistent. A rank of 4–6 identifies a system as somewhat consistent. Finally, a score of 7–10 classifies a system as highly consistent and it will be pointed out that the metaphysical systems I covered in chapter 2, all find their place in this latter category. A second aspect of the table that stands out is the large proportion of zero rankings. Even though many of the above combinations are exceedingly bizarre, I will nevertheless touch on all of them; however, I will give more space to those that are of a higher probability. A third point to mention is that I will not cover the five single-ultimate possibilities, as I have already briefly addressed these options at the end of chapter 4 through chapter 8 under the heading entitled: "Why Not Just . . ."

The Problems

There are five distinct problems that can affect any of the thirty-one possibilities: (1) the primordial content problem; (2) the interaction problem; (3) the sustained order problem; (4) the free will problem and (5) the communication and storage problem. The first problem concerns the Forms, the second Creativity, the third God, the fourth the World and the fifth, the Receptacle. What this means is that any system excluding one or more of the five ultimates must have a plausible answer as to how the system will deal with these problems *without* that particular corresponding ultimate.

The Possible Combinations

6. Forms/Creativity

The main problem with this combination is that there is no matter for the Forms to eventually "descend" into. Unless somehow creativity and the Forms work together in some sort of automatic, mechanistic fashion and just somehow happen to produce matter or a World, then there is a dilemma. Some other glaring concerns are: where are the Forms, are they free-floating and divorced from any mentality? If so, this would be a strange scenario. In other words, given this system there can be no actualization of what is merely ideal, only eternal possibilities which are somehow free-floating. This would be an inert world.

Concerning the role of Creativity, it is unclear as to what Creativity would be bringing together and pulling apart? I view the role and function of Creativity to bring together actual entities and then to pull them apart again and again, but in this system there are no actual entities and it is unlikely that any could be created. Perhaps Creativity could be randomly combining the Forms and bringing them together in different ways, but it seems that there would be no purpose for this action. Finally, without the function of the Receptacle, what would remember any of the prior combinations of Forms that may have come together through the role of Creativity? It would just be a pointless, endless cycle. Therefore, this does not seem like a tenable option to me.

Part II: Cosmosyntheism: A New Option

7. Forms/God

This is a potentially viable option that can be elucidated in two ways. In the first view, one would need to imbue God with a significant amount of powers and abilities. Essentially this possibility would require something similar to classical theism. The reason why it might work is that God could contain all the Forms and then through God's will creation occurs in an *ex nihilo* fashion thereby manifesting a wholly contingent world. In this scenario, a World or some realm of co-eternal, finite actual entities would play no role. This could be the case, but God would need to possess many of the typical classical attributes, such as, omnipotence, transcendence, aseity and presumably, immutability.

Since there is no world co-eternal with God in this scheme, then all freedoms must be derived from the will and goodness of God in some sort of kenotic fashion. There would be no need for Creativity as I have represented it because God would not necessarily need to be brought into communion with the contingent entities of God's own creation. Most likely there would be no need for a reciprocal creativity, that is, if one were to conceive God as also possessing omniscience, which as I have shown in chapter 2, is the belief of most classical theists. Finally, the whole concept of a Receptacle understood as a place or plane of mutual immanence and as a growing repository or memory bank of the totality would not be relevant because God is not in nor is God affected by space or time or by the contingent creatures. God does not directly interact with them through internal relations, nor does God gain anything from them that would need to be remembered.

The second option is that of the perennial philosophy, which claims the Ultimate to be an impersonal Infinite that contains all possibilities. One could call this first level of reality God and as I pointed out in chapter 2, the perennialists claim that if something contains all possibilities *then one of those possibilities must be the creation of a world*. Therefore, the One or the Infinite radiates out the first emanation, which allows for self-reflection, differentiation and the thought of further celestial and terrestrial worlds. This option is better defined as Forms/Infinite but it can be understood to fit in the category of Forms/God. These are both feasible options, but as I will show in part III, there are a plethora of negative repercussions that stem from both options one or two of this view of Ultimate Reality.

8. Forms/World

This possibility can be understood in one of three ways. The first conception would suggest some sort of *eternal world* with all or some of the Forms already instantiated somewhere and somehow within the world. It is very confusing to understand how the Forms would have gotten into the world or how any new Forms could be received by the world if there are no un-instantiated Forms. Where was the Form of man or of a car a few million years ago if all Forms are eternally instantiated?

The second possible conception would entail some primordial quantum world that evolved new Forms. This seems unlikely as the only Forms that a quantum world would contain would be motion, chaos and perhaps a few other abstract types of Forms. Given a primordial quantum world, how would the rest of the Forms actually arise within time if there is no force like Creativity bringing the chaotic world together and allowing for aggregations, mutations and a general complexification? How would they keep order through time without lapsing into chaos without God and the Receptacle?

A third approach would be to view these two ultimates as two distinct and fully separate realms. Once again, how would they interact without Creativity and how would the Forms be a sustainable or coherent realm without a God or entity to contain and envisage them? Forms and Ideas devoid of an actuality to think and imagine them is a strange prospect. I would think that this would result in mutually exclusive realms that in no way interact with or contribute to one another. There could be no motion, no change or process on this account, unless one viewed the primordial world as containing only a few Forms at first and then over time spontaneously creating through aggregations of entities and mutations, totally new Forms within the world. But this process would not affect the other separate realm of Forms. This approach in its second form seems potentially viable and it shares some similarities to the modern scientific view of creation.

9. Forms/Receptacle

As I have defined these terms, this option is wholly nonsensical. There is no world for the Forms to instantiate themselves. There is no entity for the Forms to reside in, unless one views the Receptacle as somehow an entity, but then it would be something other than the Receptacle. Short of investing the Receptacle with more powers than it has, this option results in an inconceivable and totally static and inert paradigm. The Forms would just be in the Receptacle—or somehow outside of it—but either way, there would be no change or motion. There could never be an act of creation resulting in the world that we are all intimately familiar with and take as an obvious fact.

10. Creativity/God

This option is also not viable. God needs some primordial mental content and the Forms provide this. Without any Forms, God is some type of vacuous entity. Why would Creativity even be needed, what multiplicity would it be bringing together? I suppose Creativity would be bringing God together with God, because there is not yet a world. First, this content-less God would need to create a contingent world and then perhaps Creativity could have a meaningful place; but how can an empty and content-less God create anything? This possibility is completely inadequate and does not deserve any further attention.

Part II: Cosmosyntheism: A New Option

11. Creativity/World

This picture would need to be a quantum-like world with Creativity bringing things like strings or simplistic sub-atomic events together and then evolution eventually taking over from there. The problem is that even strings and sub-atomic particles have or contain some Forms and so this would actually represent the scenario Creativity/World/Forms to be discussed later. As the current scenario stands, it is unthinkable without Forms. Can there be a prime-matter that combines with itself mysteriously and then produces something totally different and more complex in the process? I think not. Even still, what allows for sustained order over time through more complex aggregations of this prime matter? What retains the memory or progress of this self-sustaining, self-replicating and then self-transcending prime-matter?

12. Creativity/Receptacle

This possibility is hardly worth mentioning as it makes the least sense of all the options thus far discussed. There are no Forms, so there is no real content; there are no entities, so there is nothing to bring together and since there are not any entities or primordial content, there can be no need of a plane of mutual immanence or of a cosmic mental repository. Creativity and the Receptacle could never have initiated any sort of creation; it would be a content-less paradigm that brings together nothingness, into nothingness, and then records and remembers nothing.

13. God/World

A conception of Ultimate Reality that posits just a God and a World is bound to fall flat. As in example twelve above, without any Forms as initial content, what can actually be said of this type of God or this kind of World? It would seem that they would both be empty and meaningless. Furthermore, without some creative force operating to bring these two elements into communion, one would be left with two isolated and bare elements of Ultimate Reality. Perhaps one could claim that God is simply the entirety of the natural world as most forms of pantheism assert, but even still, in this particular scheme, there is no content with which the World can grow from and there is no creative force bringing about change and process. God is nothing more than a word in this scheme, as is the world; both are impotent. Collapsing God into the World neither changes, nor adds anything, a fully immanent but empty and powerless deity explains nothing, nor does it have any meaning. This combination is therefore, not justifiable.

14. God/Receptacle

This possibility is equally as strange as the last two and likewise it is not defensible. An empty God that is related to nothing else but its own emptiness has no need of a plane of mutual immanence, nor of an ongoing memory. This God could not create a World and even if this God could do so there would be an unbridgeable gulf between the creation and creator due to the lack of Creativity and once again the Receptacle becomes pointless.

15. World/Receptacle

A scheme positing the World and Receptacle is fraught with precisely the same difficulties as God and the Receptacle above. The World is devoid of primordial content with which to work from and there is no force working to increase complexity. The Receptacle once again becomes futile as does the whole system.

16. Forms/Creativity/God

This could be understood in two ways. The first option is that God contains *some Forms of God's own* from the beginning, but that there is also a Platonic realm of *additional Forms somewhere else* that is separated from God. In this scenario, God would act as a demiurge and Creativity could serve to bring God and the Forms together, so that God gains new ideas and perhaps during this process creates the world from the blueprints of the Forms God has encountered thus far. The creation of the world would be an *ex nihilo* affair as in classical theism, initiated by the will or desire of the creator God.

The second possibility is that God contains all the Forms from the beginning, but Creativity forces God to actualize these Forms into a more physical substrate and creation begins *with God under duress from the power of Creativity as a distinct Ultimate*. This scenario is to some extent similar to emanation theories which propose that the One or the Infinite has all the possibilities but is compelled to create by an overflowing of either love or just a bursting from the quantity of the Forms. However, in the view of the perennialists, Creativity would have to be understood *as the Form that demands there be a constant creative process, rather than as a separate, ultimate or unique superforce*. All of these options are plausible.

17. Forms/Creativity/World

Of all the options discussed up to this point, none have come close to rivaling number seven; however, a metaphysical stance that asserts the Forms, Creativity and a World is at least as probable as option seven, if not even more likely to be true. This is nearly the position of Samuel Alexander and his emergent theism addressed at the end of chapter 2. As a brief recap of Alexander's philosophy, there is a simplistic world of space-time that contains some very rudimentary Forms and there is a nisus or creative impulse that causes new combinations and aggregations of the primordial stuff and over time the world grows in its complexity and its degree of deity.

This position is also closer to the view of reality and creation espoused by mainstream cosmologists. There is some sort of cosmic superforce which holds together the singularity unifying the four fundamental forces and then spontaneous symmetry breaking occurs resulting in the inflationary big-bang scenario. This unifying superforce could be viewed as analogous to the Eros aspect of the Creativity/Eros defined in prior chapters and the Creativity aspect could be seen as parallel with de Sitter expansion, Lambda, Dark Energy or the exponential energy of the false vacuum state at the beginning of creation.

The cause of the initial symmetry breaking is a point of contention and uncertainty amongst cosmologists, but many believe that there was a quantum fluctuation in the void or in some singularity, perhaps as the result of a tachyon, which brought on creation as we know it. This is a scientific version *bordering* on *creatio ex nihilo*, but it must be pointed out that it is not complete nothingness, as there must be some extremely simple sub-atomic particles and therefore, a primordial World. *Where there is a World, there also must be at least some simple Forms.* In addition to all this, the physical constants just so happened to be perfectly balanced in our particular fledgling universe and so the cosmos continued to expand in a relatively stable fashion. This view could be grafted onto or fit into the triadic structure of Forms/Creativity/World. The fact that the scientific view of creation is similar to this option calls for serious weight and attention to be given to it and I believe it is not only plausible, but the second most likely scenario next to Cosmosyntheism.

18. Forms/Creativity/Receptacle

The only way this option makes sense is if the Receptacle is understood as containing at least some simplistic Forms in a higher-dimensional space and somehow through Creativity the Forms are ripped from the Receptacle in a sort of spontaneous symmetry breaking that may have primordially existed within the Receptacle. Perhaps some versions of Daoism, Chan, and Zen Buddhism could be related to this view of Reality with the functions of the Receptacle *combined with* the functions of Creativity taking the place of the Dao or of Sunyata. What is likely is that the Receptacle would need to be composed of actualities of some kind in order to be capable of holding any Forms, as Forms cannot reside "free-floating," or perhaps they can as Plato thought. This position would be a far more mystical or at least mysterious view than any of the others, but it is possible.

19. Forms/God/World

The main issue that arises in this scheme concerns whether or not God and the World are in any way related to and mutually influencing one another. Without Creativity there isn't a force that necessitates God interacting with the World. So this option could simply imply a domain for God containing some Forms and a separate world containing its own Forms and they never interact. Since this God would not contain all the Forms or possibilities in this scheme, then one cannot say with the perennialists that one of the infinite possibilities is a mandatory creation of a world outside oneself.

One could follow the route of ancient Greece, Persia, and that of the Bible in saying that there was always a chaotic world, the "waters" in most ancient accounts, and that God chose out of free will to bring order and complexity to the world. If this line of reasoning is taken, then the question becomes: is the influence unilaterally stemming from God, or is it a reciprocal influence involving the chaotic world affecting God? Classical theism denies the possibility of God's nature being affected or changed by any element within the world.

Essentially, this option lacks any explanation of whether or not the two—God and World—interact, why they interact, and how they interact. There is furthermore, no account of where they would or could commune with one another and how exactly each moment of togetherness is recorded and built upon during later encounters. In other words, it is uncertain whether a Receptacle would play any role at all or if it is just some sort of one-sided logos issuing forth from God that affects the world when God so pleases. However one construes this option, it could at least be worked into something feasible.

20. Forms/God/Receptacle

This makes the least sense of all the "three ultimate" options. The reason why this choice is so strange is that there is no need of a Receptacle unless God is interacting with some other entities not fully identical with God's self. God would first need to create a world that is truly free and allow for there to be a two-way communication and influence and then it could make sense. One could conceive of God panentheistically, with the Forms residing in the Receptacle, which is also a part of God and then creation coming through an emptying or kenosis of the Forms through the Receptacle envisioned as maybe in some higher-dimensional space. This position is also quite bizarre and it does not seem like this possibility is very likely, but it still remains a slim possibility.

21. Forms/World/Receptacle

The issue I have with this scheme is once again related to the interaction problem. How do the entities that comprise the "World" commingle without Creativity to draw them together and pull them apart? How do they go into or come out from the Receptacle without Creativity? Also, without God in the mix, it seems unlikely that order and continued progress towards complexity could be sustained. Even if one takes a scientific approach that excludes God, it is still unclear as to how things would aggregate and group into more sophisticated formations without some force like Creativity allowing for togetherness.

22. Creativity/God/World

At first glance, this seems like the position of Whitehead found in his *Process and Reality*. However, it is not because the eternal objects or Forms are taken for granted within his system, so in truth when he talks of Creativity, God and a World it would be like Creativity/God/World/Forms to be discussed below. With the Forms, this option might make good sense, but without any Forms, it is completely pointless and unintelligible. One would basically be asserting a "prime-God" devoid of all Forms interacting with a "prime-world" devoid of all Forms. What could this possibly lead to other than more nothingness? It is completely untenable and is not a viable option.

23. Creativity/World/Receptacle

This position is ridiculous for the same reason as the option above. What would be the point of wholly vacuous entities interacting within a Receptacle? This would lead to absolutely nothing novel and it is not a feasible view.

24. Creativity/God/Receptacle

Once again, this is meaningless. A prime-God being brought together with nothing other than itself, into a realm containing nothing is beyond bizarre. The Receptacle is empty and remains empty; God is empty and remains empty; and Creativity loses all its purpose and becomes insignificant.

25. God/World/Receptacle

With this option one encounters a totally inert, completely lifeless and static universe. God is empty; the World is empty; the Receptacle is empty. Nothing can come of this scenario either.

26. Forms/Creativity/God/World

Here one finally has the view of many process philosophers and theologians. This is a strong option with a lot going for it. First off, the continued problem of interaction *appears* to be solved because there is an explicit mention within Whitehead's works of a two-way or reciprocal relationship between God and the World, with Creativity serving to bring them together. There are Forms, so there is primordial content; there is a world with its own power and freedom; and there is God with God's own power and freedom. However, there are still some major oversights inherent in this position. The first problem I find with this scenario is that God is frequently understood to contain *all the possibilities* in God's primordial nature. An initial aim is somehow given to creatures within the temporal world from the primordial nature of God, which somehow *eternally knows* what this *supposedly free creature* has done in the past and ought to do in the present. This is a problem that has already been discussed by David Ray Griffin in his *Reenchantment without Supernaturalism*. Second, the point of the reciprocal process between God and the World is to issue in novelty within the world for the sake of enjoyment and God's gaining experiential as opposed to merely theoretical knowledge, which is all that God's primordial nature contains. However, how can God, in God's primordial nature, have all the possibilities if God is always related to some World or other of actual entities? What would this primordial world be like; some prime-world devoid of all Forms? If "it is as true to say that the God creates the World as that the World creates God"[1] then how can this assertion be upheld if the primordial world is devoid of all Forms?

How exactly does God's consequent nature interact with God's primordial nature? If the primordial nature is unchanging, it is strange that the consequent nature, which takes back the data from the world, in no way affects the primordial nature. How could anything have or envision all possibilities without a large store of pre-existing experiential knowledge? It seems that there needs to be a Receptacle that acquires more experiential knowledge and stores the data away, *while also highlighting any incoming novelty from the world, not merely experiential novelty but a more radical novelty resulting from the chaotic nature of the world*. If the Receptacle is "the foster-mother of all becoming," *then it is also where God becomes more than God was*. New Forms are brought into and out of the Receptacle. God receives new possibilities by weaving the experiential knowledge gained from the World, plus any random novelty produced by the World, with God's primordial vision. Rather than a static primordial God, this would result in there being a constantly growing deity. Nevertheless, this is a viable option as many mainstream process theologians have proven over the years.

---

1. This quote is one of the famous six antitheses found in part V of *Process and Reality,* 343.

Part II: Cosmosyntheism: A New Option

27. Forms/Creativity/God/Receptacle

This could work in one of two ways. First, is the option that all of the Forms are within God and then Creativity compels God to create a world, presumably *ex nihilo*, and then that world would interact with God in and through the Receptacle. God couldn't be understood as omnipotent here because the power of Creativity as a sort of metaphysical imperative would mean that God is still subject to something outside God's control.

The second option is that at least some of the Forms could be within God, but the rest of them could be in a separate realm that God looks to in order to bring about the creation of the world. Creativity might draw the Forms to God and pull God to additional Forms and thus inspire God to reflect upon them and utilize them as a plan. As in most accounts that have the Forms and God, there is the possibility that all the Forms are somehow within God or perhaps only a limited set are within God and the rest are distinct and unattached to God. I am not personally attracted to any system that proposes that *all of the Forms* are pre-existent either within God or in their own realm, because it is too difficult for me to accept the notion that there was a primordial Form of things like robots or airplanes.

28. Forms/Creativity/World/Receptacle

This is actually the closest approximation to the position of Samuel Alexander's emergent theism. If one will recall Alexander proposed a nisus or a creative force or lure that always urges matter on to the next level of emergent complexity. This nisus is essentially Creativity. He also mentions the Receptacle in his writings and for him it would appear that Time, as the mind of space, would fulfill this role. Space-time taken as a whole would be the primordial World and space-time contains some elementary Forms. Over time, the power of the nisus brings about more complex Forms and a more elegant world.

Some confusion arises for me in that the nisus appears to have a *telos*, which is its aim at bringing about deity, *yet it is not an actual entity and so it is strange to understand how it could be purpose driven*. It seems that Alexander's nisus can be compared to an amalgamation of the function of Whitehead's primordial nature of God and Whitehead's concept of Creativity. Finally, I question the ability of the Receptacle, understood as simply Time or space-time as a whole, to store and build upon the reality of the past. It seems that God is still required to account for the sustained order especially at the early stages of the evolution of the universe and for the apparent purposeful growth towards greater complexity. Disregarding these ambiguous elements, I believe that some form of emergent theism, not necessarily Alexander's conception, stands as the single strongest contender for a viable global metaphysical paradigm for the twenty-first century.

29. Forms/God/World/Receptacle

Here one again finds a common problem, the interaction problem. Given this view one is left wondering how God and the World interact or if they need communicate at all? Would the Receptacle be empty or would it contain just God and the Forms God beholds or would it record the interactions, if any were even possible without Creativity, of the World? This option is less plausible than some of the other four ultimate options.

30. Creativity/God/World/Receptacle

This is the least plausible of all the options containing four ultimates because the primordial content problem appears to be an insurmountable one. God and the World can interact in this view, but they are also both empty, so what is really gained? The Receptacle is also empty and remains empty and there would be no growth and progress, just emptiness communing with emptiness, within emptiness. Of all the five potential problems, the primordial content issue appears to be the most challenging to deal with.

31. Forms/Creativity/God/World/Receptacle

This is Cosmosyntheism. In this metaphysical picture, the five problems dissolve away. There is no primordial content problem, interaction problem, sustained order problem, free will problem or communication and storage problem. Supernaturalism can also be eradicated and this makes Cosmosyntheism more plausible than other feasible positions discussed that need to fall back on an ultimate imbued with unrealistic abilities. As I have discussed in prior chapters, all of these five ultimates are understood to be co-eternal and mutually pre-supposing. *This implies that there are not five separate ultimates that are just out there, completely isolated from one another.* Of all the positions surveyed in this chapter that have multiple ultimates, I am strongly inclined towards Cosmosyntheism for the simple fact that it can avoid the five problems discussed. However, in order to be a truly successful global theology, *Cosmosyntheism must be capable of dealing with much bigger questions.*

What remains to be seen is how well Cosmosyntheism responds to the major issues which have plagued philosophy and religion. The goal of the next section will be to put Cosmosyntheism into dialogue with the five rival contenders for a global metaphysical system discussed in chapter 2, in order to assess the strengths and weaknesses of each system in solving long-standing philosophical problems.

Summary

Of the twenty-six positions covered throughout this chapter, all of them can be classified according to which or how many of the five problems they encounter. For example, any option that excludes the Forms must deal with the problem of primordial content and any system dismissing God must provide a convincing account of how order is first brought about and then sustained throughout time. Without Creativity, one is left with the troubling issue of how the various entities interact with one another and without a primordial World of some kind, then it is unclear how there is any real freedom in either a God-produced or a mechanistic and deterministic world. Lastly, if there is no Receptacle, then one is left wondering how there can be communication, mutual immanence, internal relations, and a retaining of what has happened thus far.

PART III

Cosmosyntheism vs. the Five Rival Contenders:
Assessing the Strengths
and Weaknesses of Each System

CHAPTER 10

Free Will

But man is freer than all of the animals, on account of his free will, with which he is endowed above all other animals.

—ST. THOMAS AQUINAS

Mankind has a free-will; but it is free to milk cows and build houses, nothing more.

—MARTIN LUTHER

THE PURPOSE OF PART I was to introduce different philosophies of religion, some of which focused on the claim that there is only one religious ultimate, whereas others, like the systems of Whitehead, Cobb, and Griffin allow for the possibility of multiple religious ultimates. These chapters were merely intended to be descriptive presentations of each view with as little bias as possible projected onto the opinions of the respective systems. Likewise, part II was designed as a presentation and description of the key elements that comprise a system, which I call Cosmosyntheism.

The primary goal of part III is to highlight the *advances and advantages* that Cosmosyntheism has over the other five systems I have discussed thus far, especially when it comes to longstanding problems within the field of philosophy of religion. By putting these six different systems into a conversation, their best possible arguments will be revealed, along with any nagging issues which appear to go along with their respective solutions to problems, such as, the free will problem and the problem of evil. I will argue throughout part III that Cosmosyntheism's solutions to the free will problem, the problem of conflicting religious truth claims and the problem of evil are better-suited for the globalized community of the twenty-first century than the solutions of the other five contenders. My argument for the superiority of Cosmosyntheism will hinge upon the fact that its solutions are pluralistic, interdisciplinary, more

Part III: Cosmosyntheism vs. the Five Rival Contenders

consistent, coherent and multidimensional. Put differently, *Cosmosyntheism meets all of the four criteria for a successful constructive theology in the twenty-first century as outlined on pages eight through ten of the Introduction.*

The main objective of chapter 10 is to survey six potential responses to the free will problem. By examining different solutions to the free will problem culminating in Cosmosyntheism, *I am also building the case that Cosmosyntheism fulfills criterion three, logical consistency, better than any of the other five contenders.* I will begin with the perennial philosophy, followed by emanationism, classical theism, emergent theism, Cobb/Griffin and then Cosmosyntheism. This pattern deviates slightly from Part II because Cobb and Griffin's positions will be dealt with second to last, rather than first. The reason for this change in order is so that the, sometimes subtle differences, between Cobb/Griffin and Cosmosyntheism can be more readily seen and appreciated. Each system will be dealt with under its own heading with a subheading addressing the problems with each solution. But first, some general remarks on the free will problem.

The Free Will Problem

Are all events pre-determined either by a divine creator or simply by the laws of physics, or are humans truly free when they think, act and make decisions? This is the problem. A given system's view of Ultimate Reality is going to have a profound effect on this very question and it is my intention in this chapter to elucidate how the six systems examined thus far provide different answers to the free will debate. I will argue however, that five of the systems fall short and that the answer provided by Cosmosyntheism is likely the most plausible account of how the human will can truly be free, an assumption that all people explicitly or at least implicitly operate from.

Free Will and the Perennial Philosophy

The first thing that one notices when researching the solution to the free will problem within the perennial philosophy is how little space is devoted to the topic. Free will and predestination are mainly discussed in a brief two-page section found within Frithjof Schuon's *The Transcendent Unity of Religions*. Schuon recognizes the problem when he states, "if God is omniscient then He knows future events, or rather events that appear thus to beings limited by time; if God did not know these events He would not be omniscient."[1]

For perennialists, the Infinite is outside of and the initiator of time itself and the Infinite is also All-Possibility; therefore, the Infinite must also be omniscient. It is not surprising then that the Infinite is the source of all reality and freedom including the will of human beings.

---

1. Schuon, *The Transcendent Unity of Religions*, 54.

Free Will

> From the individual standpoint however, which is the standpoint of human beings, the will is real in the measure in which they participate in the Divine Liberty, *from which individual liberty derives all its reality by virtue of the causal relationship between the two*; whence it follows that liberty, like all positive qualities, is Divine in itself and human insofar as it is not perfectly itself.[2]

The individual will is only a portion of the totality and the knowledge and experiences of this isolated portion can lead to ignorance of the truth, which is holistic unity. What an individual person understands as a free decision is really only the playing out of pre-planned possibilities in the eternal timeless nature of the Infinite. "The life of a man, and by extension the whole individual cycle of which that life and the human state itself are only modalities, is in fact contained in the Divine Intellect as a complete whole, that is to say, as a determined possibility."[3] In short, your free will is an illusion, as is your ego, your creativity, sense of individuality and separateness from everything around you. Schuon is forced to admit this and he does. "If we cannot will anything other than what is predestined for us, this does not prevent our will being what it is, namely, a relatively real participation in its universal prototype."[4] This statement seems to imply that the will is just the playing out in the terrestrial realm of the pre-planned Forms residing in the celestial realm. This approach to the problem of free will is loaded with inconsistencies.

Problems with the Perennialist Solution

Almost all of the problems with the perennialist solution stem from their insistence that the Infinite is All-Possibility. Since it is All-Possibility, it must know anything that a person could imagine or experience. *But isn't one possibility that the Infinite is capable of learning something truly novel*? If it is All-Possibility, then it must manifest a situation where it learns something new, but how could this be? If this is possible, then the Infinite is not really Infinite. Here one finds a paradox and a successful theology for the twenty-first century should avoid as many paradoxes as possible.

A second, but related issue is: what is the Infinite gaining from its manifestations? *Is experiential knowledge gained in a physical substratum or a terrestrial world in no way different from an eternal, hypothetical visualization or imagination*? I think that there is a difference between theoretical knowledge and experiential knowledge. So, even if the perennial philosophy and many Indian religions are correct in asserting the centrality of *maya* and predestination, they are left with some major paradoxes within their metaphysical picture. *One of these paradoxes is that humans apparently have a form of*

---

2. Ibid.
3. Ibid.
4. Ibid.

Part III: Cosmosyntheism vs. the Five Rival Contenders

knowledge that is unique and unknown to the gods or the Infinite. Any paradoxes within a metaphysic will trickle down and infect all levels of the overall philosophy.

A final obvious problem with this picture concerns the issue of justice and evil. *How can anyone be judged guilty of any crime if all is pre-determined?* Furthermore, *why should anyone be punished if their will is not truly free?* The rapist is no better or worse than the rape victim; they are both merely playing out pre-determined possibilities for manifestation that were conceived in the Divine Intellect, the first radiation or emanation of the Infinite. Any system that advocates a strict determinism or predestination is bound to encounter these intractable quagmires.

Free Will and Emanation Theories

Daoism

For Daoism, as for most all of the ancient Chinese religions, the will (*zhi*) is understood as free.[5] Why or how the will became free if its source or ground is the Dao is unclear. I believe that the answer to this is that the will or humans are free because of their distance from the One or the Dao. It is this epistemic distance combined with an intermingling with the physical substratum of the material world that makes it so simple to fall from the path or way (Dao). Remember that the Dao first engendered Being or *de/qi* and then *yin* and *yang* or perhaps Heaven and Earth and finally humanity; this places humans far from the source.[6]

For Daoists our wills may be free, but they are nevertheless, misguided. The problem is that our wills have become polluted and debased by the prescriptions of *li* and through the process of naming things. *Li* are the rules of propriety practiced within the *Zhou* society of the time, which informed people of the proper ways to act, so that social and therefore, cosmic order and balance would be maintained. The second source of the problem is identified in the *DaoDeJing* (hereafter *DDJ*). "The way that can be told of is not the eternal way; the name that can be named is not the eternal name. The Nameless is the origin of Heaven and Earth; the Named is the mother of all things" (1). Naming is the beginning of distortion and leads to the bifurcation of nature and thereby destroys the primal unity of Dao. The focus on pre-established modes of conduct, analyzing and compartmentalizing reality, completely severs the individual from their natural state of openness, simplicity and flexibility; hence the

---

5. The best all-in-one resources for all aspects of ancient Chinese religion and philosophy are Wing-Tsit Chan, *A Source Book in Chinese Philosophy*; Graham, *Disputers of the Tao*; Fung Yu-lan, *A Short History of Chinese Philosophy*; and Schwartz, *The World of Thought in Ancient China*. Concerning the issue of freedom and free will see pp. 300–5 of A. C. Graham's work and pp. 228–30 of Fung Yu-Lan's work.

6. Cf. *DDJ* 1, 4, and 25.

repeated appearance of water and newborn babies in the *DDJ* as metaphors for right living.[7]

Daoists abhorred the rigidly Confucian aspects of society and sought to purify the individual by affecting a return or reversal to the source or Dao. The way of this return was through unlearning all of the social patterns, rules and ideals imposed by Confucian and Mohist philosophies. "Abandon learning and there will be no sorrow" (*DDJ* 20). This process culminated in a sharp distinction between Daoism and Confucianism and Mohism. The distinction can be seen in the Confucian/Mohist ideal of *yu-wei* (deliberate, conscious, goal-oriented decision making) vs. the Daoist focus on *wei-wu-wei* (lit. action without action, meaning non-calculative or spontaneous action).

The ideal form of action is action in conformity with one's *de* or natural potency and to the original or primordial Dao, which requires one to be firmly grounded in the present. Deliberative action causes one to miss the present moment, so does acting in accordance with *li*, because no two situations are precisely the same; therefore, how can a pre-established pattern created in the past be the ideal way of meeting the present unique moment? The will is free to let go of the past, tradition and the rational mind and to initiate the return to acting in accordance with nature, which is ultimately derived from the Dao itself.

Problems with the Daoist Solution

My primary concern with the Daoist solution revolves around the fact that all things are ontologically derived from the primordial Dao. This could mean that our will is free because the Dao wanted us to have free will and so the Dao may have divested itself of power. However, the Dao is not an entity or a will of any kind and the correct answer seems to be that we have free will because in the process of emanation, power is spilled over into the world as we know it. It is unclear as to whether the Dao or *Tian* (heaven) is capable of reversing this emptying out or emanation. If heaven could do this, then our will and our power are only on loan and could be overridden.

On a more practical level, the Daoist ideals of *ziran* and *wei-wu-wei* imply a complete sacrificing of one's deliberative, goal-oriented will. This may be a good thing as it could put an end to selfish desires and it can make one mindfully aware of the present and capable of responding in a timely, appropriate and novel manner; however, there is a negative dimension to this. *How can one be certain that becoming an empty vessel or conduit for the Dao won't lead to complete anarchy or evil acts*? It is a fact that the Dao is beyond good and evil as it transcends any polarizations and distinctions. In the *DDJ* it is stated, "Heaven and Earth are not humane. They regard all things as straw dogs. The sage is not humane. He regards all people as straw dogs" (5). Now obviously this does not mean that the sage is mean or unkind as some translators have assumed,[8]

7. Cf. *DDJ* 8, 10, 20, 55 and 78.
8. Cf. R.M. Blackney

but it does imply that heaven and earth are impartial and do not play favorites. Why should one align one's will with either the *Tianzhi* or the *Daozhi* (if there can be said to be such a thing) if they are not governed by any moral principles? To assert that heaven and earth do not play favorites is to tacitly suggest that a murderer is not viewed any differently than a benevolent philanthropist.

This philosophy could lead to anarchy as people simply could claim that it was not of their own will that they acted in such-and-such a manner, but rather they were merely vacuous conduits for the capricious will of heaven or the Dao. In short, the Daoists are not totally convincing in their assertion that sacrificing or annihilating one's will and becoming a receptive vehicle for the Dao is a superior lifestyle to the Confucian insistence that heaven and man are *ren* or benevolence. The *DDJ* 19 claims, "Abandon sageliness and discard wisdom; then the people will benefit a hundredfold. Abandon humanity and discard righteousness; then the people will return to filial piety and deep love." There is no reason why one should accept this claim because as we have seen heaven and earth are beyond good and evil and are impartial, so who is to say that following them will benefit the people a hundredfold? However, if heaven is benevolent, intelligent and shares its nature to a certain extent with humanity, as Confucians would assert, *then it would make more sense to act according to one's spontaneous nature*, a fact recognized and repeatedly discussed by Mencius.[9]

Hermetic Gnosis

Hermetism presents us with an intriguing case because the will can be understood as both constrained and free. First off, the will is bound because all humans are a mixture of nature or *physis* with soul *psyche* or mind *nous*; there is a body/soul dualism. Poimandres tells us how this admixture came about when explaining to Hermes that there was an archetypal or essential man that was created in the image of the first Father and this image existed above the seven heavens.

> But mind, the father of all, who is life and light, gave birth to a human being like himself . . . And the primal person took station in the highest sphere of heaven and observed the things made by its author, his brother the demiurge, who ruled over the region of fire. Now that the human had seen those things made in fire, he wished to create things of his own. And his father permitted him to do so. And since the rulers loved him too, each gave him a share of his own nature. When the human learned their characteristics, he wished to break through the bounding orbits of the rulers and to share the power of him who rules over the fire.[10]

---

9. Cf. Mencius 1A:7, 2A:2 and 2A:6.
10. Barnstone, *The Gnostic Bible*, 505–6.

Free Will

One learns from this account that the original, essential human, who was androgynous, had a free will and desired to share in creation, so it appears that man, being modeled on the first father, must have a free will.

The story continues however, to describe the descent of the essential man into the world of nature. "Then the primal person . . . leaned down through the harmony and having broken the vault, showed lower nature the beautiful form of god. When nature saw the beautiful form of god, it smiled on the human with love, for it had seen the wondrous beauty of the human reflected in the water and its shadow on the earth."[11] The story progresses and essential man and nature are immediately intermingled through the power of *Eros* and from this point on, all future generations of man are half mortal and half immortal in nature. The key point in all this is that *once one passes down through the seven heavens, then one enters the realm of fate or heimarmenē.*

The reason why the will is constrained is because mind or soul has descended into nature. "And this is why the human, of all the creatures on the earth, is twofold: mortal in his body but immortal through the eternal human. Though he is immortal and has power over all things, he also suffers mortality, since he is subject to fate. Though above the world of the spheres, he is slave to fate."[12] This is not to say that the world is evil as in other Gnostic stories. Quite the contrary, the true hermetic adept knows that one's purpose is to create something of lasting importance while in the world, but after this is accomplished, the follower of Hermetic philosophy must ascend back to the source. Just because one is under the influence of the spheres or fate, this does not mean that one cannot be the author of their own destiny. *Destiny is not the same as fate.* It is our fate that we will die, but how we live and if we find salvation is up to us. If we choose to develop our immortal side then we gain more freedoms and creative control, but if we give in to the temptations of the flesh and the body, then we descend deeper into the mire of darkness.

For Hermetism it has been shown that the will is free in the sense that the divine half of humanity, the mind and reason, are capable of transcending this world. However, if one allows oneself to be dominated by the power of sexual lust and other animal drives, then one will remain forever blind and ignorant, lacking in redemption. It is through asceticism, meditation, and philosophy that one recalls one's true nature and affects an ascent back to the source, the father of all.

Problems with the Hermetic Solution

The first problem with the Hermetic understanding of freedom is the elitist attitude suggesting that only some people possess Intellect. The question is raised by Hermes himself. "For God says, 'Let those that have intellect recognize themselves.' So do not

11. Ibid., 506.
12. Ibid.

Part III: Cosmosyntheism vs. the Five Rival Contenders

all people have intellect?"[13] This is a great question to which there is never an adequate answer. The answer that Poimandres provides Hermes is that Intellect is with those that are pious and good and pure. Those that are wicked an impure are handed over to the avenging demon, "who visits such a person with the sharpness of fire, piercing his sense sand driving him to further lawlessness so that he may incur greater punishment."[14] So, if only some people actually possess intellect as an already activated or latent power, then there are actually two classes of people, those with intellect and those without. The latter class would live a deterministic life pushed here and there by the power of fate and sexual impulses. This potential bifurcation of humanity is dangerous as a solution and is inadequate for our current time because it would allow for the possibility of sexism, racism, and intellectual elitism.

The second issue is what exactly are the abilities of the first God and the second *nous* or demiurge? Is it possible that these powers can destroy their creation and take back any free will granted? Remember that the archetypal human asks the first Father for the rights to partake in creative power and it is granted, but could the first Father reverse this decision at some point in time? This uncertainty raises serious suspicions as to the adequacy of what at first glance appears to be a feasible account of how to reconcile our deep-seated belief in free will with the apparent determinism of the material world.

Sethian Gnosticism and Free Will

Sethian Gnosticism contains numerous parallels to Hermetism, but with a few key distinctions. First, the similarities: (1) both have a body/soul dualism; (2) both suggest an elitism where only a privileged few have the divine spark; (3) both require gnosis to affect a return to the source. The differences are: (1) Sethians believe that the true God is wholly unknowable; (2) they view the Creator God or demiurge as evil; (3) the demiurge and his minions actively try to thwart the escape of the light within the Gnostics through sexual lust and fate. By contrast, in Hermetism, it is the archetypal man *that of his own volition descends into nature*, whereas for Sethians, the soul has been trapped in human form *through the in-breathing of Ialdabaoth the demiurge*. Humans find themselves thrown into this dismal scenario through the prior mistakes of Sophia and her offspring Ialdabaoth.

The will of humans is in bondage because of the activity of the demiurge who infects humans with his counterfeit spirit through his raping of Eve. "Now up to the present day sexual intercourse continued due to the chief archon. And he planted sexual desire in her who belongs to Adam. And he produced through sexual intercourse the copies of the bodies, and he inspired them with his counterfeit spirit."[15] It is this

---

13. Layton, *The Gnostic Scriptures*, 456.
14. Barnstone, *Gnostic Bible*, 509.
15. *The Nag Hammadi*, 119.

counterfeit spirit which works against the spark of light that was given over to humans earlier by Ialdabaoth when he was tricked by the heavenly luminaries of the pleroma.

> And when the mother [Sophia] wanted to retrieve the power which she had given to the chief archon [Ialdabaoth], she petitioned the Mother-Father [Barbelo] of the All who is most merciful . . . And they [the Heavenly Luminaries] said to Ialdabaoth, "Blow into his [Adam's] face something of your spirit and his body will arise." And he blew into his face the spirit which is the power of his mother."[16]

Humans are unfortunately caught in the middle of this cosmic drama with the light attempting to reclaim its lost sparks and the darkness trying to enslave the sparks. What all of this entails for free will is that only two groups: the offspring of Seth or of the true light, and the "psychical," have any free will. If you feel that you are not of this world and you come to gain acquaintance or gnosis with your inner or higher self and with its heavenly origin, then you have some free will and at that point it is your sole objective to escape the terrestrial hell that you find yourself currently enslaved in. It is unclear how one knows whether or not they are a "pneumatic" who automatically ascends back to the pleroma or a "psychic" who must choose the correct ethical path.

And what about the rest of humanity? The answer to this depends upon which group of Gnostics you would happen to ask. Some later groups that have been Christianized like the Valentinians would recognize a tripartite scheme of salvation, with the *pneumatics* or Gnostics at the top, followed by the *psychics* or Christians, and then the *hylic* or material people. Only the pneumatics are capable of rising without further assistance past the eighth sphere of the fixed stars. The implication is that even the Christians will be bound by fate and there is nothing they can do about it except wait for higher powers to descend and assist them up at the end of all time.

Problems with the Sethian Solution

The Sethian solution is plagued by some of the same deficiencies as the Hermetic one. For example, the elitism between the imperishable race of Seth, who have free will and then all the other "enslaved humans" is not a viable solution and is meaningless in today's globalized and racially mixed environment. Furthermore, any solutions which seek world renunciation and complete self-abnegation are simply too pessimistic for today's highly interconnected and fast-paced world. The final problem with the Sethian solution is that in order to truly free the will from bondage, there were rites (e.g., Sethian Baptism), which must be performed, as well as a ritual of ascent at the time of bodily death. We currently lack the information as to how these rites were performed. We are also in the dark as to the passwords and ritual spells to affect this ascent back to the pleroma.

16. Ibid., 116.

Part III: Cosmosyntheism vs. the Five Rival Contenders

Plotinus and Free will

Plotinus's philosophy distinguishes itself from some of the other emanation theories in that Plotinus specifically addresses the free will problem in relation to humans and even concerning the One itself. The general impression that one gathers from his, at times disjointed tractates is that human beings are only *minimally free*. What Plotinus means by minimally free is that the majority of the population is led astray by their senses and are weighed down by their physical body with its corresponding appetites. "We refuse to range under the principle of freedom those whose conduct is directed by such fancy: the baser sort, therefore, mainly so guided, cannot be credited with self-disposal or voluntary act" (VI.8.3). A person that gives in to these desires and external influences is therefore, not free. As Plotinus says, "How can we be masters when we are compelled" (VI.8.2)?

The only aspect of the human being that is free is *the higher aspect of the soul*, because it contemplates the Good, which is internal to its nature. "Effort is free once it is towards a fully recognized good" (VI.8.4). The fact that the soul is good and can contemplate the Good is key for Plotinus because this implies a self-reflection and it does not necessitate any external factors exerting influence on the soul. "No doubt Intellectual Principle itself is to be referred to a yet higher; but this higher is not external to it; Intellectual Principle is within the Good; possessing its own good in virtue of that indwelling, much more will it possess freedom and self-disposal which are sought only for the sake of the good" (VI.8.4). The higher soul partakes in the Intellectual Principle because soul is one degree lower on the hierarchy of being than the Intellectual Principle.

It must be remembered that, for Plotinus, soul is divided into a higher and lower aspect and it is the higher soul, which is guided by virtue that is free. However, *the higher soul is only free when it is operating from Intellection and aiming at the even higher Good*. "So understood virtue is a mode of Intellectual-Principle, a mode not involving any of the emotions or passions controlled by its reasoning" (VI.8.6). This idea of a body/soul dichotomy should already be familiar and Plotinus, like others before him, believes that matter and the physical body are the causes of bondage and of evil. Plotinus continues on throughout the remainder of the treatise to show that the One is the most free, because it is constrained by nothing external to itself.

Problems with the Plotinian Solution

Although Plotinus provides a sustained account of the nature of free will, his solution is surprisingly inadequate. The first major point of confusion is how the Good ever allowed itself or any later emanation of itself to become constrained by matter. If matter and the One are co-eternal, which Plotinus frequently alludes to in an extremely paradoxical way, then how can he state the One to be "veritably free?" If there is a genuine primordial other to the One, then there is something external to the One. It was a point of contention among Platonists as to whether creation was first planned out and then undertaken or whether the emanations or chain of being just always existed the way it is. Plotinus opts, against Plato, for the latter position, but this is so paradoxical that it strains one's ability to accept the otherwise gifted intellect of Plotinus. Put differently, it is challenging to understand what form of ontological dependence matter has in relation to the One, without there first being a temporal act of creation and then successive temporal emanations culminating in matter. If everything is derived from the One, then in the end there is no genuine other and in a real sense there is nothing "external" to the One and thus pursuing material ends should not be in itself wrong or bad.

There is a problem in Plotinus's solution that is even more poignant to the question of free will as it relates to human beings. Plotinus, once again in opposition to Plato, asserts the bizarre doctrine that all individuals have Forms, rather than the Platonic position of there being one Form for all humanity and each person is a *particular* loosely participating in this *universal* Form of man. "No: one Reason-Principle cannot account for distinct and differing individuals: one human being does not suffice as the exemplar for many distinct each from the other not merely in material constituents but by innumerable variations of ideal type" (V.7.1). I find it very challenging to accept that anyone could have any freedom if there was already a specific Form or set of Forms either pre-planned or designed for that individual's life.

Compounding the problem and the confusion is that Plotinus appears to accept the Stoic doctrine of the eternal recurrence of the same or a periodic renewal. How can one assert freedom if there is an eternal recurrence? One could say that it is cyclical, but not the precise same occurrence each time, which Plotinus appears to actually believe to be the case. However, the Forms for the individuals are still going to remain ready-made. In the end, it is the One that is limitless and infinite, a similar scenario to the Perennial Philosophy and other emanation accounts.

> Thus when the universe has reached its term, there will be a fresh beginning, since the entire Quantity which the Cosmos is to exhibit, every item that is to emerge in its course, all is laid up from the first in the Being that contains the Reason-Principles. Are we, then, looking to the brute realm, to hold that there are as many Reason-Principles as distinct creatures born in a litter? Why not? There is nothing alarming about such limitlessness in generative forces and in Reason-Principles, when Soul is there to sustain all. As in Soul, so in Divine Mind there is infinitude of recurring generative powers. (V.7.3)

It is my contention that any time one begins to assert the infinitude and limitlessness of something then paradoxes rather than lucidity will begin to emanate to the point of utter confusion.

Part III: Cosmosyntheism vs. the Five Rival Contenders

General Problems with Emanation Theories

If the One, the Father or the Dao is truly unlimited and full of all imaginable possibilities, then how can I actually be free? Even if I get to choose of my own volition from a set of alternatives, is this real freedom? What about creativity, innovation and novelty? My view of free will is not one where a person chooses from a wholly pre-determined set of possibilities, none of which would result in any effect or affect within the One Ultimately Real religious object. Just as true love is reciprocal, so to must true freedom involve the ability to create something genuinely new for others, God included.

Another point, this time specific to Plotinus, is the absurdity of his claim that all the realms of being are eternal, yet somehow they are also generated by emanations from the One. If they are eternal, then it seems that they must either be completely empty and devoid of any type of content, or they are already filled with something. If they are empty, *then they are meaningless and cannot be distinguished one level from another*, but if they are already filled, *then what are the "emanations" from the One providing*? While reading most emanation accounts, one will likely be struck by the frequent flip-flopping of opinions and mental gymnastics that occur. These inconsistencies represent a serious roadblock for emanation theories if they are to be viable contenders for a global metaphysical system in the twenty-first century.

A final point of concern that I have about most forms of emanation and a problem shared by the perennial philosophy is the insistence that the Infinite had to create because it is "All-Possibility" and creating a cosmos was just one of these possibilities. This logic can always be reversed right around and *one could just as consistently assume that one of the "possibilities" is to spontaneously destroy the cosmos or to take away free will (if it even can exist in their paradigm) or to promote evil*. If it is all simply about the playing out of an Infinitude of possibilities, then why do so many religious groups and great philosophers believe the One or the Infinite to be wholly Good? There is no logical reason to assume this. This problem concerning the idea of Infinitude and supremacy is shared by our next contender: classical theism.

Free Will and Classical Theism

In contrast to the above systems, I will treat classical theism more as one unified whole. This means that I will not go over the positions of all the individuals introduced in chapter 2; instead, I will focus on the main points shared by all of them in their conception of free will in humans. A discussion of free will and classical theism will not however, be complete without an account of the new theological movement which is afoot within Protestant and post-evangelical circles known as Open Theism.

Classical Theism and the Free Will Problems

For the most part, Jews, Christians, and Muslims all assert that humans have free will. However, there are at least three major points of confusion: (1) Exactly how much freedom do humans truly possess; (2) how does the issue of divine grace factor into the free will debate; (3) how does one reconcile humanity's supposed freedom with God's attributes, such as, omniscience and omnipotence? The manner in which a particular religious group answers these questions can be enough to label them as a new or separate sect or offshoot from a more orthodox position.

An illuminating example of the way in which the first point of confusion was answered can be found in the works of St. Augustine. Augustine distinguishes between *liberum arbitrium* and *libertas*. *Liberum aribitrium* implies that humans have the ability to choose freely between different options in given circumstances, but that humans lack the ability or the freedom to avoid sin, due to original sin and concupiscence brought on by Eve and Adam. Original sin has resulted in man becoming a *massa peccati* or mass of sin that requires divine grace in order for an individual to be saved. "The choice of the will, then, is genuinely free only when it is not subservient to faults and sins. God gave it that true freedom, and now that it has been lost, through its own fault, *it can be restored only by him who had the power to give it at the beginning*"[17] (emphasis mine).

No matter how much a person might choose to do good, it is the sole prerogative of God whether that person can or will achieve salvation. The centrality of the role of grace or unmerited favor from God becomes a contentious issue after Augustine and is a major point of difference between certain Christian sects who radicalized the notion of sovereign grace. Groups, such as the Calvinists and Arminians, advocated a doctrine of double predestination where grace is crucial to salvation, whereas, Semi-Pelagianists believed in the power of individuals to work out their own salvation.

In antiquity Augustine's ideas of free will and grace clashed with that of Pelagius who also said that the will was free, but in a more radical way in that the individual will could through good deeds, work towards achieving salvation and redemption. Augustine found this doctrine troubling for a variety of reasons, but mainly because it erased the importance of Jesus Christ as redeemer and savior of humanity because each individual does not need conversion, the sacraments or the church because they can work out their own salvation through virtue.

The bottom line for Augustine was that freedom, like grace, was a gift from God and this implies, whether we may like it or not, that our wills are limited in their freedom. Augustine is unique in that he believed we come to the good in a different way than which we come to evil. We come to evil through "neglecting eternal things." This neglect is brought on by a lack of wisdom. However, we come to the good only through God's grace, rather than through our own free will. All of

---

17. St. Augustine, *City of God*, 569.

Part III: Cosmosyntheism vs. the Five Rival Contenders

this is spelled out in Augustine's famous treatise on free will known as the *De Libero Arbitrio* or *On Free Choice of the Will*.

Another example of the confusion over the degree of free will humans possess can be seen in the history of Islam. A group known as the *qadariyyah* which came to be called the *Mu'tazilah* argued for the reality of free will and the freedom of humans from divine predestination whereas, the *jabriyyah* who came to be known as the *Asha'irah* claimed that all was pre-determined and free will was an illusion. However, the third and dominant position of both modern day *Sunni's* and *Shia's* lies between these two extremes, with humans having free will, but nevertheless, all events being predestined by God and written down in the *al-Lauh al-Mahfuz* or Preserved Tablet 50,000 years before creation.

The way that the *Sunni* and *Shi'a* doctrine works is due to the fact that God lies outside of time and so can see exactly what each person will freely choose to do in the temporal realm. These choices are all recorded on the tablet before creation takes place. The position finds similarities to Christian doctrine in that God creates the world *ex nihilo* and therefore, freedom is a gift from God and God could overrule a person's decisions, however, God chooses not to.

The issue of God's attributes and abilities brings us to the last point of confusion regarding free will within classical theism. In Judaism, there is a long tradition of dealing with what is known as the free will/omniscience paradox. Maimonides presents the problem thus,

> The Holy One, Blessed Be He, knows everything that will happen before it has happened. So, does He know whether a particular person will be righteous or wicked, or not? If He does know, then it will be impossible for that person not to be righteous. If He knows that he will be righteous but that it is possible for him to be wicked, then He does not know everything that He has created . . . The Holy One, Blessed Be He, does not have any temperaments and is outside such realms, unlike people, whose selves and temperaments are two separate things. God and His temperaments are one, and God's existence is beyond the comprehension of man . . . [Thus] we do not have the capabilities to comprehend how the Holy One, Blessed Be He, knows all creations and events. [Nevertheless] know without doubt that people do what they want without the Holy One, Blessed Be He, forcing or decreeing upon them to do so . . . It has been said because of this that a man is judged according to all his actions.[18]

The paradox is quite simple: *if God can know the decisions and outcomes of all supposedly free agents before they choose to do them, then how is anyone truly free?* Maimonides's answer is surprisingly honest; he says that he does not know and that it is a part of the mystery of God beyond the comprehension of man.

---

18. Maimon, *The Guide for the Perplexed*, section III.

This problem of God's foreknowledge and its repercussions for human free will is also addressed by Aquinas. Aquinas as well as Augustine and some Muslim theologians are willing to harbor a guess as to how divine foreknowledge and free will are compatible. Aquinas's answer is clearer than Augustine's or those of some Muslim philosophers so it will serve to highlight the defense.[19] Augustine's answer amounts to saying that God's knowledge of what we will decide in the future is not the same as God *making it happen.*

Aquinas attempts to explain the resolution of the free will/omniscience paradox through an analogy. The answer provided by Aquinas is similar to the Muslim response, which is that God is outside of time itself and can therefore know all that we will freely choose. "God acts in the timelessness of his eternity."[20] Aquinas provides an analogy of a man walking down a path not knowing that another man is walking towards him from the other side of a hill that stands between the two individuals. Neither of these men is aware of the other's proximity, *but a third man standing on top of the hill would be able to see that in a few minutes in the future the paths of the two men will cross.* This bird's eye view is supposed to be analogous to God's timeless perspective.

Open Theism and Free Will

I will only briefly mention open theism because it purports to have a superior solution to the free will problem than that of classical theism.[21] Essentially open theists disagree with the five classical attributes of deity: immutability, impassibility, omnipotence, omniscience, and omnipresence. They rightly believe that these attributes represent a later accretion from Greek philosophy into early Christian apologetics. Open theists argue that these attributes are actually non-biblical and should be done away with entirely. Instead, the true biblical attributes should be reinstated, which claim that God is: living, personal, relational, good and loving. If the classical Greek attributes are done away with, then humans can have *libertarian free will* and the omniscience/free will paradox will evaporate away and one will also have the advantage of living according to the true biblical tradition.

For open theists, humans have libertarian free will because God through a process of *kenosis* emptied himself of power, a biblical idea found in Philippians 2:5–7. "Let the

---

19. For example, in one of Augustine's defenses of divine foreknowledge found in the *City of God* one is hard-pressed to find a cogent argument. Augustine is attempting to refute Cicero who is arguing for the unreality of divination, prophecy and divine foreknowledge. Augustine's defense is so feeble that I struggle to find any actual refutation of Cicero's insightful arguments against the possibility of divine foreknowledge.

20. See Aquinas's, *Summa Theologica*, 1a.14.1–13 for one of his most comprehensive treatments of the subject of God's timelessness and the free will of humanity.

21. Open Theism first came on the theological scene in the early 1980s with the book *The Openness of God*. The main proponents of Open Theism are: Richard Rice, Clark Pinnock, Thomas Jay Oord, and William Hasker.

same mind be in you that was in Christ Jesus, who, though he was in the form of God, did not regard equality with God as something to be exploited, *but emptied himself*, taking the form of a slave, being born in human likeness." Open theists do however maintain that God created the world *ex nihilo*, *but that in the process of either creation or the Incarnation he emptied himself, giving up omniscience and omnipotence*. The result for humanity is true libertarian freedom and a God that is legitimately a God of love, not only capable of giving up power, but also of listening to and responding to prayer as well as being capable of being affected by the decisions of human beings.

Problems with Classical and Open Theism

I will begin with the main problem that plagues both classical and open theism: a belief in *creatio ex nihilo*. If before creation, there was only God and nothing else, then all power, knowledge and possibility resided with God. It is irrelevant that God emptied himself of power through kenosis because *in theory God could always reverse the decision and take back his power and his creation*. This sort of freedom is really freedom on loan, which is not truly freedom at all. It must be *metaphysically impossible* for God to take back power otherwise our freedom will always remain in doubt, if not our freedom today, the possibility that we will remain free tomorrow.

The problem is compounded when one asserts that God is love as both classical and open theists do. The issue now becomes, why doesn't God intervene and take away power either selectively or all together when it is realized that humans are committing atrocities through their new found gift of free will? If God is love, why World War I, The Holocaust of World War II, and global terrorism? Presumably, the answer is that *freedom is a greater gift and outweighs the potential evils that may come from a free will*; but tell that to the millions of murdered, raped, robbed, and disenfranchised.

Open Theism at least recognizes that the current beliefs advocated by classical theists must change, and so the open theist encounters fewer logical dilemmas. Open theism is a more plausible interpretation of theism for the twenty-first century, but it still is at a loss of how to reconcile free will with the fact that God *could* take away humanity's power. However, theism in its classical forms is racked with even more problems, like the grace/free will and omniscience/free will paradoxes. How can one rightfully claim, as Augustine does, that the will is free, but that humans are incapable of avoiding sin and that they require the gift of God's grace in order to achieve salvation? If I have *arbitrium libero* or the ability to freely choose between alternatives, why can I not choose to work toward the good and salvation and *achieve my goal by my own power*? My will is actually in bondage through sin, but if this is the case, then I am not truly free at all. In other words, how can I freely choose between good and evil if my will is already weighed down by original sin? If I act from my emotions or base desires, I am in a sense acting from a position of compulsion and slavery; it is not my free will which is operating, so how do I fall of my own will?

Free Will

The final confusion is that if I lack the freedom to rise to goodness on my own, then *why are only some people saved through grace and others not*? This appears to be predestination and preferential treatment from a supposedly fair and just God, regardless of the fact that Augustine denies that it is preferential treatment. The free will/grace predicament is also evident in Aquinas who says, "free choice without grace remains incapable of accomplishing that good which is beyond human nature."[22]

In general, the answers provided by Aquinas are not much better than Augustine's. Aquinas explains the free will/God relationship as follows,

> By free decision a human being moves himself into action; but it is not essential to freedom that the free agent should be its own first cause, just as in general to be the cause of something one does not have to be its first cause. God is the first cause which activates both natural and voluntary causes. His action on natural causes does not prevent their activities from being natural; equally in activating voluntary causes He does not take away the voluntariness of their actions. On the contrary, it is He who makes their actions voluntary; for he works in each thing in accordance with its own characteristics.[23]

What one finds here is the same sort of kenotic idea with God divesting himself of power, but still remaining the first cause in a creation *ex nihilo* scenario. I have already shown that this is a troubling basis for free will because *in theory* God could revoke our freedom at any point.

Aquinas tackles the omniscience/free will paradox by stating that God is outside of time itself and can therefore know all that we will freely choose. "God acts in the timelessness of his eternity." One may recall that he provides an analogy of a man walking down a path not knowing that another man is walking towards him from the other side of a hill that stands between the two individuals. Neither of these men is aware of the other's proximity, but a third man standing on top of the hill would be able to see that in a few minutes in the future the paths of the two men will cross.

This bird's eye view is supposed to be analogous to God's timeless perspective. However, *the analogy fails because a third man on a hill could not know for sure that either man would keep walking on the same trajectory, perhaps one will stop or turn around and then their paths will not cross*. At best, the third man on the hill could *predict what might* come to pass and God's knowledge is not prediction, it is supposedly a complete and infallible knowledge. The bottom line is that it is simply unclear as to how God's foreknowledge would in no way intrude on the free will of human beings; it seems that no matter what approach classical theists take to answering these problems their responses end up lacking a sufficiently logical solution.

---

22. Aquinas, *De Veritate*, "On Free Choice," article XIV.
23. Quoted in Ilham Dilman's, *Free Will*, 103.

Part III: Cosmosyntheism vs. the Five Rival Contenders

Free Will and Emergent Theism

Samuel Alexander rightly supposes that humans are partially free and partially determined. He draws attention to the fact that causality and determination still play a role and exert an influence on the will of humans because *the category of causality must be incorporated into the constitution of every form of finite existence*. This means that in all cases we are partially free and partially determined; however; Alexander provides some examples where the will is understood as more free and other examples where it appears to be more constrained and determined. For example, he states "We are free to open our eyes or not, or to direct them anywhere, but we are not free to see or not: we are passive or under compulsion in respect of our sensations."[24]

Alexander goes beyond examples of a free will to show how humans are free in other ways, such as, in our imagination. "For example, we have this consciousness in instinctive processes, where one mental state leads to another; or in what we call the free play of the imagination, one fancy suggesting another."[25] It seems that for every example illustrating our freedom a counter-example can be shown and Alexander does a good job of articulating both sides of the problem. Not only are we constrained by what our passive sensations receive from the external world, sometimes "an unaccountable outburst of anger, or a mental obsession, makes us feel unfree."[26] It seems that Alexander's account of free will is quite straightforward and acceptable, but his metaphysics implies some intriguing possibilities that take one far afield from common sense wisdom about freedom.

Alexander's metaphysics proposes that there are emergent levels of being starting with the simplest—space-time itself—and moving on all the way to human minds and likely beyond to even higher empirical qualities than mind. What this implies is that there may be higher degrees of freedom than that enjoyed by human imagination and willing. Just as the highest level we know—mind—can exert a downward causation on the lower level—life or a body—*so too could a higher level than mind exert a downward causation onto human minds*. It may be remembered that Alexander hypothesizes the existence of finite gods or angels and suggests that whatever they may be or whatever deity may entail, "it is not merely infinite mind, if that phrase has any meaning, but something higher."[27] So the real question now becomes precisely how much influence could this higher level be exerting downwards onto the level of human mind?[28]

---

24. Alexander, *Space, Time, and Deity*, vol. II, 316.
25. Ibid.
26. Ibid., 317.
27. Ibid., 329.
28. I must point out that this problem is far more acute for advocates of strong emergence rather than weak emergence where Alexander would be classified. Adherents of strong emergence are more committed to the idea of both upward and downward causation, whereas weak emergence focuses on the role of upward causation.

Alexander recognizes the dilemma and its potential repercussions for free will. "For instance could an angel or God foretell all the new creations of human advance? It may be not; though on the other hand the cyclical recurrence of groups of physical properties even among the elements may indicate that there is some calculable order of forms of existence."[29] Alexander does not give a definitive answer to this paradox that I will call *the finite gods paradox*. However, it seems that the answer should be that the finite gods or deity would be limited in its ability to either foretell or directly impact the lower level of mind because on analogy *the level of mind is frequently overridden by compulsions and mutations on the level of life or body*. I will close with an intriguing suggestion by Alexander. "The only meaning that can rationally be attached to the notion that God can predict the whole future is that the future will be what it will be. And there is one part of the universe which in any case even God cannot predict, and that is his own future."[30]

Problems with the Emergent Solution

I find only two problems with the emergent solution. First of all, at what point does freedom truly appear? If the belief is that only at life does it emerge, I find this possible due to the logic of emergence that new qualities and abilities are gained at higher levels that did not previously exist. However, the position of process theology and process philosophy is that of *panexperientialism or the belief that experience and therefore some degree of freedom is inherent in all levels of being*. I feel that the best solution is that new avenues of freedom open up as one goes up the chain of emergence, but that at least some rudimentary form of freedom should be asserted even down to the atomic and sub-atomic level.

The other concern that I have about Alexander's view on freedom concerns the finite gods paradox. If an angel or a god could see and know all of our future decisions or if they could radically control our decision making, then just how free are we? It may be that our free will is an illusion and we are really just actors in a game being played by some higher emergent level of reality as suggested by numerous films in the last twenty years and by Oxford scholar Nick Bostrom who believes that there is a 20 percent chance that this is the case.[31] Be that as it may, I am inclined to think that the chaotic element that seems to exist at all levels of reality would make omniscience in the narrow sense of knowing all human actions, impossible even for a higher level entity. It is not as if these finite gods are outside of time and space with some bird's eye view, they are integral parts of creation and they are affected by the lower levels, constrained by lower levels just as humans are, so it seems impossible for any finite god to know *everything*. The end result is that Alexander does not make a clear enough

---

29. Alexander, *Space, Time, and Deity vol. II*, 327.
30. Ibid., 329.
31. See Bostrom, "Are You Living in a Computer Simulation?"

Part III: Cosmosyntheism vs. the Five Rival Contenders

statement about the limitations of any higher emergent levels. In contrast, the next contender, process philosophy as espoused by Cobb and Griffin, does make a definitive statement about God's ability to tamper with human freedom.

Cobb and Griffin on Free Will

Process theologians are unique among theists in that they deny *creatio ex nihilo* and God's omnipotence and omniscience. Instead, they claim that God must always have been related to a *genuine other* normally conceived as a World or realm of very simplistic actual entities.[32] Creation was therefore, out of pre-existing material and was out of chaos rather than nothingness. The idea that God is always related to a genuine other provides a truly novel solution to the free will problem as well as to the problem of evil to be discussed later. The concept is so simple that it is unsettling to think that few other groups have been willing to make the move to multiple ultimates, in this case: God and a primordial world. The argument from process theology runs: if God is necessarily related to some "primordial other," *then power is not wholly derived from God and it is instead, shared with both God and the world, thus God also cannot know all future events because of the inherent creative self-determination within the world.*

In addition to the advance made by the shift to multiple ultimates, Cobb and Griffin also advocate a doctrine that Griffin calls panexperientialism. Panexperientialism is the belief that all things—atoms and molecules included—have experience, *with experience being distinguished from conscious experience*, which is limited to higher-order animals. Each moment of experience for a given entity unfolds in the same dipolar manner, meaning that every entity has two poles: a receptive or physical side and a self-creative and enjoying side known as the mental pole. Lower entities like atoms are primarily driven by their physical poles, with only a vanishingly small mental pole and this implies that an atom has a nearly negligible amount of freedom. An atom is instead driven by a law of averages and is thereby, rather predictable. In contrast, an occasion of experience belonging to a human being is dominated by the mental side with data coming from past occasions of one's own experience as well as data from other people and the surrounding environment. Not only does the past data arrive via our five senses, but for process theologians there is also a non-sensuous perception involving the re-enactment of the feelings of other entities in what can be understood as a sort of empathic encounter involving internal relations.

The receptive phase of experience sets limits upon what a person is going to experience and be capable of choosing in the present moment. "However, precisely how the present subject responds to its past, precisely how it incorporates the past feeling, precisely how it integrates the multiplicity of feelings into a unified experience, this is

---

32. The idea of God needing a genuine other comes from Whitehead, in particular his famous six antitheses in part V of *Process and Reality*.

not determined by the past."[33] In other words, each individual is partially determined by the past and the environment, but also partially free and self-determining. However, other people are not the limit of influencing factors on a new moment of experience, there is also the key role played by God. "The attractive possibility, the lure, in relation to which its act of self-determination is made, is derived from God. This lure is called the initial aim. God is the divine Eros urging the world to new heights of enjoyment."[34] God provides the new occasion with an ideal set of possibilities to choose from, ideal in the sense that they will result in a heightened sense of enjoyment for the occasion.

God's role as the divine persuader urging the world onwards to greater and more complex forms of value is not limited to a sorting of the available options from the past environment, but includes a presentation of truly novel possibilities that would have been unthinkable given just the past data drawn from the world. "The possibilities that were previously unactualized in the world are derived from the divine experience. One aspect of God is a primordial envisagement of the pure possibilities. They are envisaged with appetition that they be actualized in the world. This means that the divine reality is understood as the ground of novelty."[35] What is known as the primordial nature of God is the repository of all possibilities for both Cobb and Griffin. It is at this point that old problems under a new guise begin to creep in.

Problems with Cobb and Griffin's Solution

I follow Cobb and Griffin in advocating the truth and value of both multiple ultimates and the doctrine of panexperientialism. However, I am forced to part ways with both of them when it comes to God's primordial nature and the possibilities residing therein. Wouldn't initial aims coming from God's primordial nature which existed before creation represent in effect God knowing what we are going to choose in the future? The problem is: how could God, preceding creation, set up relevant aims for each *free* entity before they have even been born? If the world truly has its own inherent power, then how could God know what aims will be relevant?

In fairness, this is a problem which plagues Whitehead and supposedly not Griffin and Cobb. In fact, Griffin devotes considerable attention to these precise questions in his *Reenchantment without Supernaturalism*,[36] but what is strange is that Griffin refuses to just do away with the notion that *all possibilities* eternally reside in God. Instead, his answer appears to be that initial aims actually come from "God as a whole," meaning God's primordial nature combined with his consequent nature, which responds to and is influenced by the world moment-by-moment. *But why doesn't the*

33. Cobb and Griffin, *Process Theology*, 25.
34. Ibid., 26.
35. Ibid.,, 28.
36. See pp. 150–56 of *Reenchantment without Supernaturalism* for Griffin's explanations of the problems inherent in Whitehead's system.

experiential knowledge gained by God from the world alter and result in new possibilities within the primordial mind of God? Furthermore, if the primordial world existing with God at least exhibits chaos as a Form and God exhibits order, then how does God contain *all* possibilities? Again, if the consequent nature of God is changing moment-by-moment in response to the decisions of the world, then are the results of these changes in the consequent nature already conceived as possibilities in the unchanging primordial nature or not? Finally, one could also ask, if God truly contains all possibilities like we have seen in so many of the other contending systems, *then wouldn't one of these possibilities be to attempt to deprive humanity of freedom and persuade each person to do evil?* These questions are not answered by any of the five contenders including Cobb and Griffin.

Any system which assumes that God contains all possibilities is going to be forced into a position where humanity's freedom is an impoverished notion at best of what we feel our freedom to be like. If God has already thought of or imagined everything, then I am just one actor playing out some possibilities in a divinely envisaged drama. If there truly are multiple ultimates, with each one containing its own degree of power, then it seems impossible that God could timelessly or eternally contain all possibilities. If experiential knowledge is to have any meaning distinguishing it from theoretical knowledge, then God cannot have all possibilities primordially. The solution to this persistent problem that I have called *the infinity paradox* is so simple yet seemingly never employed: *God never did (timelessly or temporally in the past), does not now, and never will in the future, contain all possibilities.*

Cosmosyntheism and Free Will

Cosmosyntheism shares many of the solutions to the free will problem offered by previous process theologians like Cobb and Griffin. For example, I am in agreement that the idea of multiple ultimates is capable of solving numerous problems, one of which is the free will problem. Cosmosyntheism also incorporates the standard Whiteheadian epistemology with dipolar actual occasions and the doctrine of panexperientialism with all entities sharing in at least some degree of experience. Another point of agreement is the belief that a person is partially determined by the past and external environmental factors, but also partially free in their creative self-determination given the possibilities available to the person at that moment. However, Cosmosyntheism parts ways with other forms of process theology on the issue of free will because it proposes an even more radical notion of freedom than what is allowed under a typical Whiteheadian framework.

For Cosmosyntheism humans are free because: (1) as mentioned above, there are multiple ultimates, so power is distributed accordingly across the ultimates; (2) God does not contain all possibilities, or power or knowledge; (3) the World has a dominant Form of chaos or randomness that allows humans to be capable of imagining, creating and experiencing truly new possibilities that not even God had previously imagined.

In suggesting that the primordial World contains Forms of its own like chaos or randomness that are not primordially within God, a more extreme account of freedom begins to unfold. In Cosmosyntheism, *God's primordial nature is limited to a set of initial possibilities rather than being All-Possibility*. This is not to say that God's primordial nature may not include an unimaginable amount of potential Forms and Ideas, it is merely asserting that God never did, nor never will contain All-Possibilities. In other words, *there is no talk of infinity, unless one was to say that there is an infinite process.*

In former process-oriented systems like those of Whitehead, Cobb and Griffin, God is capable of receiving data in the form of feelings back from the world; God can gain experiential knowledge. What is unclear is how these feelings and experiential knowledge gained affects the initial apparently infinite set of possibilities residing in the primordial nature of God. *Cosmosyntheism says that this experiential knowledge must alter the original set of possibilities, enlarging what was supposedly already infinite*. Another more striking issue than the experiential knowledge is how the reality of chaos within the World is incapable of providing both humans and God with previously unimagined potential courses of thought and action. Cosmosyntheism says that *both experiential knowledge gained from the world and the inherent randomness and uncertainty within the world contribute to a general increase of freedom for humans as well as God.*

Throughout this chapter, I have focused on free will as it pertains to humans, but I will now shift briefly to the issue of God's free will. In classical accounts of theism, God is completely free to do whatever he wants *assuming it does not violate logical possibility*. But, is God truly free if God is incapable of true love, of being in a reciprocal relationship, of growing in response to others, of learning or imagining new possibilities in light of interactions with creation? Many forms of theism simply do not view these as limitations or they introduce sophisticated, yet unintelligible concepts like the Trinity, to explain away the problem. By contrast, the God of Cosmosyntheism is always related to others and therefore, *capable of genuine love, growth and mutual sharing and learning*. Most importantly, these others that God is related to can be and I will argue do represent *legitimate avenues for religious exploration*. Therefore, the idea of multiple ultimates should actually be viewed as multiple *religious* ultimates and this concept does not only provide superior solutions to the problem of freedom, but also to what is arguably the most pressing contemporary concern: conflicting religious truth claims.

Summary

- The free will problem is captured in the following question. Are all events predetermined either by a divine creator or simply by the laws of physics, or are humans truly free when they think, act and make decisions?

Part III: Cosmosyntheism vs. the Five Rival Contenders

- For the Perennialist, free will is ultimately an illusion just like the ego.
- Emanationist solutions range from the Daoist acceptance of free will within humans to Gnostic accounts where the will is, at least for most human beings, heavily constrained by the passions of the body.
- For the classical theist, the will is free to cling to God or to turn away towards lesser goods, but our free will is in a sense on loan to us from God, who in theory could revoke our freedom.
- Alexander believes that humans are partially free and partially determined. There are some cases in which we are freer than others. Alexander also hints at the possibility that perhaps some finite gods or angels could radically control our free will and thus our actions although appearing free would be more like those of marionettes.
- Cobb and Griffin align with Alexander in believing that humans are partially free and partially determined. Our freedom is limited by the power of the past manifesting in the present, the initial aim from God and the complexity of the organism in question.
- Cosmosyntheism allows for a more radical amount of freedom than the position of Cobb and Griffin by suggesting both that God does not contain all the Forms and that the World, as one of the ultimates, has its own degree of raw power.

CHAPTER 11

Conflicting Religious Truth Claims Part 1

Those who know only their own religion, know none.
—MAX MÜLLER, *INTRODUCTION TO THE SCIENCE OF RELIGION*

THE MANNER IN WHICH a philosophical system deals with the problem of conflicting religious truth claims is perhaps the single most important factor for whether or not that system will be pragmatically effective as a twenty-first century philosophy for a globalized community. The reality is that we live in an age of religious pluralism where a Muslim, a Buddhist and a Christian may all live on the same street. Therefore, as I pointed out in the introduction, the first criterion for any successful constructive theology in the twenty-first century is going to be dealing with religious pluralism. The purpose of this chapter is to elucidate the solutions put forth by the first five contenders for a globalized theology to the problem of conflicting religious truth claims.

The Problem of Conflicting Religious Truth Claims

The problem is: if all the different religions are making different and incompatible truth claims about the nature of Ultimate Reality and the way to salvation, then either (1) one must be right and the others all wrong (2) one is more right than another or (3) perhaps the conflicting statements are evidence that they are all wrong. For example, the monotheistic faiths claim that a personal, good and loving God is Ultimate Reality and the way of salvation is through faith in this God, with the result being an eternal life in paradise. However, other religions such as *some forms* of Buddhism and Daoism claim that Ultimate Reality is in no way an entity, but an infinite process of becoming and that after death, humans are either reborn or they just cease to exist. All of these religions claim to be correct, but *if one is correct then it stands to reason that the others are all false or at least less true.* This is the problem of conflicting religious truth claims and along with the problem of evil, it is one of the best weapons in the arsenal of neo-atheists. Since we are entering a fully globalized community, philosophers of religion must come up with adequate solutions to this pressing issue. What follows are some attempts to answer the problem of conflicting religious truth claims.

The Perennial Philosophy and Conflicting Religious Truth Claims

The perennial philosophy provides a popular and simplistic solution to the conflicting religious truth claims paradox. The perennialist's solution categorizes them as *identist pluralists*, meaning that their answer to the problem is that all the religions are not actually making different truth claims, *at least not at the esoteric level*. This is one way out of the quagmire, to simply dissolve it away and chalk up the problem to a misunderstanding stemming from an inadequate background in the actual sacred scriptures of the various religious faiths. The one truth is that all the religions are esoterically the same. "This digression was necessary in order to bring out more clearly the profoundly different natures of the exoteric and esoteric domains and to show that whenever there is incompatibility between them it can only spring from the first and never from the second, which is superior to forms and therefore beyond all oppositions."[1] In other words, all conflicts arise from the outward, dogmatic and superficial understandings of the religious faiths.

An intriguing feature of the perennial philosophy is that one can rank the levels of the exoteric forms of each religion. "Christianity, for example, is esoteric relatively to the Judaic form and Islam relatively to the Judaic and Christian forms, though this is of course, only valid when regarded from the special point of view that we are here considering and would be quite false if understood literally."[2] Well then why mention a ranking at all? What one gathers from the above comments is that Islam is the best exoteric religion, but in fact, the answer is that Islam and Hinduism are supreme due to their unique positions in a cosmic cycle. "The fact that Islam constitutes the last form of the *Sanatana Dharma* in this *maha yuga*, to use Hindu terms, implies that this form possesses a certain contingent superiority over preceding forms; similarly, the fact that Hinduism is the most ancient of the living religious forms implies that it possesses a certain superiority or centrality with respect to later forms."[3] Exactly what makes them superior is unclear and not mentioned aside from being the earliest and latest major religions.

The real test of the perennialist solution *is going to hinge upon the truth or falsity of their main claim that all the religions are deep down the same*. However, before putting this proposition to the test, I provide the following as a reminder of exactly what this universal esoteric religion is supposed to look like in the minds of perennialists.

---

1. Schuon, *The Transcendent Unity of Religions*, 47.
2. Ibid., 31.
3. Ibid., 36.

> *Reality affirms itself by degrees, but without ceasing to be "one," the inferior degrees of this affirmation being absorbed, by metaphysical integration or synthesis, into the superior degrees. This is the doctrine of the cosmic illusion: the world is not only more or less imperfect or ephemeral, but cannot even be said to "be" at all in relation to absolute Reality, since the reality of the world would limit God's Reality and He alone "is." Furthermore, Being itself, which is none other than the personal God, is in its turn surpassed by the Impersonal or Supra-Personal Divinity, Non-Being, of which the Personal God or Being is simply the first determination from which flow all the secondary determinations that make up cosmic existence.*[4]

What the above passage proposes is that Reality is hierarchical with the Infinite at the top and then the celestial followed by the terrestrial at the bottom. The celestial is the realm of the personal creator God and humans reside in the bottom layer or the terrestrial. The influence of Advaita Vedanta and its apparent superiority comes through in the above passage, but as I mentioned above, the real question is, do all religions at the esoteric level affirm this metaphysical picture?

Problems with the Perennialist Solution

I will begin with the most obvious problems and work my way towards those that are more subtle. First off, why even assert that at the exoteric level Islam and Hinduism are in some ways superior? If the goal is to pave the way for a true global community and to argue for the transcendent unity of religions, then what good is it to say: "deep down we are all the same so we shouldn't fight any more . . . but by the way Islam and Hinduism are outwardly more correct?" This is clearly a mistake and will not have a positive pragmatic effect on promoting interreligious dialogue, which is a must for any successful metaphysical system in the twenty-first century. Besides, it seems that Buddhism and Daoism are outwardly superior given the perennialist's description of Ultimate Reality, because they both assert, at least in some forms of the religions, *that Ultimate Reality is an Impersonal process.* Does exoteric Islam assert that the Impersonal aspect of Divinity is superior to the personal and creating aspect of God? I think not. For that matter, does Hinduism even assert this, well yes, in a couple of Vedantic forms, but certainly not in all its forms.

The main criticism I have of the perennial philosophy is that their central thesis for a transcendent unity of religions is untenable. The idea that all the religions are esoterically the same arises from two things: (1) an inadequate examination of the available data provided by the scriptures and (2) a failure to accept the fact that religions, even at the esoteric level, evolve over time. I will address the latter issue first, using the evolution of Jewish mysticism as an example.

---

4. Ibid., 38.

Part III: Cosmosyntheism vs. the Five Rival Contenders

Not only are all the different religions not the same deep down, *but even a single religion in its esoteric dimensions cannot be said to be advocating the same doctrines over time*. For example, in early Judaism (more accurately ancient Israelite religion), the Hebrews are not even monotheistic; they are henotheistic, meaning that they may worship one god, but they acknowledge the existence of other gods. The early Hebrew people were known to worship Baal, El, Asherah and others throughout the formative period of the religion before Yahweh usurped the power of these other major Canaanite deities.

More importantly, around the time of the destruction of the second temple in 70 C.E., there were three major groups of Jews living in the region around Jerusalem: Sadducees, Pharisees, and Essenes.[5] The Sadducees were the Hasmonean kings/high priests who presided over the workings of the temple, such as, animal sacrifices. *The Sadducees can be viewed as exoteric Judaism* at this point because they advocated a strict adherence to the written Torah, allowing only a literal interpretation. However, *the Pharisees, an esoteric group* that later became the Rabbinic strand of Judaism which is dominant today, asserted that in addition to the written Torah, there is also the Oral Torah or Talmud, which had been passed down from Moses until today. The Pharisees believed in the resurrection of the dead as well as an allegorical interpretation of Torah in distinction from the Sadducees. However, some Pharisees during the early Rabbinic period also began to develop the practice known as Merkabah mysticism, which suggested a spiritual ascension through the seven heavens culminating in a mystical vision of the throne of God or God himself. This ascent ritual required spiritual purification and intense meditations and visualization exercises as well as secret knowledge of angelic names and passwords.

The third group, *the Essenes, can also be seen as an esoteric group of Judaism* that was strictly ascetic, against marriage, celibate and against animal sacrifices, *which distinguished the Essenes from both the Sadducees and the Pharisees*. On top of these three groups there were the Jewish mystics living in Alexandria creating Jewish Gnostic texts *which claimed that Yahweh was an evil creator God*! As time goes on, Kabbalistic Judaism adds even more twists to the rich history of mystical Judaism, borrowing heavily from Sethian Gnosticism and Hermetism. The question becomes, *which one of these esoteric Judaisms is the one that is correct because it cannot be all of them? Furthermore, how is that particular esoteric form of Judaism similar to other distinct esoteric religions?*

The perennialist's do not ask nor answer such vital questions and so their solution is too simple and bound to result in failure. Given the fact that even within a *single religious tradition* there is significant diversity of opinion regarding theological and soteriological matters, it isn't even necessary for me to make the further case, which is even more obvious, that different religious traditions have wildly unique theologies, cosmologies, anthropogonies and soteriologies. In other words, Tantric

---

5. See Josephus's *Antiquities of the Jews* and the *War of the Jews* for information about first-century Judaism.

Buddhism is not the same as Zen Buddhism and even less similar to Kabbalah, Sufism or Rosicrucianism and Freemasonry.

A final related point, this one also resulting from the striking absence of something in the perennialist's texts, is the issue: are all the esoteric religions advocating merely the same metaphysics or *are they also suggesting that their paths to salvation are esoterically the same*? If the claim is that the paths to salvation are identical or at least similar then I must take issue with this as well. Zen Buddhism and Daoism stress the importance of spontaneity and unlearning what one has learned as the path to a pure and natural existence, but other esoteric ideas stemming from Neo-Confucianism, Neo-Platonism, Vedanta and certain groups of Jewish Mysticism insist upon the value of book learning, moral and intellectual cultivation. Some systems like Tantrism and certain Gnostic sects like the Carpocratians, Nicolaitans and Ophites advocate the need to break moral taboos and so stress all kinds of licentious activities to free one from deep cultural conditioning. Some Jewish, Christian, Buddhist, and Daoist esoteric groups practice ritual magic—invocations, evocations, divination and enchantment—for the purpose of gaining powers, knowledge and ultimately for salvation, either in the form of spiritual immortality, or in the case of religious Daoism, physical immortality. The list of differences between esoteric groups can go on and on, but the above should suffice to disprove any lingering beliefs that perhaps the various religions offer the same end goal and method of salvation.

Emanation and the Problem of Conflicting Religious Truth Claims

Systems which endorse only one religious ultimate or at least favor one over another are limited in their possible responses to the problem of conflicting religious truth claims. In total, one-ultimate systems have five possible ways to respond when confronted by a new religion: (1) either, they are completely right and we are totally wrong; (2) they are completely wrong and we are totally right; (3) they are more correct than we are; (4) we are more correct than they are; or (5) perhaps we are both wrong. By and large, the second option has being the dominant response and this represents taking an exclusivist stance where only your religion is valid. Since most of the examples I have been using to explain emanation up until this point would fall under option two, they would fail my first criterion for a successful global theology, which is to deal with religious pluralism. Almost no group would fall under options one and five, so that leaves options three and four to be explored. Throughout history and up until modern times option four has stood out as an attractive solution to the problem of conflicting religious truth claims.

For this chapter only, I will shift my attention away from the individual examples of emanation theory I have thus far employed and instead, highlight two systems, Advaita Vedanta, *an ancient example*, and the system of John Hick, *a modern example*, both of which can be viewed as advocating emanation or *at least a hierarchical system*

Part III: Cosmosyntheism vs. the Five Rival Contenders

of reality/truth. In both of these systems option four above comes in to play, *where religions such as Buddhism and Advaita Hinduism which focus on an impersonal and attributeless ultimate are understood as superior.* The two philosophers, Shankara and John Hick, may not view their positions as leading to this conclusion, but the evidence shows that this is precisely the only outcome that an emanation theory or a hierarchical view of reality can provide to the problem of conflicting religious truth claims.

Shankara's Solution to the Problem of Conflicting Religious Truth Claims

Shankara was an Indian philosopher living in the eighth century C.E. who championed the school of Advaita Vedanta. Advaita literally means non-dual or not-two and Vedanta means end of Vedas; therefore, Advaita Vedanta implies in its name that the true message of Hindu holy scripture is that reality is not-two or more specifically, *atman* (self/soul) is *Brahman* (Ultimate Reality/the Totality).[6] However, Shankara in his commentaries on the *Prasthanatrayi* (*Brahma Sutras*, *Upanishads* and the *Bhagavad Gita*) uncovered much more than simply the truth of *advaita*.

Shankara realized that there were levels of truth and reality. The highest level of truth is called *Pāramārthika* and consists of *jnana* or knowledge of the truth of *advaita* and Brahman is understood as Nirguna Brahman at this stage, meaning God without any attributes. The second level of reality and truth is known as *Vyāvahārika* or pragmatic truth. This derivative level is born from the magical power of *Maya* which Ishvara or Brahman with attributes wields in order to create a cosmos for the purpose of sport or play known as *leela*. Creation proceeds from Ishvara who along with *Maya* as a magic power creates the five elements and then the actual universe.

What is important for us here is that the second level is not real; it is illusory, at least in comparison to Absolute Truth. Thus there is a hierarchy created, with Nirguna Brahman at the top and then Saguna Brahman or Ishvara second and then third, the material cosmos that humans occupy. As Shankara says, any attempt to come to know Brahman through dichotomies and comparisons is fallacious and results in an I-Thou relationship with divinity. The highest that one taking this approach of devotion to God can attain is the second to last level of truth and reality. It is only when one finally dissolves away the distinctions between the I and the Thou of the divine that one realizes that I am That or I am all things; atman is Brahman.

I realize that Shankara's monistic system may not be an example of emanation in the literal sense of a flowing out from, but the point is that there are degrees of truth and reality in his system resulting more precisely from Brahman's transformations, the result of the cosmic play or *leela*. What matters is that there is one ultimate—Brahman—which through the power of *Maya* becomes or is perceived as a multiplicity of different things. This interpretation of Vedanta *is not the majority response* however,

---

6. For one of the best two-volume overviews of Indian philosophy see Radahakrishnan, *Indian Philosophy*.

with most of the Hindu population of India aligning themselves with other forms, such as Dvaita and Vishishtadvaita Vedanta. These two schools advocate devotion to Vishnu as the ultimate path to liberation rather than *jnana,* with the Dvaita school proposing that *reality is two,* with Brahman as an efficient and final cause and *prakriti* as a separate material cause. Regardless of their number of adherents, Advaita Vedanta has maintained a certain degree of philosophical prestige throughout the years and so its solutions to philosophical problems must be carefully examined.

The solution that presents itself in Shankara's system to the problem at hand is that other religions may have a lesser degree of insight into the truth because they are operating from a dualistic mindset. Shankara uses this hierarchy to explain away other philosophical opponents and his followers have appropriated this three-tiered hierarchy to show the incompleteness of other schools of Vedanta. This is one way to deal with conflicting religious truth claims, to simply argue that one religion is the most correct, but *that same religion can include other religious viewpoints as derivative truths.* This is exactly the implication of the next author's system, but he, like the perennialist's, believes that all the religions are aimed at the same religious object.

John Hick's Solution to the Problem of Conflicting Religious Truth Claims

John Hick, a twentieth-century philosopher of religion, has argued for the truth of what he calls the "Real *an sich*" or the Real in itself, as that to which all religions are *attempting* to describe and relate to. However, the best that humans can achieve due to linguistic and cognitive limitations is to describe the Real as humanly experienced. Hick invokes Kant's distinction between the *noumena* and the *phenomena* as an analogous example from philosophy for what is happening in the religious life.

> The hypothesis proposed at this point hinges upon the distinction first given philosophical prominence by Kant between something as it is in itself and as it appears to a consciousness dependent upon a particular kind of perceptual machinery and endowed with a particular system of interpretive concepts congealed into a linguistic system. An analogous distinction is drawn within each of the great religious traditions between the Real in itself and the Real as humanly thought and experienced.[7]

With this distinction between the Real *an sich* and the Real as humanly understood in place, Hick identifies two major ways of experiencing and interpreting religious experience of the Real: personal and impersonal.

Hick shows that the "personal" expressions explain the Real *as having attributes, as being a genuine other with qualities more akin to theistic descriptions,* whereas the "impersonal" descriptions focus on the Real *without any attributes or as a process rather than an entity.* Hick's goal is to prove that both of these interpretations of religion are

---

7. Hick, *An Interpretation of Religion,* 13–14.

equally valid ways of approaching the Real *an sich* because neither approach is capable of capturing the full essence of the Real in itself, as it always transcends human limitations.

Hick not only claims that all the religions are attempting to "describe the same putative transcendent reality"[8] but also are advocating the same general form of salvation. "The function of religion in each case is to provide contexts for salvation/liberation, which consists in various forms of the transformation of human existence from self-centeredness to Reality-centeredness."[9] In other words, Hick is what is known as an identist pluralist both ontologically and soteriologically.

What matters for the present inquiry is that a bizarre hierarchy begins to subtly unfold within Hick's work, a hierarchy which ultimately undermines his goal of placing all the religions on an equal footing. The top of the hierarchy is obviously the Real *an sich*. "But nevertheless the Real is the ultimate ground or source of those qualities which characterize each divine *persona* and *impersona* insofar as these are authentic phenomenal manifestations of the Real."[10] One would expect that there is only one more actual level which would consist of the personal and impersonal descriptions of the Real, but this does not actually seem to be the case.

A hidden bias for the *impersonae* descriptions of the Real can be grasped at key points throughout Hick's major work, *An Interpretation of Religion*. "We shall see later in chapter 16.4 that the Buddhist concept of Sunyata in one of its developments, namely as an anti-concept excluding all concepts, provides a good symbol for the Real *an sich*."[11] The bias for Eastern impersonal descriptions extends to Hick's former favorite: Advaita Vedanta. "Thus in this formulation the Real *an sich* is equated with *nirguna* Brahman, whilst both *satchitananda* and Ishvara are identified as forms of *saguna* Brahman."[12] Finally, as promised, one finds later in chapter 16 the following statement, "When *sunyata* is understood in this sense, as referring to the ultimate reality beyond the scope of all concepts, knowable only in its manifestations, then it is indeed equivalent to what in our pluralistic hypothesis we are calling the Real."[13]

It appears that instead of all religions being capable of claiming equal validity, what unfolds is a hierarchical view based on the presumption of there only being one ultimate, the Real *an sich,* and then slightly more accurate descriptions of this Real with the *impersonae* descriptions being superior to the *personae*. As far as conflicting religious truth claims are concerned, there are none because all the truth claims are only apparently conflicting. This apparent clash is due to the differences in cultural heritages among varied religious groups, which can be categorized according to the Wittgensteinian concept of "family resemblances." There is no conflict, but there are

8. Ibid., 10.
9. Ibid., 14. Also, see p. 240.
10. Ibid., 247.
11. Ibid., 246.
12. Ibid., 283.
13. Ibid., 291.

some religious forms of life which provide superior descriptions than others, mainly the "impersonal" understandings of the Real. However, ultimately none of the religions can be conflicting *because none of them are actually true*! This shocking result is due to the limitations of human beings; in effect, the religions are all equally false because none of them can fully grasp the Real as it truly is.

Problems with Hick's Solution

The issue of greatest concern is the fact that certain religions like Zen Buddhism and Advaita Vedanta are awarded a position of prominence over all other faiths. By suggesting that Sunyata and Nirguna Brahman are closer approximations to the Real, Hick has setup a hierarchy and this is not going to work as a pragmatic approach for dealing with religious pluralism. It is rather obvious that any interreligious dialogue based on Hick's theory would create major rifts between theistic and non-theistic religious groups.

The second striking problem is that Hick's Kantian bifurcation of the world into the noumenal and phenomenal results in the unfortunate consequence that all the religious descriptions are wrong because they are just accounts of the phenomenal manifestation of the Real *an sich,* all of which miss the true essence of the Real. This is a unique problem because in some ways Hick appears to be completely in line with Shankara in suggesting the truth of Nirguna Brahman over Saguna Brahman, but he cannot actually affirm this. All Hick can say is that human descriptions of Nirguna Brahman are *less false* than human descriptions of Saguna Brahman.

The final problem with Hick's position is his belief that all the religions are advocating the same general pattern of salvation from ego-centeredness to Reality-centeredness. This is an arbitrary choice and does not accurately reflect the various hopes and salvific goals of the myriad religions. I am not so sure that I am sold on the notion that all the theistic faiths are seeking the dissolution of the ego and I am certainly in disagreement when such religions as contemporary Paganism, Satanism, and some primordial religions are brought into the mix, as they often employ methods that bolster and increase the efficacy of one's personal will and desires.

In the end, Hick's solution is just an example of a bizarre hierarchy with the Real *an sich* at the top, followed by the less wrong Advaita Vedantists and some Buddhists and then monotheistic faiths and lastly, pre-axial shamanic faiths at the bottom. Hick's position has been heavily criticized over the years, especially by the next author I will cover: S. Mark Heim. What is fascinating is that although Heim realizes so many of the problems with Hick's position, Heim nevertheless creates another extremely cunning and subtle way of dealing with religious pluralism that results in a subjugating hierarchy and a method for ranking religions.

Part III: Cosmosyntheism vs. the Five Rival Contenders

Classical Theism and the Problem of Conflicting Religious Truth Claims

I will not be covering the opinions of Augustine, Aquinas, and the other monotheists I have previously addressed because their responses would fall under option one, which is to simply assert that all other religions are false. This may not be completely true as Christianity incorporates Jewish history and Islam utilizes insights from both Judaism and Christianity, but nevertheless most philosophers within each faith view their particular tradition as superior. For this reason, I will address the recent approach of S. Mark Heim for dealing with conflicting religious truth claims from within the tradition of classical theism.

Heim makes some major advances upon the pluralistic theories that preceded him, such as John Hick and Paul Knitter. The most important advance that I believe Heim contributes is that he fully recognizes that there are not common beliefs or a shared foundation under-girding all of the different religions. Put differently, Heim is extremely critical of all identist forms of pluralism as evidenced by part one of his 1995 book *Salvations*. One particular problem with the identist approach according to Heim is that,

> The most insistent voices calling for the affirmation of religious pluralism seem equally insistent in denying that, in properly religious terms, there is or should be any fundamental diversity at all. The assertion that major faith traditions are independently salvific means, in its most common forms, that they are equivalently effective in achieving a single human end. This conclusion undermines the distinctive value that can be attributed to the particulars of the actual faith traditions.[14]

Heim is correct in his criticism here because if all the religions are the same and aimed at the same salvation and all are equally valid expressions, then what is the point of interreligious dialogue and pluralism? When pluralists are only searching for what religions have in common, then so much of the uniqueness of each religion must be glossed over or completely ignored. Heim rightly finds this tactic unacceptable.

In contrast to identist pluralists, Heim suggests, as evidenced by the title of his book, that there are *salvations plural* rather than one common form of salvation like is found in Hick. "One set of religious ends may be valid for a given goal, and thus final for that end, while different ways are valid for other ends."[15] What Heim means here is that the Buddhist goal of attaining nirvana is valid and represents a different religious end than the Christian goal of communion with God. Up until this point, I am in complete agreement with Heim, but it is the move he makes in his next book, *The Depth of the Riches: A Trinitarian Theology of Religious Ends*, where a familiar trouble arises.

---

14. Heim, *Salvations*, 2–3.
15. Ibid., 3.

In *The Depth of the Riches* Heim introduces a novel Trinitarian form of religious pluralism.

> We can . . . see the connection between the Trinity and varied religious aims. The actual ends that various religious traditions offer as alternative human fulfillments diverge *because they realize different relations with God*. It is God's reality as Trinity that generates the multiplicity of dimensions that allow for that variety of relations. God's threefoldness means that salvation necessarily is a characteristic communion in diversity. It also permits human responses to God to limit themselves within the terms of one dimension. Trinity requires that salvation be communion. It makes possible, but not necessary, the realization of religious ends other than salvation.[16] (emphasis mine)

What Heim has done here is to utilize the classic theological model of the Trinity to provide for a plurality of religious ends. So, it is possible that the Hindu goal of *moksha* or liberation may be related to one or other of the three *personae* of the Trinity and the same goes for the Buddhist view of Sunyata and the goal of nirvana; perhaps they are related to the Holy Spirit aspect of the Trinity.

Heim's answer to the problem of conflicting religious truth claims then becomes that *they are not in conflict because they are oriented towards different personae of the Trinity*. This is why the Buddhist account of emptying and the focus on process over substance appears so different from Western theistic and substantialist accounts, because Buddhists are engaging a specific aspect of the Trinity whereas theistic faiths are focusing on others.

Problems with Heim's Solution

The first positive point of Heim's approach is that he recognizes the reality that religions are different, both ontologically and soteriologically. Another strong point is that he leans towards a truly pluralistic solution involving multiple ultimates. Unfortunately, Heim's multiplicity comes from imposing the Christian concept of the Trinity, *which is really a unity and therefore, not an adequate model to deal with real diversity*.

The negative elements of Heim's approach are numerous and they all hinge from his choice of the Trinity as a model for religious diversity. The most obvious objection is that he is forcing all other religions into a Christian superstructure and then evaluating them from the apparently self-evident superiority of the Christian faith. Heim even says that in truth only Christianity can provide salvation. "The one way to salvation and the many ways to religious ends are alike rooted in the Trinity."[17] In other words, only Christianity in its "intense" recognition of all three aspects of the Trinity has developed the supreme religious end, which is genuine salvation. This is

---

16. Heim, *The Depth of the Riches*, 180.
17. Ibid.

clearly a problem and on a practical level is going to immediately turn off any potential dialogue between Christianity and other religions.

Heim goes even further in claiming that the various religions can be ranked according to the intensity of communion they advocate with the entire Triune God. This results once again in a subjugating hierarchy, but this time with Christianity, rather than Advaita Vedanta and Buddhism at the top. Heim explains this hierarchy in the final chapter of the *Depth of the Riches*.

> I am suggesting that there are four broad types of human destiny. There is salvation, that communion through Christ with God and with others that unites an unlimited diversity of persons and opens each to a wider participation in the Triune life. Second, we have alternative religious ends, the distinctive human fulfillments of the various religious traditions. Each of these grasps some dimension of the triune life and its economic manifestation, and makes it the ground for a definitive human end . . . Third, there are human destinies that are not religious ends at all . . . The fourth destiny does not idolize some created good, but negates creation itself.[18]

The first two levels of the hierarchy pertain to the religious life, but only the first, that of Christianity, allows for salvation; this is a major problem and seems to go against Heim's earlier book *Salvations*. As a practical approach to dealing with religious pluralism, Heim's approach is destined to fail because of its elevation of Christianity over all other faiths.

Emergent Theism and the Problem of Conflicting Religious Truth Claims

Samuel Alexander never directly addressed the problem of conflicting religious truth claims; however, his philosophy nevertheless provides a unique solution. Alexander's philosophy of emergence could be utilized to argue for genuine difference yet equal validity between the truth claims of the different religions, but it could also be employed in a manner that would result in a hierarchy once again. It may be remembered that Alexander spoke of a nisus within the fabric of space-time itself. "There is a nisus in Space-Time which, as it has borne its creatures forward through matter and life to mind, will bear them forward to some higher level of existence."[19] This enigmatic and directional force could be understood to correspond with Eastern religious insights, such as, the Dao, *pratitya-samutpada*, Sunyata, *samsara* or even *maya*. In this way, many Eastern religions can be understood to be focusing on that aspect of reality that engenders an infinite process towards the manifestation of new forms.

---

18. Ibid., 272–73.
19. Alexander, *Space, Time and Deity*, vol. 2, 346.

Alexander also speaks about deity and God. "Deity is a nisus and not an accomplishment."[20] What Alexander means by this is to say that deity refers to the leading or cutting-edge of the nisus's forward and upward movement into novel qualities. God on the other hand can refer to finite gods, which are the next actually emerging or perhaps already existing qualitative level of reality, or to God as a whole, or God as Infinite. "Yet God's body is at any stage the whole of Space-Time, of which the finites that enter into God's body are but specialized complexes."[21] This distinction between deity as finite gods and God as the whole of space-time allows for a variety of pre-existing religions to be incorporated. Therefore, it could be said that the monotheistic faiths when speaking about angels are really drawing attention to the next higher level of finite existence, but when they talk of God as the One and the father they could be understood to be referencing God as the entirety of space-time.

Through the multitudes of emergent levels, all disciplines, including the various sciences, can find their appropriate location and all can be correct as they are attempting to describe a different feature of the totality. Another advantage of Alexander's system is that one does not need to suppose that one religion is superior to another, although one could argue for the superiority of some religions over others. For example, one could say that Daoism and Buddhism are superior because they identify the restlessness of Time and the reality of an indescribable nisus which drives the whole system. However, one could just as plausibly state that the monotheistic faiths are superior in that they attempt to explain the highest actually existing level of finite gods and the ultimate ideal, which is God as a whole striving towards further experiences and perfections. In other words, *it is ambiguous as to which faith would be at the "top" of the list or hierarchy and so it is more plausible to simply assert that they are all correct within their own limited foci of interests.*

Problems with Alexander's Solution

The main problem with employing Alexander's emergentist philosophy as a way of mediating various religious truth claims is that it fails to adequately deal with the monotheistic faiths. What I mean by this is that the monotheistic faiths assume that God is actual and the creator of the universe. This is a problem for Alexander, because God is an ideal, never fully achieving actuality. Furthermore, deity, finite gods and God as a whole, are growing with time. For Alexander the universe grows from simplicity to complexity, not the other way around, from an infinite God to a simplistic universe.

Alexander's system does appear to be capable of meshing well with some of the Eastern religions. However, this is a problem because if his system appears to fit well with the Eastern traditions over the Western and if his system is correct in its description of Reality, then a favoritism of the Eastern over the Western religions will once

20. Ibid.
21. Ibid., 366.

again begin to emerge. However, as I mentioned earlier, there are ways of incorporating both where neither can be seen as more correct than the other. In the end, Alexander's philosophy could represent a novel approach to dealing with conflicting religious truth claims and in fact his system always seems to waver between one ultimate, space-time, and two ultimates, space and time, with time being given a place of superiority as "the mind of space." By suggesting a nisus, space-time and the possibility of higher levels of empirical existence, Alexander's philosophy could be utilized to incorporate the benefits of multiple ultimates and the advantages of a hierarchical view. Nevertheless, there is a simpler and I believe more logically adequate solution to the problem of conflicting religious truth claims. The solution involves an explicit recognition of multiple religious ultimates.

Cobb/Griffin and the Problem of Conflicting Religious Truth Claims

In contrast to some of the "identist" forms of religious pluralism discussed so far, which all advocate that the various religions are oriented towards the same religious object and salvific goal, Cobb and Griffin advocate a "differential" or "deep" religious pluralism. This form of pluralism proposes that there are *multiple religious ultimates* and furthermore, that each one of these ultimates can be viewed as *complementary rather than contradictory*. The complementary pluralism of both Cobb and Griffin is grounded in a Whiteheadian framework. "Complementary pluralism can in turn be rooted in various perspectives, one of which is Whitehead's philosophy. And there can in turn be more than one version of Whiteheadian complementary pluralism."[22]

The version of Whiteheadian-based complementary pluralism that both Cobb and Griffin endorse is founded upon Whitehead's distinction between God, Creativity, and a World. Most of the work thus far has focused on how some Eastern religions—Buddhism in particular—resonate with the Creativity ultimate, whereas most Western faiths focus on God as ultimate. The idea is that Buddhists have correctly identified one element of the extremely complex system that comprises Ultimate Reality, and that element, when described by Buddhists, sounds similar to Whitehead's account of the nature and function of Creativity. "The connection with Whitehead's distinction between God and creativity is the idea that the term "creativity" points to the same reality to which some Buddhists point with the term "emptying" or "emptiness."[23]

Cobb and Griffin recognize that the idea of multiple religious ultimates also simultaneously brings about two forms of interreligious dialogue: *purification and enrichment*. "Dialogue with those from other traditions that are attending to the same ultimate, as when Christians talk with Jews, Muslims and theistic Hindus, can be a dialogue of purification. Dialogue with those who focus on the other ultimate can be a

22. Griffin, "John Cobb's Whiteheadian Complementary Pluralism," 39.
23. Ibid., 47.

dialogue of enrichment, in which one's comprehensive vision is enlarged. In this latter type of dialogue complementarity plays an especially central role."[24] It is during "enriching" dialogue that a person is truly capable of broadening their overall religious paradigm and hopefully coming one step closer to a complete picture of the complex truth that is Ultimate Reality.

Cobb provides a fine example of what enrichment between Buddhists and Christians might look like.

> Consider the Buddhist claim that Gautama is the Buddha. That is a very different statement from the assertion that God was incarnate in Jesus. The Buddha is the one who is enlightened. To be enlightened is to realize the fundamental nature of reality, its insubstantiality, its relativity, its emptiness . . . That Jesus was the incarnation of God does not deny that Gautama was the Enlightened One. In that vast complexity that is all that is, it may well be that God works creatively in all things and at the same time, in the Buddhist sense, all things are empty . . . To affirm both that Jesus is the Christ and that Gautama is the Buddha is to move our understanding closer to the truth.[25]

This is but one way in which the insights from Christianity and Buddhism can be found to be complementary and many more are identified by Cobb in earlier and later writings.

As I mentioned above, the vast majority of this enriching dialogue has revolved around conversations between Buddhism and Christianity. In fact, Cobb's 1981 book *Beyond Dialogue: Toward a Mutual Transformation of Christianity and Buddhism*, exclusively dealt with Christianity and Buddhism. The discussion between these two religious traditions has sought a mutual understanding and transformation through a dialogue mediated via a Whiteheadian hermeneutic. In other words, the Whiteheadian ultimates of God and Creativity have received the most attention, but it must not be forgotten that *Whitehead actually suggests three ultimates in Process and Reality*.[26]

Cobb, being a Whiteheadian, seeks to describe and classify the third ultimate.

> Today in the West there is another religious spirit at work, a reverence for the Earth and the cosmos. It, too, takes many forms. It has deep roots in many cultures. Much of primal religion has this form. It expresses itself in some forms of Taoism. Western pantheism has sometimes had this character. Surely we cannot deny that in some sense the totality of the things that are is ultimate as well! But it is not just another way of conceiving of Being Itself or of the Supreme Being, of Brahman or Ishvara.[27]

---

24. Ibid.
25. Cobb, *Transforming Christianity and the World*, 140.
26. Whitehead actually proposes four with the Receptacle being the fourth, but his discussion of this is limited to his *Adventures of Ideas* although intimations of the Receptacle can be found in germ form throughout part IV of *Process and Reality* entitled "The Theory of Extension."
27. Cobb, *Transforming Christianity and the World*, 185.

Part III: Cosmosyntheism vs. the Five Rival Contenders

This third ultimate corresponds with Whitehead's insistence that there be a World *not necessarily our particular world,* co-existing primordially with God and Creativity.

One final point must be addressed and that is the charge by some that any pluralistic position advocating multiple religious ultimates would constitute polytheism. Cobb immediately quells this argument by rightly explaining that in his system, as well as in Whitehead's, there is only one God.

> The charge of polytheism, sometimes directed against this affirmation of multiple ultimates, is misplaced. Being Itself is not God, and the cosmos is not God. There is only one God. But not all religions are theistic. To claim that in fact they are directed to God when they say they are not is one more expression of religious imperialism. To claim that all are directed toward an ultimate that lies behind or beneath these three, disparages all the religious traditions with the claim to know directly what all of them relate to only indirectly.[28]

The above remarks succinctly express what I believe, along with Cobb and Griffin, to be the best position for dealing with conflicting religious truth claims: advocating multiple religious ultimates. Only in this way can one do justice to the genuine uniqueness inherent within each tradition while simultaneously avoiding the violence stemming from an exclusivist attitude and the debilitating relativism resulting from any pluralistic theories which still hold to the belief that there is only one ultimate. Nevertheless, the position of both Cobb and Griffin can still be improved upon.

Problems with Cobb and Griffin's Solution

Of all the solutions proposed so far, I find myself most aligned with Cobb and Griffin's response of recognizing multiple religious ultimates. I commend them for taking this critical and difficult first step towards a totally new way of approaching the situation, but their initial insights can be expounded upon. I believe that there are at least two ways in which the solution advocated by Cobb and Griffin can be enhanced. The problems with their solutions arise from the fact that they are perhaps too influenced and thereby constrained by Whitehead's metaphysics. This influence leads to two limitations: (1) trying to fit the accounts of the different religions into one of only three possible slots (God, Creativity, and a World) and (2) struggling to incorporate the third ultimate, a World, as evidenced by the utter lack of treatment it has received aside from a few passing comments.

The first problem can be illustrated by examining the Buddhist/Christian dialogue which has been so fruitful over the past couple of decades. Cobb and Griffin both suggest that *sunyata* or emptiness corresponds with Whitehead's Creativity and his description of the process of concrescence and transition. However, I feel that a more adequate relation to emptiness can be found in a combination of the ideas of

---

28. Ibid.

Creativity and the Receptacle, an element missing in Cobb and Griffin's Whiteheadian triad. One important question is whether or not *pratitya-samutpada,* a central concern in Buddhism and for Cobb, is the same as *sunyata* because they are treated as synonymous terms by Cobb. I feel that emptiness or *sunyata* is referring to more than just the initial insight that all events dependently co-arise. Furthermore, *sunyata* does not necessarily need to be described as the formless ultimate, a fact recognized by Christopher Ives. "Rather as indicated by the locus classicus in the *Heart Sutra*, 'form is none other than emptiness, emptiness is none other than form.'"[29] Where do the forms come from and where are they housed? It is at this juncture that the historically later and richer term *sunyata* can shed light on the problem.

More contemporary Buddhist accounts of *sunyata* suggest that it is empty yet full and that Ultimate Reality is the storehouse consciousness. The views of D. T. Suzuki, Nishitani, Merton, and Hisamatsu suggest not only a creative process of infinite becoming, but that *sunyata* also refers to a repository where all events commingle and where all possibilities reside. For example, D. T. Suzuki says, "That is why *sunyata* is said to be a reservoir of infinite possibilities and not just a state of mere emptiness. Differentiating itself and yet remaining in itself undifferentiated, and thus to go on eternally engaged in the work of creation, this is *sunyata* the *prajna* continuum."[30] And again, "To say that reality is empty means that it goes beyond definability, and cannot be qualified as this or that. It is above the categories of universal and particular. But it must not therefore be regarded as free of all content, as a void in the relative sense would be. On the contrary, it is the fullness of things, containing all possibilities."[31]

What the above comments amount to saying is that *sunyata,* at least for many contemporary Buddhists, is more than just the process of interrelated becoming and impermanence associated with the insight of *pratitya-samutpada*. Emptiness or *sunyata* can also refer to the matrix or continuum uniting subjective experiences through successive "emptyings" of itself. This aspect of emptiness takes one beyond the way in which it is viewed by Cobb/Griffin and the early Indian Buddhist tradition. Although Creativity and concrescence do correspond well with Siddhartha Gautama's idea of *pratitya-samutapada* or dependent co-origination, they are too limited to be employed as corresponding terms for all that is meant by the later and more nuanced term: *sunyata*.

A starker problem arises concerning religions that are supposedly oriented towards a World as a religious ultimate. Cobb says, "Today in the West there is another religious spirit at work, a reverence for the Earth and the cosmos. It, too, takes many forms. It has deep roots in many cultures. Much of primal religion has this form. It expresses itself in some forms of Taoism. Western pantheism has sometimes had this

---

29. Ives, "Liberating Truth," 184.
30. Suzuki, *Studies in Zen*, 123.
31. Suzuki, "The Buddhist Conception of Reality," 103.

character."[32] The main problem here is that if the earth is taken as an ultimate, then Cobb is in violation of his own definition of an ultimate. "By an ultimate I mean that at which a line of questioning ends."[33] It is rather obvious that the earth—4.5 billion years old—is not an ultimate in the same sense as say, the cosmos itself—13.7 billion years old—or for that matter, God him/herself. However, the idea of a hypothetical, primordial chaotic world co-eternal with God *is* acceptable as an ultimate. This is not to suggest of course that the earth is not a proper religious object worthy of reverence and perhaps even worship, but *it is not ultimate in the strict sense*.

Summary

- The problem of conflicting religious truth claims is summarized as follows: if all the different religions are making different and incompatible truth claims about the nature of Ultimate Reality and the way to salvation, then either (1) one must be right and the others all wrong, (2) one is more right than another, or (3) perhaps the conflicting statements are evidence that they are all wrong.

- The Perennialist solution is that the apparent conflict is only on the surface or at the exoteric level of religion, on the esoteric level, all religions are the same.

- The emanationist solution differs depending upon the group, but more often than not, it results in option two, one religion is more correct than another.

- Classical theists would fall under either the first option or the second. Exclusivists would state that only Christianity or Islam, etc. is fully correct. An example of a classical theist taking the second option can be found in S. Mark Heim and his misappropriation of the Trinity as a symbol allowing for a hierarchy.

- An emergent theist could advocate for either the second or the third options. Under option two, the newest religion could in some ways be seen as the best while at the same time building upon that which came before it. Under option three, one could take a more scientific approach and say that all religious attempts at describing reality are flawed.

- Cobb and Griffin propose the most adequate solution to the problem by advocating for multiple religious ultimates. However, they struggle to provide a fair and realistic classification of some of the world's religions because of their over-stressing of two of the ultimates in Whitehead's metaphysics—God and Creativity—while seemingly being incapable of adequately incorporating the third: a World.

- The stance of Cosmosyntheism is that religious scriptures and religious experiences point to the reality of five religious ultimates, no more, no less.

---

32. Cobb, *Transforming Christianity and the World*, 185.
33. Ibid., 184.

CHAPTER 12

Conflicting Religious Truth Claims Part 2

The true religion of the future will be the fulfillment of all the religions of the past.
—MAX MÜLLER, *LIFE AND LETTERS II*

THROUGHOUT THE PRECEDING CHAPTERS, I have argued that Cosmosyntheism is a philosophical system composed of five ultimates. In this chapter, I shift the focus to the religious dimension of these five ultimates, showing how each of the world's religions has shed light on one or more of these five ultimates. The proposal of multiple religious ultimates is in line with both Cobb and Griffin's theories, but Cosmosyntheism distinguishes between five rather than three ultimates. I contend that various religious scriptures and experiences along with philosophical analysis point towards the existence of five rather than three ultimates. I have also stressed the *interrelatedness* of these five ultimates so, like Cobb, I argue that the different religious truth claims rather than conflicting, are capable of being complementary as they each are describing a different element of Ultimate Reality. Although I endorse much of Cobb and Griffin's work concerning the problem of conflicting religious truth claims (multiple ultimates, complementarity, purification and enrichment), my insistence on five ultimates loosens some of the kinks that have resulted from their acceptance of merely theistic, non-theistic and cosmic religions.

The primary advantage of Cosmosyntheism's five ultimates over three or one is that it allows for more religions to be accurately categorized without forcing them into a narrowly defined box which would distort the original message of that particular religion's insight into reality. I am not suggesting that each religion is simply engaged with one ultimate, however, some are. Instead, I believe that each religion makes one or two ultimates the overarching focus, often, but not always, to the exclusion of the other ultimates. This is actually a good thing because it means that a great deal of *depth* has been achieved by each religion and this gives a real purpose and meaning to dialogue: *gaining greater depth and breadth*. Remember, that if all the religions were aimed at the same religious object and they were all deep down correct, as the perennial philosophy assumes, then why bother with dialogue? The central point is that all of the religions are different, but this is not a problem; instead, it is a gift as it affords all of us with the opportunity for what Cobb calls mutual transformation and Griffin describes as purification and enrichment.

Cosmosyntheism's 5 Mutually Grounding Ultimates and the Religions

Gnosticism
Judaism
Islam
Christianity
Hinduism
Zoroastrianism
Sikhism
Confucianism
Baha'i

Neo-Confucianism
Hinduism
Jainism
Contemporary Paganism
Indigenous
Daoism
Physics / Chemistry / Biology

Buddhism
Sikhism
Theoretical Physics
Cosmology

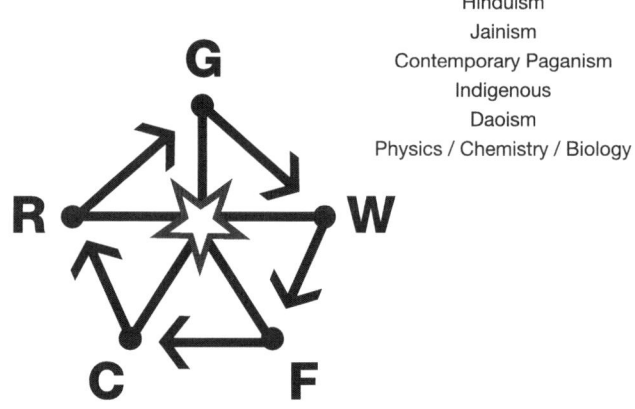

G

R   **W**

C   **F**

Buddhism
Daoism
Physics / Cosmology
Jainism

Platonic Mysticism
Indigenous / Shamanic
Neo-Confucianism
Gnosticism

Part III: Cosmosyntheism vs. the Five Rival Contenders

The rest of this chapter will be devoted to explaining how and where some of the world's religions fit within the pentad of Cosmosyntheism. I will employ the five ultimates—Forms, God, a Cosmos, Creativity, and the Receptacle—as the major headings throughout the chapter and then proceed to explicate which religions primarily focus on this specific ultimate. It should be noted that this chapter along with the preceding chapter, *both deal with the first and third criteria for any successful constructive theology in the twenty-first century: deal with religious pluralism and logical consistency*. I will argue throughout this chapter that only Cosmosyntheism adequately deals with the first criterion by more rigorously fulfilling the third criterion.

Another objective of this chapter is *to highlight the most pressing areas needed for purifying dialogue*, meaning dialogue between similar religious traditions. The reason why this task is so critical is because violence and wars often erupt *over religious views which are similar*; the similarity making each religion a potential threat to one another's truth claims. Most wars are fought with neighbors and neighbors frequently share some of the same cultural and therefore, religious and philosophical implications. In other words, *purifying dialogue must come first and then enriching dialogue with members of more distant faiths can follow*.

The Forms

By explicitly separating the Forms out as their own unique category of religious ultimacy some additional religions can properly be understood as addressing a valid and authentic element of Ultimate Reality. It must be remembered that I am using the Forms in a manner which transcends their usage in the Platonic tradition. Cosmosyntheism follows Plato in describing *some* of the Forms as eternal models and archetypes which act as blueprints for the creation of possible objects, ideas and courses of action within the material world, but it also sees *some* Forms as not being eternal and *arising within the course of time* either in the world or in the mind of God. The Forms, whether of the eternal limited set, or the novel arising variety, both act as guides for the creation of future actions and objects or as avenues for reflection and contemplation. In short, the Forms represent possibilities and ideas. The shift in language to talking of possibilities is reflected in both the perennial philosophy and in Whitehead, although both Whitehead and the perennialists seem to believe all the Forms are or must be eternal.

The three ultimate approach of Cobb and Griffin subsumed the Forms under the category of God, but since Cosmosyntheism suggests that Forms have eternally resided in *both* a cosmos and God, the Forms are instead viewed as a unique and separate, yet obviously interrelated element comprising Ultimate Reality. With the Forms distinguished in this manner, many of the indigenous religions can find a more suitable place within the overall system of Ultimate Reality. However, it is not just primal or indigenous religions which best occupy this category; Platonic mysticism and Neo-Confucianism also find their place here.

Conflicting Religious Truth Claims Part 2

The most poignant example of the Forms viewed as a distinct ultimate within primordial religious traditions is the concept of Dreamtime or the Dreaming in the religion of the aboriginal peoples of Australia. Although there are regional variations of this concept which lead to different interpretations of the Dreamtime, one dominant interpretation found among the Lardil people of Mornington Island sounds as if it could have been taken straight from Plato.

> The Lardil believe Dreamtime is something that came into being (or perhaps more accurately, has always existed) before the appearance of humans, and it is a time that will continue after humans cease to exist. In some unexplained way, a split occurred in Dreamtime and as a result, the time of this world in which we live came into existence. The two times, Dreamtime and the time of this world, exist parallel to one another so that there are two streams of time. For the Lardil, the everyday secular world in which they live is only an imitation of Dreamtime. It is not true reality. True reality is Dreamtime. The secular world is subject to changes, to growing old and dying. But Dreamtime is timeless and unchanging.[1]

This belief in a realm of eternal archetypes or Forms that parallels our world is a fairly widespread belief among many indigenous cultures. As in the above example, it is this other realm that is somehow more real than our everyday world. I disagree with this interpretation of a realm of Forms, but it only further proves my point that certain cultures have latched on to one or more of what I believe are five elements comprising Ultimate Reality.

The religious evidence supporting the existence of the Forms goes beyond ancient Australia. It can be argued that all of Chinese society is grounded in the belief that the eight trigrams of the *I Ching* or even the early characters of the Chinese language played a critical role as blueprints in the creation of the world. However, the notion of metaphysical principle or *li* in the Neo-Confucian tradition is unequivocal on the point that the primary religious ultimate is principle, which is similar to the notion of the Platonic Forms.[2] "All things under heaven can be understood in the light of their principle. As there are things, there must be their specific principles. One thing necessarily has one principle."[3] This one-to-one correspondence between a thing and a Form is actually similar to the Plotinian view found in book V.7.

The most famous Neo-Confucian—Zhu Xi—following in the tradition of Cheng Yi, makes even more explicit the fact that principle comes first and is truly ultimate. "In the universe there has never been any material force (qi) without principle (li) or

---

1. Charlesworth, Dussart, and Murphy, *Aboriginal Religions in Australia*, 9.

2. The similarities between the Neo-Confucian concept of principle, or *li*, and the Greek conception of Forms has been addressed by such major Chinese scholars as Fung Yu-lan in *A Short History of Chinese Philosophy*, 507–8.

3. Cheng Yi, *I-shu* selected sayings in *A Source Book in Chinese Philosophy*, 563.

principle without material force."[4] This is a fascinating line because it clearly proposes multiple ultimates, the material force element will be discussed below under the heading a Cosmos. What concerns us now is that Zhu Xi goes on to claim that, if pressed, principle is prior and more ultimate. "Question: Which exists first, principle or material force? Answer: Principle has never been separated from material force. However, principle exists before physical form and is therefore without it . . . Fundamentally principle and material force cannot be spoken of as prior or posterior. But if we must trace their origin, we are obliged to say that principle is prior."[5] It must be understood that the Neo-Confucians are not referencing an aspect of God, rather they are suggesting similar to Plato, that there are principles that are just somehow out there, but very much real and exercising a dramatic effect on the world and individual things.

Back in Greece, one finds the mystical accounts of the Neo-Platonic philosopher Plotinus, whom we have encountered in the preceding chapters. Plotinus advocated an ascent to the Form of the Good reminiscent of what one finds in Plato's *Symposium*. This return to the Monad or the One is known as *henosis* and for Plotinus it took the form of an ecstatic mystical union. He describes the experience leading from delusion to the soul, to Intellect and finally to *henosis* in book VI of the *Enneads*.

The first stage of ascent consists in a turning away from a selfish and isolated delusion. "If a man could but be turned about, by his own motion or by the happy pull of Athene, he would see at once God and himself and the All. At first no doubt all will not be seen as one whole, but when we find no stop at which to declare a limit to our being we cease to rule ourselves out from the total reality; we reach to the All as a unity" (VI.5.7). Once this first step has been taken, then one opens oneself up to the higher soul which in turn partakes of Intellect where the multiplicity of Forms reside. "Entered there [Intellectual space] and making herself [the Soul] over to that, she at first contemplates that realm, but once she sees that higher still she leaves all else aside" (VI.7.35). The higher still is the One and Plotinus beautifully describes the distinction between the realm of Forms/Intellect and the Monad through the metaphor of a richly adorned house. "Thus when a man enters a house rich in beauty he might gaze about and admire the varied splendor before the master appears; but, face to face with that great person, no thing of ornament but calling for the truest attention, he would ignore everything else and look only to the master" (VI.7.35). This final stage results in the soul, briefly detracted by the opulence of the multiplicity of Forms, finally gazing upon and therefore, wholly identifying itself as one with the Monad, the Form of the Good.

Cosmosyntheism and the Forms in Other Religions

While Cosmosyntheism shares with all of these traditions the belief in the primordial reality of Forms, it is distinguished in two important ways. First, Cosmosyntheism

4. Ibid., 634.
5. Ibid.

advocates that there is genuine novelty, not only for our world, but also for God, and this means that there is not some eternal realm containing *all* Forms or possibilities like Plotinus believes and possibly suggested by the Dreamtime and Neo-Confucians. Second, in contrast to Neo-Confucianism which suggests that principle can somehow be prior to matter and does not require an actual entity, such as God, Cosmosyntheism follows Whitehead in believing that *the type of principle the Neo-Confucians are asserting* requires a deity. I agree that *certain simplistic Forms* do not require a deity, I have been arguing that all along, but Neo-Confucians often mean by *li* moral principles. The moral principles of humanity, righteousness, wisdom etc. are more complex "Ideas" and they seem to demand an actual entity in which they primordially reside. It is for this reason that Neo-Confucians could perhaps benefit from enriching dialogue with our next category of religions, which primarily dwell on God.

God

It is rather clear that the Abrahamic faiths (Judaism, Christianity, and Islam) all belong within the God category due to their shared conviction that there is but one God, the Supreme Being. However, it is less obvious, at least to some Western scholars, that other religions: the Baha'i faith, Sikhism, theistic Hinduism (Vaishnavism) and the early Chinese religions Mohism and Confucianism, all express a generally monotheistic attitude. For example, in Sikhism there is the central proclamation known as the Mul Mantra: *ek ong kar, sat nam, karta purkh, nirbhao, nirvair, akal moort, ajuni, sai bhang, gur prasad, jap, ad such, jugad such, habhe such, nanak hosi bhee such.* Translated this can read, One universal Creator God, the name is truth, creative being personified, no fear, no hatred, image of the timeless one, beyond birth, self existent, by guru's grace. True at the beginning, true through the ages, is yet true, O Nanak, will remain true.

Confucianism in its ancient forms can be understood as expressing theistic elements. In the *Analects*, the concept of *Tian* or Heaven can be seen as being deified. Confucius states in the *Analects* 7:23, "Heaven is the author of the virtue that is in me" and in the *Mencius*, Heaven or Tian even makes decisions, "In that case who gave the empire to Shun? Heaven gave it him . . . In antiquity, Yao recommended Shun to Heaven and Heaven accepted him . . . Heaven sees with the eyes of its people. Heaven hears with the ears of its people" (*Mencius*, 5A:5). Even before the rise of Confucianism during the Zhou dynasty, the preceding Shang dynasty was characterized by the worship of the one high God Shangdi, a fact the early Jesuits exploited to convert the Chinese people to Christianity. The true role and status of *Tian* in ancient China has been debated for millennia. Is *Tian* an existing Supreme Being, some sort of sky God or is *Tian* simply referring to a natural principle of order? This type of nominal or minimalist theism could make for an intriguing dialogue partner with the more explicitly theistic Abrahamic faiths and perhaps suggest ways of reconceiving deity in a more acceptable way for a larger audience in the twenty-first century.

Part III: Cosmosyntheism vs. the Five Rival Contenders

Theistic Hinduism provides another fruitful route for theistic dialogue. One fascinating aspect of certain Hindu texts is the pantheistic or at times panentheistic expressions of deity. In a famous set of lines from the *Bhagavad Gita*, Lord Krishna instructs Arjuna of the royal secret. "I [Krishna] pervade the entire universe in my unmanifested form. All creatures find their existence in me, but I am not limited by them. Behold my divine mystery!"[6] The monotheism of the text is revealed throughout with Krishna being the supreme Lord, however, in some verses it is especially clear that Krishna is the one true God. "I am the father and mother of this universe and its grandfather too; I am its entire support . . . I am the beginning, the staying and the end of creation I am the womb and the eternal seed."[7]

Aside from panentheism, another intriguing talking point for purifying dialogue between theistic Hinduism and Abrahamic faiths can be found in these profound words of Krishna. "Those who worship other gods with faith and devotion also worship me, Arjuna, even if they do not observe the usual forms."[8] This early pluralistic and open view is one of the great strengths evident in many forms of Hinduism. Other religions could do well to incorporate this accepting stance, perhaps shifting the focus from proselytizing and conversion to a mutual respect and deepening of faith.

The above religions should be allowed into and thoroughly engaged in any future interreligious dialogue among monotheists. The discussion needs to broaden beyond dialogue between members of only the Abrahamic monotheisms. By including these other religious traditions, their unique perspectives on monotheism can be understood and hopefully, used to purify and enhance the views of Abrahamic faiths. Although any dialogue is good dialogue, there are certain themes which stand out with a sense of urgency for the theistic religions in particular.

I propose that the following six philosophical and doctrinal issues should be given a place of prominence within any future dialogues between theistic faiths because of the major rifts or just sheer confusion that these topics have caused.

1. Trinity
2. Eschatology
3. Incarnation
4. Messiah
5. Paraclete
6. God's Transcendence, Immanence or Both

---

6. *The Bhagavad Gita*, 173.
7. Ibid., 175.
8. Ibid., 176.

Trinity

The Trinity is perhaps the most unique and mind-boggling aspect of some theisms because it suggests a monotheism that is at the same time a plurality of personas. The issue gets very complicated, at least with the Christian Trinity, because the three personas of Father, Son and Holy Spirit are not different modes (heresy of modalism) nor different entities (heresy of tritheism), but as Tertullian states, "one in essence but not one in person." This idea of *homoousis* or of the same substance between the Father and the Son sounds too similar to polytheism to some of the other Abrahamic faiths.

The Qur'an states in multiple passages that the Christian Trinity represents polytheism and false teaching. "O followers of the Book! Do not exceed the limits in your religion, and do not speak lies against Allah, but speak the truth; the Messiah Isa [Jesus] son of Marium is only an apostle of Allah and his Word which he communicated to Marium and a spirit from Him; believe therefore in Allah and His apostles, and say not, Three. Desist, it is better for you; Allah is only one God; far be it from his glory that He should have a son" (Qur'an 4:171). This anti-Trinitarianism is also seen reflected in the following verse of the Qur'an, "Certainly they disbelieve who say: Surely Allah, He is the Messiah, son of Marium; and the Messiah said: O children of Israel! Serve Allah, my Lord and your Lord. Surely whoever associates others with Allah, then Allah has forbidden to him the garden, and his abode is the fire" (Qur'an, 5:17). In addition to these two verses there are two other Qur'anic passages which express a strictly monotheistic view.[9]

The Trinity is a critical issue for dialogue especially among Christians and Muslims because it represents one of the few major doctrinal differences[10] and it is likely that through dialogue a more accurate understanding on both sides can be reached concerning precisely what each religion believes about the Trinity and about the nature of God in general. However, discussion about the Trinity should not be limited to Muslims and Christians because a Trinitarian structure can be found in many of the world's religions. For example, in Hinduism there is the *Trimurti* or Trinity of Brahma the creator, Vishnu the preserver and Shiva the destroyer or transformer. In Buddhism, there is the notion of the *Trikaya* or three Buddha bodies doctrine consisting of *nirmanakaya* or the physical body, *sambhogakaya* or body of mutual enjoyment and the *dharmakaya* or body of truth. These various trinities share some similarities to each other but are also radically different and this remains a fruitful area for further interreligious dialogue.

---

9. See Qur'an 5:75 and 5:116.

10. Another major difference is the view of Jesus' crucifixion where Islam takes a docetic view arguing that he only appeared to die on the cross. See Qur'an 4:156.

Part III: Cosmosyntheism vs. the Five Rival Contenders

Eschatology

The study of the end times or eschatology has become vitally important within 21st century interreligious dialogue. The problem is that certain groups are convinced that recent events such as increasing natural disasters, terrorism, climate change, technology and the Jews returning to the Holy Land represent the beginning of the end foretold in Revelation and other prophetic literature. Christian Zionists, Millenialists and other groups should at least make an effort to engage with differing opinions and interpretations of texts like the book of Revelation in order to avoid some possibly dangerous consequences. Perhaps recent events are signs of the coming apocalypse, but that does not mean that anyone should attempt to further this process by say trying to rebuild the Jewish Temple complex on top of the Temple Mount in Jerusalem. Another example of potentially damaging understandings of the end times is the tactic so often misunderstood of the promise of seventy-two virgins given to the faithful. This particular Hadith has an *extremely weak chain of transmission* meaning that it is almost certainly inauthentic and therefore, Muslims and Christians should both stop using it for polemical purposes.

Incarnation

Incarnation or God becoming flesh is usually understood as a Christian issue but once again, there are important parallels to Hinduism and Buddhism. In Hinduism, the avatars of Vishnu in particular represent the ongoing role of Vishnu as preserver of creation. Vishnu at least according to the *Garuda Purana* takes on many different forms over successive avatars or descents from heaven, ranging from a fish, to a boar, to the historical Buddha. Likewise, in Buddhism, the idea of bodhisattvas and lamas suggest the notion of intentional reincarnation for the purpose of guiding additional sentient beings to enlightenment. Once again, all of these ideas are similar yet quite different and provide fertile ground for debate and discussion.

Messiah

Was Jesus the messiah or was it Simon bar Kochba or someone yet to come? The proper answer to this question all depends upon what one expects of the messiah or anointed one. Obviously, Jesus' mission did not reclaim the Holy Land as many Jews had hoped for, but suggested a Kingdom of Heaven instead. However, the differences in opinion as to what the messiah actually is and is supposed to do has resulted in extremely unfortunate consequences—mainly for Jews—who have been persecuted for centuries often times because of their "lingering sin for killing the messiah." Luckily we live in a more enlightened age, a global age, where we can actually talk with one another to come to a clearer understanding of what we all mean when we speak about a particular word or concept. As Cobb says, "We must work together repeatedly to clarify the difference between what Jews mean by Messiah and what Christians legitimately mean by Christ." When we have done this then "we need to join the Jews in their longing for the coming of the Messiah and the messianic age."[11]

Paraclete

Similar to the debate between Jews and Christians over the meaning of messiah is the debate that has resulted between Christians and Muslims over the term *paraclete*. In Christianity, the paraclete refers to the "comforter or advocate," which is identified as the Holy Spirit. However, in John 14:16 Jesus suggests that he will ask the Father to send another comforter. "And I will ask the Father, and he will give you another Advocate, to be with you forever." Whereas most Christians simply understand this to mean the Holy Spirit, later religious figures such as Mani, Montanus and most importantly, Muhammad, have either self-identified as the paraclete or in the case of Muhammad, have been seen by interpreters to be the paraclete. This attempt to go back into older religious texts to justify a current prophet or religious founder is a familiar practice. Christians appropriated passages from the Hebrew Bible in order to prove Jesus' authority as the messiah and some Muslims have done the same with the common result that this practice always increases the likelihood of future trouble between the two faiths.

God's Transcendence, Immanence or Both

One final point of confusion between theistic truth claims concerns whether or not God's nature is either wholly external and transcendent or fully immanent and internal. In general, the Abrahamic faiths have opted for the former answer whereas Hinduism and some forms of Western pantheism have suggested the latter. The third option, which represents the position of Cosmosyntheism, Process Theology, and some forms of Hinduism like that expounded by Ramanuja, is that God is both transcendent and immanent. The idea that God has a unique, transcendent character while also being immanent within the other creatures of the world is often associated with the theological position known as panentheism or all things within God. There are advantages and disadvantages to each one of these theological approaches to the nature of divinity and whichever approach one takes will color much of the remaining theology. Since this issue exercises such immense influence on how the rest of a religion's theology and doctrine unfolds, it should represent a significant topic for any purifying dialogue.

---

11. Cobb, *Transforming Christianity and the World*, 86–87.

Part III: Cosmosyntheism vs. the Five Rival Contenders

Cosmosyntheism and the Other Theisms

Regardless of the differences that are apparent among the existing theistic religions, they all share the important insight that there is a divine being of some kind that is capable of agency and plays an integral role in our lives and the universe at large. Cosmosyntheism shares this general assertion as well as the insights that God is somehow a critical element for the creation, sustaining and transforming of the cosmos. Beyond these basic points of similarity Cosmosyntheism parts ways with other forms of theism in ways that I have already discussed in part II.

A Cosmos

When I employ the term a Cosmos, I am referring to some quantity of "primordial chaotic stuff" co-existing with God and not to our particular well-ordered and evolved universe. I have already mentioned how John Cobb Jr. and David Ray Griffin in following Jack Hutchison identify three main types of religion: theistic, acosmic and cosmic. Cobb believes that certain primal religions and Daoism fall under this third category, but I disagree. It is not that primal religions cannot be classified under this heading, it is just that they do not fit under this category for the reason that Cobb thinks they do. Cobb believes their focus on nature and the totality of things constitutes an ultimate cosmic religious perspective, but this is too ambiguous.

As I said in the previous chapter and in chapter 1, focusing on the earth as a whole or even our universe in its current state is technically too specific to constitute a worship of one of the five ultimates. However, that does not mean that these religious perspectives are without value. Aside from this point, I still feel that primal or indigenous religions along with some other traditions should still find a place under the ultimate of a cosmos. Primal religions recognize *the inherent, unique power and capriciousness of the world* and when they understand the cosmos in this more abstract and fundamental manner, they can then properly be understood as being in line with a true religious ultimate.

The following six traditions all appear to recognize and respect the raw power intrinsic to the cosmos: Manichaeism, Greco-Roman religions, primal/indigenous religions, Dvaita Vedanta, Neo-Confucianism, and contemporary paganism. The ordering of these six religions is no accident either because I feel that these traditions can be sub-classified as negative, neutral or positive towards a cosmos as a religious ultimate. In general, Manichaeism and some other Greek and Roman religions/philosophies like Stoicism are going to have a negative view of a cosmos. Many indigenous religions along with Dvaita Vedanta take a neutral or cautious, but respectful position on the issue. However, some groups like Neo-Confucians and contemporary pagans tend to have a positive view of the chaotic power residing in a cosmos.

Negative Views

There is no doubt that Manicheans advocated a primordial dualism between light and dark or spirit and matter. These two principles are both co-eternal and in conflict with one another from the very start. What is interesting is that in the beginning, matter or what is similar to what I mean by a cosmos, gains the upper hand in the battle, defeating and imprisoning the light.

> At the beginning stands the undeducible antithesis of the world of light and the world of darkness or of the good and the evil principle. The ruler of the realm of light, which is located in the North, has various names: Father of Greatness, King of the Paradise of Light . . . Darkness, or Hyle (matter), which is located in the South, also has a king and five worlds . . . Driven by its [matter's] inherent agitation, the night of darkness comes to the borders of the realm of light and begins, filled with jealousy, to fight against it . . . The primeval man now descends to fight the darkness but is vanquished and leaves his fivefold soul to the underworld.[12]

What I find particularly intriguing is that it was matter's *inherent agitation* that led to the initial conflict and commingling of light and dark; this conception resonates well with the contemporary view of a wildly restless quantum realm.

Mani's attempt at synthesizing all of the existing world religions was one of the great success stories in religious history, but it was his fundamental dualism that got him into trouble with Christians. Nevertheless, his proposal of two primeval powers represents a fine example of a religious group that at least recognized the truth and pragmatic value of multiple ultimates, although Mani undoubtedly had an extremely negative view of matter and its effects like many other Greek philosophers of the day. "The body is the dark, evil, component of man, which in death returns to its origin, the darkness, in order to let the soul ascend, in its liberated state, to its place of origin."[13] The dualism of the two ultimates of matter and spirit may seem misguided to some like St. Augustine, but in truth, it allows for a simple and lucid theodicy.

This straightforward bifurcation of reality into body and soul or matter and spirit was rather ubiquitous throughout philosophical circles of the day and was not original to Mani. The idea that matter imprisoned the soul and that all of creation consists of matter mixed with Forms goes back to at least Plato. The role of *arche* or material principle as an ultimate in its own right, uncreated by God, can be seen in the Pre-Socratic's concern over which element was primary: water (Thales), fire (Heraclitus), earth or air (Anaximenes, Diogenes of Apollonia) and all the way through to Aristotle's hypothesized prime matter. Perhaps the most interesting of the Pre-Socratics were Empedocles and Anaxagoras who both suggested a plurality of material elements and some sort of ordering and transforming principle such as love/strife for Empedocles

12. Rudolph, *Gnosis*, 336.
13. Ibid., 338.

Part III: Cosmosyntheism vs. the Five Rival Contenders

and *Nous* for Anaxagoras. The positions of Empedocles and Anaxagoras represent another prime example of early systems advocating multiple ultimates and their views on matter bridge the gulf between negative and neutral views on a cosmos as an ultimate.

Neutral Views

In ancient India and China, dualistic philosophies were flourishing which claimed that there must be both a material cause and an efficient or final cause. This dualistic belief can be seen in three of the six classical Indian schools of philosophy (Sankhya, Yoga, and Vedanta) as well as in Neo-Confucianism from the Song-Ming through to the Ch'ing dynasty. Unlike the Gnostic and Greek views which were strongly against the body and saw it as an evil, the Indian schools of Sankhya, Yoga and Dvaita Vedanta understood the body and matter as neutral in its own nature. It is ignorance of the true pluralistic nature of reality which causes one's *jiva* or self to become self-identified with the body and the material world.

It is interesting to note that Indian philosophy is not universally monistic and world-negating as it is often portrayed to Westerners due to the strong hold of Advaita Vedanta on the minds of influential Western scholars. In fact, some of the oldest interpretations of the Vedas and Upanishads suggest that the greatest truth is a dualism between *Purusha* or spirit/consciousness and *Mula-Prakriti* or primordial matter. Sankhya philosophy like Mimasa and Dvaita philosophy suggest that there are a plurality of *jiva* or *purusha*. This belief in multiple souls/centers of consciousness is directly opposed to the Advaita belief in the fundamental Monistic unity described in the formula—*Atman* is *Brahman*. The truth of the matter is that most Indian philosophy (Sankhya, Yoga, which follows the Sankhya metaphysics and Dvaita) is dualistic rather than monistic, with one of the elements in the dualism always being something akin to what I mean by a cosmos.

The most recent of these Indian dualistic schools is Dvaita Vedanta, which reveres Srimad Ananda Tirtha as their main guru who is better known as Madhvacharya. Dvaita does differ somewhat from both Sankhya and Yoga philosophy mainly in its strongly monotheistic character, but they all share a belief in the dual yet interrelated nature of reality. What Madhva points out against the beliefs of the Advaitans is that the world is not illusory and it is also not the result of Brahman breaking himself apart. Instead, the world is a product of Vishnu or Ishvara's conscious will to create, wherein Vishnu utilized *prakriti* to form and shape the material world. However, rather than simply two elements comprising Ultimate Reality, Madhva suggests, in line with older Sankhya tradition, that there are three. Madhva posits a doctrine of real difference between each of the individual souls or *jiva* and between all of the various souls and the Supreme Lord. "Five fundamental, eternal and real differences exist in his system: 1.) Between the individual soul (or *jîva*) and God (Ishvara or Vishnu). 2). Between matter (inanimate, insentient) and God. 3). Among individual souls (*jîvas*)

4). Between matter and *jiva*. 5). Among various types of matter. These five differences are said to make up the universe."[14]

The Dvaita philosophy of three entities and five differences is succinctly summarized by a disciple of Madhva in the Prameya-shloka which outlines the nine tenets of Dvaita Vedanta.

> In Sriman Madhva's doctrine: 1. Hari (Vishnu) is Supreme. 2. The world is true and real. 3. The differences are real 4. The classes of souls are cohorts of Hari. 5. The souls reach different ultimate states. 6. Liberation is the experience of the joy of one's own nature; 7. Liberation is achieved by flawless devotion 8. Correct understanding and observation, these are indeed the sources of knowledge, 9. Hari alone is praised in all the Vedas.[15]

Of these nine tenets the first three stand out because they show that both God and a world are real and finally that the differences between them are also real.

The Indian belief in the fundamental necessity of more than one ultimate can also be seen reflected in all forms of Neo-Confucianism. I have already addressed the impact that Zhu Xi had on Chinese culture, but he can provide even further clues as to precisely how Confucians of the Song-Ming dynasty understood the role of matter or a Cosmos. "Principle attaches to material force and thus operates . . . What are called principle and material force are certainly two different entities. But considered from the standpoint of things, the two entities are merged one with the other and cannot be separated with each in a different place. However, this does not destroy the fact that the two entities are each an entity in itself."[16] The point for Zhu Xi is that principle needs material force so that it can be efficacious, principle needs a substratum with which to adhere and this is material force.

The proof that both principle and material force are intermingled is also expressed by Zhu Xi. "Question: What are the evidences that principle is in material force? Answer: For example, there is order in the complicated interfusion of the yin and yang and of the Five Agents (wood, metal, earth, fire and water). Principle is there. If material force does not consolidate and integrate, principle would have nothing to attach itself to."[17] In other words, the evidence that both exist is that there are tangible things as is self evident to our five senses, but the phenomenal world is clearly well-ordered and this proves that principle is there as well.

For Zhu Xi, principle is superior to material force and has a logical priority, but for later Neo-Confucians such as, Wang Fu-Chih and Yen Yuan, this idea is turned upside down and we come one step closer to an actual worship of a Cosmos as a religious ultimate. Wang Fu-Chih states, "The world consists only of concrete things. The way is

14. Taken from Madhvacharya's Hindu commentary on the *Paramopinshad*.
15. The Prameya-shloka of Vyasatirtha.
16. Zhu Xi, *I-shu*, in *A Source Book in Chinese Philosophy*, 636–37.
17. Ibid., 635.

Part III: Cosmosyntheism vs. the Five Rival Contenders

the Way of concrete things."[18] Wang continues saying, "Principle depends on material force. When material force is strong, principle prevails. When Heaven accumulates strong and powerful material force, there will be order, and transformations will be refined and daily renewed."[19] This shift to favoring material force over principle can be viewed as admiring the raw power of a Cosmos over that of a realm of Forms.

It should be noted that although I have classified Neo-Confucianism as neutral in its attitude toward the role of matter, it is true that at times even the great masters like Zhu Xi identify the material world as the cause of evil. As Yen Yuan notes, even Zhu Xi said, "What is called evil is due to material force."[20] However, Yen Yuan correctly points out that the problem with this belief is based on the fact that material force and principle are either united or material force is produced from principle. "If we say that material force is evil, then principle is also evil, and if we say that principle is good, then material force is also good, for material force is that of principle and principle is that of material force. How can we say that principle is purely and simply good, whereas material force is inclined to be evil?"[21] Instead of placing the source of evil within matter, Yen Yuan rightly suggests that *matter is merely the means through which evil enters*. By this Yen Yuan means that matter can lead to obsessive attractions and agitations and these can result in the rise of evil. "Evil is due to attraction, obscuration and bad influence."[22] This shift towards a more positive view of matter or a Cosmos as an ultimate puts Yen Yuan on the brink between a neutral view and an explicitly positive view.

Positive Views

Contemporary paganism is a blanket term covering a diverse and fertile ground of new religious movements, many of which are positively inclined towards nature as a religious ultimate. Wicca represents the largest sub-group under the heading of contemporary paganism.[23] For Wiccans, the power of nature and objects within nature and the cosmos at large play a pivotal role. Wiccans accept and utilize the classical five elements of earth, air, fire, water and spirit in the opening of many of their rituals. The elements are often called out during the consecration of sacred space, which regularly takes the form of a magical circle, which is the shape most frequently employed for ritual work. Each element corresponds to one of the four cardinal points, with spirit taking its place at the center of the circle.

In addition to working with the five classical elements, Wiccans have two central rites that show their reverence for the power of nature. The first rite is the drawing of the

18. Ibid., 694.
19. Ibid., 697.
20. Zhu Xi, *Chu Tzu yü-lei* (Classified Conversations of Chu Hsi), 1880 ed., 4:9b.
21. Yen Yuan, in *A Source Book in Chinese Philosophy*, 704–5.
22. Ibid., 706.
23. Cf. Gardner, *Witchcraft Today*; and Gardner, *The Meaning of Witchcraft*.

moon which involves the high priestess "aspecting" the deity Hecate and the powers of the moon. During this invocation, the high priestess temporarily becomes the god form, either through full trance, or more frequently, a partial trance state. While in trance, counsel, divination, healing, or enchantment can be accomplished. The second rite is the Great Rite, which is either a symbolic (dipping of an athame within a chalice) or literal (sexual congress) merging of the male and female powers within nature. Sometimes this rite and others can be incorporated with the Rite of Pan which is a powerful invocation of the capricious power of nature and the cosmos whereby Pagans pay homage to the unpredictable and random elements of life. In fact, all forms of contemporary paganism share the belief that *"magic" is real and represents an unpredictable but natural, not supernatural, force within the world; a power which pervades all of nature and which the practitioner can access and manipulate through imagination and willpower.* In Wicca, there is an acceptance of both the body and the phenomenal world. The body and nature are understood as sacred rather than something evil which should be controlled or transcended; this qualifies Wicca as having a positive view of a cosmos.

This positive view towards the inherent energy and freedom within nature is shared by other contemporary pagans such as Neo-Druids and the Church of Satan. Whereas Wicca and Druidism can be seen as theistic, either polytheistic, duotheistic, pantheistic or panentheistic, the Church of Satan represents an atheistic philosophy. Nevertheless, Satanists are keenly aware of the power within nature and the liberating effect of embracing the phenomenal world to its limits and the liberation that can come through transgressing cultural taboos.

> Satanists do not believe in the supernatural, in neither God nor the Devil. To the Satanist, he is his own God. Satan is a symbol of Man living as his prideful, carnal nature dictates. The reality behind Satan is simply the dark evolutionary force of entropy that permeates all of nature and provides the drive for survival and propagation inherent in all living things. Satan is not a conscious entity to be worshipped, *rather a reservoir of power inside each human to be tapped at will.* Thus, any concept of sacrifice is rejected as a Christian aberration—in Satanism there is no deity to which one can sacrifice.[24] (emphasis mine)

What the above amounts to saying is that Satan is merely a symbol for humanity's innate nature, which is unpredictable, at once simple and savage and also complex and intellectual. Rather than repressing a major portion of our being which is still very much linked to animalistic behaviors and impulses, we should instead embrace the power inherent within our material nature.

All of the groups mentioned thus far as having a positive view of an ultimate that can be defined as a cosmos or as "nature" more generally, are frequently focusing on a particular aspect of nature, either a force within the natural world, or a power innate in man. There is however, one group that makes explicit positive references to a religious

---

24. See Lavey, *Satanic Bible*.

Part III: Cosmosyntheism vs. the Five Rival Contenders

ultimate that can be identified with what I mean by the more abstract term a cosmos and that group is known as the Illuminates of ThanatEros. The founder of the Illuminates of ThantEros (IOT) is Peter Carroll and he helped inaugurate what could be understood as post-modern occultism. There is a strong emphasis on the role of Chaos and on applied paradigm shifting, which is actually a form of worship of the erratic power of chaos. Many of the IOT's beliefs are indebted to the quasi-religion: Discordianism.

> The force which initiates and moves the universe, and the force which lies at the center of consciousness, is whimsical and arbitrary, creating and destroying for no purpose beyond amusing itself. There is nothing spiritual or moralistic about Chaos. We live in a universe where nothing is true, although some information may be useful for relative purposes. It is for us to decide what we wish to consider meaningful or good or amusing. The universe amuses itself constantly and invites us to do the same. I personally applaud the universe for being the stupendous practical joke that it is. If there were a purpose to life, the universe, and everything, it would be far less amusing. We could only go sheepishly along with it or fight an heroic but futile battle against it. As it is, we are free to grasp whatever freedoms are available and do whatever we fancy with them.[25]

Immediately following these statements, the author breaks out into a laudatory hymn in which chaos is thanked and even worshiped. "Oh let me worship the randomness of things, for all that I have ever loved has come forth from it and will be taken away by it. Chance!"[26]

These seemingly bizarre remarks are not as strange as they may at first appear. The point that Peter Carroll is trying to drive home is that the nature of the universe is chaotic, and so we should embrace rather than fight a losing battle against this fact. Through embracing randomness, there is true liberation and freedom. As Carroll states, "hell is the condition of having no alternatives."[27] The IOT provides rituals and methods for enriching one's life through embracing chaos. "The purpose of Chaos rituals is to create beliefs by acting as though such beliefs were true. In Chaos rituals, you fake it until you make it, to obtain the power that a belief can provide. Afterword, if you have any sense, you will laugh it off and seek the requisite beliefs for whatever you want to do next, as Chaos moves you."[28]

This sort of radical paradigm shifting which suggests that, "it is better to build upon the shifting sands than the rock, which will confound you on the day it shatters,"[29] allows an individual to "turn and face the tidal wave of Chaos from which philosophers have been fleeing in terror for millennia."[30] Undoubtedly this lifestyle is

25. Carroll, *Liber Null & Psychonaut*, 154.
26. Ibid.
27. Carroll, *Liber Kaos*, 79.
28. Ibid., 75.
29. Ibid., 77–78.
30. Ibid., 79.

not for everyone, but it is undeniably clear that chaos is viewed as the only thing truly ultimate and at times, although Carroll would likely disagree to be classified in such a way, this chaoism with its rituals of invocation and laudatory hymns sounds awfully religious in nature. As far as I am aware, it is only with this group that the power of chaos is worshipped, revered and recognized as the Ultimate Reality.

Cosmosyntheism and the Traditions that Focus on a Cosmos

Cosmosyntheism is in agreement with all of these religions and philosophies that one element of what can be called Ultimate Reality is a primordial world of "stuff" that behaves chaotically. However, unlike the majority of these traditions which have a negative attitude toward this ultimate, *Cosmosyntheism strongly emphasizes the need to sanctify the role of chaos within the bigger picture*. We know nowadays that existing on the edge of chaos is the ideal state for maximum productivity and creativity and so the Dark Age view that chaos and matter are the roots of all evil must be overturned.

Concerning Neo-Confucianism, Cosmosyntheism shares the belief that principle cannot exist without matter to act as a material substratum for the principle to inhere into. This idea found in Cheng Yi, Zhu Xi, and others is similar to Whitehead's famous ontological principle where Forms of necessity require an actual entity of some kind. However, it is with the IOT and their positive appraisal of the role of Chaos that Cosmosyntheism finds the most parallels. Although both the IOT and Cosmosyntheism share the belief in the positive role of chaos within the universe, the IOT is dangerously one-sided and paradigm shifting is not something that just anyone should engage in. Instead, paradigm shifting is only a tool that is effective once a person already has a fairly strong moral and intellectual foundation. Without this prior grounding, radical paradigm shifting can quickly cause one to spiral out of control and result in total chaos and anarchy, which leads to destruction rather than further novelty. The IOT explicitly draws parallels between the capriciousness and spontaneity of Chaos and the ever-changing Dao and indeed there are similarities, but as I will show, Daoism is more adequately classified under our next heading: Creativity.

Creativity

Throughout history, Daoism and Buddhism have paid special attention to the ephemeral and fleeting nature of all things. For Daoists an in-depth analysis of the world awakened the insight into the ever-elusive concept of the Dao or Way. In making the Dao the central subject of concern, Daoists uncovered the importance of *wu-wei* and *ziran*. The Buddhists likewise have stressed the crucially important insight of *pratitya-samutpada* or dependent co-origination. This fundamental breakthrough led to other key Buddhist concepts, such as *anatman* and *anicca* or the doctrines of no enduring soul substance and impermanence. I contend that the Dao and *pratitya-samutpada* both represent an awakening into another necessary element of Ultimate Reality: Creativity. I have defined Creativity as a metaphysical force or principle that oscillates, pulling all things together and then back apart, repeatedly. By examining what Daoists and Buddhists have to say about the Dao and *pratitya-samutpada* it will become clear that both of these religions have made explicating the nature of Creativity *at least one of their central tasks*.

In prior chapters, I have explained the basic metaphysics and cosmogony of Daoism and the main point was the unceasing creative power of the Dao. One need look no further than the opening lines of verse 1 of the *DaodeJing* to capture the central concept of creative change. "The Way that can be the way is not the abiding Way." The idea of a ubiquitous, transforming and oscillating or pulsating force is presented in many other points in the *DDJ*. For example, Laozi says, "How Heaven and Earth are like a bellows! While vacuous, it is never exhausted" (*DDJ* 5),[31] and again, "The great Dao flows everywhere" (*DDJ* 34), and also, "In order to contract it is necessary to first expand" (*DDJ* 36). Such is the nature of the great or primordial Dao, to operate on all things, moving them together and apart.

In verse 25 of the *DDJ*, one finds a famous account of the nature of Dao.

> There was something undifferentiated and yet complete, which existed before heaven and earth. Soundless and formless, it depends on nothing and does not change. It operates everywhere and is free from danger. It may be considered the mother of the universe. I do not know its name; I call it Dao. If forced to give it a name, I shall call it Great. Now being great means functioning everywhere. Functioning everywhere means far-reaching. Being far-reaching means returning to the original point. (*DDJ* 25)

This beautiful verse illuminates the similarities between the Dao and what I have been referring to as Creativity. First of all, the Dao is formless yet complete; it is not an informed ultimate like a personal deity. The Dao furthermore, depends upon nothing and does not change, suggesting that it is the one true ultimate requiring no other ultimates. I interpret "it does not change" to mean that its cyclical or oscillating nature is eternal and unceasing. The Dao can be considered the mother of the universe because it gives birth to the ten thousand things and nourishes them. However, the Dao in its far-reaching nature also seems to be capable of pulling all things back in a process of return and renewal. To me this signifies that Daoists are primarily concerned with what I have defined as Creativity, an impersonal ultimate that is an infinite oscillating process rather than an infinite or Supreme Being.

The other major figure in the Daoist tradition, Zhuangzi, provides further evidence in favor of the Dao being associated with Creativity. "Although the universe is vast, its transformation is uniform. Although the myriad things are many, their order

---

31. In this chapter, all references from the *DaodeJing* are taken from *A Source Book in Chinese Philosophy*. I will continue to use the standard in-text abbreviation of *DDJ* followed by verse number.

is one."³² This suggests that the entire universe is subject to the same process of uniform or oscillating transformation. Zhuangzi uses the metaphor of a galloping horse to further explain the nature of Dao as ceaseless transformation.

> Dao has neither beginning nor end. Things are born and die, and their completion cannot be taken for granted. They are now empty and now full, and their physical form is not fixed in one place. The years cannot be retained. Time cannot be arrested. The succession of decline, growth, fullness, and emptiness go in a cycle, each end becoming a new beginning. This is the way to talk about the workings of the great principle and to discuss the principle of all things. The life of things passes by like a galloping horse. With no activity is it not changing, and at no time is it not moving. What shall we do? What shall we not do? The thing to do is to leave it to self-transformation.³³

This passage makes it abundantly clear that Reality is a constant succession of events, the ending of one event merely being the birth of the next. Here one finds a system completely focused on the role of process rather than substance or Being.

The nature of the Dao is motion and this is precisely why one must not get caught up in stagnate rituals and rules of propriety like the Confucians because it severs you from the living flow of the Dao. In order to return to the flow, one must embrace naturalness or spontaneity and non-calculative action or *wei-wu-wei*. As Zhuangzi says, "it is better to leave it to self-transformation." He also famously stated, "In dealing with things, he would not lean forward or backward to accommodate them. To him everything was in the process of destruction, everything was in the process of perfection. This is called tranquility in disturbance."³⁴ The idea of not leaning forward or backward means that one should act spontaneously in the present, rather than leaning on the past or the future.

Many of the foundational concepts of Daoism find a parallel in Buddhism. I will focus on Theravadan Buddhism in this section because it is the oldest form of Buddhism and stands closer to the historical Buddha. The historical Buddha, Siddhartha Gautama, said that the core content of his enlightenment experience was the realization of *pratitya-samutpada* or the dependent co-origination of all phenomena. In the *Majjhima-Nikaya* the Buddha says,

> And I discovered that profound truth, so difficult to perceive, difficult to understand, tranquilizing and sublime, which is not to be gained by mere reasoning, and is visible only to the wise. The world however, is given to pleasure, delighted with pleasure, enchanted with pleasure. Verily such beings will

---

32. *A Source Book in Chinese Philosophy*, 204.
33. Ibid., 206.
34. Ibid, 196.

hardly understand the law of conditionality, the Dependent Origination of everything.[35]

It is reasonable to assume that Siddhartha was primarily concerned with causality and his great revelation was exactly that *all things mutually affect and influence one another through an intricate web.*

Siddhartha identified twelve causal links or *nidana* which engender one another: ignorance, mental formations, consciousness, name and form, six sense gates, contact, sensation, craving, attachment, becoming, birth and death. As the Tibetan *bhavachakra* (wheel of life or transformation) illustrates so well, the twelve *nidanas* and the six worlds[36] with all of their objects, are all interrelated. This mutual dependence creates a massive web or a wheel with a near infinite amount of spokes, each one connecting different portions of the wheel with another point; this is samsara. What Gautama so wisely realized is that each element of reality affects every other aspect of reality and therefore, the idea of any unchanging or eternal substances or objects must be an illusion.

The foundational insight of *pratitya-samutpada* led to three major philosophical implications for early and Theravadin Buddhism: *anatman*, *anitya* and the five *skandhas*. *Anatman* implies that there is no enduring soul substance. The Buddha guides one from first realizing the illusory nature of the body's permanence, to awakening to the fact that one's soul is also an ephemeral or more accurately, a totally false construct. In the *Dhammapada*, the Buddha is found saying the following somewhat macabre words, "Oh, see this beautified image; a mass of sores erected. Full of illness, highly fancied, Permanence it has not, or constancy. Quite wasted away is this form, a nest for disease, perishable. This putrid accumulation breaks up. For life has its end in death."[37] And again, "Knowing this body to be like foam, awakening to its mirage nature, cutting out Mara's flowers, one may go beyond the sight of the King of Death[38]."[39]

Anitya or *Anicca* identifies all things as impermanent, including the soul. "All formations are transient (*anicca*); all formations are subject to suffering (*dukkha*); all things are without an Ego-entity (*anatta*)." Lastly, the five *skandhas* refer to the aggregates which make up a particular thing, which Siddhartha also explains are impermanent. "Form is transient, feeling is transient, perception is transient, mental formations are transient, consciousness is transient."[40] Dwelling on the nature of cau-

---

35. Goddard, *A Buddhist Bible*, 22.

36. The six worlds are the realm of the *devas* or gods, the *asuras* or demi-gods, the world of humans, the world of animals, the world of *pretas* or hungry ghosts and finally, hell. These six worlds represent the possible locations one could be reincarnated into upon death.

37. *The Dhammapada*, trans. Carter and Palihawadana, 28.

38. The King of Death can be understood to be Mara or Yama who spins the wheel of becoming, but if one can exit from the wheel, *a highly disputed issue*, then one may go beyond the sight of the King of Death.

39. *The Dhammapada*, 10.

40. Goddard, *A Buddhist Bible*, 27.

sality was not unique to early Theravadin Buddhism and the later Mahayana texts also thoroughly discuss causality, impermanence and emptiness.[41]

Disregarding the specific implications of the initial insight, what matters most is that Gautama awakened to the truth of how the samsaric wheel operates. Causality functions through an infinite process of momentary events, with each event being the product of the internal relations of all other past events of one's own life, plus the experiences of all the other myriad things. *Pratitya-samutpada*, just like Creativity, ensures that all things are in a state of flux between two modes, one being influenced by the past and the other influencing the near future. This apparent truth allows Siddhartha to prescribe a cure for the ailment plaguing humanity. The ailment is falsely attributing permanence to all things, so the solution is not to attempt to cling or grasp to anything because everything is *anitya* or impermanent and the way to achieve this state of serenity is through the eightfold path.

Cosmosyntheism and the Religions that Focus on Creativity

Cosmosyntheism incorporates the Daoist and Buddhist insistence that nature is in a constant state of flux through the inclusion of Creativity in its metaphysics. The Dao of Daoism is explicitly not a thing, but rather an enigmatic and dark force, constantly performing its task of creating change and novelty within the world. It is the impersonal and processive nature of the Dao which causes me to classify Daoism under Creativity. Daoism also presents a possible solution to a question which has frustrated many process theologians working on epistemology and the process of concrescence. If one is supposed to align one's will with the initial aim received from God, *how is one capable of being sure that they are operating in accordance with God's wishes*? In process epistemology, which Cosmosyntheism for the most part shares, there is incoming data from a multitude of actual entities, not just God, so it is not clear exactly how one can know the source of a message. However, Daoism proposes that through spontaneity, *which is pre-calculative action*, one can be in line with the Dao. This sort of immediate and effortless response to various situations may be one way of dealing with the problem.

Buddhism, process theology and Cosmosyntheism all share a belief in dependent co-origination and the implication that there is no enduring soul substance. The doctrine that all phenomena dependently co-arise is virtually the same doctrine as Creativity, which functions to bring all things into a state of novel togetherness and mutual immanence. However, process theology and Cosmosyntheism do not necessarily accept the notions of karma and reincarnation. In fact, the idea of reincarnation and the assertion that all humans have a "Buddha Body" lead to certain philosophical paradoxes within the Buddhist tradition. It is not that reincarnation is a problem in

---

41. Nagarjuna the great Madhyamaka philosopher provides sustained reflections on causality and emptiness and the famous *Diamond Sutra*, an early Mahayanist text, discusses impermanence and emptiness repeatedly.

and of itself; it only becomes a problem when accepted along with the idea that there is no enduring soul substance. I now turn to the answer to this particular problem.

Receptacle

By the sixth century C.E. there were some real problems being exposed within the Buddhist tradition. Most of these troubles stemmed from ambiguities and inconsistencies concerning certain key doctrines like *anatman/anatta* or the doctrine that there is no enduring soul substance and the precise nature of consciousness. These problems gave rise to a dominant Buddhist school known as Yogacara.

> This school, [Yogacara] which was influential in Tibet and China, represents in part a reaction to the philosophy of Nagarjuna and his failure to resolve certain philosophical questions such as accounting for the nature of error, explaining how the mind creates and objectifies fictions, *accounting for memory within the flux of time*, making sense of suffering, and explaining what or who experiences ultimate truth devoid of discrimination.[42] (emphasis mine)

The Yogacara School came up with an ingenious way of dealing with and integrating prior attempts to explain impermanence and emptiness: the *alaya-vijnana*.

Alaya-vijnana means storehouse consciousness and in the Yogacara tradition this is the eighth and final consciousness. The storehouse consciousness is the only true consciousness and hence it is frequently viewed as synonymous with other key Buddhist notions concerning truth such as, *dharmakaya* and the *tathagata-garbha*. The seven other consciousnesses are: eye, ear, nose, tongue, body, mind and *manas* or self. The seventh—*manas*—is very difficult to comprehend, but in general, it unites all of the other six consciousnesses and *interprets them according to a share of the storehouse consciousness*. This "share" creates the illusion of separateness and a substantial self. Thich Nhat Hanh beautifully describes the role of *manas* and its relationship to the storehouse consciousness. "Manas arises from store consciousness, *turns around and takes hold of a portion of store consciousness,* and regards this grasped part as a separate, discrete entity, a self."[43]

In Yogacara literature the seven consciousnesses are understood as waves on the ocean, with the depth of the ocean being analogous to the eighth or storehouse consciousness, which is the source of all the others. The storehouse consciousness is described as the last to go and first to come, meaning it is the final consciousness to break up at death and the first to arise during rebirth, which makes sense as it is the repository of all one's karma and so *it is the source of identity over time, the sense of self and of memory.*

---

42. Olson, *The Different Paths of Buddhism*, 175.
43. Nhat Hanh, *Transformation at the Base*, 20.

The storehouse consciousness is "perfumed" by the actions and perceptions of the individualized and lower levels of consciousness and this perfuming, results in the future germination of the *bijas* or karmic seeds deposited in the storehouse, which will affect your future actions and perceptions. There are universal and private seeds. The universal seeds explain how we all seem to share common perceptions, such as the sun, moon, stars, trees, cars, etc. The private seeds are what differentiate each of us from one another; they are our body image, personal perceptions, conceptions and actions. What is of central importance is the recognition that the negative seeds deposited do not solely influence and impact you at a later time; they also work destructively on all other people and things.

Sikhism and the Akashic Records

In addition to Yogacara Buddhism, there is at least one other religious tradition that speaks about a cosmic memory bank that pervades higher-dimensional space. Sikhs make mention of something called the Akashic Records. A simplistic definition of the Akashic Records can be found on SikhDharma.org: "The Akashic Records are an etheric record where all actions and deeds are recorded." It is this "cosmic library" that holds all of the information concerning what you have done throughout your life, but also everything that has happened anywhere at any point in time in the universe. This notion of an ethereal plane where hidden knowledge is stored was also extremely attractive to the Theosophical Society and the Anthroposophists of the late 19th and early 20th centuries. Another famous figure who claimed to have worked with the Akashic Records was the twentieth-century prophet and medium Edgar Cayce, who supposedly used the records to heal people, as well as to uncover long lost knowledge, such as the supposed whereabouts of the fabled Atlantis.

The possibility of a repository or receptacle of knowledge is not limited to Eastern traditions. Even in Islam, there is the idea of the *"al-Lawhu 'l-Mahfuz"* or the tablet of destiny. The idea for Sunni Muslims is that all that has happened or ever will happen is written down on this ancient tablet. This does not suggest that a person's action is caused by what is written down on the tablet; instead, it suggests that God, being outside of time and omniscient, knows what one will freely choose throughout one's life.

Cosmosyntheism and the Religions that Focus on the Receptacle

The Yogacarin description of the *alaya-vijnana* is strikingly similar to how I have defined the process of Creativity as *pulling all things into a Receptacle or plane of mutual immanence where everything influences everything else and is then released back out*. The parallels between the Storehouse and the Receptacle are even more dramatic

Part III: Cosmosyntheism vs. the Five Rival Contenders

when one examines the famous verses on consciousness of Vasubandhu[44] and other Buddhists of a similar persuasion. "The function of store consciousness is to receive and maintain seeds and habit energies, so they can manifest in the world, or remain dormant."[45] It is made clear that the Storehouse contains not just some things, but all things, as is evident in the following two verses. "Although impermanent and without a separate self, store consciousness contains all phenomena in the cosmos, both conditioned and unconditioned, in the form of seeds,"[46] and again, "In us are infinite varieties of seeds, seeds of samsara, nirvana, delusion, and enlightenment, seeds of suffering and happiness, seeds of perceptions, names and words."[47]

The idea of mutual immanence is also represented in many verses. "Whether transmitted by family, friends, society or education, all our seeds are, by nature, both individual and collective."[48] Again, "Seeds and formations both have the nature of interbeing and interpenetration. The one is produced by the all. The all is dependent on the one."[49] Finally, one learns that the collective and individual seeds through their interaction result in an unceasing transformation of the Storehouse. "Store consciousness is neither the same nor different, individual nor collective. Same and different inter-are. Collective and individual give rise to each other."[50]

From all of these verses there is a growing body of evidence for a religious ultimate that cannot properly be understood as Creativity within the Buddhist tradition; instead, it appears to fit far more precisely with the idea of a universal Receptacle or repository, such as the one I have suggested as one of the five elements comprising Ultimate Reality. The following key point cannot be overstated—when Buddhists speak about "emptying" that corresponds with what I understand as "Creativity"; however, when Buddhists speak of either "Emptiness/*Sunyata*" or the "*Alaya-Vijnana*" that matches with what I am calling the "Receptacle." *Thus, emptying and emptiness are not synonymous terms within Buddhism and do not refer to the same religious ultimate.* The reason they are not synonymous is because emptying is the never-ending process of coming-to-be and perishing, or breaking off from and returning to the storehouse consciousness. However, Emptiness can mean one of two things: all entities and things lack an unchanging soul or essence, or it can be a reference to the storehouse consciousness, which is empty in its own nature, but full of all the entities, thoughts, ideas, and actions that have entered or "perfumed" it. The only other religion that briefly seems to recognize the need of a cosmic repository or memory bank that accounts for the transformations of all things is

---

44. For more of Vasubandhu's works which have been translated into English, see Anacker, *Seven Works of Vasubandhu*.

45. Nhat Hanh, *Transformation at the Base*, 10.

46. Ibid., 11.

47. Ibid., 9.

48. Ibid., 10.

49. Ibid., 11.

50. Ibid.

Daoism. "Dao is the storehouse of all things" (*DDJ* 62). However, Daoism appears to focus more on the Dao's shifting and capricious nature and its unceasing movement rather than *the Dao as actively remembering all of the events that have unfolded within the world.*

One final point of interest is that Yogacarins, although not wishing to attribute a separate and partially transcendent aspect to the storehouse consciousness, never the less explicitly state that the Storehouse has all five of the mental operations working in a unique way at the eighth level of consciousness, thus suggesting something akin to a deity. "Unobstructed and indeterminate, store consciousness is continuously flowing and changing. At the same time, it is endowed, with all five universal mental formations."[51] I point this out because it seems that anywhere one finds a predominance of interest on just one of the religious ultimates, *aspects of another religious ultimate are implicitly or explicitly grafted on, suggesting the necessity for additional ultimates in order to allow for a more consistent and plausible overall paradigm.*

Cosmosyntheism also finds a parallel with Sikhism and Theosophy with their understandings of the Akashic Records. However, if the suggestion is that the Akashic Records also contain all that will happen in the future, then Cosmosyntheism would be forced to part ways at that critical juncture, as it would seem to submerge us again in the intractable debate over free will. The free will problem also arises when looking for a comparison with Islam's tablet of destiny. For Sunnis everything that ever will happen is written down and their lack of concern for the implications towards free will is most certainly not shared by Cosmosyntheism.

Summary

- All of the religions focus on and discuss the nature and functions of one or more of Cosmosyntheism's five ultimates.

- Purifying dialogue is dialogue with other religions that share the same religious ultimate, whereas enriching dialogue is dialogue with religions that hold to a different religious ultimate.

- Purifying dialogue is a more immediate concern, due to the fact that most wars are fought with neighbors who share a similar cultural and religious background.

- This chapter provided a survey of some of the world's religions and then classified them according to which ultimate is their primary concern. This classification can help to pave the way for future dialogue.

- In addition to categorizing some of the world's religions, I also pointed out how and where Cosmosyntheism either agrees or disagrees with some of the world's religions.

---

51. Ibid., 10.

CHAPTER 13

The Problem of Evil

God is omnipotent; God is wholly good; and yet evil exists.

—JOHN MACKIE, *EVIL AND OMNIPOTENCE*

IN THE PREVIOUS PAGES, I have covered two major problems which arise for most religions and philosophers of religion: the problems of freedom and conflicting religious truth claims. The chapter on the problem of freedom dealt with criterion number three for any successful constructive theology in the twenty-first century, which is to attempt to eliminate or minimize any logical inconsistencies and paradoxes from the proposed system. Chapters 11 and 12 addressed the first criterion, which is to adequately deal with the reality of religious pluralism. The current chapter is related to the concerns of chapter 10 in that both survey possible approaches to eliminating logical problems which confront most all religions and constructive theologies. Whereas chapter 10 dealt with the problem of freedom, this chapter tackles a related but even graver concern, an issue which has presented what has been perhaps the most insurmountable problem for religions and philosophers of religion: evil.

The Problem

Simply stated, the problem is how to reconcile the supposed goodness and unlimited power and knowledge of God or Ultimate Reality, with the obvious fact that there is genuine evil in this world.

The Perennial Philosophy and the Problem of Evil

In typical fashion, the perennial philosophy attempts to distinguish an exoteric solution and an esoteric solution for the existence of evil. The exoteric solution is as follows, "Now as regards the problem of the existence of evil itself, the religious point

The Problem of Evil

of view gives only an indirect and somewhat evasive answer, declaring that the Divine Will is unfathomable, and that out of all evil good will ultimately come."[1] In fact, this is often the answer one hears given as a simple theodicy by members of the monotheistic faiths and I agree it is an unacceptable answer. However, the apparently superior solution offered by the esoteric perspective is hardly any better.

Schuon is under the impression that the esoteric solution can be properly grasped by answering two questions. "From an esoteric point of view the problem of evil resolves itself into two questions: firstly, why do things created necessarily imply imperfection? And secondly, why do they exist?"[2] Schuon proceeds to explain why the answer to these two questions clears up any uncertainties about the necessity of the existence of evil.

> To the first of these questions the answer is that if there were no imperfection in the Creation nothing would distinguish it from the Creator, or in other words, it would not be effect or manifestation, but Cause or Principle; the answer to the second question is that Creation or Manifestation is necessarily implied in the infinity of the Principle, in the sense that it is so to speak an aspect or consequence of this infinity. This amounts to saying that if the world did not exist the Infinite would not be Infinite...The existence of the world is strictly implied in the infinity of the Divine Principle, and the existence of evil is similarly implied in the existence of the world. God is All-Goodness, and the world is His image; but since the image cannot by definition, be that which it represents, the world must be limited relatively to the Divine Goodness, hence the imperfection in existence.[3]

This apparent solution however, is loaded with problems. I may add that it is telling that Huston Smith does not address the problem in his book—*Forgotten Truth*—perhaps because he realizes the perennialist solution is inadequate or possibly because he thinks Schuon and other perennialists have sufficiently answered it.

Problems with the Perennialist Solution

The first issue I have is the equation of imperfection with evil. It is in no way clear to me how imperfections necessarily imply evil. It does not follow that an imperfect world that is a copy of a perfect world must therefore be evil, perhaps the imperfections provide an impetus for ambition and striving toward that which is greater; in this case imperfections would be a good thing. More importantly however, is the problem of God being "All-Goodness," yet also "All-Possibility," and Infinite. If the creation of a world is but one possibility that must reside within an Infinite, *then how is the creation of evil not another genuine possibility residing in that very same Infinite?*

1. Schuon, *The Transcendent Unity of Religions*, 52.
2. Ibid.
3. Ibid., 52–53.

It is not a logical impossibility for God to manifest evil, as it would be for him to say create a stone so heavy that even he could not lift it. It is fully consistent with Schuon's own logic that God should and must create or manifest evil. The likelihood of evil should be equal to that of the manifestation of good, if not; *then God is not All-Possibility*. If God is not All-Possibility, then it becomes apparent that God need not have manifested a world either.

Emanation and the Problem of Evil

As I have shown in the previous chapters, not all emanation theories are the same; sometimes they come up with radically different solutions to problems and sometimes there are significant similarities. Regarding the problem of evil, the solutions once again cover a broad gamut of possible responses. In sticking with the pattern that has been employed thus far, I will begin with the Daoist solution followed by the Hermetic, Gnostic and Plotinian approaches.

Daoism and the Problem of Evil

Everyone is familiar with the iconic image of the *Taiji* circle and the *yin/yang* symbolism. This ubiquitous image can help to explain the first way to deal with the concept of evil. Good and evil are obviously polar opposites and any concept like goodness requires an opposite so that the initial concept can be understood by its relation to the opposing concept. Thus, in order for there to be good in the world, there must be evil as its counterpoint. "When the people of the world all know beauty as beauty, there arises the recognition of ugliness. When they know the good as good, there arises the recognition of evil" (*DDJ* 2). However, the *yin/yang* symbolism also shows how polar opposites are in constant transformation and are mutually engendering, so evil contains the seed of goodness and will eventually transform into it and vice-versa, good will become evil. "Calamity is that upon which happiness depends; happiness is that upon which calamity is latent" (*DDJ* 52).

The question still remains: what role does the Dao play and is it culpable for the calamities which arise from a dualistic perspective? It must be remembered that the Dao engendered all things, including the dynamism of *yin* and *yang*. The answer would appear to be that the polar opposites of good and evil are but linguistic conventions. We name and decide what is good and bad, but the Dao itself is beyond good and evil. The Dao does not play favorites; it just continuously flows and engenders new things, situations and circumstances.

There is a more practical dimension to the problem of evil in Daoism. Undoubtedly, living in line with the Dao is good and fighting against it brings what is normally considered to be bad consequences. This is why Daoists stress *wei-wu-wei* and *ziran* so much because *yu-wei* or calculative thought and *li* or ritual propriety cuts one off from the natural response one would otherwise have had to the present moment. "Therefore, only when Dao is lost does the doctrine of virtue arise. When virtue is lost, only then does the doctrine of humanity arise. When humanity is lost, only then does the doctrine of righteousness arise. When righteousness is lost, only then does the doctrine of propriety arise. Now, propriety is a superficial expression of loyalty and faithfulness, and the beginning of disorder" (*DDJ* 38). It may be true that propriety *can become vacuous ritual* and the beginning of disorder, but what is never clear in any of the Daoist works is exactly how the Dao itself represents order or harmony.

Problems with the Daoist Solution

My primary concern with the Daoist insistence on returning to Dao and unlearning what one has learned is that the Dao is completely unpredictable and erratic. There is no guarantee whatsoever that following the Dao will benefit you, others or anyone. Daoists recommend returning to one's original nature, but *isn't calculative thought one of the defining characteristics that distinguish human nature from the nature of other creatures*? If this is true, then why should we at all times seek spontaneous action? I can accept that there are circumstances where this would be ideal, especially if the Dao was understood to have consciousness or a plan, a sense of purpose; however, this is not how the Dao is conceived in philosophical Daoism. In short, I am far from convinced that the primary cause of evil is calculative thought, ritual and book learning.

Hermetism and the Problem of Evil

Hermetism is unique among early forms of gnosis in that the world is not inherently evil and not the result of an evil demiurge. Instead, creation is the result of the second *nous* as we have seen earlier. This demiurge is not evil and is closer to the craftsman of Plato's *Timaeus*. "In terms of cosmology, there is in Hermetism no idea that the cosmos is bad, or that it has been created by an evil demiurge. Indeed, in some Hermetic texts one can find a kind of cosmic religiosity, the possibility of a mystical experience involving a feeling of oneness with the universe."[4] Evil is therefore, not the result of a nefarious creator God who is intentional seeking to trap human souls from ascending back to the light.

Evil is nonetheless very real and the body, although not necessarily evil, is viewed as imprisoning. The source of evil can be chalked up to three things: (1) the literal distance of the earth from the source; (2) the imperfection inherent in the world as a copy of a perfect original; and (3) an exclusive identification with one's mortal half, the body. Regarding the first point, it must be remembered that the earth lies at the outer boundary of the tenth and final emanation so there is a vast gulf between the one true god and humanity. As for the second point, we have already encountered this

---

4. Pearson, *Ancient Gnosticism*, 276.

idea in the perennial philosophy, that a copy is automatically flawed in comparison to the original. The reason for the third point comes from the archetypal man stooping down and showing himself to nature below and this created a love bond. This love bond between the archetypal man and nature means that humans are half spirit and half matter and evil is the result of over-identification with our material half. "People who have recognized themselves have reached the choicest good. But those who love the body, which derives from the error of burning desire, remain wandering aimlessly in the darkness, perceptibly experiencing the realm of death."[5]

The solution is clearly to obtain gnosis or acquaintance with one's true nature and this frequently requires an ascetic lifestyle. Once one realizes that they are a creature of the light and life rather than darkness and death, then they can ascend back to the one. This ascent is described in the *Poimandres* as passing back beyond the seven controllers or heavenly spheres and at each sphere a vice is given back and one ascends ever higher all the way up to the tenth sphere where one "becomes god." However, while one is still alive, one must adopt an ascetic stance to prepare for the final ascent after bodily death. "First, you must tear off the tunic that you are wearing, the robe of unacquaintance, the foundation of imperfection, the bond of corruption, the dark enclosure, the living death, the perceptible corpse, the portable grave, the resident brigand, who acts in hatred through what he loves and with his instruments of hatred causes corruption."[6]

Problems with the Hermetic Solution

If the One, the source, was co-existing with the "darkness" and "the moist nature," then there would be a plausible way to deny the One's culpability for evil by holding a theological dualism similar to the Manichaeans, but this is emphatically not the case. "That light, it said, is myself, intellect, your god, who is prior to the moist nature that appeared out of the darkness."[7] It seems that the light or intellect emanated everything and therefore, should be culpable for what proceeds out of it.

A separate issue concerns the distance from the One to earth. Why should distance automatically entail a deprecation of the goodness of the source? The same problem exists for the notion of imperfection within a copy. Even if a copy is less perfect than an original, it does not follow that the copy is therefore, evil or inclined towards evil, especially given the fact that the second *nous* (itself a copy) is not evil or ignorant in Hermetism. Finally, the issue of the body being evil may be true in the sense that an over-identification with one's body does lead to selfish and possibly evil acts, but there isn't strong enough evidence that there even is a soul or spirit which would justify such extreme asceticism. In sum, the theodicy of this classical religion/philosophy is not well-suited for the demands and the milieu of the twenty-first century.

5. Layton, *The Gnostic Scriptures*, 456.
6. Ibid., 462.
7. Ibid., 453.

Sethian Gnosticism and the Problem of Evil

The Sethian tractates provide a cunning solution to the problem of evil—split God into two. In truth, there is only the one original God, the Father of All, but during the process of emanation, the final emanation within the pleroma—Sophia—decided to create without the consent of her consort or of the consent of the Father. This breach of the heavenly order resulted in dire consequences. Sophia gives birth to Yaldabaoth, a monster who is cast out into the darkness of the abyss beyond the limit of the pleroma. Evil is the result of Yaldabaoth's further creations in the lower world and his later attempts to enslave humanity in the lower realm through sexuality. It is Yaldabaoth who creates the cosmos with the seven planetary spheres of the classical tradition. It is also Yaldabaoth that creates humanity.

It becomes evident that Yaldabaoth is none other than Yahweh the God of Judaism and that the Hebrew Bible and the Judaism stemming from it is actually the work of this lesser God. "And he [Yaldabaoth] is impious in his arrogance which is in him. For he said, 'I am God and there is no God beside me,' for he is ignorant of his strength, the place from which he had come."[8] Yaldabaoth's association with Yahweh is brought up again later in the text. "And when he saw the creation which surrounds him and the multitude of the angels around him which had come forth from him, he said to them, 'I am a jealous God and there is no God beside me.' But by announcing this he indicated to the angels who attended him that there exists another God. For if there is no other one, of whom would he be jealous?"[9]

The Sethian theodicy consists then in the reinterpretation of the book of Genesis resulting in a demonization of Yahweh by associating him with the ignorant creator: Yaldabaoth. This Gnostic hermeneutic flips the entire Hebrew Bible on its head. This new Gnostic understanding requires that one achieve gnosis and the first step in attaining this gnosis is becoming aware of the real players within the Bible. The One True God, the Father of All in Sethian Gnosticism is twice exonerated from culpability for the world's evils because not only does Sophia fail, but then Yaldabaoth also transgresses the will of the True God. God, much like humans, is nothing more than an innocent bystander in what amounts to a heavenly and then cosmic, drama or tragedy.

Problems with the Sethian Solution

If one is to take the Sethian myth seriously then their theodicy can still be called into question. For example, why wasn't the One True God who is "total perfection" aware of Sophia's intentions and why if he is "goodness giving goodness" doesn't he step in to intervene? In other words, it is not clear how the Monad is exonerated from guilt if the Father could have prevented Sophia's mistake. Even assuming some sort of free will

---

8. *The Nag Hammadi Library*, 111.
9. Ibid., 112.

defense where God could not have intervened to suspend Sophia's will, there is nothing to stop God destroying Yaldabaoth as soon as he was born thus setting straight the pleroma once more.

Plotinus and the Problem of Evil

With Plotinus, one has the advantage of a sustained treatise on the topic of evil, tractate I.8. Plotinus first discusses absolute evil, which would be prime matter. Why is matter associated with evil? The answer to this question for Plotinus is that prime matter lacks form and being formless it is therefore, without the Good because the Good is not only a Form, but the highest Form. As non-being and formlessness, matter does not partake in the Good at all. "Evil is not in any and every lack; it is in absolute lack. What falls in some degree short of the Good is not Evil; considered in its own kind it might even be perfect, but where there is utter dearth, there we have the Essential Evil, void of all share in Good; this is the case with matter" (I.8.5). From this statement, one learns that matter is an absolute lack of the Good and also by implication, the body is not in-and-of-itself evil, because it shares in some Forms like the Form human being. "No, if the body is the cause of Evil, then there is no escape; the cause of evil is matter" (I.8.8). Matter is completely distinct in kind from Form. "In truth it [matter] is a Kind contrary to Form" (I.8.10).

In sum, *Matter is the only thing that is truly evil, whereas derivative evils are only partially evil in that they participate in matter*. However, the reason why matter is evil is that it partakes in less of a share of Being than higher levels like soul. For humans, evil is the result of a turning of the will to lesser goods, which can result in negative or evil consequences for oneself and others. Evil is non-being or nothingness and any willful approach towards nothingness is evil; this idea is taken up and elaborated on by St. Augustine.

Problems with the Plotinian Solution

Plotinus appears to jump around between emanationism and metaphysical dualism in his solution to the problem of evil. The reason that he does this is because if the Monad is the source of everything, then it must be the ground of evil as well. I have shown in the previous chapters that, in general, the position of emanation is the one that Plotinus adopts, but in this section, he appears to waver. Plotinus probably wavers because he recognizes the difficulty that an emanation theory has in explaining evil. Perhaps this is why in a surprising quotation Plotinus appears to suggest a metaphysical dualism.

> But why does the principle of Good necessarily comport the existence of the Principle of Evil? Is it because the All necessarily comports the existence of matter? Yes: for necessarily this All is made up of contraries: it could not exist

> if Matter did not. The nature of this Cosmos is, therefore, a blend; it is blended from the intellectual Principle and Necessity: what comes into it from the God is good; evil is from the Ancient Kind, a phrase which means underlying matter not yet brought to order by Ideal-Form. (I.8.7)

If this was Plotinus's actual metaphysical position then he might have a simple way out of the dilemma: there are two ultimates.

In the end, Plotinus does not advocate two ultimates, instead he sticks with his emanationist framework. "There is another consideration establishing the necessary existence of evil. Given that the Good is not the only existent thing, it is inevitable that, by the outgoing from it or, if the phrase be preferred, the continuous down-going or away-going from it, there should be produced a Last, something after which nothing more can be produced: this will be Evil" (I.8.7). This statement conflicts with Plotinus's earlier suggestion that the All could not exist without matter. One is left wondering which position Plotinus actually holds, presumably the latter, as he frequently advocates a doctrine of emanation. If Plotinus does hold the second position, then the question arises as it always does, if everything came from the One, then how is it not to blame at least in part for the rise of evil? Furthermore, can one even make any sense of a prime matter totally devoid of any Forms that is *either* co-eternal or as the *terminal point* of a temporal chain of emanation; this is rather difficult to imagine.

Classical Theism and the Problem of Evil

When the problem of evil is discussed, it is normally in regard to the classical theism represented in orthodox forms of Judaism, Christianity and Islam. Rather than survey what Jewish, Christian and Islamic authors have said concerning the problem of evil, I will only focus on one author: St. Augustine. The reason for sticking to one author is twofold. The first reason is that all of the Jewish, Christian and Islamic responses more often than not revolve around some form of *free will defense*, so looking at one example will suffice. The second reason for utilizing Augustine's work in particular is that he was preoccupied with the problem of evil his entire life and his response has exerted a tremendous influence over later theologians. Due to the fact that I will only be covering one representative of classical theism, I will alter my normal approach just a bit and examine St. Augustine's solution to the problem of evil on two levels. First, I will provide a quick, yet broad, overview of his thought on the topic and then I will transition into a more in-depth look at the intricacies of his solution.

Augustine's general explanation of the problem of evil highlights three main points: (1) evil is the privation of good; (2) evil is deficient rather than efficient causation and (3) the possibility of evil is always present due to *creatio ex nihilo*. Realizing that God's creation is completely good, Augustine is hard-pressed to account for the origination of evil, but he finds his answer in the freedom of the will which higher beings, such as angelic entities and humans, possess. "I likewise know that when an evil choice happens in any being, then what happens is dependent on the will of that being; the failure is voluntary, not necessary and the punishment is just."[10] It is not that the human body, soul or will are evil in their own natures, this is impossible, as they are both the product of God, but evil arises because of humanity's ability to turn away (*auersio*) from the harmonizing will of God. "I did not know that evil has no existence except as a privation of good."[11] This privation or diminution of the good, first occurred due to the self love and pride of some of the angels in the heavenly retinue who as a result, rebelled against God. The angelic fall causes Satan to envy humanity and to lure Adam and Eve into the original sin of eating of the tree of the knowledge of good and evil.

This is the gist of Augustine's solution, that the will is by nature good and so God allowed humans to have a will, knowing full well that some of us would eventually transgress his divine decrees. When Augustine is pressed even further about how something originally good could fall, he simply responds that we should not be looking for an efficient cause of the fall, but rather for a deficient cause.

> The truth is that one should not try to find an efficient cause for a wrong choice. It is not a matter of efficiency, but of deficiency; the evil will itself is not effective but defective. For to defect from him who is the Supreme Existence, to something of less reality, this is to begin to have an evil will. To try to discover the causes of such defection, deficient not efficient causes, is like trying to see darkness or to hear silence.[12]

In the end, Augustine admits that he does not know how the original fall or turning away from God could have taken place and quotes Psalm 19:12 "who can detect his defects?"

It immediately becomes evident that Augustine is not pleased with his inability to provide an adequate answer to how privation of the good could have originally taken place because he turns right around and attempts to provide some sort of quasi-efficient or material cause for the origin of evil. "This I do know; that the nature of God cannot be deficient, at any time, anywhere, in any respect, *while things which were made from nothing are capable of deficiency.*"[13] This point about being created from nothing is raised repeatedly by Augustine in *The City of God* and it makes sense when interpreted through a Neo-Platonic lens. Augustine was deeply influenced by Plotinus, so it is not surprising that he would have turned to him to attempt to uncover the root of evil. Augustine, in saying that God created out of nothing, was in effect suggesting that matter in the Plotinian sense was involved in the creation of the lower order beings and since prime matter is Formless, it is absolute evil. Humans are contingent and

---

10. St. Augustine, *The City of God*, 480.
11. St. Augustine, *Confessions*, 43.
12. St. Augustine, *The City of God*, 479.
13. Ibid., 480.

a mixture of matter and soul and are thus susceptible to perversion, whereas, God is a necessary and *immaterial being* and therefore, is incapable of any evil.

Since Augustine's solution to the problem of evil becomes the gold standard for nearly all classical theists into the Middle Ages, it is necessary to dig even deeper into his answer to bring out the more subtle and nuanced arguments. At a more specialized level, Augustine's response to the origin of evil actually involves six elements.

1. All of creation whether spiritual or corporeal are made *ex nihilo* or out of sheer nothingness and thus are mutable, but still good in their own way and place.
2. There is a hierarchy of being with some parts of creation partaking in a greater amount of form, measure, number and order.
3. There are at least three classes of goods: material, spiritual (will, reason, memory), and virtues.
4. Evil is not a positive substance or nature but rather, a privation (an absence of goodness where goodness might have been).
5. Evil is the result of *auersio* or the movement by which the mind on its own turns the *freundi voluntas* away from the creator and toward created being.
6. Thus evil is a tending or turning away from God towards non-being. Evil is complete nothingness or non-being.

I will cover all of these in turn as well as incorporate primary and secondary sources where relevant.

Concerning the first point, Augustine frequently states his belief that God created matter itself out of nothingness in contrast to the Greek tradition which allowed for matter to be coeval with God (*Conf.* 13.33.48, *C.Secundinum* 8 etc.). William Mann points out that Augustine's adoption of *creatio ex nihilo* implies, "that God cannot create anything equal to himself. Because every created thing has its origin in non-being, it is mutable. But God is essentially immutable, and any immutable being is superior to a mutable being."[14] The issue of creatures being comprised or fashioned out of non-being is important because it allows for an ontological basis for both a difference from the nature of God and the turning or *auersio* which will be important later. Furthermore, God, *being simple*, is immutable and the highest good and thus provides a security for our reason and our will, that God is the ultimate good.

Augustine, undoubtedly influenced by the Neo-Platonism of his day, especially that of Plotinus, asserts that there is a hierarchy of being and thus, angels are higher than humans and humans than brute animals etc. (*City of God* 11, 16; *In Joann. Ev.* 23.5). The notion of an order and hierarchy within creation is important because the higher the level of being, the greater its partaking of form, measure and order and thus, goodness. However, all things, even the lowest material elements, partake to some degree in being

---

14. Mann, "Augustine on Evil and Original Sin," 42.

(*De lib. arb.* 2.2.54; *De nat. boni c. Man* 3). "No creature then is evil, in spite of the fact that some creatures are worse than others. The word evil when predicated of creatures, refers to privation."[15] One could sum up this point by saying that *no existence is contrary to God, non-existence is contrary to God* (*City of God* 12, 2).

It is a possibility inherent in the nature of the will and the *men* to become deluded and to change from a state of cleaving to the immutable good and turning downward to the lesser created goods. Augustine points out in both *De Libero Arbitrio* (2.20.54, 3.17.48) and in the *City of God* that there is no efficient cause to be found for this turn, instead, it is a deficient cause (*City of God* 12.7) which leads the will down. As with the angels, it is pride that comes before the fall; it is the will and reason desiring to be *causa sui* and to be their own master. Thus, the will turns away from eternal truth and looks within and/or below meaning a focus on either the *psyche* or even lower still: *physis* and *hyle*.

One might object at this point and state, "why would God create us out of nothingness and make our wills capable of defect?" Augustine responds to this by saying, "God judged it better to bring good out of evil than not to let evil exist" (*Enchiridion* 27.8). In other words, God gave us genuine freedom which is better than merely having a mechanical clockwork universe where everything simply unfolds according to an original master plan. We as rational human beings are in a unique position within the hierarchy of beings because our wills are capable of "using a good evilly" (*De nat. boni c. Man* 36). As Emilie Zum Brunner says, "there is a mysterious nihilating power possible in the spiritual created being."[16]

A "conflict of interest" can arise within the mind of men and the deluded pursuit of power, sex and simply curiosity can bring one to commit evil. Thus, the power we have to love and cling to God can become the love of one's own excellence and a desire for perverse elevation, or it can become depraved to the point where the will is led around by the capricious passions of one's brute sexual nature. But why exactly is the act of turning towards these lesser goods evil? It is because they are *ephemeral* and they owe their very existence to the one true God. If one forgets this fact and attempts to find happiness and well being in impermanent and perishable objects and desires, then one will never find the security and permanence which alone can be the proper abode of rest for the soul. Of course, this proper abode is God.

Even in the state of *auersio* all hope is not lost for the soul of man. There is still a semblance of the true form left and this can help one to recognize and accept the call of the Word (*De lib. arb.* 2, 17, 46). Unlike his Neo-Platonic counterparts, Augustine only finds a final consolation in the Christian message because it alone provides a *mediator* between the unbridgeable gulf that lies between our fallen state and True Being or God. "Although these books [the Platonic sources] contain according to him, almost the entire truth concerning God and the soul, in them the mediator is missing.

15. Ibid., 44.
16. Zum Brunn, *St. Augustine*, 42.

This attitude radically distinguished Augustine's Neo-Platonizing Christianity from all doctrine that is exclusively philosophical."[17]

The process and result of an evil will and act can be put in the philosophical language of Augustine's day. *Minus esse*, or partaking in less being is the result of turning away from God, but the soul nevertheless still wants to be (*quia esse uis* and *esse uelle*) and wants to attain rest, it longs for *magis esse* or greater being. However, the soul requires the intermediary, which is Christ, to pull one back up to one's rightful abode and thus attain one's final goal of rest and beatification. Ultimately, it is by the grace of God that we are pulled off the path towards annihilation which was initiated by the will.

In the end, if it is God that is the *bonum supremum* and God is identified as the ground of all being and existence, then evil is non-being and all desires and acts which pursue lesser goods and set up anything other than God as the standard of goodness only result in the hastening of the soul and the body towards complete destruction and nihilation. There can be no conflict of interest, the will must will one thing only and that must never be anything less than God himself. "Only God as the sovereign good is to be enjoyed for its own sake, and only the love of God as the eternal, spiritual and unchangeable good causes the individual to live well and virtuously."[18]

"As I have said, therefore, sin is not a desire for naturally evil things, but an abandonment of better things. And this itself is evil, not that nature which the sinner uses evilly. For evil is to use a good evilly" (*De nat. boni c. Man* 36). Sometimes a man's will to sin is caused by a cognitive defect, say ignorance of the way things are (*De natura et gratia* 29.33). The will is on a par with reason and memory and thus it has the inherent power to reject sound reasoning, justice and memory. However, not all sins originate from ignorance, a point that Augustine admits in *De Libero Arbitrio*. "From whence then will it [the movement down] come? If I respond to your querying that I do not know, perhaps you will be disappointed but nevertheless I will respond truly. For that which is nothing cannot be known."

This is the final point of the ontology of evil: "evil is nowhere because evil is nothing."[19] There is nothing for us to find, nothing for us to know. There is no positive evil substance as in Manichaeism, there is only the improper use of what is itself good, but caught midway between its proper object God and its improper possible obsessions: lesser psychical and physical goods. The failure begins when we confuse love of God with love of self, memory of God with memory of self, willing of God for self-will.[20] The turning away or *auersio* creates a twist which over time becomes knots and entanglements. The mind becomes further confused and mired in despair and

---

17. Ibid., 70.
18. Banner, *The Path of St. Augustine*, 47.
19. Evans, *Augustine on Evil*, 6.
20. For a discussion of this mirrored Trinitarian structure of mistaken loves leading to the fall, see Augustine's *De Trinitate* books IX–XIV.

sin, at this point there is nothing one can do but fall upon the mercy of God who can untie the knots through conversion and the redeeming power of grace.

Problems with Augustine's Solution

The first problem with Augustine's solution applies to the majority of free will defense theories. The problem is that God can *in theory* take away the freedom that he originally gave to humans; there is nothing metaphysically restraining God in his omnipotence from performing this feat. Since this is at least theoretically possible, then it is challenging to accept that we are truly free; instead, we have been given freedom on loan and that loan can be revoked. This is not just a problem for Augustine, but for Jewish and Islamic theologians that assert God's creation out of nothingness and God's omnipotence.

Another difficulty with Augustine's response stems from his inability to adequately account for the reason why an originally good creation could ever have gone awry in the first place. His answer that evil is the privation of good and that this privation is possible due to the fact that angels and man are created *ex nihilo* is confusing and does not appear to explain anything. If God knew that non-being or matter or nothingness would somehow be an affliction affecting the freedom and goodness of the creatures, *then why did he allow this*? It seems that God is still culpable as long as he is viewed as omniscient. It is also strange that God would be incapable of something that humans are, namely, *willing evil*; this seems like a limitation of God's power.

As I have shown, the original Fall is made possible due to our inferior natures created from nothingness and thus allowing privation, but does it follow that we should both be punished and further inclined to sin (concupiscence) because of this? Augustine seems to think so as he states, "all evil is either sin or the punishment for sin."[21] Hence natural evils like hurricanes and earthquakes represent God's exacting judgment and punishment for humanity's moral evils. The whole concept of sin however, is traced back *illogically* to Adam and Eve by Augustine. It is completely unclear why Adam and Eve were deemed guilty for eating from the tree of the knowledge of good and evil when obviously they were unaware of the difference between good and evil *when the decision to eat the fruit was made*. It is only after eating the fruit that they recognize the mistake, but how can someone be judged guilty if they are genuinely ignorant of any wrong-doing and their intention is innocent?

It is bad enough that humanity is responsible for the sins of our earliest ancestors, but the problem of evil is compounded for Augustine by his insistence that a large portion of the population will suffer eternal torment in hell. This idea of a permanent perdition goes completely against the notion of God as love portrayed throughout the New Testament and books IX–XIV of Augustine's own work *De Trinitate*. If Augustine were to say that the torment is only a temporary purgation, this might be feasible, but

---

21. St. Augustine, *De Genesi Ad Litteram*, Imperfectus liber, 1.3.

there is no constructive purpose behind an unceasing punishment in the flames of hell. These are all serious dilemmas for the classical tradition and it is these problems that have led so many to seek a naturalistic explanation for creation and the rise of evil.

Emergent Theism and the Problem of Evil

It should be stated up front that the problem of evil is not really a key concern for Samuel Alexander, just as it isn't for Daoists, because he does not believe in a creator God transcending the world and containing all power and goodness. Nevertheless, he finds himself tempted to provide an account of the meaning of various evils and how they came about. Basically, evil on the human and practical level arises through the misdistribution of satisfactions. "The problem of morality is to secure a coherent distribution of satisfactions among persons. Evil is misdistribution, and vice is a feature of character which wills such misdistribution."[22] Alexander believes also that there is progress in morals, so that new moral institutions arise that incorporate a larger and larger number of the population. The evil man is subject to either elimination, or at a minimum, exclusion from society if deemed guilty. One sinks or swims based on the collective will of the people and the most successful moral institutions of the time.

My primary concern, however, is not Alexander's opinions on morality but his manner of describing the relationship of evil in a more general sense to God, deity and humanity. What Alexander comes up with is the notion that evil is, "the name of the imperfection through whose defeat the perfect types acquire their value."[23] Evil on one level of the evolutionary hierarchy is not seen as evil on the higher level because it has been surpassed and made subservient to the next higher level. Thus, "evil is in a certain manner redeemed and made subservient to deity."[24] It is not that the evil is eradicated on the next level it is just that the imperfections of value on the lower level serve as indicators of that which should be overcome and thus, become useful to the higher level.

Alexander recognizes the fact that the world can be cruel, but as he repeatedly states, "There is no overruling and pre-existing purpose in the world upon which we should throw the blame for what we cannot help."[25] In other words, there is no God as an actual and transcendent being; there is only space-time and its restlessness or nisus towards deity, the always higher level of perfection. The solution to the problem of evil is then *a rational acceptance of the workings of nature and a faith in the nisus which always compels us and pushes us towards better forms of value and living.* It is the nisus of space-time within us that can slowly but surely affect a better world as it progresses to more refined levels of deity.

---

22. Alexander, *Space, Time and Deity*, vol. 2, 280.
23. Ibid., 420.
24. Ibid., 421.
25. Ibid., 422.

Part III: Cosmosyntheism vs. the Five Rival Contenders

Problems with the Emergent Solution

I am not at all convinced that evil is the "misdistribution of satisfactions" because it seems that Alexander means a quantitative equality of distribution of goods. A certain degree of equality is undoubtedly an essential element of a just society, *but a culture of sameness which is what Alexander appears to be arguing for is not good and goes against his fundamental notion that the universe is seeking to instantiate through the restlessness of space-time as many new forms of experience as possible.* With sameness and homogeneity there is stagnancy rather than restlessness, which is supposedly necessary for evolutionary growth. I am also deeply concerned about the ambiguity behind the term "the collective will" and its role in deciding what is good and bad. Which collective is Alexander referring to: government agencies or the entire polis?

The other major problem that I find with Alexander's solution is that one should have faith in the nisus of space-time to bring about a better situation. By Alexander's own admission, the nisus is not an entity or a consciousness, but rather a blind, endless and restless motion. It is intriguing to me that Alexander at this point shares a problem with Daoism, which also suggests that one should be open to the present movement of the Dao, which is understood in non-theistic terms. An argument needs to be made by both emergent theists and Daoists for precisely why humanity *should act in accordance with this purposeless and capricious force.* It is primarily for this reason that I share the opinions of our next candidates who feel that some form of pre-existing God is required.

Griffin on the Problem of Evil

I will focus my attention on the work of David Ray Griffin as he has written at length on the topic of evil within a process theology paradigm. Griffin treats the problem of evil at length in his book *God, Power and Evil: A Process Theodicy*, but he succinctly summarizes this earlier work in a chapter of *Reenchantment without Supernaturalism*. Griffin points out that the problem of evil is not really a problem at all in a process framework because *there are multiple ultimates* and thus everything, including the origin of evil, need not be traced back to a single all-powerful God. The beginning of Griffin's solution can be summed up in the following lines.

> In contrast to traditional theism's simple doctrine, which posits God as the sole formative factor in our world, Whitehead's position has "additional formative elements," namely, creativity (as embodied in creatures as well as in God), the eternal forms or possibilities, and the metaphysical principles. It is the addition of these other, equally eternal elements that makes this a naturalistic, as distinct from a supernaturalistic, theism.[26]

---

26. Griffin, *Reenchantment without Supernaturalism*, 223.

Griffin is here attempting to drive home the point that there is a genuine distribution of power across multiple entities and thus, the possibility for conflict is inevitable.

Griffin's response to the problem of evil requires that divine power be reconceived. The reason why this reconception is necessary is because there are multiple ultimates and therefore, power must always have been spread between God and a world. "Because our universe was created out of chaos rather than out of absolute nothingness, so that creative power is inherent in the world (as well as in God), the creatures' twofold creative power of self-determination and efficient causation cannot be canceled, overridden, or completely controlled by God."[27] This is the basic solution, *God is not omnipotent and the majority of evil has come about through the free decisions of the creatures of the world, a freedom which God can never take away.*

Griffin recognizes that even with this novel conception of Ultimate Reality, God can still be somewhat to blame for the evils that have arisen because God continually lures the world on towards ever-higher forms of value and complexity. As Griffin points out, with every increase in the capacities and complexities of organisms there is a corresponding increase in the ability to choose and create more heinous evils. Griffin calls this, "the law of the variables of power and value," and this law holds for all advances made in the evolutionary process. God is still partially responsible for the world's ills then because *God could have stopped luring the world on to greater complexity and thus God could have avoided some of the vilest evils that have only come about with the rise of humanity.*

In the end, Griffin does not feel that most people would find God indictable for evil under a process paradigm, even given the fact that God could have stopped luring the world forward, because a world without human beings would just be a far poorer world. In other words, the evils that have happened are worth it in the light of the greatness and goodness that has also come about. "When the choice is put in these terms, either a world with the risk of the kinds of evils our world has or a world with no humanlike beings at all, there are probably few who could indict God for making the wrong choice. As great as the evils caused and experienced by humans have been, a world without human (or at least humanlike) beings would be a far poorer world."[28] This particular opinion of Griffin has landed the most severe criticism.

Problems with Griffin's Solution

I will begin with the criticism that Griffin's solution results in a morally unacceptable elitism. Some individuals, such as Edward Madden and Peter Hare, have suggested that Griffin's process theodicy represents a disturbing elitism wherein God is content with all of the world's suffering and evil because it has allowed the creation of a select few fine specimens of humanity and that this elite group has justified all the carnage

---

27. Ibid., 224.
28. Ibid., 229.

that resulted just so that they could exist. Basically they are attacking the idea that God is supposed to be according to Whitehead, "the fellow sufferer who understands," yet God is also apparently at ease with all the human suffering and waste of life that has had to occur just so an elite group of individuals could come about.

It seems to me that the solution to the above criticism for a process theologian should consist in the role of Creativity as a metaphysical force. *If God is compelled by Creativity or a nisus, to use Alexander's phrase, then God cannot simply decide at some point during the evolutionary process to just stop luring the world onwards and upwards.* God has no choice in the matter; God is compelled by the power of Creativity as a force just as the creatures are compelled by Creativity. With this solution, the charge of whether or not God could be indictable for what appears to be an elitism, would vanish because God is incapable of putting on the brakes.

There is another problem however, with Griffin's solution that I believe no one else has addressed and it hinges upon a familiar problem: infinity. The primordial nature of God is said by both Whitehead and Griffin *to hold all possibilities and thus is infinite*. If one takes this premise along with Whitehead and Griffin's belief that the purpose of the totality is to issue into the world novelty of ever increasing complexity, then a serious problem occurs. The problem is: why would God favor the good experiences over the evil ones? If God and the world are simply playing out all possibilities, then God must contain all the evil possibilities and furthermore, *equally wish for their manifestation*. This is a serious concern, which I do not believe any process theologian discusses and it is just another reason why I feel that Cosmosyntheism is more consistent than former process theologies.

Cosmosyntheism and the Problem of Evil

At the outset, my solution to the problem of evil is the same as Griffin's, in that I feel that the only adequate way to answer the problem is to argue for the reality of multiple ultimates and in particular: God, a World and Creativity. Any solution based on one all-powerful and completely good ultimate like most emanation theories and classical theism is bound to end up mired in logical inconsistencies at best and at worst, it will appear laughable. However, even Whitehead and Griffin are not immune from the obsession of the infinite and this is where Cosmosyntheism differs from previous process theologians on the problem of evil.

Cosmosyntheism's contribution to the solution is simple: God is not infinite and does not contain all possibilities, thus *there is no need to ever play out evil scenarios in the real world*. If God only has some possibilities, even if it is an unimaginably large set of potentialities, then evil can logically be said to be wholly absent from God's nature. This is not to say that evil therefore resides in a primordial world that is in conflict with God, like some form of Manichaeism. There is no reason whatsoever to claim that the World is evil. Instead, as I have said, the world embodies randomness and chaos. This randomness can lead to what are *perceived as evils* on earth, such as earthquakes or storms, but rather than being penal consequences for sin, they are just a part of the unpredictability of the overall system of Ultimate Reality.

The majority of real evil is simply the result of free choices made by complex entities like humans *and God* who either intentionally or unintentionally willed something or other that brought about negative situations, either for themselves or others. Even God is capable of making mistakes with the "initial aims" due to the erratic nature of the primordial world and its chaotic structure. Not every variable can always be accounted for. In the end, *evil is either the result of intentional selfish and malicious behavior; the unpredictability of nature; or the result of innocent mistakes based upon faulty data.*

The good news of Cosmosyntheism is that we are all capable of creating a better world than the one we currently find ourselves in. However, in order to increase the likelihood of the emergence of a healthy global community, we must reinstate a strong sense of meaning and purpose to our existence as human beings. The investigation of meaning and the aim of life will require a transition from discussing good and evil in broad and abstract terms, to a more pragmatic examination of how we can apply these initial broad insights into a working practical program. For this reason, I will now commence a slow descent from a survey of the heavens, back to *terra firma* and more worldly concerns.

Summary

- The problem of evil arises from two major claims. (1) There is genuine evil in this world. (2) The divine reality whether conceived of as God, a Monad or the Infinite, is almost always understood to be wholly good and at least very powerful if not all powerful. Thus, why does the divine not eradicate evil?

- All of the attempts at a solution which posit only one ultimate are forced into complicated and often logically inconsistent theodicies.

- The Whiteheadian family of thought and in particular, the Cobbian/Griffian school, points out a novel solution based upon multiple ultimates and a reconception of God where God is no longer omnipotent.

- Cosmosyntheism differs from Cobb/Griffin however, in that there is no infinite set of Forms in the primordial nature of God and thus, there is no need to play out all possibilities, some of which may result in unnecessary pain, suffering or evil.

- In Cosmosyntheism evil arises from three possibilities: (1) intentional selfish and malicious behavior; (2) the unpredictability of nature; (3) the result of innocent mistakes based upon faulty data.

PART IV

Implications and Applications of Cosmosyntheism

CHAPTER 14

Ethics

A religion which takes no account of practical affairs and does not help to solve them is no religion.

—MOHANDAS GANDHI

THE FIRST TWO PARTS of this work strictly dealt with the theoretical dimensions of both Cosmosyntheism and five other metaphysical systems. Part III explored the applications of these theories to some longstanding problems within the field of philosophy of religion. This final part continues this expansion into the practical realm by making clear both the ethical and religious implications of Cosmosyntheism's metaphysics. The remainder of this work is *highly speculative and imaginative* and parts ways from the previous pages, in that it begins to move progressively farther away from the traditional academic style and tone. It is my sincere hope that the arguments I have put forward thus far in the preceding three sections be scrutinized via the same litmus test applied to all rigorous academic pursuits. However, in this final part, and the appendix which follows, I request that the reader temporarily suspend the normal criteria employed while reading academic work and instead, allow this last section and in particular, the material on worship in the appendix, to be deemed a success or a failure based on the following four criteria: *intuition, emotional impact, probable efficacy of a proposed exercise or technique to affect a profound religious experience, and common sense.*

    I realize that this is a rather dramatic shifting of gears, but I am confident that if one can read the rest of this work with this new set of hermeneutical lenses, then the reward will be far greater. How else can I prove Cosmosyntheism can live up to my fourth criterion if I do not make an appeal to the heart-strings of humanity, to the practical concerns of our everyday life, as well as the greatest hopes and ecstatic feelings we experience during profound periods of religious fervor and worship? To reiterate, the first three parts were laid out logically, argued for academically and thus, stand or fall based upon the strength or weakness of the proposed premises and

Part IV: Implications and Applications of Cosmosyntheism

conclusions. However, the heart has its own criteria, which may or may not align well with those suggested by the head. Nevertheless, in an effort to be multidimensional (my fourth criterion for a successful constructive theology), this final material is critical because it demonstrates the full power and scope of Cosmosyntheism.

In order to ease the transition, the current chapter on ethics does stay for the most part within the same style applied thus far, in that it is logically structured and engages some authors that one should by now be familiar with: Whitehead and Griffin. My discussion of ethics will be divided into three main headings: cosmic aim of life, social aim of life and individual aim of life. It is not my intention to get into a drawn-out debate between process ethics and say, utilitarian or deontological ethical systems; instead, I wish to merely present Whitehead's thoughts on ethics and then to address areas where I either modify his ideas or simply apply Whitehead's insights in a novel way. Therefore, what follows is not designed as a systematic presentation of process ethics or as an exercise in comparative ethics.

Before diving into the cosmic aim of life, it is worth mentioning that the final heading, the individual aim of life, is where I present something completely new from any prior thinkers, process or otherwise. The last heading reflects my passionate belief that any metaphysical system worth discussing must also have as a corollary to its metaphysics an ethical system or systematic framework for self cultivation, which provides the individual with a sense of meaning and purpose and the means with which to attain such purposes. With this final caveat in place, I now turn to Whitehead's understanding of the cosmic aim of life and the role of ethics within philosophy and religion.

The Cosmic Aim of Life

When I employ the phrase "cosmic aim of life," I am referring to the bridge between a proposed cosmology or metaphysics and the ethical implications, value judgments, and action guidance inherent within and unfolding from the suggested metaphysical system. In prior chapters, I have briefly touched upon Whitehead's generic answer to the cosmic aim of life, which is that life exemplifies an "upward trend,"[1] towards greater—more complex—forms of life capable of higher grade experiences of value realization. Whitehead further clarifies what the cosmic aim of life is in the following points. "Beauty, moral and aesthetic, is the aim of existence."[2] "The teleology of the universe is directed to the production of Beauty."[3] "The purpose of God is the attainment of value in the temporal world."[4] Whitehead understands beauty in broadly aesthetic terms, such as the creation of intensity and harmony, or one could say an

---

1. Whitehead, *The Function of Reason*, 24.
2. Whitehead, *Essays in Science and Philosophy*, 8.
3. Whitehead, *Adventures of Ideas*, 265.
4. Whitehead, *Religion in the Making*, 97.

Ethics

optimized harmonious intensity. This harmonious intensity ideally seeks the greatest degree of complexity possible given the circumstances.

David Griffin explains some of Whitehead's remarks on value and the purpose of the universe or existence in general. Griffin points out that it is not merely about the attainment of value, but rather the growth towards entities which are capable of experiencing higher and higher forms of value. "The order of the world, in other words, reflects the divine purpose of evoking individuals with increasingly greater degrees of intrinsic value. *The world is a locus for value realization.*"[5] What all of this boils down to is that the cosmic aim of life is to issue in novelty of increasing complexity for the sake of the enjoyment of the creatures of the world and for God.

Whitehead does provide a further explanation of his meaning that the aim of life is the production of value and beauty. In *Modes of Thought*, Whitehead's last major book, one finds him advocating that each actual entity should strive to maximize importance. "Morality consists in the control of process so as to maximize importance. It is the aim at greatness of experience in the various dimensions belonging to it . . . Whether we destroy, or whether we preserve, our action is moral if we have thereby safeguarded the importance of experience so far as it depends on that concrete instance in the world's history."[6] Of course, this statement requires a definition of precisely what Whitehead means by importance.

> Importance is a generic notion which has been obscured by the overwhelming prominence of a few of its innumerable species. The terms *morality, logic, religion, art*, have each of them been claimed as exhausting the whole meaning of importance . . . The generic aim of process is the attainment of importance, in that species and to that extent which in that instance is possible.[7]

In the end, this is the cosmic aim of life: to maximize importance given the circumstances one finds oneself in. Thus, it could mean at one moment to pursue a harmonized intensity of moral experience and an hour later a harmonized intensity of aesthetic or religious experience.

Since the cosmic aim of life is the production of more complex forms of value and experience Whitehead wisely states, "thus the pure conservative is fighting against the essence of the universe."[8] While I completely agree with this statement, I am inclined to disagree with both Whitehead and Griffin that the best way to maximize importance is to follow the initial aim from God. This may make good sense to follow the will of God since God has the most comprehensive vision of all that has happened, but Griffin and Whitehead fail to convince for two reasons. First, there is the problem of *how one even knows for sure if they are following the initial aim from God*. A solution

---

5. Griffin, *Reenchantment without Supernaturalism*, 91.
6. Whitehead, *Modes of Thought*, 13–15.
7. Ibid., 11–12.
8. Whitehead, *Adventures of Ideas*, 274.

to this problem is never really provided by either Whitehead or Griffin. I have suggested earlier that perhaps a Daoist approach of *ziran* or *wei-wu wei* could help one be assured that their will is in line with God's, but in the end, who can know with one hundred percent certainty?

The second critique I have concerning initial aims stems from Griffin's statement that, "Given Whitehead's doctrine of the God-human relation, there can be, in the language of Kierkegaard, no 'teleological [religious] suspension of the ethical.' The divine aim for us is directed toward the production of moral beauty."[9] I agree that due to the fact that we are all interrelated and that the aim of life is to maximize importance for ourselves and for others, God included, that there can thus be no religious suspension of the ethical, since following the initial aim from God is being holy and religious. However, my problem is that even if one could identify the initial aim of God with complete certainty, *there may be a time where denying it would actually radically increase the possibilities for value realization for oneself and others, God included.* Since God is not omniscient and humans have free will and their own true power, humans can create their own novel forms of value and thus experience a teleological suspension of the ethical for the sake of the religious, i.e., even greater value than the initial aim.

One must never forget that God's function is to "provide order and possibilities." This order is critical over time so that the universe does not lapse into total chaos, but there may be brief critical moments where an organism *randomly* or *willfully* breaks with or disobeys the ordering principle and thus allows for totally unforeseen possibilities to play out. This is completely within the metaphysical scheme of Cosmosyntheism and furthermore, it is suggested by the fact that God does not contain all the Forms and the World contains a degree of chaos.

Creativity and the Cosmic Aim of Life

If the above discussion has left one asking the questions: why does God seek to impress an order onto the world; why the endless pursuit of value and why the need to maximize importance, then it is necessary to reflect back on the role of Creativity within both process metaphysics and Cosmosyntheism. As Whitehead says, "God is not to be treated as an exception to all metaphysical principles, invoked to save their collapse. He is their chief exemplification."[10] Thus God is obliged or compelled by the power or force that is Creativity as one of the ultimates to engage in a continuous oscillating process, which automatically results in the creation of value and satisfactions.

The general concern that arises from all of the above hypothetical questions is what is the point? Why, why, why? The chain or line of questioning does have an end, and that end is found in the different ultimates which act as terminal points of any regressive chain of questions. One answer to the why is that God is compelled to engage

---

9. Griffin, *Reenchantment without Supernaturalism*, 309.
10. Whitehead, *Process and Reality*, 343.

Ethics

in a process due to the ultimate power of Creativity, which is a *metaphysical* principle. Another answer to a different why, is that God and other entities seek satisfactions which can be understood through broadly aesthetic criteria. God has a vision, but so do more advanced entities and the greater the complexity, the more avenues that are available for experience and satisfaction. God is primarily that entity which provides order because there must be a great degree of balance and harmony if one is to keep building higher and higher. As Whitehead says, "opportunity leads upwards or downwards" and thus there is always a corresponding increase of risk for every higher level of existence. But, God also encounters chaos, chance, unforeseen events and choices and this adds to his own enjoyment as well as to the possibilities available to him and others for further exploration.

This whole discussion has dramatic implications within the realm of religion and interreligious dialogue because if there is truth to the thesis of multiple religious ultimates and in particular, the system I have been expounding, then a new solution presents itself to the quagmire of interreligious *ethical* dialogue. The problem can be found in Hans Küng's attempt at a World Ethos as well as in the work of Paul Knitter.[11] Both of these men believe that all religions have an equal claim to legitimacy, but they also think that there is a sort of universal prescriptive ethic that can be uncovered in all of the religions. They point to certain deontological statements—don't steal, kill or lie. The problem is that even if all of the religions would agree on some limited set of prescriptive "ought statements," there is the issue of *how to mediate between the ethical claims that conflict with each other*. If all the religions are equally valid, then what does one turn to in order to mediate or judge which particular ethical claim is more correct?

Enter Creativity. *Any religion that proposes an ethical axiom that contradicts a metaphysical principle is automatically ruled out as incorrect.* This might seem outrageous or at least harsh to some, but as Whitehead says, "the pure conservative is fighting against the essence of the universe."[12] Thus certain religious codes of ethics that might hint at or outright profess something like extreme escapism or radical asceticism or extreme selfishness can be deemed less appropriate to the overall picture of Reality which can be pieced together through the various ultimates found in the world religions and via empirical evidence.

Therefore, I suggest a new form of *categorical imperative*[13] informed by the possibility of multiple ultimates and the cosmic aim of life. Kant's famous formulation of the categorical imperative runs thus: "Act only according to that maxim whereby you can at the same time will that it should become a universal law." By contrast, my formulation runs: Act only in accordance with the cosmic aim of life whereby you can be assured to be following a universal law.

11. Küng, *A Global Ethic*.
12. Whitehead, *Adventures of Ideas*, 274.
13. The concept of the categorical imperative is taken from Immanuel Kant's *Groundwork for the Metaphysics of Morals*.

Part IV: Implications and Applications of Cosmosyntheism

Given this new categorical imperative, any proposed action which would run counter to one or more of the natures of the five ultimates is unethical. Thus, any religion or secular philosophy, which advocates either stasis or a return to an earlier time, or a culture of sameness, is in blatant violation of the way that Reality is setup and operates. In short, any actions taken in the pursuit of goals which would violate one or more of the five ultimates *is motivated by second order concerns and is thus either unethical or at least less than optimal as a course of action to pursue.* This proposed new categorical imperative leads us on to our next topic, which is the social aim of life.

The Social Aim of Life

If the cosmic aim of life is continuous process issuing in novel forms of life and value of ever-increasing complexity, then it follows that the social aim of life is to help facilitate this cosmic adventure. Humans are the apex creatures on earth and thus, the responsibility lies with us to make sure that our planet does not lapse back into complete chaos. However, our duty is more than just maintaining the current status quo; we must also attempt to further the pursuit of progress on all fronts: intellectual, technological, moral, artistic, medical, etc.

If humans are to retain the role of both the stewards and the adventurers of earth then we must make it across a critical threshold, which is looming in our near future. In order to continue to maximize importance on all fronts, there is going to need to be a continued trend towards globalization and away from nationalism, racism and sexism. We must become true global citizens sharing our knowledge, labor and resources for the good of the whole. However, attempting to achieve a truly globalized society will be the most daunting task that has ever confronted our species. Nevertheless, the social aim of life that unfolds from Cosmosyntheism's metaphysics is the pursuit of what physicists define as a type I civilization.

The Russian physicist Nikolai Kardashev first introduced a planetary civilization ranking system based upon the total energy output and consumption of a civilization.[14] The idea was that any sufficiently advanced civilization would not be able to mask the entropy they create in the form of waste heat and the entropy created could be detected by other civilizations. A civilization is ranked type I, II, or III based upon their total energy consumption. Thus,

> A type I civilization is one that has harnessed planetary forms of energy. Their energy consumption can be precisely measured: by definition, they are able to utilize the entire amount of solar energy striking their planet, or 10^{16} watts. With this planetary energy, they might control or modify the weather, change

---

14. Kardashev,"Transmission of Information," 217. See also Kardashev, "Cosmology and Civilizations," 252.

the course of hurricanes, or build cities on the ocean. Such civilizations are truly masters of their planet and have created a planetary civilization.[15]

A type II civilization has learned to harness the power of their entire star or 1026 watts and a type III civilization has accessed the entire energy output of their solar system or 1036 watts and likely has colonized significant portions of their own galaxy.

What matters for the present discussion is only what constitutes a type I civilization as humans and the earth we live on currently represent a type 0 civilization. Although a type 0 civilization is too imprecise; hence, Carl Sagan introduced a refinement to the Kardashev scale by adding sub-divisions so a civilization could be 0.1 or 2.3 etc.[16] However, Sagan further divided things making an alphanumeric scale which places our planet far more precisely as a type 0.7H civilization. What this means is that earth while in striking distance of becoming a type I civilization is still 1,000 times smaller in terms of energy production than a truly type I civilization.

With the radical exponential increase in telecommunications, worldwide trade, population, etc., we may find ourselves on the cusp of creating a genuinely global civilization, but as Whitehead pointed out, "opportunity leads upwards and downwards." Hence, we live at a crucial turning point in the evolution of our species. Theoretical physicist Michio Kaku sees signs of the emerging type I civilization already present in our society.

> The Internet is a type I emerging telephone system. It has the capability of becoming the basis of a universal planetary communication network. The economy of the type I society will be dominated not by nations but by large trading blocs resembling the European Union, which itself was formed because of competition from NAFTA. The language of our type I society will probably be English, which is already the dominant second language on Earth. Information will be almost free, encouraging society to be much more democratic, allowing the disenfranchised to gain a new voice, and putting pressure on dictatorships.[17]

Dr. Kaku who wrote the above in 2004 is certainly correct, especially in regard to the Internet, which has continued to grow at an exponential rate since 2002 with things like Wikipedia, YouTube, social networking sites like Facebook, micro-blogs like Twitter, etc., making communication instantaneous worldwide and opening the floodgates to unprecedented free access to knowledge. The recent Arab Spring has proven the veracity of the above points.

I propose that *the social aim of life is to keep humanity on track to achieving a type I civilization sometime in the next one to two hundred years*. We have an ethical obligation to perform this task since the social aim of life should conform to the most general and cosmic aim of life. Although we are almost certainly not the only intelligent civilization

---

15. Kaku, *Parallel Worlds*, 307.
16. See Sagan, *Cosmic Connection*.
17. Kaku, *Parallel Worlds*, 309.

in the universe, there is the slim possibility that we are and then our duty becomes that much more important as the sole custodians of intelligent life. As the astronomer Sir Martin Rees said, "It's quite conceivable that, even if life now exists only here on Earth, it will eventually spread through the galaxy and beyond. So life may not forever be an unimportant trace contaminant of the universe, even though it now is. In fact, I find it a rather appealing view, and I think it salutary if it became widely shared."[18]

Even if the ideal social aim of life is to pursue a type I civilization, many people in our world today feel lost, disillusioned, living a meaningless and purposeless existence. The questions that the average person likely has are: how do I fit in to this picture; what is my role to play; and how do I even go about beginning to uncover and then pursue a sense of personal destiny? It is my firm belief that no matter what age, race or gender a person is, everybody follows a somewhat similar process to achieving a sense of purpose, destiny and well-being. Assuming that the above is true, then it is possible to create a universal guide that assists all people in the discovery of their personal or individual aim of life.

The Individual Aim of Life

I have compiled a system for self cultivation that is a guide rather than a manual or rule book, which would tell one precisely what and how to do something in order to achieve a certain result. I call this system the *Compass Path* and it is a fully comprehensive and unique approach to self cultivation that is wholly grounded in the wisdom of the various religious traditions and philosophies, but it is especially informed by the metaphysical principles of both process thought and Cosmosyntheism. Due to limitations of space, I will only be able to provide a synopsis of the overall program. However, for anyone who wishes a deeper grasp of the system, then I refer them to: *The Compass Path: A Guide to Self Cultivation*.

What follows is a brief overview of the entire Compass Path system. The work opens with a prologue: *the death of wonder*. The prologue simultaneously creates a sense of nostalgia because of the child book style it is written in, but it also alludes to many of the problems and adult themes that the rest of the book covers. Next, is an introduction that aims at elucidating the primary questions that the book will later answer.

The Questions:

1. What are the roles of wonder and creativity?

2. What is excellence?

3. What is the meaning of life?

4. How can we find lasting happiness?

5. How can we cultivate our true destiny?

18. Quoted in Lightman and Brawer, *Origins*, 169.

6. Is there an afterlife?

After discussing the importance and relevance of these issues for our times, previous attempts at solutions are examined.

Section I

Now that the stage has been set by the prologue and introduction, the first of four sections begins. The overarching objective of Section I is to address "the fundamentals" which precede the actual 16 step program. Chapter 1 illustrates the major factors that hinder an individual from being able to achieve meaning and purpose. Chapter 2 highlights the true function of emotions: to make one act. E-motions are meant to set one into motion, so chapter 2 explains that supposedly "negative emotions," such as, despair, guilt and fear, are not meant to be destroyed. Instead, like an alarm, these emotions are supposed to be shut-off, so that they can function again when needed.

The third chapter is of central importance, as its content is symbolized by one of the four cardinal points in the primary image for *the Compass Path*: an elaborate mariner's compass. Chapter 3 stresses the necessity of having five elements in your life as a foundation for further growth: (1) family (2) friends (3) health (4) action and rest (5) choice. The fourth chapter is only one page in length and it suggests a period of rest after the initial work of section I. An illustration of a lighthouse accompanies this chapter as a symbol of safe harbor, rest, and a base of operations.

Section II

The second section opens with a parable: the parable of the compass. This parable enigmatically incorporates the information of section I and the entirety of what is to follow throughout section II. Chapter 5 is another crucial chapter because it explains the methodology of the refined step program. Readers are told to expect three headings in each chapter: *sequentials, consistents, and repeatables*. It should be noted that this refined step method is the single most important aspect of the entire program, because all prior solutions to existential crises fail to account for precisely when, how and for how long or how many times a step should be worked with. The aforementioned problem is eradicated by my three headings which refer to material to be dealt with sequentially or *at that particular step*, consistently *from that step on* and repeatedly or elements of a step that can be done again, but only *infrequently*.

At this point, the actual step program begins with chapter 6, step one: *engage your sense of wonder*. The objective here is to swing the doors open wide and experiment with as many ideas, jobs, skills, sports and hobbies as possible. The Hindu story of Leela or play is used as illustrative of the proper frame of mind associated with this beginning step. It is stressed that the death of wonder is the birth the sorrow.

Part IV: Implications and Applications of Cosmosyntheism

Chapter 7, step two: *discover your proclivities and interests*, builds upon the exploratory and playful nature of step one. Interests exist where wonder persists. The objective of this step is to identify an individual's strengths, weaknesses and most importantly, what they feel magnetically drawn or inclined towards. Each and every one of us is naturally skilled or talented in at least a couple of different areas. It is only when one discovers these innate powers that one can begin to find lasting purpose and contentment.

The third step dealt with in chapter 8, focuses on the benefits one can reap from *a period of preliminary study* of one's chosen interests. The goal at this stage is to achieve the dawning of precision in one's understanding of a particular subject. Whereas before this stage, one was immersing oneself in a multiplicity of activities to see what felt right, here one is starting the narrowing and refining process.

After a period of initial study, one arrives at chapter 9, step four: *find a companion*. This is a one page chapter, which points out that even great religious figures like Jesus required a network or support group as evidenced by his twelve apostles. It is pointed out that the ideal companion should share one's interests and possess roughly the same level of skill. Companions keep us motivated through healthy competition and can also pick us up when we are down.

Chapter 10, step five, *seek a mentor*, complements the previous suggestion of finding a companion. However, in this case, one is actively seeking an individual who vastly exceeds one's current skill level. At these early stages of the program, it may at times appear that many of the steps are quite obvious, but what is not so apparent is the crucial ordering of each step. For example, seek a mentor is presented after a period of preliminary study because it happens all too often that a mentor at the very beginning can actually stifle one's creativity and prematurely limit their interests to those of the mentor. Little aspects such as these make *the Compass Path* highly pragmatic and workable as a realistic program of self cultivation.

The next two steps reflected in chapters 11 and 12, are also paradigmatic of the point made above about a logical progression or sequence of steps. It is not merely the refined step method of sequentials, consistents and repeatables that separates *the Compass Path* from its predecessors. It is also the realistic unfolding of the steps. Step six: *begin moral self cultivation*, is intentionally placed later in the program. If it was step one or two, it would likely result in disinterest and a quick failure of the program. Step six concludes with an extensive suggested further reading list of classic books on the topic of virtue.

The same rationale applies for step seven: *self cultivation journal*. Other programs have advocated the need for journal keeping, but have suggested it be performed at the beginning. However, the truth is that most people, especially at the start of a journey of personal improvement, simply lack the requisite discipline to write out a journal. Example categories from my own self cultivation journal are provided in the chapter, which propose one way that a journal can be structured.

Chapter 13 presents the final step in section II: *begin implementing meditation techniques*. The aim of this chapter is not to get into specific techniques for spiritual awakening. Instead, the purpose of the methods presented, are to aid one in relaxation and catharsis. Simple exercises are suggested along with straightforward instructions of how to perform them.

Section III

This penultimate section represents a real transition period on the journey of self cultivation. The steps contained in this section are either more complex or unorthodox. After another opening allegory: the allegory of the heart, readers arrive at chapter 14, step nine: *practice with altered states of consciousness*. It is in this chapter, that the truly novel approach of *the Compass Path* begins to become clear. Techniques drawn from religious rituals and esoteric traditions are made easily accessible. These methods are presented as profound tools for enhancing one's creativity and visionary insight. The most prized states of religious leaders, mystics, saints and occultists are classified into four forms of awareness:

1. Receptiveness/Emptiness
2. Single-Mindedness
3. Intentional Trance
4. Interrelatedness/Impermanence

This chapter alone presents more concrete exercises to try than one might find in the entirety of many self-help books.

The next two chapters find the readers transitioning from students who have for the most part been passive learners up until this point now becoming active creators. Readers learn in chapters 15 and 16, or steps ten and eleven, how to go about making the shift to professionalism and transforming their interests that they have been cultivating into lifelong commitments. Wonder reveals interests; interests lead to commitments; commitments are the dawning of destiny and purpose.

Chapter 17, step twelve: *active paradigm shifting*, introduces the most potent technique of the whole program. Active paradigm shifting is classified in three forms: (1) understanding another person's point of view by living their lifestyle; (2) allowing your lesser inner drives and impulses "out to play"; and (3) extreme shifting, which involves attempting to crack fears, deep habits and taboos. The television show *30 Days* is a prime example of type one paradigm shifting. The author shares some personal anecdotes on the importance and potential risks involved with this empowering step.

Chapter 18, step thirteen is, *learn the secret language*. This chapter applies insights from the field of communication theory to the spiritual realm. Readers find that God is capable of communicating to us both subconsciously through feelings and emotions and

Part IV: Implications and Applications of Cosmosyntheism

consciously via omens, visions, revelations and epiphanies. A wide variety of divination techniques are presented. The classic methods of divination are enhanced through the application of seven laws of communication theory. Regardless of whether one believes in a higher power, the exercises are unparalleled for inspiring creative thinking.

Chapters 19 and 20 or steps fourteen and fifteen, represent the culmination of the reader's efforts. At this stage, one has uncovered their true calling in life and has gotten a good idea about what their magnum opus will be. Another element that readers learn in step fourteen is the difference between destiny and fate. The individual is now working with the universe and has therefore, formed a trinity between heaven, earth and humanity. However, there is still an essential distinction between knowing one's destiny and manifesting it. Step fifteen, manifestation, elucidates the importance of continuing on and bringing your creative projects to fruition as creativity is revealed to be one of the keys to true contentment.

Chapter 21, step sixteen, although the last step of the official program, is actually the second to last step. Extension is the theme of the chapter and it brings *the Compass Path* full circle. The essence of the universe is extension or expansion. It draws us forward and branches off new avenues of interest for us over time. In this final step readers are encouraged to become mentors themselves, as well as to keep learning and engaging wonder continually because one never knows where creativity and wonder may lead.

Section IV

The last section is devoted to death and the afterlife. One of the five constants discussed in section one: choice, is invoked to explain that one's afterlife depends upon personal decision and intention. Three options are discussed: Heaven/hell, reincarnation and reabsorption/dispersion. These possibilities for the post-mortem state represent the beliefs of the various religions and the scientific community.

The book concludes with a final meditation, which is an allegory explaining the need for multidimensional and interdisciplinary approaches in order to find lasting and far-reaching success. An epilogue complements the initial framing device of the prologue, bringing the work to a close on an edifying note.

Summary

- The cosmic aim of life is to issue in novel forms of value of ever-increasing complexity.
- Creativity can act as a criterion for mediating between the ethical claims of the various world religions.
- The social aim of life should be to bring about a type I civilization or a truly planetary society.

- Having a sense of destiny and purpose is the single most critical ingredient to the life well lived; the Compass Path can provide the roadmap to achieving a sense that one has an individual aim to their life.

Appendix

Cosmosyntheism and Applied or Practical Religion

Indian religion has always felt that since the minds, the temperaments and the intellectual affinities of men are unlimited in their variety, a perfect liberty of thought and of worship must be allowed to the individual in his approach to the Infinite.

—SRI AUROBINDO

Congress shall make no law respecting an establishment of religion, or prohibiting the free exercise thereof . . .

—CONSTITUTION OF THE UNITED STATES, *FIRST AMENDMENT*

I CANNOT HELP BUT feel that over the last few hundred years something has slowly faded away from the core of the religious spirit. What has changed? *Nothing really*, and that strikes to the very heart of the problem. So many people think it, but no one dares to say it. I will risk proclaiming what is in the back of the minds of so many of the faithful in the various traditions. *Religion has become boring*! This may seem taboo or blasphemous to many, but it should not be. Is it really surprising that anachronistic dogmas and vacuous rituals have anaesthetized the masses? However, it was not always this way and religion does not have to persist as a lingering and ineffective cultural relic. Religion, at its best, is supposed to fill us with hope, love and awe. There is, nevertheless, still one remaining vestige of religious services that fulfills the purpose of genuine religion, as well as the needs of the faithful: worship.

Why do people still attend religious services? Perhaps, they are seeking assurance, communion with the like-minded, truth or wisdom. Maybe some people merely attend out of habit or because they fear what may happen if they don't. It is likely that there is not simply one answer to the question, but one thing is for sure, many people go to religious services because of the unique feeling it ignites within their souls. Nothing seems to light a fire within or transport one to another state of mind quite like worship. It is through engaging and multidimensional forms of worship that the individual is re-connected with that which they deem sacred. This is the quintessence of religion, to rebind with the holy. What better way to restore a sense of nearness and togetherness than through "worth-ship" or as we call it worship; to show worth to that which is most sacred and divine.

I have shown throughout this work how most religions predominantly dwell on one religious ultimate and naturally, this narrows the focus of their worship. For a Christian, who aspires to worship God alone, there is a very specific method for how this is done. For most Christians, worship consists of attending church on the Sabbath, prayer, a sermon and music, perhaps accompanied by a ritual, such as the Eucharist. Recently, many evangelical churches have focused on the music component with great success and this is not surprising, as new songs and updated music inject a stronger emotional impact into the worship ceremony. However, there are other methods and techniques for showing honor and worth to that which is sacred.

Cosmosyntheism—being oriented around multiple religious ultimates—allows for a far richer and more diverse repertoire of forms of worship. The purpose of the remainder of this work is to highlight what "applied religion" might look like within the paradigm of Cosmosyntheism. Through emphasizing practical or applied religion, I am also highlighting how Cosmosyntheism meets criterion four as outlined in the Introduction. Criterion four states that any successful constructive theologies must be multidimensional, meaning that they must be intellectually, emotionally and spiritually engaging. In addition to dealing with criterion four, this appendix also helps to meet criterion one by dealing with the practical aspects of religious pluralism, mainly through incorporating rituals and techniques from many of the different world's religions.

In following with the metaphysics of Cosmosyntheism, I will discuss five areas of worship or what can be understood as applied religion. For each of the five ultimates, I will divide the types of worship and the religious exercises into two categories: *individual and group*. I will then give brief descriptions of the techniques or methods listed. After dealing with the topic of worship in Cosmosyntheism, I will provide an account of a sample religious service grounded in the principles of Cosmosyntheism.

Worship in Cosmosyntheism

I have two visions. The first is a vision where religion will once again play a central role in the lives of most people. No longer will religion be a taboo topic of discussion; the word religion will become cleansed of its negative connotations and associations. In this vision, the people of the world will no longer view life through nationalistic lens, but instead will have received the gift of foresight; they will finally realize that we are all one people, a global community on the verge of a true golden age. However, there is another, far darker vision. In this second scenario, people continue to become disillusioned and disenchanted with the world. There is a runaway spike in existential angst. It is a world of productivity without purpose, truth without trust, labor without love, growth without goodness and materialism without meaning. However, both of these are just dreams.

We stand at the proverbial crossroads; our future is open; what will we create? As for myself, I would much rather live within the first scenario, but for this to become a reality I am aware that much work is needed. I am nonetheless convinced that if there is to be religious peace and therefore, a shot at world peace, there must be an active engagement with other religious traditions, not just their texts, but their rituals, techniques and exercises. What follows is merely one manner in which this goal of religious synthesis and also religious progress can be achieved. What better way to show honor, respect and worth, or in other words—worship—than through incorporating the practices of all the world's religions into one profound system for personal and global transformation. We have much to learn from each other and by worshiping all of the five ultimates, we can kick start a religion of vitality that is overflowing with potential for all of us living in the twenty-first century.

For just as there are five ultimates, there are five human pursuits that give us a passion for life, create meaning for us and make us feel whole—*truth, hope, flourishing, creativity/novelty, and love*. Religion, science and philosophy at their best provide us with these vital ingredients for a meaningful and fulfilled life. However, it is only when religion, science and philosophy are applied and no longer theoretical that they can achieve such greatness. What follows are some of the best exercises, techniques, and practices that religion has given to humanity so that we can be complete.

Worship and the Forms

There are a multitude of methods for experiencing and worshiping the Forms.

- (Tratak) Single-minded concentration on a physical object or sound
- (Samatha/Vipassana) Silent and inward meditation on a Form, concept, or Idea
- (Vision Quest) The creation or unveiling of a power animal or totem
- (Lucid Dreaming) Awareness that one is in a dream state and the ability to control objects or forms within that state
- (Astral Projection) Ecstasy or *Ex-stasis*
- (Ladder of Love) Guided meditation
- (Artistic masterpiece) Working on a novel creative contribution

Cosmosyntheism and Applied or Practical Religion

Individual	Group
Tratak	Attunement
Samatha/Vipassana	Creative Visualization
Vision Quest	Totems/Egregores
Lucid Dreaming	Lucid Dreaming
Astral Projection	(Ladder of Love) Guided Meditation
Artistic masterpiece	Collaborative Art

It is evident that one of the primary distinctions between humans and other animals is the creation, implementation and manipulation of symbols or forms. We use forms to communicate, identify, encrypt, imagine, visualize and in general, to expand our range of possibilities for experience. As human beings we are caught up in a deluge of symbolism, a semiotic web that seems to be all-encompassing with one sign always relating to or pointing to some other group of forms. However, *we rarely take the time to isolate one particular form, sign or symbol and meditate on it to the exclusion of all others.*

The goal of *tratak* is to achieve this important state of single-mindedness. The ability to attain complete concentration is critical for living a successful life. Think about how often we hear about ADD and ADHD nowadays; it is no wonder why so many people are incapable of concentration, but this does not mean that there is something wrong with them. We are simply losing the art of concentration. *Tratak* is an Indian practice that is unbelievably simple to practice yet impressively difficult to master. The practice merely consists of single-minded concentration on a physical object (candle, mandala, image of deity) or sound (bell, seed syllables, mantras) to the exclusion of all others. The effect created is a sort of inhibitory trance where all other images, thoughts and sounds fade away and one is left feeling extremely connected and in tune with the one object or sound. Through this technique, one can gain not only concentration but a depth of knowledge about a given object or sound that would have otherwise slipped past one's awareness.

Tratak on a group level could take the form of attuning a large group of people by the simultaneous focusing of awareness on the same object or sound. I can envision a congregation using fire, if an object is chosen, as its flickering has a natural hypnotic effect. If sound is employed, which would be in some respects easier than fire, then a brief period of chanting seed syllables such as *om, aum* or Greek vowel chanting like the IAO formula found in Gnosticism could be quite effective for attuning a large group. This tuning creates a sense of togetherness right away that will likely be useful in other types of worship for different ultimates. Not only does this practice serve as a way of worshiping the Forms, it has the practical effect in a large group of a sort of banishing of the groups' prior concerns and the creation of a sacred space and time. *Tratak* naturally leads to a state of trance, which is ideal for the next type of worship: *samatha and vipassana.*

Samatha is similar to *tratak* in that one is calming or slowing the mind in order to gain attention and concentration on one specific object or idea. If one adds to this concentration an inquiry into the nature of that object or idea then *samatha* transitions into a higher form of meditation known as *vipassana* or insight meditation. One can focus on just about anything from an image of a religious figure, to a decaying corpse, to simply focusing on one's breathing, which is the most common and is known as *anapanasanti* meditation. Traditionally, there are forty objects of Buddhist meditation (*kammatthana* or *karmasthana*) that are chosen by a master for a student based upon the temperaments of the student. The key idea is that *it is meditation with form or with forms*, images, symbols, etc., thought-form aides. However, for the purposes of worshiping the Forms, I envision *samatha and vipassana* as a sort of prerequisite, which can be the initial step before embarking on an individual or group creative visualization.

The idea of creative visualization is dramatically experienced during Native American vision quests which were primarily rites of passage to adulthood. The technique commences with a period of fasting, however, for modern times the most sensible way to attempt this would be to fast Friday and Saturday with the purpose of attaining a vision on the third day, Sunday. In addition to fasting, temporary isolation is required so that one's thoughts turn inward and one is severed from one's normal mundane life. If one adds sleeplessness into the equation, then there is a powerful but admittedly dangerous recipe for vivid and profound visions. The ultimate goal of a vision quest is the revealing of some symbol, usually in the form of a power animal, which from that point on, one has an intimate connection with.

It should be noted that if one attempts a vision quest, one must anchor the climax of the experience. Anchoring consists of employing a certain hand or body gesture like crossing or touching fingertips in a particular manner at the moment when a desired experience has first been achieved. The many images of the Buddha in bizarre postures with his unique hand gestures are one example of anchoring.[1] What this means is that not only will the vision or form of that particular power animal always reenact the feelings of the ritual, but just performing the hand gesture or whatever anchor you choose, will also help to recreate the feelings of the experience. Anchoring is like a short-cut to attuning to a desired state of mind.

For a large group, the counterpart to a vision quest is the creation of a totem or egregore. Totems and egregores are powerful thoughtforms that are established through repeated visualization or a group mind created through the coming together for a common purpose. A totem or egregore can be a symbol or form such as an animal, an abstract symbol or mythical figure or character. The idea is that a totem or egregore has a sort of separate identity or consciousness that is created through repeated group work on a single project.

---

1. *Mudras* and *bandhas*, or hand and body gestures, are essentially synonymous with the concept of anchoring.

One way of interacting with a totem or egregore is via astral projection. Astral projection is an ancient technique of *ecstasy* utilized by shamanic cultures and other religious groups (Theosophists, new-agers, Thelemites) whereby an individual's consciousness leaves the confines of the body and travels to distant locations. The concept can be found in groups as diverse as Inuit shamans to ancient Egyptian religion, to Kabbalah, to modern day occultism and New-Age movements. OBE's or out of body experiences and NDE's or near death experiences can be understood as rough analogues to this discipline. The actual method involved for achieving astral projection ranges from *lucid dreaming, to the construction of an astral double by way of visualization exercises and then the transfer of consciousness from the earthly body to the body of light or astral body double.*

Lucid dreaming is in some respects the easiest way to achieve a form of astral travel or astral work. There are a plethora of books available on the subject nowadays, but in general there are five techniques for achieving this state of awareness that you are dreaming. The point is that if you can become aware that you are dreaming without waking up, then you can begin to become the architect of your dreams and work with idealized perfect forms or models (e.g., a more Platonic understanding of Forms) and with various possibilities (e.g., Forms as understood by the perennial philosophy, Cosmosyntheism and many process thinkers) in a nearly infinite way. The primary techniques are as follows:

1. *Reality Checking*: Anytime something seems out of the ordinary or extremely frustrating in real life, perform at least three checks. For example, try flipping a light switch; in a dream it should not change the lights. Also, try leaning against a wall in a dream; you will fall through walls. Try jumping; in a dream you can fly. The list goes on, but by performing these during your everyday waking state it will become a habit that will carry over into your sleep patterns.

2. *Keep a Dream Journal*: Every night when you wake up immediately record as much information as you can from your dreams. This trains the mind to recognize patterns of thought that occur in your dreams thus making you more likely to recognize that you are dreaming in the future.

3. *Wake Back to Bed Method*: This method requires you to set an alarm for five hours after you are likely to fall asleep. Wake up and spend one hour awake meditating on the desired dream you wish to have then go back to bed.

4. *W.I.L.D.*: Attempt to go straight from a state of conscious meditation into a dream state where awareness is not lost during the transition. WILD stands for wake induced lucid dreaming.

Earlier, I discussed the idea of soul separation as it pertains to emanation philosophies like Gnosticism and Neo-Platonism; however, I never explained the actual method in detail by which one leaves the body. There is evidence in the *Three Steles of Seth* and in Platonic and Neo-Platonic sources for an experience of ecstasy which can take either individual or communal form.[2] By adapting the Platonic notion of the ladder of love encountered in the *Symposium*, with insights from Plotinus and Gnosticism, I think that a profound new technique for worshiping the Forms can be constructed.

The technique I envision would begin with the Gnostic use of vowel chanting which is essentially nothing more than a mantra that helps to focus and still the mind. The next step would be that provided by Plato and Plotinus whereby a large group now sits in stillness and complete quiet while one person narrates a dramatic guided meditation through higher and more abstract levels of being, culminating in the Form of the Good itself or some other ethereal and sublime Form. This would be similar to using Diotima's vision of the ladder of love in the *Symposium* as narrated by Socrates, but with the addition of more embellishments—visual, auditory, and kinesthetic—cues to provide detail and draw people deeper into the hypnotic-like experience. As everyone is led in their imagination up the hierarchy of Being, passwords and specific Forms are visualized just as Gnostics used specific passwords and signs to gain access past each archon who controlled the various emanations. Finally, the leader would guide people back down to the mundane realm where quiet and a period of stillness would again ensue.

One last way of showing reverence for the realm of Forms is via artistic endeavors of all kinds: music, painting, poetry, creative writing, etc. What better way to show honor to the Forms than by manifesting them in new and creative ways in individual projects and group endeavors. The concept of the great work or the *magnum opus* is something that we need to revive now more than ever as so many individuals feel at a loss in this world. Nothing creates a sense of meaning and purpose like large-scale artistic undertakings.

What all of the above methods have in common is that they all make a Form or set of Forms the focus of either individual or group attention. The above list is by no means exhaustive. There are a plethora of ways in which one could show honor to the Forms as an ultimate. It can be argued that engaging creatively with archetypal Forms through art and writing represents one of the oldest sacred disciplines.[3] Primitive man from time immemorial until the present has used Forms and signs for divination and for attempting to either uncover or express the inscrutable will of the divine or the sacred. From the I Ching to the Delphic Oracle, to Runes, to the Tarot, humanity has been fascinated by signs, symbols and Forms and so it is high time that they are

---

2. As for the Neo-Platonic or more precisely Late Platonic accounts of how this is achieved, see the work on theurgy by the last great Platonic philosophers Iamblichus and Proclus. A great book dealing with and cross-referencing both the Gnostic and Platonic sources on ritual and theurgy is *Gnosticism and Later Platonism: Themes, Figures and Texts*, ed. John Turner and Ruth Majercik (Atlanta: SBL, 2000).

3. The ritualistic and religious applications of artistic Forms goes all the way back to our Paleolithic ancestors as evidenced by the Lascaux cave paintings, aboriginal cave art, and the many Venus statuettes and votive figurines found throughout Europe and Central Asia. Even Neanderthals may have grasped the religious significance of shapes and forms as is made clear from the Shanidar IV cave site in Iraq where skeletons were placed in fetal positions within the earth and decorated with flowers.

Cosmosyntheism and Applied or Practical Religion

singled out as a religious ultimate within their own right. After all, what is it that rebinds us and reconnects us to each other and to God other than the Forms? Lastly, it is worth pointing out that the oldest images on cave walls are of human hands with fingers spread apart . . . five ultimates?

Worship and God

Traditionally, the concept of worship has been associated with showing reverence and honor to one or more deities. Due to the fact that Cosmosyntheism recognizes God as one of the five religious ultimates, this tradition of paying respect to God continues. However, as people of the twenty-first century, we no longer need to view the worship of God as *propitiation and appeasement*. God is not all-powerful and is not waiting to punish us for our wrongdoings or our lack of offerings. If God's purpose is understood as issuing in order and continued growth into complexity, then the simplest type of worship we can show him is to assist in facilitating the peaceful upward trend towards growth and complexity. However, there is still a place for the old practices of worship as they help to solidify our relationship to a reality which is greater than ourselves. There are seven general methods by which one can still worship God.

- Prayer
- Scriptural Study
- Evangelism
- Pilgrimage
- Sacrifices
- Invocations
- Offerings
- Unveiling/Revealing

Individual	Group
Prayer	Prayer
Scriptural Study	Sermons and Study Groups
Evangelism	Missionary
Pilgrimage	Pilgrimage
Self-Sacrifice (Abstention, Altruism etc.)	
Invocation	
	Unveiling/Revealing
Offerings of Food and Valuables	Offerings of Music, Hymns and Praise

The most common form of worship shown towards God is prayer. However, there are many forms of prayer: petitionary, supplicatory, thanksgiving, and praise. When it comes to worship, the only forms that fit the bill are the last two. I am by no means asserting that there is no place within the paradigm of Cosmosyntheism for petitionary or supplicatory prayer; instead, I am merely pointing out that only prayers of thanksgiving and praise adequately show the necessary reverence involved for acts of worship.[4] Prayer is of course an integral aspect to all of the monotheistic faiths, but it is also of secondary importance for the Eastern religions, following meditation and other spiritual exercises.

One aspect of prayer that is intriguing is the method in which it is practiced. For Jews, one frequently rocks back and forth during prayer, whereas for Muslims, one prostrates towards Mecca. Christians bow their heads and fold their hands in a penitent gesture, whereas some Sufi groups whirl in circles. Being that Cosmosyntheism is an inclusive philosophy, it only stands to reason that all of the varieties of prayer methods should be experimented with in order to experience the subtle differences which each outward performance yields. On a related note, Cosmosyntheism advocates the use of different languages during prayer, as it is frequently the case that each language can induce a unique feeling when used in prayer.

Prayer can be deeply personal, but it is also common to rely on the power of group prayer, especially when it comes to worship. Frequently prayers of thanksgiving and praise are done in communal settings and the power that a group brings to these forms of worship is often palpable. Within the framework of Cosmosyntheism, group prayer that incorporates the techniques employed by the various faiths all within one grand system is likely to enhance the effects of any prayers.

In addition to prayer, scriptural study is a critically important way within which an individual shows reverence for God, especially within those religions where the sacred scriptures are understood as the very word of God. This is necessarily true in Judaism and Islam, where the study of scripture outweighs almost any other divine imperatives. What better way to show that you value God than by gaining a richer depth of understanding of his laws and will.

Cosmosyntheism stands out from all prior religions in that it not only passively suggests, *but rigorously encourages people to delve into all of the sacred texts from throughout the various world religions.* If everyone would do this, at the very least, one would have a more profound awareness of the cultural heritages of other peoples, but most likely, one will also become increasingly convinced of God's presence within their lives.

The study of scripture in isolation can be an arduous task at times. It is imperative that one is connected with a larger group in order to comprehend Scriptures, which at times seem anachronistic and arcane. This is the point of sermons and group study. Sermons are important because a religious expert discourses on select passages and

---

4. With perhaps the exception of petitionary prayer that is aimed at *selfless* goals such as aiding the hungry or world peace.

then provides a deeper interpretation and contextualization than most individuals could otherwise have achieved through self-study. If Cosmosyntheism were structured as a religion, a key difference would be *that the sermon could be on Buddhism just as easily as it could be on Christianity*. This format is already practiced in some Unitarian churches and by the Unity movement.

It is important to note that sermons within the confines of Cosmosyntheism would never be polemical in the sense of doing apologetics for one particular religious tradition. This leads us to the next issue of evangelism. There is nothing inherently wrong with spreading the good news, which in this case would be *the reality of multiple religious ultimates*, but proselytizing is another matter. In short, evangelism is good, but forced conversion is always bad. Evangelism is a necessary counterpart to scriptural study, one learns about God and then one wishes to share this news to others. This is perhaps the greatest form of worship one can practice in the twenty-first century in that merely spreading the news that God still matters to the millions in despair or apathy lost in this disenchanted world is crucially important. For this reason, missionary work is also a productive means of disseminating the good news and thus, also easily finds a place within Cosmosyntheism.

Another ubiquitous religious tradition is pilgrimage. The most famous pilgrimage is of course the *Hajj* or journey to Mecca, which all Muslims must attempt to make. However, every religious tradition has at least one holy site of pilgrimage. Once again, in the spirit of globalism and pluralism, Cosmosyntheism differs in suggesting that *all of the holy sites are equally as valuable as they all stand as sacred spaces within which one should consciously reflect on the nature and necessity of God or perhaps some other religious ultimate*.

A practice that is frequently associated with pilgrimage is self-sacrifice—either in the form of fasting or abstention from displays of status—to grueling means of transportation, such as continuous prostration on every step of the pilgrim's path. The notion of sacrifice within Cosmosyntheism however, is specifically limited to forms of self-improvement, abstentions and altruism. In other words, the old days of blood sacrifices of either animals or humans must be done away with. More often than not, blood sacrifices were done for the sake of propitiating, which suggests a master/slave dialectic between God and his subjects, which is emphatically not the structure advocated in Cosmosyntheism. Thus said, blood sacrifices are not necessarily to be condemned, such as those practiced in Santería or by other West African diasporic religions. If these sacrifices are seen as gifts and as a symbolic gesture of giving up something of value in exchange for say, information, then this is acceptable. Each culture has its own standards for what is deemed socially acceptable or a moral practice, but for any global religion seeking acceptance in the twenty-first century, sacrifice should take on a more personal and metaphorical role.

I have deliberately left blank a group counterpart to sacrifice as this is often where physical ritual sacrifices would be placed and as I have said above, Cosmosyntheism finds this unnecessary and an archaic practice. Of course, there is still the possibility of an entire congregation or group of adherents all sacrificing something of either literal or symbolic importance to the group. However, for the most part, one shows reverence to God through individual sacrifices such as abstentions and altruistic acts.

For some people an intimate I-Thou relationship is not enough and these individuals seek an even closer relationship in the form of complete identification through invocation. Literally, invocation or *invocare* is *to call a deity into oneself*. Invocations are commonly practiced in contemporary paganism, primal religions, West-African diasporic religions such as Vodoun, Santería, and Candomblé. This is certainly not for everyone, but the effect is extremely intense and so it may be viewed as the ultimate form of worship or by some, the ultimate sin. Regardless of one's moral inclinations towards the practice it is useful and potentially life transforming and *certainly not boring*!

As far as Cosmosyntheism is concerned, there is no specific deity or godform that one should seek to invoke, but regardless of the choice, the method is pretty much universal. For best results one should follow a five-step process. (1) Decide on the deity one wishes to invoke and then surround oneself with symbolic correspondences associated with that deity. For example, if one wishes to invoke the war god Mars, then they should immerse themselves in the color red, harsh battlefield type smells, weapons, images of the god etc. (2) Do something to assist in achieving a trance state (ingest drugs,[5] fast, aggressive exercise like boxing, dance repeatedly, etc.) (3) Formally call upon the God through incantations and perhaps utilize "sigils" or seals that represent that deity. (4) Fake it until you make it. (5) Ground yourself and banish any excess energies. Invocation or "aspecting" of a deity is one of the most cherished parts of many pagan ceremonies because once the priest or priestess has achieved the requisite state, then people treat the priest or priestess as the actual deity incarnate and often seek divination, counseling, healing as well as using the priest or priestess to perform enchantments or spell-casting.

The bottom line with invocation is that it provides a profound religious experience, one which the Western world has all but forgotten or consciously eliminated. This is the real value of many African and pagan religions, *they harness religious rituals to bring about extreme altered states of consciousness*. As I have said, for some there is no greater form of worship, whereas for others there is no greater sin than attempting to become God.

Regardless of one's stance on the doctrine of sin, Cosmosyntheism recognizes the importance and efficacy of the central theme behind confession—unveiling or unburdening. It is true that pastoral care and counseling is still a major part of most Christian organizations, but I believe that a more regular program of revealing our

---

5. I personally do not recommend ingesting drugs under any circumstances because there is the potential for doing permanent damage or harming other people. Also, it is not a good idea to become reliant on an external aid; what will happen if that aid is no longer available but you need to attain that state of consciousness?

troubles, fears, taboo desires, etc., can prevent the creation of obsessions and other neurotic behaviors. Through unveiling, we either let go and extinguish some of our problems, or we transform and sublimate some negative energy into something useful for our continued flourishing. It is not that you need a priest or pastor to confess to, rather, there is a human need to share painful or private information and thus, unburden ourselves of shame, guilt, remorse or whatever the case may be. Therefore, Cosmosyntheism wholeheartedly endorses the need for a therapeutic and cathartic process that involves some member or members of the larger group hearing the troubles of others and vowing to keep the information secret.

The final method of worship is through ritual offerings of food and valuables. This is similar to the issue of sacrifice, but it differs in that it is something tangible and may not represent a significant sacrifice or relinquishing of something cherished as is the case in self-sacrifice. Virtually all religions provide offerings to God or the gods, with Hinduism providing the most striking example. Common offerings range from Hindu ceremonies and festivals where clarified butter, rice, and eggs are used, to first and second temple Judaism where there were burnt offerings of bulls, goats and birds all the way to alcohol and cigarettes for certain spirits within various African diasporic religions.

In the contemporary religious scene, offerings have taken a more acoustic turn where worship services at evangelical church events frequently incorporate Christian Rock or even Metal music. The offering of music and song is a simple yet moving manner in which one can establish a feeling of nearness with the divine, or at least an easy way to show praise. To be sure, there are other forms of offerings, but one in particular—charity—or almsgiving belongs to another religious ultimate to be addressed later: Creativity/Eros. However, there is an even greater offering or gift that humans can provide for God and that is the unpredictability of our free choices and *the resulting novelty that can occur not only for God but also for all entities.* The inherent spontaneous power within the world itself is also worthy of worship in its own right and it is high time that we reinstate chaos and the role of the unforeseen to a place of high prominence on par with the ordering power of God.

Worship and a World

This is perhaps the most difficult "ultimate" to treat when it comes to the issue of worship and applied or practical religion. One reason is that it has never adequately been treated by any religion, although some have provided hints at ways in which to show reverence to the awesome power of chaos; however, more often than not, randomness has been seen as evil and anathema to the proper study of religion. The truth is that chaos is not evil and it must be embraced; *it is the main piece of the puzzle that has been missing.* The primary purpose of all the techniques I will suggest below, are to allow the forces of spontaneity, chaos and randomness to inspire the truly new: new Forms, ideas, concepts and ways of living.

Cosmosyntheism and Applied or Practical Religion

- Invocation of chaos
- *Ars combinatoria*
- Kabbalah (*gematria, notaricon, temurah*)
- Nature Worship (five elements and five phases/agents)
- Dice ritual/Lullian Circle for the purpose of sermon selection

Individual	Group
Invocation of Chaos	
Ars Combinatoria	Dice/Lullian Circle Rite
Kabbalah	Kabbalah
Nature Worship	Nature Worship

The goal of the first three forms of worship under the individual category is to induce what is known as *apophenia* or the experience of seeing patterns and connections where others don't. An invocation of chaos would literally be a calling in or invitation for the forces of spontaneity to work through you. The method could take an infinite variety of forms. Peter Carroll suggests the following basic ritual structure:

- Banishing ritual if desired.
- Ignite incense and consume a sacrament if desired.
- Statement of Intent
- Appeal to *Apophenia*
- Draw and visualize and suffuse oneself with the *Apophenia* symbol.
- *Apophenia* incantation in any barbarous tongue or gibberish.
- A nod to *Eris* (strife) and *Pareidolia* (perceiving random stimulus as significant)
- Working with tables or other creative aids.
- Banishing ritual if necessary.[6]

There are more mundane ways in which one can seek inspiration and true creativity and thus manifest the truly new. The simplest would range from forms of divination such as *kledonomancy* (asking a question, then plugging your ears and going into a public place and then unplugging your ears) and *bibliomancy* (using a book for creative inspiration or divination) all the way to more complex systems like the *I Ching*, Tarot and the *ars combinatoria*. The *ars combinatoria* was elucidated by Gottfried Leibniz but is based on the prior work of Raymond Lull and possibly the Arabic Zaijr.

The technique for creating a Lullian circle involves the construction of a device consisting of concentric circles with words, letters or concepts on the various rings.

---

6. This ritual can be found on pp. 120–21 of Carroll's *The Apophenion*.

Cosmosyntheism and Applied or Practical Religion

Through the random spinning of the rings or dials, one can come up with previously unforeseen possibilities and combinations. Utilizing a Lullian Circle may also provide a fundamentally new way to approach group religious services *in that one could use the device or any other device that would create random results like throwing dice to be the deciding factor in how the ritual service or the sermon might unfold*. Thus, instead of having a typical Sunday service where the sermon is already announced ahead of time, one could have a list of either the names of various religions or philosophical concepts on a Lullian circle and thus by spinning the dials, a random combination would unfold. The pastor, priest, leader or whatever would then have to spontaneously discourse on that particular combination of ideas. Granted, this would require a tremendous amount of knowledge—not to mention creativity—on the part of the religious leader, but you should not be leading if you are not already learned and experienced. This would make for an intriguing service every time *with only a minimal possibility of ritual stagnation and boredom*.

I am not suggesting that the aforementioned divinatory tools are meant to provide some precise answer to what will happen in the future (that's impossible, especially the farther out in time one projects), but rather, act as creative amplifiers allowing one to draw new conclusions or ideas on one's own. The classic method by which to obtain hidden messages and new religious inspiration is found in the Kabbalistic practices of *gematria, notaricon* and *temurah*. In ancient times most languages were "isopsephic" meaning that each letter also had a number value. Thus, Hebrew and Greek along with Arabic and even Latin, to a lesser extent, could involve the transformation of words, phrases and sentences into numerical values. For centuries, Jews have sought to employ *gematria* in order to access hidden information. One example would be from Genesis 18:2 where three unnamed men come to visit Abraham. The passage starts *Ve-hineh shelshah* "And behold, three" which adds up to 701. The sentence *Elu Michael Raphael ve-Raphael* also equals 701, thus, there is a gematric connection here and the three unnamed men were really the three archangels: Michael, Raphael and Gabriel.

Kabbalists also employ the techniques of *notaricon* and *temurah*. In *notaricon*, a phrase like <u>c</u>hokmah <u>n</u>istorah is condensed by taking the first letters of each word in the phrase into an acronym. In this case, one gets the acronym ChN or *chen*, which is grace in Hebrew. Thus, wherever the word grace or *chen* appears in the Hebrew Bible, it is actually a code to inform one that secret wisdom is being divulged. *Temurah* means permutation and involves the transformation of each letter in a word into a different letter. Thus, in the system of temurah known as AThBSh or *Atbash*, each letter turns into its opposite, so Aleph, the first letter of the Hebrew alphabet would become Tau, the last letter and so on. As an example, the word Baphomet BPhVMTh infamously associated with the Knights Templar would become SVPhIA or Sophia meaning wisdom who is a central figure in Jewish Wisdom literature and Gnosticism.

The practices of Kabbalah seek to creatively uncover hidden messages from God, but *what if one wished to implant a hidden message into the very mind of God?* The following technique may be considered by some the most demoniacal of all suggestions, but the real question is whether or not what follows is possible. Just as cells within our own bodies go awry and cause changes that we didn't necessarily want to have happen, so too may it be possible for human beings to influence higher levels than ourselves, perhaps, even God. In a panentheistic system where the world has its own real power and God is not omnipotent, all things are interrelated and thus, *all influences all*.

I do not want to get into too much detail, but there might be a way where one could create and implant what is known as a sigil in a very specific manner, where the result would be the radical transformation of events within the everyday world by apparently magical means. The precise technique is critical and if one accepts the intricacies of Whiteheadian epistemology, actual entities and the process of concrescence and transition, then it may be possible to bring about totally unforeseen changes in the real world. I will say no more on this matter as it is too complicated and undoubtedly too contentious to be taken seriously by most "normal" individuals. Besides, this method moves one beyond worshiping the power of a world or chaos and into the realm of hubris.

The final form of worshiping the power of a world is not technically showing honor or reverence to an ultimate, but instead to that which is penultimate: the earth. Just because the earth may not be a proper religious ultimate, it is certainly an extremely important and valuable object of religious concern for millions of people, and rightfully so. Many contemporary pagans make a place for one, if not all five of the classical elements in their ritual sabbats and esbats. The powers of fire, earth, air, water and spirit have been revered in religious rites since the dawn of history and by incorporating them in creative ways into rituals it helps to provide us with an identity of who we are, where we come from, and the great debt we have to the planet at large, without which, we are nothing.

The Chinese have also made great use of a paradigm of five phases or five agents, however, theirs is slightly different in that it includes: wood, fire, earth, metal and water.[7] The interactions and mutual engendering of each of these elements has led to insights in TCM or Traditional Chinese Medicine, cosmology, philosophy, religion, cooking and just about everything in between. In other words, the theory of the five agents and their interrelatedness can be used to create rituals that are in harmony with the natural courses and patterns of the earth. The issue of impermanence and interrelatedness leads us to a discussion of the next ultimate: Creativity/Eros.

Worship and Creativity/Eros

The function of Creativity/Eros is to bring all things together into a state of mutual immanence and then pull them back apart. Creativity is the force, the engine which

---

7. Tsou Yen (305–240 BCE) is frequently cited as the originator of this theory.

drives the advance into novelty, but it also suggests two fundamental insights into the nature of reality: impermanence and interrelatedness. In the West, these two notions have often been overlooked and instead, there has been an obsession with permanence and individualism. A proper harmonious balance needs to be reinstated and that can be achieved by incorporating some simple methods and techniques for cultivating an awareness and appreciation for the twin truths of impermanence and interrelatedness.

The following suggestions, exercises and techniques for worshiping Creativity fall under either the category of impermanence or interrelatedness.

- Updated *vipassana* meditation on the 31 objects of repulsion and the ten kinds of foulness
- Amending of Scripture
- Charity/Almsgiving
- *Tonglen*
- *Brahma-viharas*

Individual	Group
Updated Vipassana	
Amending Texts	Amending Texts
Charity/Almsgiving	Charity/Almsgiving
Brahma-viharas	Brahma-viharas
Tonglen	Tonglen

The first technique on the list needs revision if it is to be utilized in the twenty-first century. The reason for the revision is the simple fact that most people do not have access to corpses or skeletons and the secondary fact that the risk for disease transfer is a genuine concern. In one classic form of insight meditation found in the *Sattipattahana Sutta*, the Buddhist practitioner contemplates the nature of impermanence by staring at rotting corpses or skeletons for the purpose of gaining a deep existential awakening to the reality of death and impermanence. There are other variations that are delineated in the *Visuddhimagga* along with a commentary on all the forty proper objects of Buddhist meditation.

Rather than making use of actual corpses, I believe that it is far more effective to combine a multitude of examples ranging from the subtle, mundane and ephemeral, to the dramatic and the slowly disintegrating. The following suggestions however, *would necessitate a common meeting place for worship over a sustained period of time.* The method would consist in activating the three primary senses: visual, auditory, and olfactory.

Beginning with the subtle, the place of worship should be adorned with beautiful and highly fragrant flowers and garlands. This first aspect satisfies both the visual and the olfactory because over a few weeks, the flowers and garlands will of course slowly die out, losing their beauty and their scent, which will undoubtedly be noticed by any people attending on a regular basis. As for the auditory dimension, any meditations should begin with a large deeply resonant bell which provides a lingering sound that only slowly diminishes with time; each meditation should open and close with a bell. Another method is to employ Tibetan sand mandalas on the ground or in the aisles of the place of worship and over time watch as they are swept away by both people and by the natural elements.

The final and most lasting example of impermanence should be the most profound because of the length of time it takes to disintegrate. A large detailed anthropomorphic statue should be set in a prominent place outside of the area of worship; however, unlike the bronze and marble statues of ancient Greece and Rome which sought immortality, this statue should be made out of the most delicate, yet still workable stone so that over a period of years the human figure morphs and transmogrifies, slowly wasting away at about the same time as a human life fades. This would provide an enduring reminder of the reality of impermanence and thus, implant this truth forever within the minds of any practitioners.

One additional way in which the importance of the doctrine of impermanence can be incorporated is through applying the principle to the creation and restructuring of canonical texts and established dogma. Too often in religions and in law and politics, ideas become so rigidly codified and entrenched that it is nearly impossible to move beyond them. The founding fathers of America recognized this fact and thus allowed for the Constitution to be amended as the times changed and circumstances necessitated it. Zen masters have also pressed a similar point home that can be seen reflected in phrases like, "if you see the Buddha on the road, kill him" and in the story of the three monks who burned sacred texts and icons for warmth. It is clear why applying this principle to revealed religions is problematic, but Cosmosyntheism insists on the idea of constant flux, so amending or altering texts and fundamental ideas would be a necessary enterprise over time and it also serves as a unique reminder of the centrality of impermanence.

Experiencing and showing reverence to the power of Creativity as an ultimate must not be unduly limited to the truth of impermanence which results from the function of Creativity. There is also the function of Creativity/Eros—more specifically Eros—to bring all things together. The significance and the degree to which all things are interrelated is a truth which stands out as perhaps the most important piece of wisdom lacking in the Western mentality.[8] With issues such as climate change and the worldwide economic crisis, it should become increasingly more obvious just how tightly all things are interwoven and mutually influence one another. Cultivating a deep awareness of this crucial truth is of the utmost importance for any constructive theology.

---

8. There are encouraging signs of progress in this area within the West such as the experiment resulting in the six degrees of separation theory, which states that we are only separated from any random person by no more than six other individuals.

Cosmosyntheism and Applied or Practical Religion

In the East and the West there are multiple techniques, which are based upon an insight into the truth and importance of the interrelatedness of all things. The most ubiquitous practice is *charity or almsgiving*. It may seem odd to suggest that charity or almsgiving should be classified under the worship of Creativity/Eros; however if one thinks back to the primary function of Creativity/Eros it makes sense. Creativity/Eros' role is to bring all things into communion and then pull them apart again and again. Thus, freely giving to those who are less fortunate and in need shows that one has grasped that if one group is suffering and falling behind, then it is going to have an impact on the larger whole. Charity/Love is the chief among the three theological virtues of Catholicism and almsgiving or *zakat* is one of the Five Pillars of Islam.[9] The concept of charity plays a large role in Buddhism as well, with the practice of the bhikku's begging bowl. Charity or loving kindness to all things, must also be just that, loving kindness to *all things*. Buddhism is far beyond the other monotheistic faiths in its recognition of all sentient beings as intimately interconnected. The biosphere and the overall ecosystem must be kept in harmony and hopefully, we can take a cue from the Eastern religions on this point and make the required corrections before it is too late.

However, charity and almsgiving without a prior system of moral and intellectual self-cultivation is bound to be misguided charity or in other words, ultimately self-motivated charity. If one is giving of their time or money only because they believe it will grant them eternal life or some other spiritual gift, then they clearly are lacking in an experiential insight into the depths of interrelatedness. This is where some specific programs come into play. Classical Confucianism was one of the first religions to provide a systematic approach to moral and intellectual self-cultivation and then extension to all other sentient beings. The Confucian step-program is delineated in the *Da Xue* or Great Learning. However, this idea of first self-cultivation and then extension is also reflected in Buddhist practices such as, *tonglen* and the *Brahma-vihara*s.

The Buddhist practice of *tonglen* is a simple, yet effective way of worshiping the truth of Creativity as an ultimate. *Tonglen* consists of a combination of breathing exercises combined with visualization. For example, you may begin with confronting one of your own fears and visualizing it in your mind and then on each in breath you take in the pain or fear and confront it. Then on the out breath you visualize and focus the mind on sending out healing. The idea is that the practice should be extended to include close friends, family and ultimately, the whole world by breathing in their problems/pains and sending out solutions and healing intentions.

The practice of *tonglen* has similarities with another set of Buddhist practices known as the *brahmaviharas* or the four divine abodes. The four divine abodes or sublime emotions are *metta* (loving kindness), *karuna* (compassion) *mudita* (altruistic joy) and *upekkha* (equanimity). In the fifth century C.E. Buddhaghosa suggested in the *Visuddhimagga* that each of the four practices aside from *mudita* should be practiced first on oneself and then extended out in a radiating circle to

---

9. See 1 Corinthians 13 for Paul's discussion of the theological virtues.

close friends and family and then onwards to include all sentient beings. All of these practices cultivate an experiential knowledge of the truth of both impermanence and interrelatedness, but through our final religious ultimate there is one additional manner in which to both truly understand other people and to broaden the scope of our values and our overall artistic creativity.

Worship and the Receptacle

The religious traditions that deal with what I have defined as the Receptacle are Yogacara Buddhism and Tibetan Buddhism or Vajrayana Buddhism. However, Sikhism and many Western esoteric movements (the Theosophical Society, Hermetic Order of the Golden Dawn/Thelema, and the New Age Movement) have all discussed the existence of astral/mental planes or an Akashic Record which appear to function similarly to how I have defined the Receptacle. The function of the Receptacle is to provide a plane of mutual immanence and to store all that has happened. The techniques that provide one with an awareness of this religious ultimate are the most esoteric.

Individual	Group
Akashic Record Reading	Akashic Record Reading
Tantric Techniques: 6 Yogas of Naropa, Dark Retreat, Dzogchen or Mahamudra	
Zazen	
Applied Paradigm Shifting	Applied Paradigm Shifting

The first technique is a fascinating blend or pastiche of a multitude of exercises. The goal or point of trying to access the Akashic Records is to find out information about the past, present or future. It does not have to be your past, present or future. If you seek knowledge concerning another person, then you will need their full name, date of birth and place of birth, an image would be helpful as well. The process for reading the records normally consists of entering into a hypnotic-type trance through a self-guided meditation. Normally, you would walk yourself through a strongly visualized scene. For example, you may envision yourself walking up stairs to a massive building with colossal columns and golden doors. As you enter the doors you keep your question or intention in the forefront of your mind. As you pass into the building you walk through what seems like miles of hallways filled with books. You pick up a book with your name on it and then open it. At this point of the guided meditation you may find the answer to your question through any sense, visually on a virtual page or as an auditory sensation from a disembodied voice or you may even somehow feel the answer to your question through involuntary muscle spasms or twitching. It is possible that you may have fallen asleep by this point, but either way, in a trance or asleep you must write down all of your sensations immediately upon returning to normal waking consciousness. Many of these techniques carry over into the next practice, which comes from later forms of Buddhism.

To put it briefly, one can gain an awareness of the Storehouse or Receptacle through the final three inner tantras of the completion stage of Vajrayana Buddhism. In total, the six yogas of Naropa provide an outline of the completion stage of this lesser-known form of Buddhism. However, the final three known as the inner tantras are *milam* (dream yoga), *bardo* (intermediate state yoga), and *phowa* (transference of consciousness). These secret practices allow one to interact with the Receptacle and to manipulate the information that is within it through lucid dreaming, visualizations, and the uniting of mindstreams. The point is that these practices allow you to deal with *information* that is stored within the Receptacle, *not with the Receptacle itself as it is in its own nature*.

The practice of *Dzogchen* (great perfection) or *atiyoga*, the last of the nine *yanas* or vehicles in Nyingama Tibetan Buddhism along with "the dark retreat" can bring one to an experience of the primordial state of consciousness. This primordial state is one of emptiness pure receptivity and clarity; *it is bare witnessing rather than bearing witness to something*. You are not trying to glimpse information; you are not trying to create a change within the world; you are just dwelling in the ground or root consciousness as it is in itself: empty. I will not go into these practices in any more detail here due to the complexity involved, but I will say that it is frequently believed that *milam*, *bardo* and *phowa* yoga are viewed as prerequisites to achieving ground consciousness. I personally do not feel that one must go through the other inner tantras in order to experience Mahamudra or Dzogchen, but I can see why it may be a good idea to master the other tantras first.

Zazen, which is literally seated meditation, is simply that, just sitting. *Zazen* is primarily found practiced by the Soto school of Zen Buddhism, in contrast to the *koan* method used by the Rinzai school. The technique consists of just sitting in a variety of possible postures (half lotus, full lotus, *seiza,* a kneeling posture) while concentrating on one's breathing. *Tratak* is single-minded concentration, but *zazen* (as well as *koans*) although beginning as single-minded concentration, *culminates in a state of utter receptivity, openness or emptiness*. By itself, *zazen* can create a powerful feeling of empty calm or it can lead to the awareness of *sunyata*. Thus, zazen can in theory lead to the same experience of the Receptacle as it is in itself, as one finds in Dzogchen and Mahamudra.

For the purposes of Cosmosyntheism, there is a much simpler way to interact with and to maintain an awareness of the Receptacle: Active Paradigm Shifting. This concept is simple and fun, yet if done too frequently or improperly could become dangerous. One of the tell-tale signs of a well cultivated individual is the ability to understand the validity of another person's position or belief. We can respect someone else's opinions, but that is not the same as actually *understanding them in the sense of having first-hand experiential knowledge*. This experiential knowledge is what Active

Paradigm Shifting (APS) is all about. The best way of practicing this is to fully immerse oneself in a new philosophical, cultural, religious or secular paradigm for about two weeks, not too much longer or shorter. If you exceed two weeks you may lose your grounding and if the experience is too short, it may not acquire the realism that only truly begins to form after a few days. The truth here is that everyone's ability to shed worldviews like they do clothes is different, some actors and artistic personalities may find this much easier to perform than a rigid scientist, or conservative religious personality would.

You must try your best to fully live the lifestyle of the worldview you are practicing with. There was a television program on the FX channel called *30 Days* that basically is all about Active Paradigm Shifting and the results that the participants experienced was incredibly powerful. Most of the people that participated went through a drastic change of perspective, but then after the show, often went back to their old paradigm, but I imagine *with a much healthier respect for another point of view*. Reverting back to your old paradigm is often good, unless your dominant paradigm is currently a destructive one.

As for the actual technique, the best advice I can give is one that is often repeated in occult circles, "*Fake it until you make it*." At first, it may require a bit of method acting, but eventually it will start to feel natural and you will notice ideas and perceptions that you may have never thought possible before. For example, if you are a creationist try to live for two weeks as if the evolutionary view of life is completely correct. If you are financially well off, then try living on minimum wage. Completely disregard your old habits. The possibilities are truly endless. However, I firmly believe that Active Paradigm Shifting can have the largest global impact when dealing with religions.

What better way is there to promote religious tolerance than to actually experience what it is like to be Jewish, a Muslim, a Hindu, a Buddhist etc.? I assure you that you will have no trouble finding people who are willing to assist you in this task, as it is a great honor and sign of respect to approach someone of another faith and ask them to teach you their ways and customs. Everyone loves the opportunity to showcase their knowledge every once and awhile and in this case it is all for the best. Active Paradigm Shifting could also be called "miximizing" because you are maximizing your experience of various realities or points of view.

Active Paradigm Shifting can also be extremely liberating, but I must warn: dangerous. It is up to you to decide just how extreme you want to let this become. For example, attempting to do something that would normally revolt you can be immensely liberating, but it can also put you into a state of chaos and confusion. Disregarding your morals for an alternative set, engaging in taboo behavior for your culture and breaking the law are just a few extreme examples. I would not advise this, as it takes one too far off track and most cultivated individuals will see that *the negative consequences of such actions will outweigh any knowledge gained.*

Active Paradigm Shifting is a process that can and should be repeated in innumerable ways. However, as mentioned above, there are some forms that are dangerous if done even once let alone repeated. To summarize, I propose that there are three main forms of APS: *(1) understanding another person's point of view by living their lifestyle; (2) allowing your lesser inner drives and impulses out to play; and (3) extreme shifting, which involves attempting to crack fears, deep habits and taboos.* This third form is extremely risky and should not be repeated often if done at all. The first two should be done on a consistent basis, meaning whenever you feel that you do not really know something or understand something that is a frequent reality in your life or the lives of those around you, or whenever you feel that you are suppressing some strong inner impulse or desire.

My recommendation is that if you want to experiment with the third form, you should make it more about working with your fears, because they can be a genuine roadblock to progress. There are often good reasons for many things being taboo or illegal and you must take into consideration the ramifications of your proposed actions if you decide to shift your paradigm. You may end up doing irreparable damage to yourself and others, not to mention *it can become a convenient excuse for licentious, immoral and deviant behavior, which is certainly not the long term intended purpose of APS.*

The Receptacle contains all the past experiences, feelings and memories of all things. Thus, through APS either an individual or a group can alter their identity, their sense of self or community. The Yogacarins say that when consciousness is first coming out of the storehouse, a segment begins to separate or bud off and so at any given moment as we are going in and out of the Receptacle, we can bring our intention to a point where we either *grab a different piece of the whole or a larger piece of the Receptacle thus recognizing and experiencing it as a religious ultimate.*

A Sample Religious Service

The question still remains: what would all of these forms of worship look like if worked into a unified and holistic religious service or ceremony? I think the best way to answer this is by providing a *guided meditation* where one can visualize what this new type of ceremony would look like, sound like and feel like. What follows is a sustained guided meditation incorporating some of the techniques and methods discussed earlier in the chapter, but this time each form of worship provides one experiential piece of the larger whole that is a full-fledged religious service representing the philosophical principles of Cosmosyntheism.

Guided Meditation

Please find a comfortable position. Begin to calmly breathe in and exhale out. Now breathe in a little deeper and slower and then exhale slower and slower. Feel the

Cosmosyntheism and Applied or Practical Religion

tension in your body dissolve away as you begin to relax. With each outgoing breath gradually let your eyelids get heavier and heavier until they are fully closed. A moment ago, before you closed your eyes you could see everything within your room, but now there is only serene darkness. Any ambient noise begins to fade as you start to notice your breathing and your heartbeat. You can feel the chair beneath you and the carpet under your feet as you become totally relaxed. You begin to journey further within as each breath comes and goes . . .

In your mind's eye, you may find yourself driving up a gentle incline, moving slowly but surely up a long and winding driveway towards the top of a hill. As you continue to climb farther and farther, you notice the perfectly manicured hedges which pass by your vision on both sides of the driveway. You round one final bend in the road and start to slow down from 40 to 30 . . . 20 . . . 10 all the way down to five miles per hour as you ease your way into a parking space.

Upon exiting your vehicle your awareness is immediately drawn towards a magnificent structure, which appears to be shimmering from the sun's rays, reflecting back to you a profound sense of warmth and beauty, as if the structure itself was a precious stone. As your eyes adjust to the radiant light, you notice that the inviting structure at first glance seems to be a perfect dome, but it is actually a dome constructed of thousands of five-sided plates of glass.

As soon as you begin to make your way towards the structure a deep tonal sound rings out from a giant bell and you can feel it resonate throughout your entire body. With the sound of the bell still lingering, your senses are drawn towards an intriguing human shaped statue. Approaching the statue you recognize that the closer you get, the less human-like it appears. It is as if it was ever so slowly wasting away in front of you. Reaching out, you touch the now barely recognizable form and are surprised by the soft and porous texture as if it was made of sandstone. Continuing past the statue, you move forward across a meandering path of flagstone experiencing all of the ornate landscaping around you and the vibrant moss beneath your feet.

The path is leading you directly into the gem-like structure through two wide open doors. As you cross the threshold, you pick up on the subtle scent of fresh-cut flowers whose odor is wafting on the breeze suggesting hints of roses, juniper and lavender. Continuing into the heart of the structure you make your way down one of the aisles which is sloping downwards as you notice a large altar in the foreground which is decorated with unfamiliar symbols. While still in the aisle you turn all the way around taking in a panoramic view of the entire structure. You cannot help but notice the garlands and flowers, which you had smelled earlier decorating the walls and banisters of a second story level. You may also take note of the fact that the layout of the structure is reminiscent of a Greek amphitheatre, but with 360-degree seating encompassing the entire center stage and altar.

As you continue taking in the sights of the interior, such as the numerous images of various deities, statues and cryptic looking diagrams, you notice some of your close

Cosmosyntheism and Applied or Practical Religion

friends filing in to the structure and taking their seats, so you may choose to go sit with them. As soon as you take your seat, you become aware of all the people around you who have taken their seats and gotten situated; it is a full house. While you are looking around a slow hypnotic drumbeat commences playing a very simple rhythmic pattern. Your attention moves back towards the altar as you realize that a man is approaching it.

The drumbeat dies down as a very faint chant begins to slowly crescendo: IIIIIIIIIIII, AAAAAAAAAA, OOOOOOOOOO. You can feel the vowels pulsing throughout your head, throat and chest eliciting a hypnotic and serene effect. You are now feeling calm and centered as you become aware that the man at the altar has begun to speak. He welcomes everyone and thanks them for coming. Next, you see him place his hands on a large device with concentric rings on it. He takes the outer ring and spins it as you hear a repeated click . . . click . . . click as the dial slowly settles into place under the power of chance. The man announces that the first ring says: ancient Egypt. The man now turns the second dial at random and once again it slowly clicks to a stop, this time the window on the dial reads: soul. Finally, he spins the last ring and it comes to a slow halt on the word: afterlife.

The man at the altar then begins to give a short sermon on the topic selected at random, but as he nears the end of his sermon, he transitions to more poetic and artistic language. He asks everyone to close their eyes and imagine that they are in ancient Egypt. Notice the heat in the air and the grains of sand that are slowly being wisped about by the dry desert winds. You turn west and see the setting sun and the pyramids across the Nile. He invites you to cross the river on a large barge that is in front of you. Across the water you find yourself transported to another realm. You go through fields of reeds and find yourself face-to-face with the god Osiris, who leads you to reunite with your *ka* allowing you to become a complete *Akh*. By chanting the sacred spells given to you by Osiris, you can sense a change as you feel a remarkable sense of joy and completeness as if all of your body, mind and soul were operating in perfect harmony. Osiris tells you that if you ever need to find him again, simply cross your arms over your chest and position your hands as if you were gripping a crook and flail. Osiris fades away as you once again notice the words of the man at the altar who slowly guides you back home across the shore and suggests that you open your eyes and rejoin the congregation.

Now, back with your friends around you, the man proposes one last technique before the closing of the service. As he says this, a slow melodic drumbeat begins again and the man instructs you that when you breathe in, to breathe in a specific problem, physical, psychological or emotional that has been plaguing you lately. On every exhale he tells you to visualize that problem as healed and then to send the transformed energy back out into space. He then asks you to breathe in the problems of certain members of the congregation that may be sick and then to breathe back out healing energy for that person.

Before departing, the leader of the congregation requests that everyone perform one or more exercises over the next week. He suggests either reversing the order in which you normally do something. So perhaps try eating dinner in the morning and breakfast in the evening or sleeping all day and staying up one night or at a minimum, to take a different route home after work. With these thoughts in mind, you make your way back to your car.

As you begin to drive home, you once again notice the hedges on the winding road down the hill back towards your house. You speed up from 10 to 20 . . . 30 . . . all the way up to 40 miles per hour and before you know it, you are back home. You take a few deep breaths as you arrive home and then you open your eyes wide feeling refreshed, energized and ready to take on another week.

Summary

- Many people are simply bored by religion, but through incorporating numerous methods of worship from the various religions, a new and intriguing form of religious service can be created.

- Cosmosyntheism is open to virtually any technique that can provide a profound religious experience of one or more of the five ultimates.

- With such an open attitude, any given religious service from one week to another could be radically different, yet still fixed within a broad format that remains the same; thus, people still have some idea of what to expect.

- Some techniques are dangerous however, and that is why they would either not be used at all or set aside for people who are in the right place to attempt them, say people that have completed the Compass Path program of self cultivation.

Final Meditations

A little philosophy inclineth man's mind to atheism, but depth in philosophy bringeth men's minds about to religion.

—FRANCIS BACON, *ESSAYS OF ATHEISM*

WHAT IF THIS NEW era with the ever-strengthening grip that science has over the keys of truth, results in the dwindling of religion to the point of extinction? In other words, will religion or philosophies of religion, remain relevant in the twenty-first century? Should religion simply be allowed to fade away or should it be done away with altogether? I have argued throughout this work that religion will not die out and furthermore, should not be extinguished. However, religion must grow with the times and *one* way it can do that, is through the acceptance and incorporation of multiple religious ultimates; this has been the overarching thesis I have endeavored to prove. In addition to this central argument, I leave you with five propositions, which can serve as further meditations.

1. As long as mystery persists, the divine will still exist . . . and mystery will always persist.
2. By abandoning the infinite, one can embrace the infinite journey.
3. Hope is the quintessential human virtue; it will never be fully extinguished.
4. Seek a culture of equality, but not sameness.
5. The death of wonder is the birth of sorrow.

Bibliography

Alexander, Samuel. *Space, Time and Deity.* 2 vols. Gifford Lecture Series 1916–1918. Reprint. New York: Dover, 1966.
Al-Ghazali, Abu Hamid. *The Revival of the Religious Sciences.* Translated by Nabih Amin Faris. Lahore: Sh. Muhammad Ashraf, 1999.
The Ancient Egyptian Pyramid Texts. Translated by James P. Allen. Atlanta: Society of Biblical Literature, 2005.
Anacker, Stefan. *Seven Works of Vasubandhu: The Buddhist Psychological Doctor.* Delhi: Motilal Banarsidass, 2008.
Anselm. *Proslogion.* Translated by M. J. Charlesworth. Oxford: Clarendon, 1965.
Aristotle. *The Complete Works of Aristotle.* Edited by Jonathan Barnes. Princeton: Princeton University Press, 1984.
Aquinas, Thomas. *Quaestiones Disputatio, Volumen I: De Veritate.* Edited by Raymundi Spiazzi, P. Bazzi, M. Calcaterra, T. S. Centi and E. Odetto. Rome: Marietti, 1949.
Augustine. *City of God.* Translated by Henry Bettenson. London: Penguin, 1984.
———. *Confessions.* Translated by Henry Chadwick. Oxford: Oxford University Press, 1998.
The Bhagavad Gita. Translated by Eknath Easwaran. Berkeley, CA: Nilgiri, 2007.
Banner, William Augustus. *The Path of St. Augustine.* Lanham, MD: Rowman & Littlefield, 1997.
Barnstone, Willis, and Marvin Meyer, editors. *The Gnostic Bible.* Boston: Shambhala, 2003.
Basinger, David et. al. *The Openness of God: A Biblical Challenge to the Traditional Understanding of God.* Downer's Grove, IL: InterVarsity, 1994.
Bohm, David. *Wholeness and the Implicate Order.* London: Routledge, 2002.
Bostrom, Nick. "Are You Living in a Computer Simulation?" *Philosophical Quarterly* 53 (2003) 211–230.
Campbell, Joseph. *The Masks of God.* 4 vols. London: Penguin, 1991.
Caputo, John D. "Love Among the Deconstructibles: A Response to Greg Lambert." *JCRT* 5:2 (April 2004) 37.
———. *The Prayers and Tears of Jacques Derrida: Religion without Religion.* Bloomington, IN: Indiana University Press, 1997.
Carroll, Peter. *The Apophenion.* Oxford: Mandrake, 2008.
———. *Liber Kaos.* San Francisco: Weiser, 1992.
———. *Liber Null & Psychonaut.* San Francisco: Weiser, 1987.
Charlesworth, Maxwell John, Francoise Dussart, and Howard Murphy, editors. *Aboriginal Religions in Australia.* Aldershot, UK: Ashgate, 2005.
Chown, Marcus. "You Are a Hologram." *New Scientist* (January 17–23) 2009.
Clayton, Philip, and Arthur Peacocke. *In Whom We Live and Move and Have Our Being: Panentheistic Reflections on God's Presence in a Scientific World.* Grand Rapids: Eerdmans, 2004.
Cobb, John B. Jr. *Transforming Christianity and the World: A Way beyond Absolutism and Relativism.* Edited and introduced by Paul F. Knitter. Faith Meets Faith. Maryknoll, NY: Orbis, 1999.
Cobb, John B. Jr., and David Ray Griffin. *Process Theology: An Introductory Exposition.* Louisville: Westminster John Knox, 1976.

Bibliography

Cornford, Francis. *Plato's Cosmology: The Timaeus of Plato*. Indianapolis: Bobbs-Merrill, 1957.
Davis, Caroline Franks. *The Evidential Force of Religious Experience*. Oxford: Clarendon, 1989.
Deleuze, Gilles. *Pure Immanence: Essay on a Life*. Cambridge: Zone, 2005.
Derrida, Jacques. *On the Name*. Translated by Thomas Dutoit. Stanford, CA: Stanford University Press, 1995.
The Dhammapada. Translated by John Ross Carter and Mahinda Palihawadana. New York: Oxford University Press, 2000.
Dilman, Ilham. *Free Will: An Historical and Philosophical Introduction*. London: Routledge, 1999.
Evans, Gillian. *Augustine on Evil*. Cambridge: Cambridge University Press, 1990.
Gardner, Gerald. *The Meaning of Witchcraft*. London: Aquarian, 1959.
———. *Witchcraft Today*. New York: Citadel, 1970.
Goddard, Dwight, editor. *A Buddhist Bible*. Boston: Beacon, 1994.
Graham, A. C. *Disputers of the Tao: Philosophical Argument in Ancient China*. La Salle, IL: Open Court, 1989.
Greene, Brian. *The Elegant Universe: Superstrings, Hidden Dimensions, and the Quest for the Ultimate Theory*. New York: Vintage, 2000.
———. *The Fabric of the Cosmos: Space, Time, and the Texture of Reality*. New York: Vintage, 2005.
———. *The Hidden Reality: Parallel Universes and the Deep Laws of the Cosmos*. New York: Knopf, 2011.
Griffin, David Ray. "John Cobb's Whiteheadian Complementary Pluralism." In *Deep Religious Pluralism*, edited by David Ray Griffin, 39–68. Louisville: Westminster John Knox, 2005.
———. "Religious Pluralism: Generic, Identist and Deep." In *Deep Religious Pluralism*, edited by David Ray Griffin, 3–38. Louisville: Westminster John Knox, 2005.
———. *Reenchantment without Supernaturalism: A Process Philosophy of Religion*. Cornell Studies in the Philosophy of Religion. Ithaca, NY: Cornell University Press, 2001.
———. *Whitehead's Radically Different Postmodern Philosophy: An Argument for Its Contemporary Relevance*. SUNY Series in Philosophy. Albany, NY: SUNY Press, 2007.
Hartshorne, Charles. *Creative Synthesis and Philosophic Method*. Chicago: Open Court, 1970.
———. *Omnipotence and Other Theological Mistakes*. Albany, NY: SUNY Press, 1984.
Heim, S. Mark. *The Depth of the Riches: A Trinitarian Theology of Religious Ends*. Grand Rapids: Eerdmans, 2001.
———. *Salvations: Truth and Difference in Religion*. Faith Meets Faith. Maryknoll, NY: Orbis, 1995.
Hick, John. *An Interpretation of Religion: Human Responses to the Transcendent*. New Haven, CT: Yale University Press, 1989.
———. *Philosophy of Religion*. 4th ed. Prentice Hall Foundations of Philosophy Series. Upper Saddle River, NJ: Prentice-Hall, 1990.
Ives, Christopher. "Liberating Truth: A Buddhist Approach to Religious Pluralism." In *Deep Religious Pluralism*, edited by David Ray Griffin, 178–93. Louisville: Westminster John Knox, 2005.
Josephus, Flavius. *Jewish Antiquities*. 3 vols. Loeb Classical Library. Cambridge: Harvard University Press, 2001.
Kaku, Michio. *Parallel Worlds: A Journey through Creation, Higher Dimensions, and the Future of the Cosmos*. New York: Anchor, 2005.
Kardashev, Nikolai. "Cosmology and Civilizations." *Astrophysics and Space Science* 7 (March 1997) 252–70.
———. "Transmission of Information by Extraterrestrial Civilizations." *Soviet Astronomy* 8 (1964) 217–28.
Katz, Stephen. "Language, Epistemology and Mysticism." In *Mysticism and Philosophical Analysis*, edited by Stephen Katz, 22–74. New York: Oxford University Press, 1978.
Küng, Hans. *Christianity: Essence, History and Future*. The Religious Situation of Our Time. New York: Continuum International, 1996.
Lao-tzu. *The Tao-Te-Ching*. Translated by Jonathan Star. New York: Tarcher/Penguin, 2003.
Layton, Bentley. *The Gnostic Scriptures*. Garden City, NY: Doubleday, 1987.
Lavey, Anton. *Satantic Bible*. New York: Avon, 1969.

Levenson, Jon. *Creation and the Persistence of Evil: The Jewish Drama of Divine Omnipotence.* Princeton: Princeton University Press, 1994.
Lightman, Alan, and Roberta Brawer. *Origins: The Lives and Worlds of Modern Cosmologists.* Cambridge: Harvard University Press, 1990.
Maimon, Moses ben. *The Guide for the Perplexed.* Translated by M. Friedlander. New York: Hebrew Literature Society, 1904.
Madhvacharya and Vyasatirtha. "The Prameya Shloka." Online: http://www.dvaita.org/shaastra/prameya.shtml.
Mann, William. "Augustine on Evil and Original Sin." In *The Cambridge Companion to Augustine*, edited by Eleonore Stump and Norman Kretzmann, 30–46. Cambridge: Cambridge University Press, 2001.
May, Gerhard. *Creatio ex Nihilo: The Doctrine of "Creation out of Nothing" in Early Christian Thought.* Edinburgh: T. & T. Clark, 2004.
Myths from Mesopotamia. Translated by Stephanie Dalley. New York: Oxford, 2000.
The Nag Hammadi Library in English. 3rd revised edition. Translated by members of the Coptic Gnostic Library Project of the Institute for Antiquity and Christianity. Edited by James M. Robinson. San Francisco: Harper and Row, 1988.
Nhat Hanh, Thich. *Transformation at the Base: Fifty Verses on the Nature of Consciousness.* Berkeley, CA: Parallax, 2001.
Olson, Carl. *The Different Paths of Buddhism.* New Brunswick, NJ: Rutgers, 2005.
Pearson, Birger. *Ancient Gnosticism: Traditions and Literature.* Minneapolis: Fortress, 2007.
Plato. *Complete Works.* Edited by John M. Cooper. Indianapolis: Hackett, 1997.
Plotinus. *Enneads.* Translated by Stephen Mackenna. New York: Penguin, 1991.
The Qur'an. Translated by M. H. Shakir. 13th ed. Elmhurst, IL: Tahrike Tarsile, 2002.
Radhakrishnan, Sarvepalli, editor. *Indian Philosophy.* 2 vols. Oxford: Oxford University Press, 2009.
Redford, Donald, editor. *The Ancient Gods Speak.* New York: Oxford, 2002.
Rudolph, Kurt. *Gnosis: The Nature and History of Gnosticism.* Translated by Robert McLachlan Wilson. San Francisco: Harper & Row, 1987.
Sagan, Carl. *Cosmic Connection: An Extraterrestrial Perspective.* Edited by Jerome Agel. Cambridge: Cambridge University Press, 2000.
Sallis, John. *Chorology: On Beginning in Plato's Timaeus.* Bloomington: Indiana University Press, 1999.
Schuon, Frithjof. *The Essential Frithjof Schuon.* Edited by Seyyed Hossein Nasr. Bloomington, IN: World Wisdom, 2005.
———. *The Transcendent Unity of Religions.* Wheaton, IL: Quest, 2005.
Schwartz, Benjamin. *The World of Thought in Ancient China.* Cambridge: Harvard University Press, 1985.
The Shepherd of Hermas. Edited by James Donaldson et. al. Ante-Nicene Fathers 2: Fathers of the Second Century. Reprinted, Peabody, MA: Hendrickson, 1996.
Smith, Huston. *Forgotten Truth: The Common Vision of the World's Religions.* San Francisco: HarperCollins, 1992.
A Source Book in Chinese Philosophy. Translated by Wing-Tsit Chan. Princeton: Princeton University Press, 1963.
Suzuki, D. T. "The Buddhist Conception of Reality." In *The Buddha Eye: An Anthology of the Kyoto School*, edited by Frederick Franck. New York: Crossroad, 1991.
———. *Studies in Zen.* Edited by Christmas Humphreys. New York: Dell, 1955.
Talbot, Michael. *The Holographic Universe.* New York: HarperCollins, 1991.
Tatian. *Address to the Greeks.* Edited by James Donaldson et. al. Ante-Nicene Fathers 2: Fathers of the Second Century. Reprinted, Peabody, MA: Hendrickson, 1996.
Theogony. Translated by Apostolos N. Athanassakis. Baltimore: John Hopkins University Press, 2004.
Whitehead, Alfred North. *Adventures of Ideas.* Cambridge: Cambridge University Press, 1933.
———. *Essays in Science and Philosophy.* New York: Philosophical Library, 1947.
———. *The Function of Reason.* 1929. Reprinted, Boston: Beacon: 1958.
———. *Modes of Thought.* 1938. Reprinted, New York: Free, 1968.

Bibliography

———. *Process and Reality.* Corrected edition. Edited by David Ray Griffin and Donald W. Sherburne. New York: Free Press, 1978.

———. *Religion in the Making.* 1926. Reprinted, New York: Fordham University Press, 2005.

Yang, Lihui, and Deming An, with Jessica Anderson Turner. *Handbook of Chinese Mythology.* New York: Oxford University Press, 2008.

Yu-lan, Fung, *A Short History of Chinese Philosophy.* New York: Free Press, 1948.

———. *Hsin li-hsueh.* Changsha, Hunan: Commercial, 1939.

Zaehner, R. C., editor and translator. *Hindu Scriptures.* 1966. Reprinted, Everyman's Library 64. New York: Knopf, 1992.

Zum Brunn, Emilie. *St. Augustine: Being and Nothingness.* Translated by Ruth Namad. New York: Paragon House, 1988.

Subject Index

Abraham, 45
Abram, 48
acosmic ultimate, 5–6, 12
active paradigm shifting, 233, 256–58
Acts, 48–49
Adam, 33, 140, 145, 210, 214
Adams, Henry, 92
Address to the Greeks (Tatian), 44
Advaita Vedanta, 8, 21, 159, 161–65, 168
advancements of cosmosyntheism, 60–61
Adventures in the Spirit (Clayton), 64n3
Adventures of Ideas (Whitehead), 5, 59, 87, 107, 110–13, 171n26
Against the Gnostics (Plotinus), 35
agape, 104–105
Akashic Records, 199, 201, 255–256
Akhenaton, 34n40
Akkadian creation myths, 94
alaya-vijnana, 196, 200
Alexander, Samuel
    generally, 13, 50n67, 51n71, 123–24, 128
    on conflicting religious truth claims, 168–70
    emergent theism and, 49–51, 53–55
    on evil, 215–16, 218
    on free will, 150–51, 150n28, 156
Allah, 42, 45–49, 183
Allegory of the Cave (Plato), 74
almsgiving, 254
amendment of texts, 253
An, Deming, 94n5
Anacker, Stefan, 200n44
Analects, 181
ananda, 20
anapanasanti, 241
anatman, 196
Anaxagoras, 187–88
Anaximander, 23n18
The Ancient Gods Speak (Redford), 93n3
anitya, 193, 196–97
Anselm of Canterbury, 83
anthropic principle, 84
Antiquities of the Jews (Josephus), 160n5

Apocalypse of Paul, 27
Apocryphon of John, 31
apophenia, 249
The Apophenion (Carroll), 249n6
applied religion, 237–261
    guided meditation, 258–261
    overview, 237–38, 261
    sample religious service, 258–61
    worship (*see* worship)
Aquinas, Thomas
    generally, 166
    on *creatio ex nihilo*, 45
    on free will, 133, 147, 147n20, 149
    on God, 49
    on trinity, 42, 42n47
Arbib, Michael, 51n73
arguments in favor of cosmosyntheism
    compatibility with science, xix
    global appeal, xix
    immunity to atheistic criticism, xix
    integration of religious concepts, xviii–xix
    overview, xviii–xix
Aristarchus of Samos, 38n45
Aristotle
    on forms, 63
    prime matter, 96–97, 102–3
    on world, 92, 96–97, 99, 187
Arjuna, 182
Arminianism, 145
ars combinatoria, 249
artificial intelligence, 89–90
artistic endeavors, 243–44, 243n3
ascent, 34–35
Asha'irah, 146
Asherah, 160
assumptions regarding cosmosyntheism, xvi–xviii
astral projection, 242
atheism, xix, 10, 84–85, 90, 191
atiyoga, 256
atman, 5, 162, 188
attunement, 240
Atum, 93

269

auersio, 210–13
Augustine
    generally, 166, 213*n*20
    auersio, 210–13
    on *creatio ex nihilo*, 44–45, 44*n*54
    on evil, 208–15
    on free will, 145–47, 147*n*19, 149
    on God, 42, 42*n*47, 49
    on original sin, 41
Aurobindo, Sri, 3*n*1, 237
Autogenes, 31
Averroes, 46
Avicenna, 46

Baal, 160
Bacon, Francis, 263
Baha'i, 181
bandhas, 241*n*1
Barbelo, 31, 33
bardo, 256
Barrett, Tom, 92
Basilidian Gnosticism, 23, 31, 43
Bhagavad Gita, 182
Bhakti Yoga, 8
bhavachakra, 196
bibliomancy, 249
Big Bang theory, 116
bijas, 197
Bohm, David, 114*n*19
bonum supremum, 213
Bostrom, Nick, 151
Brahma, 94, 183
brahman, xv, 5, 20, 94, 162–63, 188
brahmaviharas, 254–55
Broad, C.D., 51*n*73
Buddha, 195–97
Buddhaghosa, 254
Buddhism. *see also specific branch or sect*
    charity in, 254
    conflicting religious truth claims and, 157, 159, 161–62, 164–73
    creativity in, 193–98
    incarnation in, 184
    meditation in, 241, 252
    receptacle in, 198–200
    religious ultimates in, 20–21
    ritual magic in, 161
    scriptural study in, 246
    trinity in, 183
Bukhari, Sahih, 46

Cain, 31
Calvin, John, 45
Calvinism, 145
Campbell, Joseph, 93*n*1

Candomblé, 247
Caputo, John, 113
Carpocratians, 161
Carroll, Peter, 192–93, 249
categorical imperative, 227, 227*n*13
Catholicism
    charity in, 254
    trinity in, 7*n*15
Chan, 124
Chan, Wing-Tsit, 136*n*5
charity, 254
Cheng Yi, 179, 193
Chinese creation myths, 94
Christianity. *see also specific branch or sect*
    confession in, 247–48
    conflicting religious truth claims and, 158, 166–68, 170–72
    creatio ex nihilo in, 44–45, 146
    eschatology in, 184
    evil in, 209
    free will in, 145–47
    God in, 42, 47–48, 181
    incarnation in, 184
    messiah in, 40, 184–85
    paraclete in, 185
    prayer in, 245
    religious ultimates in, 10
    ritual magic in, 161
    trinity in, 7*n*15, 40, 167–68, 183
    worship in, 238
Christianity: Essence, History and Future (Küng), xiii*n*1
Chronology (Sallis), 110*n*8
Chronos, 95
Church of Satan, 191
Cicero, 147*n*19
City of God (Augustine), 45, 147*n*19, 212
classical theism, 40–49
    generally, 59–60
    attributes of God in, 47–49
    conflicting religious truth claims in, 166–68
    creatio ex nihilo in, 43–46, 211
    evil in, 209–15
    free will in, 144–49, 156
    one true God in, 42–43
    overview, 40–42, 55
    pantheism compared, 41
Clayton, Philip, 51*n*73, 64*n*3
Cobb, John B., Jr. *see also* pluralistic metaphysics
    generally, xx, 3, 59, 61
    on conflicting religious truth claims, 170–76
    on evil, 219

Subject Index

on forms, 78–79, 178
on free will, 133–34, 152–56
on messiah, 185
on pluralistic metaphysics, 3–8, 10, 12
on world, 100, 186
collaborative art, 243–44
The Compass Path: A Guide to Self Cultivation (Iammarino), 230–35
Compass Path system, 230–35, 261
Compendium Theologicae (Aquinas), 42*n*47
confession, 247–48
Confessions (Augustine), 45
conflicting religious truth claims, 157–201
    Alexander on, 168–70
    Buddhism and, 157, 159, 161–62, 164–73
    Christianity and, 166–68, 170–72
    classical theism and, 166–68
    Cobb on, 170–76
    creativity and, 193–98
    Daoism and, 157, 159, 161, 166–69
    emanationism and, 161–65
    emergent theism and, 168–70
    forms and, 178–81
    God and, 181–86
    Griffin on, 170–76
    Hinduism and, 158–59, 162–63, 167
    Islam and, 158–59, 166
    Judaism and, 158–60, 166
    Neo-Platonism and, 161
    overview, 157, 174–76, 178, 201
    pantheism and, 173–74
    in perennial philosophy, 158–61
    perennial philosophy and, 158–61
    pluralistic metaphysics and, 170–74
    problem of, 157–58
    receptacle and, 198–201
    sunyata and, 164–65, 167–68, 172–73
    Whitehead on, 168–73, 171*n*26
    world and, 186–93
Confucianism, 137–38, 181, 195, 254
Cornford, Francis, 110*n*8
Corpus Hermeticum (Hermes), 27
cosmic aim of life, 224–28
cosmic ultimate, 5–6, 12
cosmos. *see* world
cosmosyntheism. *see specific topic*
creatio ex nihilo
    Aquinas on, 45
    Augustine on, 44–45, 44*n*54
    in Christianity, 44–45, 146
    in classical theism, 43–46, 211
    in Islam, 45–46, 214
    in Judaism, 43, 45, 214
    Neo-Platonism and, 46
Creatio ex Nihilo (May), 95*n*8

Creation and the Persistence of Evil (Levenson), 95*n*8
Creative Synthesis and Philosophic Method (Hartshorne), 89*n*22
creative visualization, 241
creativity, 102–106
    agape and, 104–5
    in Buddhism, 193–98
    conflicting religious truth claims and, 193–98
    in cosmosyntheism, 197–98
    dao and, 193–95, 197
    in Daoism, 193–95, 197
    defined in cosmosyntheism, 63–64, 104–5
    elements of, 103–4
    ethics and, 226–28
    Griffin on, 103
    insufficiency of creativity alone, 105
    logical inconsistency of alternatives to cosmosyntheism lacking, 117–30
    necessity of, 102
    overview, 102, 105–6
    prime matter distinguished, 102–3
    as religious ultimate, 4, 7–9, 12
    Whitehead on, 102–5
    worship and, 251–55
cyborgs, 89–90

Dalley, Stephanie, 94*n*4
dao
    generally, xv, 124, 168
    creativity and, 193–95, 197
    emanationism and, 22–23, 26
    evil and, 204–5, 216
    free will and, 136–38, 144
    receptacle and, 201
DaodeJing, 22–23, 26, 136–37, 194, 194*n*31
Daoism
    generally, 124
    conflicting religious truth claims and, 157, 159, 161, 166–69
    creativity in, 193–95, 197
    emanationism in, 21–27, 156
    ethics and, 226
    evil in, 204–5, 215–16
    free will in, 136–38
    receptacle in, 116, 200–201
    ritual magic in, 161
    world in, 186
dark energy, 115
Da Xue, 254
de (Daoist force), 26, 136–37
Deep Religious Pluralism (Griffin), 10
definition of cosmosyntheism, xvi
Deleuze, Gilles, 113

De Libero Arbitrio (Augustine), 146, 212–13
The Depth of the Riches: A Trinitarian Theology of Religious Ends (Heim), 166–68
Derrida, Jacques, 112–13
De Trinitate (Augustine), 42n47, 213n20, 214
Deuteronomy, 42–43
Dhammapada, 196
dharmakaya, 183, 196
Diamond Sutra, 197n41
Diotima, 243
dipolar process theism, 85–87
Discourse on the Eighth and Ninth (Hermes), 27
Disputers of the Tao (Graham), 136n5
The Divine Matrix (Bracken), 87n17
dreamtime, 179, 181
drugs, 247n5
Druidism, 191
Dvaita Vedanta, 163, 186, 188–89
dzogchen, 256

Eckhart, Meister, 8
egregores, 241–42
Egyptian creation myths, 93
Einstein, Albert, 117
El (Canaanite deity), 160
The Elegant Universe (Greene), 97n14
emanationism, 22–40
    generally, 59–60
    conflicting religious truth claims in, 161–65
    dao and, 22–23, 26
    in Daoism, 21–27, 156
    evil in, 204–9
    free will in, 134–44, 156
    Hermetic Gnosticism (*see* Hermetic Gnosticism)
    "old paradigm" versus, 38–40
    ontological dependence, 36–37
    overview, 22–23, 55
    pantheism and, 22, 26
    Plotinus (*see* Plotinus)
    Sethian Gnosticism (*see* Sethian Gnosticism)
emergent theism, 49–54
    generally, 59–60
    Alexander and, 49–51, 53–55
    conflicting religious truth claims in, 168–70
    evil in, 215–16
    free will in, 150–52, 150n28, 156
    key emergent levels, 52–53
    logical inconsistency of, 123–24, 128
    overview, 55
Empedocles, 23n18, 187–88
Enneads (Plotinus), 35n44, 180

2 *Enoch*, 27
enrichment, 3, 10, 12, 170–71, 175–76
Enuma Elish, 94
Eratosthenes, 38n45
Erebus, 95
eros (force). *see* creativity
Eros (Greek deity), 95
eschatology, 184
Essays of Atheism (Bacon), 263
Essenes, 160
eternal objects, 75–77, 79–80
eternal three-story universe, 23n19
ethics, 223–35
    Compass Path system and, 230–35
    cosmic aim of life, 224–28
    creativity and, 226–28
    Daoism and, 226
    Griffin on, 224–26
    individual aim of life, 230–34
    overview, 223–24, 234–35
    social aim of life, 228–30
    Whitehead on, 224–27
Eugnostos the Blessed, 31
evangelism, 246
Eve, 33, 140, 145, 210, 214
evil, 202–19
    Alexander on, 215–16, 218
    Augustine on, 208–15
    in classical theism, 209–15
    Cobb on, 219
    in cosmosyntheism, 218–19
    dao and, 204–5, 216
    in Daoism, 204–5, 215–16
    in emanationism, 204–9
    in emergent theism, 215–16
    Griffin on, 216–19
    in Hermetic Gnosticism, 205–6
    imperfection as, 203
    in Islam, 209
    in Judaism, 209
    Neo-Platonism and, 210–13
    overview, 202, 219
    in perennial philosophy, 202–4
    Plato on, 205
    Plotinus on, 208–11
    in pluralistic metaphysics, 216–18
    problem of, 202
    in Sethian Gnosticism, 207–8
    Whitehead on, 218–19
Evil and Omnipotence (Mackie), 202
exclusivism, xiv

The Fabric of the Cosmos (Greene), 97n14
Facebook, 229
First Amendment, 237

Subject Index

Five Element Theories, 61n1
Five Pillars of Islam, 42, 254
Forgotten Truth: the Common Vision of the World's Religions (Smith), 13–14, 203
forms, 71–81
    Cobb on, 178
    conflicting religious truth claims and, 178–81
    in cosmosyntheism, 180–81
    defined in cosmosyntheism, 62–63
    eternal objects, 75–77, 79–80
    expanding set of forms in cosmosyntheism, 78–80
    Griffin on, 78–79, 178
    Hartshorne on, 79
    hylomorphism and, 75–76
    insufficiency of forms alone, 80
    logical inconsistency of alternatives to cosmosyntheism lacking, 117–30
    necessity of, 71–72
    Neo-Platonism and, 242–43, 243n2
    overview, 71, 80–81
    Plato on, 62–63n2, 71–82, 124, 178–79
    "theory of the forms" (Plato), 72, 74–75, 79–81
    Whitehead on, 71, 75–82, 178, 181
    worship and, 239–44
Freemasonry, 161
free will, 133–56
    Alexander on, 150–51, 150n28, 156
    Aquinas on, 133, 147, 147n20, 149
    Augustine on, 145–47, 147n19, 149
    in Christianity, 145–47
    in classical theism, 144–49, 156
    Cobb on, 133–34, 152–56
    in cosmosyntheism, 154–55
    dao and, 136–38, 144
    in Daoism, 136–38
    in emanationism, 136–44, 156
    in emergent theism, 150–52, 150n28, 156
    Griffin on, 133–34, 152–56
    in Hermetic Gnosticism, 138–40
    in Islam, 145–47
    Jesus and, 145
    in Judaism, 145–46
    in open theism, 144, 147–49, 147n21
    overview, 133–34, 155–56
    panexperientialism and, 152
    in perennial philosophy, 134–36, 156
    Plato on, 143
    Plotinus on, 142–44
    in pluralistic metaphysics, 152–56
    problem of, 134
    in Protestantism, 144
    in Sethian Gnosticism, 140–41
    in Shi'a Islam, 146
    in Sunni Islam, 146
    Whitehead on, 153–55

Gaia, 95
Gandhi, Mohandas, 223
Garuda Purana, 183–84
gematria, 250
Genesis, 29, 43, 49, 95, 250
Al-Ghazali, Abu Hamid, 46
Glaucon, 74
global appeal of cosmosyntheism, xix
Gnostic baptism, 34
Gnosticism
    Basilidian Gnosticism, 23, 31, 43
    Hermetic Gnosticism, 27–30 (*see also* Hermetic Gnosticism)
    Sethian Gnosticism, 30–35 (*see also* Sethian Gnosticism)
    Thomas Gnosticism, 31
    Valentinian Gnosticism, 30n32, 31, 141
Gnosticism and Later Platonism: Themes, Figures and Texts (Turner and Majercik), 243n2
God, 82–91
    Aquinas, Thomas on, 49
    attributes of in classical theism, 47–49
    Augustine on, 42, 42n47, 49
    in Christianity, 42, 47–48, 181
    conflicting religious truth claims and, 181–86
    in cosmosyntheism, 88–91, 186
    defined in cosmosyntheism, 63
    dipolar process theism and, 85–87
    eschatology and, 184
    gender of, 83n1
    Griffin on, 82, 84, 86–88, 91
    Hartshorne on, 82, 86–89, 88n21, 91
    in Hinduism, 182
    immanence of, 185
    incarnation and, 184
    in Islam, 42, 181
    Jesus and, 44n54, 48
    in Judaism, 42, 48, 181, 207
    logical inconsistency of alternatives to cosmosyntheism lacking, 117–30
    messiah and, 184–85
    necessity of, 82–85
    one true God in classical theism, 42–43
    overview, 82, 91
    in pantheism, 182
    paraclete and, 185
    in pluralistic metaphysics, 87–88
    as religious ultimate, 4–5, 7–9, 12

God *(cont.)*
    as serially ordered society of actual occasions, 87–88
    transcendence of, 185
    trinity and, 183
    Whitehead on, 82, 85–88, 91
    worship and, 244–48
God, Power and Evil: A Process Theodicy (Griffin), 216
Gospel of the Egyptians, 34
Gospel of Thomas, 59
Graham, A.C., 136n5
Greek creation myths, 95
Greene, Brian, 97n14, 114n19
Griffin, David Ray. *see also* pluralistic metaphysics
    generally, xx, 59, 61, 127
    on conflicting religious truth claims, 170–76
    on creativity, 103
    on ethics, 224–26
    on evil, 216–19
    on forms, 78–79, 178
    on free will, 133–34, 152–56
    on God, 82, 84, 86–88, 91
    law of non-contradiction, 11n27
    on pluralistic metaphysics, 3–5, 7–12
    on world, 100, 186
Groundwork for the Metaphysics of Morals (Kant), 227n13
Guénon, René, 14
guided meditation, 242, 258–61

hajj, 246
Handbook of Chinese Mythology (Yang and An), 94n5
Hare, Peter, 217
Hartshorne, Charles
    generally, 89n22
    on forms, 79
    on God, 82, 86–89, 88n21, 91
Hasker, William, 147n21
Hebrew creation myths, 95
Hebrews, 44
Hegel, G. W. F., xiv
Heidegger, Martin, 112
Heim, S. Mark, 7, 7n15, 165–68, 174
Heliopolitans, 93
Hermes (Greek deity), 103
Hermes the Thrice Great, 27–29, 138–40
Hermes Trismegustus, 27–29, 138–40
Hermetic Gnosticism, 27–30
    generally, 22, 41, 160
    cosmology in, 28–29
    evil in, 205–6
    free will in, 138–40
    Judaism and, 27
Hesiod, 95
Hesse, Mary, 51n73
Hick, John, xiv, 7, 7n15, 161, 163–66
Hidden Reality (Greene), 114n19
Higgs field, 50n67
Hinduism. *see also specific branch or sect*
    conflicting religious truth claims and, 158–59, 162–63, 167
    God in, 181–82
    incarnation in, 184
    ritual offerings in, 248
    transcendence or immanence of God in, 185
    trinity in, 183
    world in, 188
Hippolytus, 43
Hisamatu, Shin'ichi, 173
hologram model, 114, 114n19
The Holographic Universe (Talbot), 114n19
Holy Spirit, 42, 44n54, 167, 183, 185
Homer, 40, 95
homoousis, 183
horizon problem, 100
Horus, 93, 93n3
Hsin li-hsüeh (Yu-lan), 3n1
Hu, 94
Hundun, 94
Hutchison, Jack, 5
Huxley, Aldous, 14
hylomorphism, 75–76, 97, 99–100

Ialdabaoth, 30, 33, 140–41, 207–8
I Ching, 179, 249
identist pluralism, 158
Illuminates of ThanatEros, 192–93
immanence of God, 185
immunity of cosmosyntheism to atheistic criticism, xix
imperfection as evil, 203
incarnation, 184
Indian creation myths, 94
Indian Philosophy (Radahakrishnan), 162n6
individual aim of life, 230–34
integration of religious concepts in cosmosyntheism, xviii–xix
internal relations, 77
An Interpretation of Religion (Hick), 164
Introduction to the Science of Religion (Müller), 157
invocation, 247
Irenaus, 44
Isaiah, 42, 47–48
Ishvara, 162, 188

Subject Index

Islam. *see also specific branch or sect*
    charity in, 254
    conflicting religious truth claims and, 158–59, 166
    creatio ex nihilo in, 45–46, 214
    eschatology in, 184
    evil in, 209
    Five Pillars of, 42, 254
    free will in, 145–47
    God in, 42, 181
    Jesus and, 183n10
    pilgrimage in, 246
    prayer in, 245
    predestination in, 199, 201
    receptacle in, 199
    scriptural study in, 245
    trinity in, 40, 183

Jeremiah, 48
Jesus
    apostles of, 232
    free will and, 145
    God and, 44n54, 48
    Islam and, 183n10
    as messiah, 40, 184
jiva, 188–89
jnana, 163
John (Gospel), 44, 49, 185
1 John (Epistle), 49
Josephus, 160n5
Judaism. *see also specific branch or sect*
    conflicting religious truth claims and, 158–60, 166
    creatio ex nihilo in, 43, 45, 214
    eschatology in, 184
    evil in, 209
    free will in, 145–46
    God in, 42, 48, 181, 207
    Hermetic Gnosticism and, 27
    messiah in, 40, 184–85
    mysticism in, 161
    paraclete in, 185
    prayer in, 245
    ritual magic in, 161
    ritual offerings in, 248
    scriptural study in, 245
    Sethian Gnosticism and, 31, 33

Kabbalah, 8, 160–61, 242, 250–51
Kaku, Michio, 97n14, 229
Kant, Immanuel, 84, 163, 165, 227, 227n13
Kardashev, Nikolai, 228–29
Kauffman, Stuart, 64n3
kenosis, 147
khora, 5, 109, 112–13

King of Death, 196n38
kledonomancy, 249
Knitter, Paul, 7, 7n15, 14, 166
Krishna, 182
Küng, Hans, n1, xiii, xix, 14

Laozi, 23, 26–27, 194
Lardil people, 179
Large Hadron Collider, 50n67
al-Lauh al-Mahfuz, 146, 199
law of non-contradiction, 11n27
Laws of Manu, 94
Layton, Bentley, 30
leela, 162, 231
Leibniz, Gottfried, 50, 249
Levenson, Jon, 43, 95n8
li (Daoist rules), 136–37, 179–81
libertas, 145
liberum aribitrium, 145, 148
Life and Letters II (Müller), 175
logical inconsistency of alternatives to cosmosyntheism, 117–30
    chart, 118–19
    overview, 129–30
Lotus Sutra Buddhism, 8
lucid dreaming, 242–43
Lull, Raymond, 249
Lullian Circle, 249–50
Luther, Martin, 45, 133

2 Maccabees, 43
Mackenna, Stephen, 35n44
Mackie, John, 202
Madden, Edward, 217
Madhvacharya, 188–89, 189n14
Magus, Simon, 22
mahamudra, 256
Mahayana Buddhism, 8
Maimonides, 43, 45, 48, 146
Majjhima-Nikaya, 195–96
Malachi, 47
manas, 196
Mani, 185, 187
Manichaeism, 31, 44, 187
Mann, William, 211
Mara, 196, 196n38
Marduk, 94
Marsanes, 35
The Masks of God (Campbell), 93n1
massa peccati, 145
Matthew, 48
May, Gerhard, 43, 95n8
maya, 20, 135, 168
meditation
    anapanasanti, 241

275

    in Buddhism, 241, 252
    guided meditation, 242, 258–61
    samatha, 241
    vipassana, 239–41, 252
membrane theory, 114
Mencius, 138, 181
Merkabah mysticism, 160
Merton, Thomas, 173
messiah, 40, 184–85
Metaphysics (Aristotle), 63, 96–97
Meyer, Marvin, 34*n*41
milam, 256
Miller, Henry, 92
Mimasa Vedanta, 188
minus esse, 213
Mishnah, 47
missionary work, 246
Modes of Thought (Whitehead), 225
Mohism, 137, 181
moksha, 167
Montanus, 185
Morgan, C.L., 51*n*73
mudrus, 241*n*1
Muhammad, 45, 185
mula-prakriti, 188
Müller, Max, 157, 175
Mul Mantra, 181
multiverse theory, 90–91
Mu'tazilah, 146
mutually grounding ultimates of cosmosyntheism
    creation and cosmosyntheism, 68–69
    creativity (*see* creativity)
    definitions, 62–64
    forms (*see* forms)
    God (*see* God)
    grounding of, 64–68, 177–78
    logical inconsistency of alternatives to cosmosyntheism lacking, 117–30
    overview, 61–62, 69–70
    reality as complex adaptive system, 68
    reasons for, 61–62
    receptacle (*see* receptacle)
    world (*see* world)
Myths from Mesopotamia (Dalley), 94*n*4

Nagarjuna, 197*n*41
Nag Hammadi Library, 30
naropa, 256
nature worship, 251
Naufal, Waraqa, 45
near death experiences, 242
Nefertiti, 34*n*40
neo-atheism, 8, 158

Neo-Confucianism, 161, 178–81, 179*n*2, 186, 188–90, 193
Neo-Druidism, 191
Neo-Platonism
    generally, 41
    conflicting religious truth claims and, 161
    creatio ex nihilo and, 46
    evil and, 210–13
    forms and, 242–43, 243*n*2
    Sethian Gnosticism and, 35
A New View of Science (Kauffman), 64*n*3
Nicene Creed, 42
Nicolaitans, 161
nidanas, 196, 196*n*36
Nirguna Brahman, xv, 162, 164–65
nirmanakaya, 183
nirvana, 20, 166–67, 200
Nishitani, Keiji, 173
notaricon, 250
nous, 138
Nyingama Buddhism, 256
Nyx, 95

objective immortality, 86
Oceanus, 95
On Free Choice of the Will (Augustine), 146, 212–13
ontological dependence, 36–37
ontological principle, 63, 65, 76–77, 83
Oord, Thomas Jay, 43, 147*n*21
The Openness of God (Basinger et al.), 147*n*21
open theism, free will in, 144, 147–49, 147*n*21
Ophites, 161
original sin, 41
Osiris, 260
out of body experiences, 242
overview, xx

paganism, 44, 165, 186, 190–91, 247
Paley, William, 83–84
panentheism, 27, 63, 88, 191
panexperientialism, 152–53
Pan Gu, 94
pantheism
    generally, 122, 191
    classical theism compared, 41
    conflicting religious truth claims and, 173–74
    emanationism and, 22, 26
    God in, 182
    perennial philosophy compared, 41
    religious ultimates and, 5–6
    transcendence or immanence of God in, 185

Whitehead on, 85
paraclete, 185
Parallel Worlds (Kaku), 97*n*14
Paramopinshad, 189*n*14
Parmenides (Plato), 72*n*1
Pearson, Birger, 27*n*25
Pelagians, 41
perennial philosophy, 14–22
    generally, 59–60
    chain of being, 19–20
    conflicting religious truth claims in, 158–61
    creation in, 21–22
    ethics in, 16–17
    evil in, 202–4
    exoterics versus esoterics, 17–18
    free will in, 134–36, 156
    hierarchical nature of reality, 18, 20–21
    overview, 14, 55
    pantheism compared, 41
    reality in, 14–16
Phanes, 95
Pharisees, 160
Philippians, 147–48
phowa, 256
physis, 138
pilgrimage, 246
Pinnock, Clark, 147*n*21
plane of mutual immanence. *see* receptacle
Plato
    generally, 5, 29, 71, 107
    divided line, 73–74
    on evil, 205
    on forms, 62–63*n*2, 71–82, 124, 178–79
    on free will, 143
    on God, 41
    on receptacle, 107–11
    "theory of the forms," 72, 74–75, 79–81
    on world, 187
    worship and, 243
Plato's Cosmology (Cornford), 110*n*8
Plotinus
    generally, 22, 35*n*44, 41
    emanationism and, 30, 35, 36–38
    on evil, 208–11
    on forms, 180–81
    on free will, 142–44
    worship and, 243
pluralistic metaphysics, 3–12
    generally, 59
    acosmic ultimate, 5–6, 12
    Cobb on, 3–8, 10, 12
    conflicting religious truth claims in, 170–74
    cosmic ultimate, 5–6, 12
    creativity as religious ultimate, 4, 7–9, 12
    enrichment and, 10, 12
    evil in, 216–18
    free will in, 152–56
    God as religious ultimate, 4–5, 7–9, 12
    God in, 87–88
    Griffin on, 3–5, 7–12
    overview, 3, 12
    purification and, 3, 10, 12
    relativism, avoiding, 10–12
    theistic ultimate, 5–6, 12
    Whitehead on, 3–5, 7–12
    world as religious ultimate, 4–5, 12
Poimandres (Hermes), 27–28, 27*n*25, 138–40
Polanyi, Michael, 51*n*73
practical religion, 237–61
    guided meditation, 242, 258–61
    overview, 237–38, 261
    sample religious service, 258–61
    worship (*see* worship)
prakriti, 163, 188
pratitya-samutpada, 168, 173, 193–96
prayer, 245
predestination, 134–136, 144–45, 149, 199, 201. *see also* free will
prime matter, 96–97, 102–3
Process and Reality (Whitehead), 4–5, 82, 86–87, 102, 126, 127*n*1, 152*n*32, 171*n*26
process theology, 185
Proslogion (Anselm of Canterbury), 83
Protestantism, free will in, 144
Psalms, 47–48, 210
psyche, 138
Ptah, 93
Pure Immanence (Deleuze), 113
purification, 3, 10, 12, 170, 175–76
purusha, 94, 188
Pyramid Texts, 93, 93*n*2

qi (Daoist force), 179–80
Qur'an, 42, 45–47, 49, 183

Radahakrishnan, Sarvepalli, 162*n*6
Ramanuja, 185
Re (Egyptian deity), 93
"*real an sich*," 163–64
receptacle, 107–16
    in *Adventures of Ideas*, 110–13
    Big Bang theory and, 116
    in Buddhism, 198–200
    conflicting religious truth claims and, 198–201
    in cosmosyntheism, 113–15, 199–201
    dao and, 201
    in Daoism, 116, 200–201

receptacle *(cont.)*
    dark energy and, 115
    defined in cosmosyntheism, 64
    hologram model, 114, 114*n*19
    insufficiency of receptacle alone, 116
    in Islam, 199
    logical inconsistency of alternatives to cosmosyntheism lacking, 117–30
    membrane theory and, 114
    necessity of, 107–8
    overview, 107, 116
    Plato on, 107–11
    sunyata and, 200, 256
    in *Timaeus*, 108–10
    wave/particle duality model, 113–14
    Whitehead on, 107, 110–13, 116
    worship and, 255–58
Redford, Donald, 93*n*3
Reenchantment without Supernaturalism (Griffin), 7, 9*n*19, 78*n*18, 127, 153, 153*n*36, 216
Rees, Martin, 230
Reeves, Gene, 8–10, 9*n*19
Reinventing the Sacred: A New View of Science, Religion and the Sacred (Kauffman), 64*n*3
relativism, avoiding, 10–12
Religion in the Making (Whitehead), 85–87
religious ultimates
    acosmic ultimate, 5–6, 12
    in Buddhism, 20–21
    cosmic ultimate, 5–6, 12
    creativity (*see* creativity)
    forms (*see* forms)
    God (*see* God)
    mutually grounding ultimates of cosmosyntheism (*see* mutually grounding ultimates of cosmosyntheism)
    receptacle (*see* receptacle)
    theistic ultimate, 5–6, 12
    world (*see* world)
ren, 138
Republic (Plato), 71–72, 75*n*7
Revelation, 48–49
The Revival of the Religious Sciences (Al-Ghazali), 46
Rice, Richard, 147*n*21
Rig Veda, 94
Riley, Gregory, 30
ritual magic, 161
ritual offerings, 248
Rosicrucianism, 161

sacrifice, 246–47
Sadducees, 160
Sagan, Carl, 229
Saguna Brahman, 162, 164–65
Sallis, John, 110*n*8
Salvations (Heim), 166, 168
samatha, 241
sambhogakaya, 183
samsara, 168, 196, 200
Sanatana Dharma, 158
Sankhya Vedanta, 188
Santeria, 247
sat, 20
Satan, 210
Satanism, 165, 191
satchitananda, 164
Sattipattahana Sutta, 252
Schuon, Fritjhof, xiv, 14, 17–18, 20–21, 134, 203–4
Schwartz, Benjamin, 136*n*5
science, compatibility of cosmosyntheism with, xix
scriptural study, 245
secularism, xiv, xx, 8
serially ordered society of actual occasions, God as, 87–88
sermons, 245–46
Seth (Biblical son of Adam and Eve), 31
Seth (Egyptian deity), 93, 93*n*3
Sethian Gnosticism, 30–35
    generally, 22, 41, 160
    evil in, 207–8
    free will in, 140–41
    Judaism and, 31, 33
    myth in, 32–33
    Neo-Platonism and, 35
Seven Works of Vasubandhu (Anacker), 200*n*44
Shahadah, 42
Shakir, M.H., 42*n*48
Shangdi, 181
Shankara, 21, 162–63, 165
Shema Yisrael, 42
Shepherd of Hermas, 44
Shi'a Islam, free will in, 146
shit, 20
Shiva, 183
A Short History of Chinese Philosophy (Yu-lan), 136*n*5, 179*n*2
Shu, 94
Siddhartha Guatama, 195–97
Sikhism, 181, 199, 201, 255
Simon bar Kochba, 184
six degrees of separation theory, 253*n*8
skandhas, 196
Smith, Huston, xiv, 13–14, 17–18, 20–21, 203
social aim of life, 228–30
social media, 229
Socrates, 75*n*7, 243
Sophia, 33, 207–8

Sophia of Jesus Christ, 31
A Source Book in Chinese Philosophy (Chan), 136n5, 194n31
Space, Time and Deity (Alexander), 13, 49
Sperry, Roger, 51n73
string theory, 97-98, 97n14
study groups, 245-46
Sufi Islam, 17, 161, 245
Sumerian creation myths, 94
Summa Theologica (Aquinas), 42n47, 147n20
Sunni Islam
    determinism in, 199, 201
    free will in, 146
sunyata
    generally, xv, 124
    conflicting religious truth claims and, 164-65, 167-68, 172-73
    receptacle and, 200, 256
    religious ultimates and, 20
Suzuki, D.T., 173
Symposium (Plato), 180, 243

taiji circle, 204
Talbot, Michael, 114n19
Talmud, 160
Tantric Buddhism, 160-61, 255-56
Taoism. *see* Daoism
Tarot, 243, 249
Tartarus, 95
tathagata-garbha, 196
Tatian, 44
temurah, 250
Tertullian, 44
theistic ultimate, 5-6, 12
Theogeny (Hesiod), 95, 95n10
Theophilus of Antioch, 43
"theory of the forms" (Plato), 72, 74-75, 79-81
theosophy, 201
Theravadan Buddhism, 195-97
Thich Nhat Hanh, 198
30 Days (television program), 233
Thomas Gnosticism, 31
The Three Steles of Seth, 34-35, 242-43
Tiamat, 94
Tian, 181
Tibetan Buddhism, 255-56
Timaeus (Plato), 29-30, 71, 76, 107-10, 205
tonglen, 254
totems, 241-42
Traditional Chinese Medicine, 251
traditional school. *see* perennial philosophy
transcendence of God, 185
Transcendent Unity of Religions (Schuon), 14, 134

Transforming Christianity and the World (Cobb), 3
tratak, 240
trikaya, 183
trimurti, 183
trinity, 7n15, 40, 167-68, 183
Tsou Yen, 251n7
Twitter, 229
type I civilizations, 228-29, 234
type II civilizations, 228-29
type III civilizations, 228-29

ultimates. *see* religious ultimates
Unitarianism, 8, 246
unveiling, 247-48
Upanishads, 8, 188

Vaishnavism, 181
Vajrayana Buddhism, 255-56
Valentinian Gnosticism, 30n32, 31, 141
Valentinus, 22-23
Vasubandhu, 200, 200n44
Vedas, 188
vipassana, 239-41, 252
Vishishtadvaita Vedanta, 163
Vishnu, 183-84, 188
vision quest, 241-42
Visuddhimagga, 252, 254
Visvakarman, 94
Vodoun, 247

Wang Fu-Chih, 189-90
War of the Jews (Josephus), 160n5
wave/particle duality model, 113-14
wei-wu-wei, 137
Whitehead, Alfred North
    generally, xx, 50, 59, 64n3, 82, 102, 107, 126-28
    on conflicting religious truth claims, 168-73, 171n26
    on creativity, 102-5
    dipolar process theism, 85-87
    eternal objects, 75-77, 79-80
    on ethics, 224-27
    on evil, 218-19
    on forms, 71, 75-82, 178, 181
    on free will, 153-55
    on God, 82, 85-88, 91
    internal relations, 77
    objective immortality, 86
    ontological principle, 63, 65, 76-77, 83
    on pantheism, 85
    on pluralistic metaphysics, 3-5, 7-12
    on receptacle, 107, 110-113, 116

Whitehead *(cont.)*
    universal reality, 77
    on world, 98, 100
Whitehead's Radically Different Postmodern Philosophy (Griffin), 10–11
Wholeness and the Implicate Other (Bohm), 114n19
Wicca, 190–91
Wikipedia, 229
Wittgenstein, Ludwig, 164
world, 92–101
    Aristotle on, 92, 96–97, 99, 187
    Cobb on, 100, 186
    conflicting religious truth claims and, 186–193
    in cosmosyntheism, 193
    creation out of chaos, 93–96
    in Daoism, 186
    defined in cosmosyntheism, 63
    Griffin on, 100, 186
    in Hinduism, 188
    insufficiency of world alone, 100–101
    logical inconsistency of alternatives to cosmosyntheism lacking, 117–30
    negative views, 187–88
    neutral views, 188–90
    overview, 92, 101
    Plato on, 187
    positive views, 190–93
    prime matter and, 96–97
    primordial world in cosmosyntheism, 98–100
    as religious ultimate, 4–5, 12
    string theory and, 97–98, 97n14
    Whitehead on, 98, 100
    worship and, 248–51
The World of Thought in Ancient China (Schwartz), 136n5
worship, 238–58
    active paradigm shifting, 256–58
    almsgiving, 254
    amendment of texts, 253
    artistic endeavors, 243–44, 243n3
    astral projection, 242
    attunement, 240
    brahmaviharas, 254–55
    charity, 254
    collaborative art, 243–44
    confession, 247–48
    creative visualization, 241
    creativity and, 251–55
    dzogchen, 256
    egregores, 241–42
    evangelism, 246
    forms and, 239–44
    God and, 244–48
    guided meditation, 242, 258–61
    invocation, 247
    lucid dreaming, 242–43
    Lullian Circle, 249–50
    mahamudra, 256
    missionary work, 246
    naropa, 256
    nature worship, 251
    out of body experiences, 242
    overview, 238–39
    pilgrimage, 246
    Plato and, 243
    Plotinus and, 243
    prayer, 245
    receptacle and, 255–58
    ritual offerings, 248
    sacrifice, 246–47
    samatha, 241
    scriptural study, 245
    sermons, 245–46
    study groups, 245–46
    tonglen, 254
    totems, 241–42
    tratak, 240
    unveiling, 247–48
    vipassana, 239–41, 252
    vision quest, 241–42
    world and, 248–51
    zazen, 256
wu-wei, 193

Yahweh, 160, 207
Yaltabaoth/Yaldabaoth, 30, 33, 140–41, 207–8
Yama, 196n38
Yang, Lihui, 94n5
Yen Yuan, 189
yin/yang, 136, 204
Yogacara Buddhism, 198–99, 201, 255
Yoga Vedanta, 188
YouTube, 229
Yu-Lan, Fung, 3n1, 136n5, 179n2
yu-wei, 137

Zaijr, 249
zakat, 254
zazen, 256
Zen Buddhism, 124, 161, 165, 253, 256
Zhuangzi, 94, 194–95
Zhu Xi, 179–80, 189–90, 193
ziran, 137, 193
Zum Brunn, Emilie, 212